ISSA

Auditing IT Infrastructures for Compliance

THIRD EDITION

Robert Johnson | Marty M. Weiss | Michael G. Solomon

JONES & BARTLETT
LEARNING

World Headquarters
Jones & Bartlett Learning
25 Mall Road
Burlington, MA 01803
978-443-5000
info@jblearning.com
www.jblearning.com

Jones & Bartlett Learning books and products are available through most bookstores and online booksellers. To contact Jones & Bartlett Learning directly, call 800-832-0034, fax 978-443-8000, or visit our website, www.jblearning.com.

Production Credits

Vice President, Product Management: Marisa R. Urbano
Vice President, Content Strategy and Implementation: Christine Emerton
Director, Content Management: Donna Gridley
Manager, Content Strategy: Carolyn Pershouse
Content Strategist: Melissa Duffy
Content Coordinator: Mark Restuccia
Director, Project Management and Content Services: Karen Scott
Manager, Project Management: Jackie Reynen
Project Manager: Roberta Sherman
Senior Digital Project Specialist: Angela Dooley
Marketing Manager: Mark Adamiak

Content Services Manager: Colleen Lamy
VP, Manufacturing and Inventory Control: Therese Connell
Product Fulfillment Manager: Wendy Kilborn
Composition: Straive
Project Management: Straive
Cover Design: Briana Yates
Text Design: Briana Yates
Media Development Editor: Faith Brosnan
Rights & Permissions Manager: John Rusk
Rights Specialist: James Fortney
Cover & Title Page Image: © SidorArt/Shutterstock
Printing and Binding: Gasch Printing

Library of Congress Cataloging-in-Publication Data

Names: Johnson, Rob (Robert), author. | Weiss, Martin (Martin M.) author. | Solomon, Michael (Michael G.), 1963- author.
Title: Auditing IT infrastructures for compliance / Robert Johnson, Marty M. Weiss, Michael G. Solomon.
Description: Third edition. | Burlington, MA : Jones & Bartlett Learning, [2024] | Series: Information systems security & assurance | Includes bibliographical references and index. | Summary: "Auditing IT Infrastructures for Compliance provides a unique, in-depth look at recent U.S. based information systems and IT infrastructures compliance laws in both the public and private sector"– Provided by publisher.
Identifiers: LCCN 2022026856 | ISBN 9781284236606 (paperback)
Subjects: LCSH: Computer security. | Computer networks–Security measures. | Compliance auditing.
Classification: LCC QA76.9.A25 W428 2022 | DDC 005.8–dc23/eng/20220716
LC record available at https://lccn.loc.gov/2022026856.

6048

Printed in the United States of America
27 26 25 24 23   10 9 8 7 6 5 4 3 2 1

Contents

CHAPTER 7   Writing the IT Infrastructure Audit Report   161

CHAPTER 8   Compliance Within the User Domain   181

To my family and father Chester Johnson, for his 96th birthday, a humble man who has dedicated his life to his children, serving his community and country as a war veteran.
—Rob Johnson

Preface

Purpose of This Book

This book is part of the Information Systems Security & Assurance Series from Jones & Bartlett Learning (*www.jblearning.com*). Designed for courses and curriculums in IT Security, Cybersecurity, Information Assurance, and Information Systems Security, this series features a comprehensive, consistent treatment of the most current thinking and trends in this critical subject area. These titles deliver fundamental information-security principles packed with real-world applications and examples. Authored by professionals experienced in information systems security, they deliver comprehensive information on all aspects of this field. Reviewed word for word by leading technical experts, these books are not just current, but forward-thinking—putting you in a position to solve the cybersecurity challenges not just of today, but of tomorrow as well.

Part 1 of this book identifies and explains what each of these compliance laws requires in regard to safeguarding business and consumer privacy data elements and the design and implementation of proper security controls. Once these safeguards and security control requirements are defined for your organization, you have a yardstick of measurement for conducting an audit of your IT infrastructure for compliance.

Part 2 presents how to audit an IT infrastructure for compliance based on the compliance laws themselves, on the need to protect and secure business and consumer privacy data, and on the need to have properly documented and implemented security controls within the organization. Auditing standards and frameworks are also presented, along with what must be audited within the seven domains of a typical IT infrastructure. In addition to discussing the planning and conduct of an audit, Part 2 also reviews how to document what was identified during the audit and how to determine whether compliance requirements are being met throughout the IT infrastructure. Specific security controls and countermeasures are presented for each of the domains of a typical IT infrastructure.

Part 3 provides a resource for readers and students who desire more information on becoming skilled at IT auditing and IT compliance auditing. This final chapter provides additional content on ethics, education, professional certifications, and IT auditing certifying organizations.

This book not only addresses the tools and techniques for auditing IT infrastructure for compliance, it also examines key risk drivers. While much of the content is related to information security, the text considers and provides examples of the broader and higher-level principles around information governance and risk management. It brings together the core disciplines of auditing, accounting, and information technology.

Learning Features

The writing style of this book is practical and conversational. Each chapter begins with a statement of learning objectives. Step-by-step examples of information security concepts and procedures are presented throughout the text. Illustrations are used both to clarify the material and to vary the presentation. The text is sprinkled with Notes, Tips, FYIs, Warnings, and sidebars to alert the reader to additional helpful information related to the subject under discussion. Chapter Assessments appear at the end of each chapter, with solutions provided in the back of the book.

Chapter Summaries are included in the text to provide a rapid review or preview of the material and to help students understand the relative importance of the concepts presented.

Audience

The material is suitable for undergraduate or graduate computer science majors or information science majors, students at a two-year technical college or community college who have a basic technical background, and readers who have a basic understanding of IT security and want to expand their knowledge.

New to This Edition

This edition's updates reflect the enormous change in auditing and cybersecurity in recent years due to the worldwide pandemic, which has forced many businesses to operate remotely and expand the use of digital technologies. Work from home is now often the norm versus the exception for many workers. More than ever, data are distributed outside the confines of the corporate network. Revisions in this text reflect current techniques of auditors and cybersecurity professionals to help their organizations control risks and keep pace with the changing risk landscape, such as data breaches, ransomware, and regulatory misses.

This edition also reflects the expanding role of the auditor as organizations reimagine their business and technology needs in this changed world. This text explores key audit and cybersecurity disciplines needed as organizations go through digital transformation. This text reflects recent trends and changes in the technology such as the exponential expansion of cloud services. It discusses not only an organization's transformation but also the transformation of the auditor's tools and techniques.

Cloud Labs

This text is accompanied by Cybersecurity Cloud Labs. These hands-on virtual labs provide immersive mock IT infrastructures where students can learn and practice foundational cybersecurity skills as an extension of the lessons in this textbook. For more information or to purchase the labs, visit go.jblearning.com/auditingit3elabs.

Acknowledgments

Frank Lloyd Wright has been quoted as saying, "Youth is a quality, not a matter of circumstances." I more fully appreciate that quality after my son helped me with this book. At 14, Donald Johnson became a national chess master and has represented the United States in international games. At 16, he is an inspiring cyber expert in his own right, having already achieved certifications and written a commercially successful app to solve cryptographic challenges for a local healthcare company. I owe him an enormous debt of gratitude for sharing his experience beyond his years, offering constructive critique, fresh insights, and suggested edits through the long writing process. I am deeply touched by the gift of time we have shared together in completing this text.

I would also like to thank Melissa Duffy with Jones & Bartlett Learning for her relentless pursuit to accomplish this project through a most difficult set of pandemic challenges. Her professionalism and constant support will always be fondly remembered. I would like to once again express my personal gratitude to Carole Jelen with Waterside Productions, a wonderful and supportive literary agent who works so hard behind the scenes to make projects like this a success.

Rob Johnson

About the Authors

ROB JOHNSON has more than 25 years of experience in information risk, IT audit, and global cybersecurity. He has a diverse background that includes hands-on operational experience as well as executive experience and board-level reporting responsibilities.

Rob currently serves as the head of Information Technology Auditing at Equitable, a Fortune 500 company. Rob has held various technology and executive positions throughout his career, including as senior vice president and technology executive at a Bank of America with global audit and cybersecurity responsibilities. Additionally, during his career, he has served as chief information security officer and the chief product architect for a major software house where he led security, audit, and product implementation engagements across 15 countries.

Rob is a published author and speaker at conferences. He has served on a number of global audit and security industry committees, including formerly being the chair of the ISACA Education Committee, serving on the ISACA Assurance Committee, and being 1 of 12 members who served on the standards task force to create the COBIT 5 global standard.

Rob holds a BS in interdisciplinary studies at the University of Houston with a focus on mathematics and computer science. He holds multiple certifications including, Certified Information Systems Auditor (CISA), Certified Information Systems Security Professional (CISSP), Certified Information Security Manager (CISM), and Certified in Risk and Information Systems Control (CRISC).

MARTY M. WEISS has years of experience in auditing, information security, risk management, and compliance. Marty holds a BS in computer studies from the University of Maryland University College and an MBA from the Isenberg School of Management at the University of Massachusetts Amherst. He has several certifications, including Certified Information Systems Auditor (CISA), Certified Information Systems Security Professional (CISSP), and CompTIA Security+. He has authored and coauthored more than a half-dozen books on information technology. Occasionally he molds minds as an adjunct professor. Originally a Florida native, he now lives in New England somewhere between Boston and New York City.

MICHAEL G. SOLOMON, PhD, CISSP, PMP, CISM, CySA+, Pentest+, is an author, educator, and consultant focusing on privacy, security, blockchain, and identity management. As an IT professional and consultant since 1987, Dr. Solomon has led project teams for many Fortune 500 companies and has authored and contributed to more than 25 books and numerous training courses. Dr. Solomon is a professor of cybersecurity and global business with blockchain technology at the University of the Cumberlands and holds a PhD in computer science and informatics from Emory University. He has also authored and contributed to many IT Jones & Bartlett Learning security books, including *Fundamentals of Communications and Networking*, *Fundamentals of Information Systems Security*, and *Security Strategies in Windows Platforms and Applications*.

PART ONE

The Need for Compliance

The Need for Information Systems Compliance

TECHNOLOGY GAINS IN THE LAST DECADE have changed our daily lives. Technology innovation seems to be everywhere. Technology has helped us to be better connected from a maze of mobile phone applications to social media sites. Breakthroughs have helped us to live healthier lives through early detection of diseases and monitoring of health conditions, During the COVID-19 pandemic, many relied on telepresence to reduce the effects of social isolation and to continue working remotely over the Internet. Technology innovations have even changed the approach to health care to provide us choices not possible just a few years ago such as the surge in home-based hospital care in 2020 (Leventhal 2021). Consider how technology innovations have allowed patients' health to be remotely monitored by doctors and nurses while allowing the patient to be home with family and loved ones. A study in the *Annals of Internal Medicine* reviewed 43 hospital-at-home patients and 48 patients receiving traditional hospital care. Home-based hospital care reduced costs by 38%. More importantly, the patients receiving home-based hospital care were readmitted to the hospital after discharge at a much-reduced rate of 7% versus 23% for those that received traditional hospital care.

Yet benefits from technology innovation do come at a price. Our information is everywhere. Every click produces an electronic record of our likes and dislikes and records our private information such as personal health information. This information can be used to our benefit or our detriment. Fortunately, organizations are often required to adhere to strict rules of conduct in the handling and processing of customer information. This leads us to the need for information systems compliance audits and assessments to ensure our data are collected, processed, and stored appropriately. The stakes for organizations are high with noncompliance to these rules can lead to a loss of customer confidence, loss of business, regulatory fines, and even the potential of jail time for company executives.

Chapter 1 Topics

This chapter covers the following topics and concepts:

* What the difference between an information system compliance and information system security compliance is
* What different types of IT audits and assessments are there
* What compliance is
* What the confidentiality, integrity, availability triad is
* What the importance of governance and compliance is
* What the consequences of not complying with compliance laws are

Chapter 1 Goals

When you complete this chapter, you will be able to:

* Understand the difference between information system compliance and information system security compliance
* Understand how to apply the concept of confidentiality, integrity, and availability to compliance
* Identify different forms of mandates to measure compliance
* Examine the role of an IT assessment
* Examine the role of IT auditing
* Compare the differences between an audit and an assessment
* Summarize compliance and explain why it is important

What Is the Difference Between Information System and Information Security Compliance?

The Institute of Internal Auditors (IIA) is considered the gold standard for establishing professional practices guidance for auditors. The IIA defines an internal **audit** as "an independent, objective assurance and consulting activity designed to add value and improve an organization's operations." In context to auditing the **IT infrastructure**, it could be considered as providing reasonable assurance to management that the IT controls are complete and working effectively.

The terms *assurance* and *consulting* are used in the IIA definition. *Assurance* is a traditional term often used to describe a very formal audit.

An assurance audit will typically examine controls that have been deployed to assess their completeness and effectiveness. The results of an assurance audit are typically delivered in a report format with a narrative of any findings and an overall rating. The rating scale and verbiage can vary dramatically across industries and companies. Assurance audits can be challenging. While not the intent, an audit report rating is often viewed as a test grade at a university, i.e., did I get an "A" or "F" or something in between. They are not always seen as welcoming by the individuals who often view an audit as grading their work. Senior management on the other hand welcomes audits as a way of gaining independent insights to improve their internal controls.

The IIA recognized that management not only wants to learn the internal auditor's opinion on existing controls but also wants to get advice on emerging topics and initiatives. Thus was born the concept of audit consulting. The term *consulting* in recent years has been replaced in many organizations with the term *advisory*. We will use the term *advisory assessments* to reflect this less formal advice provided to management.

An advisory assessment by an auditor is less formal than an assurance audit. An advisory assessment may or may not result in a report being produced. Advisory assessment results can be delivered in any format mutually agreed upon with management, such as verbal, memorandum, or a report. An advisory assessment typically has no rating. The real distinction from an assurance audit is that an advisory assessment typically deals with emerging risks or future initiatives. Consequently, there are no controls to test or assess. Advisory assessments tend to focus on the completeness of designs and management plans. It is an opportunity for the auditor to add value by raising the quality of the conversation on risks that may not have been fully considered.

Difference Between Information System and Information Security

Information technology (IT) infrastructure is typically defined as everything needed to operate and manage the IT environment. It is simply all installed technologies, including all hardware, software, network devices, storage, storage, cables, printers, monitors, and such. Typically a series of smaller more management audits or assessments are performed examining different aspects of the IT infrastructure For example, one audit may examine the physical security of the data center that houses the server hardware. Another audit may examine how servers are configured. While another audit may look at specific cybersecurity threats to ensure the readiness of the IT infrastructure to defend against certain **attack vectors**.

NOTE

To simplify and enhance the reading of the chapters, we will use the term *audit* to mean either an assurance audit or an advisory assessment.

TIP

Think of an assurance audit as a detective control. An assurance audit looks at deployed controls and detects problems, while advisory assessments can be viewed as a preventative control. Advisory assessment attempts to prevent problems by identifying risks before they occur.

For example, suppose you manufacture a part that has a high defect rate. An assurance audit will tell you what control is failing, and thus, what caused the defect. An advisory assessment could have potentially told you that the design of the control to manufacture the part was risky before it was implemented and thereby prevented defects from ever occurring.

NOTE

Attack vector is a cybersecurity term used to describe the pathway used to gain unauthorized access. For example, a weak password is an attack vector that can be exploited by a hacker to gain unauthorized access to a server containing customer information.

NOTE

We will use the terms *information security* and *cybersecurity* interchangeably for this book. The definitions can vary. Some view the term *cybersecurity* as dealing primarily with Internet connectivity. As such, *cybersecurity* could be viewed as a subset of information security, while others use *cybersecurity* as a generic broader term. For the goal of this book, any distinction is not important.

There are subtle differences between information systems and information security terms. Consider the following:

- Information systems typically refer to the IT infrastructure components (hardware and software) that collect, store, and process data.
- Information security can refer to the protection against unauthorized access to the IT infrastructure components during the collection, storage, and processing of data.

In both cases, there is a significant overlap. Most notably, how information systems are configured directly impacts how the data are processed and protected. Consequently, many IT infrastructure audits are in essence cybersecurity audits and vice versa.

On occasion, auditors will need to recognize the subtle differences between information systems and information security findings during an audit. For example, suppose an application that analyzes a customer's financial records takes hours because servers having a minimal amount of memory. Yet the company's competitors could produce a similar report in minutes. Assume both systems were appropriately secure. An audit may raise an information systems finding but not an information security finding, i.e., lack of server memory impacts company competitiveness but does not put the customer data at risk.

Auditing Information Security

IT security is typically part of a larger security program within an organization. Specifically, an IT security assessment is a key activity that involves the management of **risk**—an uncertainty that might lead to a loss. Information systems provide numerous benefits and efficiencies within organizations. However, these benefits come with risks. A risk-based approach to managing information security involves the following:

- Identifying and categorizing the information and the information systems
- Selecting and implementing appropriate security **controls**—actions or changes to be applied to systems to reduce weaknesses or potential losses
- Assessing the controls for effectiveness
- Authorizing the systems by accepting the risk based upon the selected security controls
- Monitoring the security controls on a continual basis

This approach is a continual cycle as organizations evolve and as activities such as assessments and monitoring reveal gaps and ineffective controls relevant to requirements and acceptable levels of risk.

The benefits provided to organizations as a result of information technology involve complex systems and processes. These systems not only benefit organizations, but they have also become critical components to the success of the organization. As a result, the continued and secured operation of these systems contributes largely to that success.

To understand their effectiveness, organizations must assess security controls. Security controls include the physical, procedural, and technical mechanisms to safeguard systems. First, are the controls appropriately designed and implemented? Second, are they functioning as expected? If so, are they operating effectively to produce the required results? Third, do they align to the policy of an organization?

You should not use a security assessment simply as a method for proving the strength of system security or as a reason to immediately provide greater security. Rather, a security assessment should produce information required to do the following:

- Identify weaknesses within the controls implemented on information systems
- Confirm that previously identified weaknesses have been remediated or mitigated
- Prioritize further decisions to mitigate risks
- Provide **assurance**, a level of confidence that effective controls are in place and that associated risks are accepted and authorized
- Provide support and planning for future budgetary requirements

The personnel who conduct security assessments can be internal or external to an organization. While the procedures for assessments may vary widely by organization, the **National Institute of Standards and Technology (NIST)**, the technology agency of the U.S. Department of Commerce, provides a framework for effective security assessment plans in *NIST Special Publication 800-53* (NIST 2013). This publication defines a recommended assessment procedure, which includes a set of assessment **objectives**, or goals. Each objective has a set of assessment methods, including examination, interview, and test, and each objective has a set of assessment objects, including specification, mechanism, activity, and individual.

An assessment objective includes one or more statements that are directly related to a corresponding control to determine the validity and effectiveness of the control. For example, consider a common control that most users of computer systems have experienced: being locked out of an information system or application after too many unsuccessful logon attempts. The following illustrates the relationship between the control and the assessment objectives, methods, and objects.

Unsuccessful Logon Attempts

Control: The system enforces a limit of four consecutive invalid access attempts on the same username within a period of 15 minutes. The system automatically locks the account for 30 minutes. Subsequently, four more consecutive invalid access attempts within 15 minutes lock the account indefinitely, which requires manual intervention by the system administrator.

Assessment objectives:

- Determine if the system enforces the defined threshold of consecutive invalid access attempts
- Determine if the system enforces the delayed logon after the initial account lock
- Determine if the system enforces the defined threshold for locking the account indefinitely

 TIP

NIST Special Publication 800-53 rev 5 contains a catalog of all NIST controls in the form of an Excel spreadsheet. This spreadsheet can be easily modified as an assessment control tracking tool.

Assessment methods and objects:

- Examine access control policy statement and procedures addressing failed logon attempts
- Examine associated information system documentation and configuration settings
- Examine associated information system log records
- Test the automated mechanism implementing the access control policy for failed logon attempts

Methods for Conducting a Security Control Assessment

You can use several methods to conduct an assessment of security controls:

- **Examination**—Verify, inspect, or review associated assessment objects to understand or obtain evidence to support the existence and effectiveness of the security control. Examples include reviewing security policies and procedures and observing physical security mechanisms.
- **Interview**—Discuss associated assessment objects with groups or individuals to understand or obtain evidence to support the existence and effectiveness of the security control. Interviews can include senior officials, information system owners, security officers, information system operators, and network administrators.
- **Test**—Put associated assessment objects under specific conditions to compare actual behavior with what is expected to obtain evidence to support the existence and effectiveness of the security control. Objects can include hardware or software mechanisms or system operations or administration activities. Examples include testing actual security configuration settings and conducting penetration tests.

 TIP

During the audit, it is helpful to document and share the potential observations from examinations, interviews, and tests. For example, having weekly sync (synchronization) meetings with stakeholders is an effective way to validate your findings and avoid pushback when issuing the final report.

Assessment objectives should be part of your organization's IT security assessment plan. After executing the plan, you can create a report. The IT security assessment report documents the findings of the assessment and provides the information necessary to determine the effectiveness of the controls. Senior management uses the report to provide assurance that risks are appropriate to the goals of the organization and to help create, if necessary, another document for an action plan based on the results of the assessment.

Not all IT security assessments need to be comprehensive to cover all security controls or even all information systems. In fact, security assessments are often performed partially across controls and information systems. Although this chapter has laid out a best-practice framework for a comprehensive IT security assessment, security assessments vary in scope, depth, and breadth. The following is a list of some sample audits you might encounter:

- Network security architecture
- Security policies, procedures, and practices
- Vulnerability scanning and testing
- Physical security
- Security risk
- Social engineering
- Application
- Access management

Another common type of assessment, and one that seems to be more popularized in the media, is a penetration test. A **penetration test** is an assessment method that attempts to bypass controls and gain access to a specific system by simulating the actions of a would-be attacker. However, penetration tests operate under specific constraints and rules of engagement, so they simulate the process a real adversary may take while avoiding any business disruptions or outages.

As a result, a penetration test is not necessarily the best means by which to judge the security of an information system. The test helps an organization understand its systems and gain insight into the level of effort an attacker might need to go through to penetrate the system. Penetration tests often reveal weaknesses or easily exploited vulnerabilities within a system. It is not uncommon for penetration tests to be a catalyst for selling management on the need to invest more money and/or effort in information security.

> **NOTE**
>
> If an audit determines a control is poorly designed, then typically there is no need to test if the control is effective. A poorly designed control will not will not yield the correct outcome, and thus, there is no need to test the outcome.

What Is the Confidentiality, Integrity, and Availability (CIA) Triad?

The **CIA triad** is a well-known cybersecurity model. It helps an organization think through the various layers of security that are needed to protect the IT infrastructure.

Figure 1-1 depicts the CIA key concepts as follows:

1. Confidentiality—To ensure only authorized users and processes can read the data
2. Integrity—To ensure only authorized users and processes can modify the data
3. Availability—To ensure the data are readily available to authorized users and processes

FIGURE 1-1

The CIA Triad

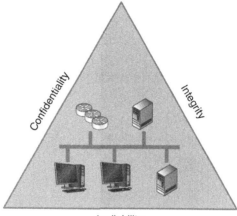

The CIA triad is a very powerful model because it can be used to understand the different layers of controls that exist within an IT infrastructure. Let's explore several scenarios in which a company collects, stores, and processes customer personal information:

- Scenario 1: How do we maintain confidentiality over the customer data? While the data are stored, we could encrypt the data. That would limit access to authorized users and processes with the encryption key. In essence, no one can read the data without the encryption key.
- Scenario 2: How do we maintain integrity over the customer data? We could limit access to authorized users through the use of IDs and passwords, i.e., allowing selected authenticated users with limited authorization to modify the data.
- Scenario 3: How do we maintain availability over the customer data? During a server hardware failure, we could failover to back up the server. The failover to servers in high availability environments are often performed in real time and may not be noticeable to the customer trying to access their account,

In each of the above scenarios different IT infrastructure technologies are used. This is very typical in a complex IT environment. The CIA triad allows us to quickly scope audits and assessments into manageable chunks of work. This is important because we want to assess the most amount of risk in the shortest amount of time. A good example is auditing and assessing access management controls. The use of authentication and authorization controls (typically in the form of IDs and passwords) can cover risks related to both confidentiality and integrity of data.

> **TIP**
>
> This chapter intends to introduce the reader to the basic CIA triad model and concepts. The reader is encouraged to surf the web and learn more. YouTube is one source with many video lessons on the subject.

What Is Compliance?

Despite being a relatively simple term, the term **compliance** has become something of an enigma within many organizations. Different people view and define compliance in different ways. This is evident across different industries, within the same industries, and even within organizations.

The Merriam-Webster Online dictionary defines compliance as "the act or process of doing what you have been asked or ordered to do." Where do these compliance rules for organizations come from? They come in many forms such as laws and regulations, industry norms and frameworks, and ethical standards established through internal company policies and standards. An information systems compliance assessment or audit not only considers each of these forms of rules but also measures the effectiveness of the governance and management oversight to ensure the rules are being followed.

Regarding IT compliance, compliance pertains to two broad areas: internal and external. **Internal compliance** refers to an organization's ability to follow its own rules, which are typically based on defined policies and standards. **External compliance** refers to the need and desire for an organization to follow rules and guidelines set forth by external organizations and authorities. Although many external-compliance mandates are regulatory, other compliance requirements include standards and guidelines that must be followed as set forth by industry frameworks.

The credit card industry is a prime example, which developed a set of security standards in an attempt to provide self-regulation which is typically enforced through contractual obligations. The majority of external compliance mandates are, however, laws and regulations. There are numerous compliance mandates to which organizations may be required to adhere. In most cases, regulations do not provide specifics and are open for interpretation. Compliance frameworks, such as **Control Objectives for Information and Related Technology (COBIT)**, and standards, such as NIST, help interpret how to comply with the regulations.

Unlike a simple traffic law, such as the requirement to stop at a red light, compliance laws and regulations are not always so clear. This is often another source of frustration for those responsible for helping an organization comply. The general steps to meeting compliance include the following:

1. Interpret the regulation and how it applies to the organization.

2. Understand how regulators are interpreting the regulation through fines and penalties assessed across an industry group.

3. Identify any gaps in controls or determine where the organization stands with the compliance mandate.

4. Align the view of gaps and risks with key stakeholders across the organization such as legal, operational risk, risk management, and compliance departments.

5. Identify accountability at the governance, department, and executive levels.

6. Ensure management devises a plan to close the gap.

7. Monitor management's execution of the plan.

 NOTE

Given the complexity of external law and regulatory obligations, most companies ensure internal policies and standards to meet these external mandates. In this way, it simplifies compliance as employees need only to follow policies to ensure external mandates are met.

Compliance is closely related to **risk management** and **governance** on all levels, be it technical, procedural, or strategic. Risk management seeks to mitigate risk through controls. For example, an organization identifies, evaluates, and takes action to lessen its risk. Compliance helps risk management by verifying that the desired controls are in place. Governance seeks to better run an organization using complete and accurate information and management processes or controls. For example, a sound security policy and comprehensive procedures are in place to implement the policy.

Compliance helps governance by ensuring such information and controls also satisfy applicable standards or regulations. On a strategic level, compliance ensures an organization can effectively meet organizational goals and objectives as planned. This means IT must ensure it is capable of delivering services to satisfy business needs and to stay compliant with external laws and regulations.

Why Are Governance and Compliance Important?

Without proper governance in place, an organization can have neither effective risk management nor compliance. A common theme thus far has been the reliance on IT throughout the organization. As a result, IT can have a tremendous impact on either the success or failure of an organization. The interest in formally governing the use and application of IT should come as no surprise. IT is now woven into the fabric of business and has made organizations dependent on information and the systems that help generate and store information. In addition, IT will continue to provide opportunities for competitive advantage and reduction of costs throughout the organization. On the other hand, IT systems are subject to numerous threats that continue to evolve and seek to exploit vulnerabilities.

At a fundamental level, internal compliance to corporate policies is critical to the success of any business. Risk management means deeming some risks acceptable so a company may accomplish its business goals. Compliance, therefore, embraces the organizational mission, and noncompliance can harm or even impede business.

Regulatory compliance benefits organizations, consumers, and shareholders. Regulatory compliance protects an organization's reputation and integrity. It considers the interests of the consumer and shareholders. Regulatory compliance also has a further-reaching economic impact on ensuring public confidence in organizations and capital markets.

Policies by themselves do not reduce risk. Policies must be implemented and maintained. Governance that provides the management oversight ensures policies are not only written but effectively implemented. Compliance audits must include a detailed assessment of the various governance forums that ensure policies are in place and appropriately implemented. At a minimum a compliance audit should examine the following:

- The compliance governance structure is documented and understood.
- The governance goals are fit for the purpose.
- Incentive structures do not create a conflict of interest.
- Desired outcomes are being measured and reported on a timely basis.
- Accountability is clear.

Case Study: Cetera and Cambridge

Consider what happens when governance is not in place or not effective. The Securities and Exchange Commission (SEC) on August 30, 2021, sanctioned eight investment firms and issued fines of $750,000 for failing to effectively implement cybersecurity policies.

In the case of Cetera, the fines resulted from an email breach. Between November 2017 and June 2020, more than 60 employees' cloud-based email accounts were hacked. This breach exposed the personal information of at least 4,388 customers. Cetera compounded the problem by issuing misleading notifications to its customers. Additionally, Cetera had clear security policies published in 2018 that required dual-factor authentication to ensure email accounts remained secure. These policies were never fully implemented.

The case of Cambridge was also an email breach. Between January 2018 and July 2021, more than 121 employees' cloud-based email accounts were hacked. This breach exposed the personal information of at least 42,177 customers. Cambridge compounded the problem because it discovered the breach in 2018 but failed to enhance and implement additional security measures until 2021.

What is equally telling about the SEC view on governance and compliance is its rationale statement that was issued about the sanctions:

"Investment advisers and broker-dealers must fulfill their obligations concerning the protection of customer information," said Kristina Littman, chief of the SEC Enforcement Division's Cyber Unit. "It is not enough to write a policy requiring enhanced security measures if those requirements are not implemented or are only partially implemented, especially in the face of known attacks."

While this statement was directed toward "investment advisers," it applies to all industries. Consider how governance and compliance (or the lack thereof) played a role in this case study. An audit could potentially have discovered and, thus, prevented these control gaps:

- Compliance to dual-factor authentication policy in the Cetera case
- Governance over the incident response in the Cambridge case

The regulator statement makes the obligation clear that organizations must protect the privacy and information of their customers. Finally, it's not good enough to have policies. Governance must ensure compliance through effective governance.

> ▶ **TIP**
>
> Examining governance dashboards and related reports presented to governance forums is a good way to assess the scope of risks that management considers and debates.

What If an Organization Does Not Comply with Compliance Laws?

Of course you wouldn't break a law, right? But asking what would happen if your organization doesn't comply with compliance laws is a fair question. Let's look at an example of an individual compliance issue to understand why.

It is a law to come to a complete stop at a stop sign, yet many people ignore it. This scenario is a form of risk management. Many people consider it an acceptable risk to

NOTE

Don't forget about the other negative effects that noncompliance can have on an organization, beyond the threat of fines and imprisonment:

- Legal fees resulting from infringements contained within many regulations
- Brand damage and lost revenue as consumers abandon a business
- Negative effect upon stock price, hurting shareholder value
- Increases in the cost of capital

approach slowly and, if there is no traffic, continue without coming to a complete stop. The threat of another car exists, yet many people feel safe enough with the slow approach and rolling stop. There is always the threat of a police officer pulling you over and issuing a ticket. Yet how often is this enforced? If it were, what is the punishment? Given the likelihood of being pulled over by law enforcement, combined with what is likely a bearable fine, many people decide the risk is low and the benefit of noncompliance outweighs the risk.

Organizations have spent and continue to spend large sums of money to achieve and maintain regulatory and industry compliance. This is especially true as regulations have placed greater accountability on individuals within an organization. Noncompliance can result in huge fines as well as jail time. Some regulations are subject to strict liability. Strict liability means even if there wasn't intent, government agencies can levy huge fines on organizations and some individuals can spend years in prison. Even greater punishments are in store where intent can be proven!

In addition to the financial and reputational consequences of noncompliance, organizations can also experience operational consequences. This can happen, for example, in the case of compliance standards imposed by the payment card industry. Potential consequences include payment card–imposed operational restrictions and even loss of card-processing privileges.

The **Payment Card Industry Data Security Standard (PCI DSS)** is an industry-created standard that applies to organizations that process credit cards. Companies that meet a specific threshold for large volumes of credit card transactions are required to achieve compliance.

Regulators are typically charged with performing their own audits of an organization to ensure compliance with applicable laws. It is not surprising that regulators may perform such a regulator exam following the publicity of a major data breach. This may seem unfair. A company just went through a major information security breach, and then a regulator performs an exam. But consider the regulator's intent. Regulators need to understand the type and nature of a breach so other organizations can benefit. New laws or regulators may be needed to keep pace with hacker innovations. Additionally, companies that have been hacked may not be fully transparent about the incident. Consequently, a regulator may be seen as "getting to the truth" to restore public confidence.

Regardless of the regulator's motivation, when violations of laws and industry norms are found the penalties can be significant. Consider the article published on March 5, 2021, entitled "The biggest data breach fines, penalties, and settlements so far" (Swinhoe 2022). The article included $1.3 billion in regulator fines. The article identified some of the biggest companies in the United States, including the top five fines, as follows:

- Equifax: Fined (at least) $575 million
  - Result from a 2017 breach of personal and financial information of nearly 150 million people due to unpatched databases.
- Home Depot: Fined ~$200 million
  - The result from a 2014 breach of 50 million customer credit card and personal information from its payment system.
- Uber: Fined $148 million
  - The result from a 2016 breach of 57 million user accounts in its web app and failure to report. In fact, the company reportedly paid the hacker $100,000 to keep the breach under wraps.
- Yahoo: Fined $85 million
  - The result from a 2013 breach of 3 billion accounts. Additionally, Yahoo settles a class-action lawsuit from its customers for $50 million.
- Capital One: Fined $80 million
  - The result from a 2019 breach of 100 million customers in the United States and 6 million in Canada through a configuration vulnerability in a web application firewall.

The complete list of companies' fined is too large to enumerate and include many household names such as Morgan Stanley (fined $60 million in 2020), British Airways (fined $26.2 million related to a 2018 breach), Marriott International (fined $23.7 million in 2020), Target (fined $18.5 million in 2017), Ticketmaster (fined $10 million in 2021), and Google (fined $7.5 million in 2020).

While many of these companies have deep pockets, many small companies do not. A recent study suggests that 60% of small businesses fold within 6 months of a cyberbreach (Galvin 2018). Small businesses may not have the expertise to protect their IT infrastructure or resources to survive the aftermath.

 CHAPTER SUMMARY

Conducting audits and assessments of IT infrastructure has increasingly become more important and visible given the large number of breaches in recent years. Although they might share similar qualities, the differences between an audit and an assessment can be great. Likewise, internal auditors and external auditors have many of the same functions yet have some important differences in their roles and expectations. Regardless, assessments, audits, auditors, and regulators are all key components to ensuring a successful risk-management and compliance strategy. Adequate governance and oversight of these activities help ensure that businesses can live up to their obligations to protect customer information.

KEY CONCEPTS AND TERMS

Assurance

Attack vector

Audit

CIA triad

Compliance

Control Objectives for
Information and Related
Technology (COBIT)

Controls

External compliance

Governance

Internal compliance

IT infrastructure

National Institute of Standards
and Technology (NIST)

Objectives

Payment Card Industry Data
Security Standard (PCI DSS)

Penetration test

Risk

Risk management

CHAPTER 1 ASSESSMENT

1. A security assessment is a method for proving the strength of security systems.

A. True

B. False

2. Categorizing information and information systems and then selecting and implementing appropriate security controls is part of a(n) _____.

3. Whereas only qualified auditors perform security audits, anyone may do security assessments.

A. True

B. False

4. The _____ is typically defined as everything needed to operate and manage the IT environment. It is simply all installed technologies, including all hardware, software, network devices, storage, storage, cables, printers, monitors, and such.

5. Which one of the following is *not* a method used for conducting an assessment of security controls?

A. Examine

B. Interview

C. Test

D. Remediate

6. Which of the following is an assessment method that attempts to bypass controls and gain access to a specific system by simulating the actions of a would-be attacker?

A. Policy review

B. Penetration test

C. Standards review

D. Controls audit

E. Vulnerability scan

7. Internal written policies by themselves reduce risk?

A. True

B. False

8. Which of the following best describes an audit used to determine if a Fortune 500 health care company is adhering to HIPAA regulations?

A. IT audit

B. Operational audit

C. Compliance audit

D. Financial audit

E. Investigative audit

9. The internal audit function may be outsourced to an external consulting firm.

A. True

B. False

10. Compliance initiatives typically are efforts around all except which one of the following?

    A. To adhere to internal policies and standards
    B. To adhere to regulatory requirements
    C. To adhere to industry standards and best practices
    D. To adhere to an auditor's recommendation

11. Only internal audit function can perform an audit?

    A. True
    B. False

12. Which one of the following is true with regard to audits and assessments?

    A. Assessments typically result in a pass or fail grade, whereas audits result in a list of recommendations to improve controls.
    B. Assessments are attributive and audits are not.
    C. An audit is typically a precursor to an assessment.
    D. An audit may be conducted independently of an organization, whereas internal IT staff always conducts an IT security assessment.
    E. Audits can result in blame being placed upon an individual.

13. Noncompliance with regulatory standards may result in which of the following?

    A. Brand damage
    B. Fines
    C. Imprisonment
    D. All of the above
    E. B and C only

14. Which component is not part of the CIA triad?

    A. Confidentiality
    B. Integrity
    C. Access
    D. Availability

15. A compliance assessment or audit should not only consider controls but also measures the effectiveness of the governance and management oversight to ensure the controls are being followed.

    A. True
    B. False

Overview of U.S. Compliance Laws

TO STAY COMPLIANT WITH REGULATIONS means you must interpret the regulation. Equally important, you must understand how regulators interpret the laws. Ultimately court cases and judges decide if a company is compliant, but rarely do regulatory compliance cases ever come to court for a ruling. The vast majority of the time, company representatives will demonstrate compliance through the appropriate regulator. Consequently, three core tenants to sustain compliance include understanding the norms of the industry for compliance, having a good working relationship with regulators, and being able to evidence compliance.

A researcher from Harvard Business School published a study in 2021 that indicated the market impact of the Internet on the U.S. gross domestic product was $2.45 trillion, an eightfold increase from $300 million in 2008. The study was commissioned by the Interactive Advertising Bureau (IAB). The study found that the Internet economy grew seven times faster than the total U.S. economy during the past four years at a rate of 22% per year.

The Internet economy is driven through the exchange of personal information as well as goods and services. No government can sit on the sidelines with so much at stake, such as personal privacy and the economic impact to name a few. state governments and the federal government establish laws (referred to as "regulations") that define how to control, handle, share, and process sensitive information that this Internet economy relies on. Much of that information is about you! "Regulators" are the individuals who help enforce these rules. Industries also try to "self-regulate," which means they create standards their members must follow. Failure to follow regulations or industry standards can result in fines or limits placed on the ability to operate. Gross violations of regulations can be seen as a violation of criminal law. These violations can result in the arrest of company officers and potential jail time.

In this chapter, we discuss major government laws and their compliance requirements. When we refer to regulations in this chapter, we mean those that relate to U.S. laws. We see how these requirements will influence security policies. We examine major drivers for the regulations and the importance of protecting personal privacy. Many industry standards and government regulations affect information technology (IT) operations. Remember, each country has its own laws and regulations. Thus, the number of compliance laws and regulations expands greatly. Keep in mind that we are only scratching the surface. Other compliance regulations exist and are often specific to a particular industry.

Chapter 2 Topics

This chapter covers the following topics and concepts:

- What public and private sector regulatory requirements are
- What the Federal Information Security Management Act is
- What the Red Flags Rule is
- What the Cybersecurity Information Sharing Act is
- What the Sarbanes-Oxley Act is
- What the Gramm-Leach-Bliley Act is
- What the Health Insurance Portability and Accountability Act is
- What the Children's Internet Protection Act is
- What the Children's Online Privacy Protection Act is
- What the California Consumer Privacy Act is
- What the Family Educational Rights and Privacy Act is
- What the Payment Card Industry Data Security Standard is

Chapter 2 Goals

When you complete this chapter, you will be able to:

- Describe the goals and requirements for key acts of Congress
- Describe the goals and requirements of the Payment Card Industry Data Security Standard
- Describe various regulations concerning the protection of health, accounting, and other information

Introduction to Regulatory Requirements

There are government concerns with consumer protection, promoting a stable economy, and maintaining a reliable source of tax revenue. All three of these drivers are linked. If people feel safe using the Internet to buy goods and services, a stable economy emerges. When you have a stable sector of the economy, the government has a reliable source of tax revenue. This is not to imply that any one of these drivers is the primary goal of government regulation. However, government regulations do exist, and the question is what to regulate and how much.

When you implement security policies, remember that there are pressures and trade-offs. For example, you may have to place restrictive controls on data to comply with a regulation that limits how your business operates. As you balance competing interests, you must be talking to the business. Security policies reflect how the business wishes to balance competing interests.

Nevertheless, it is first important to understand why these requirements exist. Equally important is to understand how the regulator within your industry interprets these regulations. It is the regulator interpretation that will set expectations on what controls the organization must deploy.

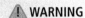 **WARNING**

There is an irony in regulatory compliance laws. Although the laws might appear complicated, they make high-level points that are simple to understand. A problem occurs when people interpret regulations in different ways.

technical TIP

Your internal policies should define what controls must be deployed to meet regulators' expectations. Policies should follow a framework that is easily understood and promotes compliance. Having a framework demonstrates a company's planned approach. Meanwhile, the policies demonstrate a company's drive and support to be compliant. Take the time to properly build your internal policies. This rids you of many headaches in the event you must undergo an audit. In other words, ensuring your policies follow a solid framework to comply with different regulations really pays off.

An example is the General Data Protection Regulation (GDPR), which was adopted by the European Union (EU) in May 2018. GDPR brings greater obligations on companies processing and handling personal data of individuals who live in Europe. Why is this important to U.S. companies? EU citizens buying products over the Internet or EU citizen traveling to the United States would be covered by the GDPR regulations. While this chapter only focuses on U.S. laws, a broader view of regulations would be needed.

Regulatory compliance is nothing new. However, government oversight and strong compliance regulations greatly increased due to the expansion of the Internet. Consider how quickly the Internet has become part of our daily lives. It's not just the browser we

 WARNING

If you do business in other countries, you need to consider the requirements and compliance laws of those foreign countries. In addition, many U.S.-based companies rely on foreign, third-party service providers. This could result in noncompliance with U.S. or foreign regulations.

use to surf the Internet that impacts our lives daily. Our doorbell may have an Internet camera, we may be using an Internet phone (smartphone), or those unwanted robot calls are usually generated through data obtained through the Internet.

Regulatory Acts of Congress

Congress enacts major legislation known as *statutes*. The president of the United States signs these **acts of Congress** into law. Examples of such acts include the Cybersecurity Information Sharing Act (CISA) of 2015, E-Government Act of 2002, the Sarbanes-Oxley (SOX) Act, and the Health Insurance Portability and Accountability Act (HIPAA).

After such acts become law, various government agencies create and enforce the federal regulations authorized by those acts. Some examples of these government agencies are the Food and Drug Administration (FDA), Environmental Protection Agency (EPA), U.S. Securities and Exchange Commission (SEC), Federal Trade Commission (FTC), and Federal Communications Commission (FCC), to name a few.

Congress first typically passes a statute to address a problem, such as a social or economic issue. These are considered enabling legislation that allow **regulatory agencies** to create the necessary regulations to implement the law. (A regulatory agency is a public or government agency that has authority over some area of activity in a regulatory or supervisory capacity.) For example, the FCC creates regulations under CIPA. The SEC creates regulations under SOX.

Federal Information Security Management Act

The **Federal Information Security Management Act of 2002 (FISMA)** is contained within the **E-Government Act of 2002**, Public Law 107-347, as Title III. This act grants the importance of sound information security practices. It also controls the interest of national security and the economic well-being of the United States. This act was amended in 2014 by the Federal Information Security Modernization Act of 2014, which provides several key changes.

The purpose of FISMA is to do the following:

- Provide a framework for effective information security resources that support federal operations, data, and infrastructure
- Accept the interconnectedness of IT. Ensure effective risk management is in place
- Ensure coordination of information security efforts between civilian, national security, and law enforcement communities
- Facilitate the development and ongoing monitoring of required minimum controls to protect federal information systems and data
- Provide for increased oversight of federal agency information security programs
- Recognize that information technology solutions may be acquired from commercial organizations but leave the acquisition decisions to the individual agencies

FISMA tasked the National Institute of Standards and Technology (NIST) to develop and set standards and guidelines. These apply to federal information systems. Standards help categorize information and the systems. They are developed using a risk-based approach. They include the minimum information security controls. For example, standards include the management, operational, and technical controls to apply to information systems.

NIST publications outline a complete set of security standards and processes. To be compliant, your policies must include key security control requirements. Regardless of the publication, often these requirements include the following:

- **Inventory**—The standards require an inventory of hardware, software, and information. The inventory identifies the type of information handled, interfaces to the systems, and special attention to national security systems.

- **Categorize risk level**—The publication outlines an approach to classify risk. It outlines how to map risk levels to computer systems and information. The risk drives what security to be applied.

- **Security controls**—The publication outlines what controls should be applied and when. It outlines how these controls are documented and approved. It is a risked-based approach giving some flexibility to the agency to tailor controls to meet their operational needs.

- **Risk assessment**—The standard defines and outlines the process to conduct risk assessments. Risk assessments are an essential part of a risk-based security approach. The risk assessment results drive the type of security controls to be applied.

- **System security plan**—The standards require a formal security plan for major systems and for the agency as a whole. The security plan serves as a roadmap. It is updated to keep current with threats and is an important part of the certification and accreditation process.

- **Certification and accreditation (C&A)**—This process occurs after the system is documented, controls tested, and risk assessment completed. It is required before going live with a major system. Once a system is certified and accredited, responsibility shifts to the agency to operate the system. This process is also referred to as the "security certification" process.

- **Continuous monitoring**—All certified and accredited systems must be continuously monitored. Monitoring includes looking at new threats, changes to the system, and how well the controls are working. Sometimes a system has so many changes that it must be recertified.

In support of FISMA, NIST developed the following publications:

- Federal Information Processing Standard (FIPS) Publication 199, "Standards for Security Categorization of Federal Information and Information Systems"

- FIPS Publication 200, "Minimum Security Requirements for Federal Information and Information Systems"

- NIST Special Publication 800-18, "Guide for Developing Security Plans for Federal Information Systems"

- NIST Special Publication 800-30, "Risk Management Guide for Information Technology Systems"

- NIST Special Publication 800-37, "Guide for Applying the Risk Management Framework to Federal Information Systems: A Security Life Cycle Approach"
- NIST Special Publication 800-39, "Managing Information Security Risk: Organization, Mission, and Information System View"
- NIST Special Publication 800-53, "Recommended Security Controls for Federal Information Systems"
- NIST Special Publication 800-53A, "Guide for Assessing the Security Controls in Federal Information Systems"
- NIST Special Publication 800-59, "Guideline for Identifying an Information System as a National Security System"
- NIST Special Publication 800-60, "Guide for Mapping Types of Information and Information Systems to Security Categories"

To comply with FISMA, the appointed inspector general of the agency performs a separate, annual evaluation. The evaluation first tests the value of the IT security policies, procedures, and practices. A subset of the information systems within the particular agency is tested. If no inspector general exists, an independent external auditor performs it. The external auditor submits the results to the Office of Management and Budget (OMB). The OMB is a cabinet-level office within the Executive Office of the President of the United States with oversight responsibilities. The OMB compiles the data from each agency. The OMB then prepares an annual report to Congress on compliance with the act.

At first, it appears only federal agencies need to worry about compliance, but this is not true. Federal agencies, for example, must care about their own systems as well as the systems of other contractors or organizations supporting the agencies. Any company or organization that expects to conduct business with the federal government needs to concern itself with FISMA.

The changes signed into law in 2014 authorize the Secretary of the Department of Homeland Security (DHS) to assist the OMB. In addition, the changes affect reporting and notification requirements. Agencies are required to provide timely notification of major security incidents to the OMB. Agencies also are required to provide much more specific information related to threats and compliance.

 TIP

The annual reports submitted to Congress from the OMB concerning FISMA compliance are publicly available online. You can find them at FISMA FY2020 Annual Report to Congress (whitehouse.gov).

Red Flag Rules

The Red Flags Rule (RFR) was developed by the Federal Trade Commission with other agencies to establish a set of United States federal regulations that require financial firms and creditors to protect consumers from identity theft. The term red flag refers to having processes that look for suspicious indicator of identity theft and to "flag" those accounts for further review and verification of customer identity. These extra checks and supporting processes are referred to as the Red Flag Rules.

An RFR program must include process to identify the red flags of identity theft that may occur in opening and accessing an account. For example, if a customer has to provide some form of identification that does not match their physical appearance or doesn't look genuine would be a "red flag." An RFR program:

* Should have policies and training to detect identify theft and red flags accounts.
* Should have clear process on how to respond to red flags.
* Must be updated regularly.

Cybersecurity Information Sharing Act

CISA was passed in October 2015. The law is considered significant as it provides legal boundaries for the sharing of sensitive **cybersecurity** information within and between the private and government sectors. The law solves a core problem that organizations are reluctant to share cybersecurity information that may expose them to civil or criminal liability, embarrassment, and loss of trust. This is especially true for companies that just suffered a cybersecurity data breach.

The objective of CISA is to improve cybersecurity in the United States through sharing of information about cybersecurity threats and breaches as well as for other purposes. The law authorizes private companies to share cybersecurity threat information for "cybersecurity purposes" with the federal government and with other private entities. A "cybersecurity purpose" is defined as "the purpose of protecting an information system or information that is stored on, processed by, or transiting an information system from a cybersecurity threat or security vulnerability."

CISA contains four titles:

* Title I establishes a centralized mechanism for cybersecurity information sharing.
* Title II instructs DHS to take measures designed to strengthen cybersecurity in the federal government and at federal agencies as well as to facilitate the implementation of Title I.
* Title III calls for a cybersecurity-focused assessment of the federal workforce.
* Title IV provides for other measures intended to identify and address threats to critical information

    Key components of the act are as follows:

* It limits the use of shared information by federal and state governments. The permissible purposes are to respond to, prevent, mitigate, investigate, or prosecute events that are considered a "threat of serious economic harm".
* It does not create a duty to share. CISA does not require private companies to share sensitive information. In fact, the act expressly prohibits the federal government from attempting to coerce sharing by withholding cybersecurity information or other benefits such as awarding government contracts.

- It provides authorization to use defensive measures. CISA also authorizes private entities to use defensive measures to protect information systems and data. However, the CISA expressly prohibits private companies from attacking or "hacking back."
- Liability protections require sharing "in accordance" with CISA. To benefit from CISA's safe harbor from civil liability, antitrust, private entities' sharing activity must be "conducted in accordance" with CISA rules.
- Communications with regulatory authorities are permitted. Communication with regulators does not result in loss of CISA's liability protections.

Sarbanes-Oxley Act

The Sarbanes-Oxley Act of 2002, also known as Sarbox or SOX, is a U.S. federal law. It is the result of the Public Company Account Reform and Investor Protection Act and Corporate Accountability and Responsibility Act. SOX dramatically changed how public companies do business.

The bill stems from the fraud and accounting debacles at companies such as Enron and WorldCom. Former President Bush characterized the act "as the most far reaching reforms of American business practices since the time of Franklin Delano Roosevelt." The act's primary purpose was to restore public confidence in the financial reporting of publicly traded companies. As a result, the act mandated many reforms to enhance corporate responsibility, enhance financial disclosures, and prevent fraud. SOX consists of the following 11 titles:

- **Title I, Public Company Accounting Oversight Board**—This title establishes the **Public Company Accounting Oversight Board (PCAOB)**. The PCAOB has several responsibilities, including overseeing public accounting firms, defining the process for compliance audits, and enforcing SOX compliance.
- **Title II, Auditor Independence**—This title establishes the conditions of services an auditor can perform while remaining independent. For example, a public accounting firm that performs external auditing services cannot provide financial information systems design or internal audit outsourcing services.
- **Title III, Corporate Responsibility**—This title requires the formation of audit committees. It also establishes the interactions between the committee and external auditors. Perhaps one of the more notable mandates of SOX is contained in Section 302, which requires the chief executive officer and the chief financial officer to take individual responsibility in certifying and approving the integrity of the company's financial reports.
- **Title IV, Enhanced Financial Disclosures**—This title addresses the accuracy and features of financial disclosures. For example, this title specifically addresses and prevents what Enron did, such as selling liabilities on its balance sheet as assets to special purpose entities. This title also contains the controversial Section 404, which requires companies to report the adequacy of their internal controls.

- **Title V, Analyst Conflicts of Interest**—This title fosters public confidence in securities research and defines code of conducts between firms.
- **Title VI, Commission Resources and Authority**—This title provides greater authority to the SEC to fault or bar a securities professional from practice. This title also addresses the prevention of fraud schemes involving low-volume, low-price stocks.
- **Title VII, Studies and Reports**—This title requires the comptroller general and the SEC to conduct studies and report their findings. Examples include studying the effects of the consolidation of public accounting firms as well as studying previous corporate fraud and accounting scandals.
- **Title VIII, Corporate and Criminal Fraud Accountability**—This title provides the ramifications for corporate fraud and addresses the destruction of corporate audit records. This is a direct response to the auditing firm, Arthur Andersen, which shredded documents.
- **Title IX, White Collar Crime Penalty Enhancement**—This title reviews the rules and penalties regarding white-collar criminal offenses.
- **Title X, Corporate Tax Returns**—This title simply states that the CEO should sign the company tax return.
- **Title XI, Corporate Fraud Accountability**—Also known as the Corporate Fraud Accountability Act of 2002, this title provides additional guidelines regarding the consequences of corporate fraud. It also provides the SEC with the authority to freeze the funds of companies suspected of violating laws.

SOX is quite large and contains many reforms to rally public confidence. It also improves corporate accountability and helps to avoid corporate fraud and dishonesty. Two sections receive much of the attention, especially of IT. The first is Section 302, "Corporate Responsibility for Financial Reports." The second is Section 404, "Management Assessment of Internal Controls." These two sections place vast constraints on IT security. Although neither section mentions IT or IT security, financial accounting systems rely heavily on IT infrastructure. Thus, it has strongly driven the subject of IT security into the boardroom.

Section 302 requires the CEO and CFO to personally certify the truthfulness and accuracy of financial reports. They start and make internal controls. Then, they must assess and report upon the internal controls around financial reporting every quarter. Section 404 goes a step further. Section 404 requires the company to provide proof. Again, they must assess the effectiveness of their internal controls, which a public accounting firm must audit and attest. They then publish this information in the company's annual report.

SOX is lengthy and is specific in many areas—for example, criminal penalties for noncompliance. It still is very high level and leaves a lot of room for interpretation, especially concerning IT controls. SOX does not directly address IT control requirements. As a result, you need to become familiar with a couple of publications. These include the auditing standards created by the PCAOB and the SEC's release on management guidance—17 CFR Part 241. In this codification, the SEC issued further interpretation and guidance regarding Section 404. It provides "an approach by which management can conduct a top-down, risk-based evaluation of internal control over financial reporting." PCAOB also made a formal process to further define the criteria within Section 404. This process became Auditing Standard No. 2. This standard is now superseded by Auditing Standard No. 5, "An Audit of Internal Control over Financial Reporting That Is Integrated with an Audit of Financial Statements." Some notable changes to provide greater clarity and a more prescriptive approach include the following four areas:

- Aligning Auditing Standard No. 5 with the SEC's management guidance, mostly with regard to prescriptive requirements and definitions
- Adjusting the audit to account for the particular circumstances regarding the different sizes and complexities of companies
- Encouraging auditors to use professional judgment, particularly in using a risk-assessment methodology
- Following a principles-based approach to determining when and to what extent the auditor can use the work of others to obtain evidence about the design and effectiveness of the control

The standard also states that the auditor should use the "same suitable, recognized control framework" as the management of the company they are auditing. Furthermore, it even goes as far to suggest a suitable framework. That framework is the Committee of Sponsoring Organizations (COSO) of the Treadway Commission.

Gramm-Leach-Bliley Act

Also known as the Financial Modernization Act of 1999, the **Gramm-Leach-Bliley Act (GLBA)** repeals parts of the Glass-Steagall Act from 1933. The Glass-Steagall Act prohibited banks from offering investment, commercial banking, and insurance services all under a single umbrella. GLBA deregulates the split of commercial and investment banking. GLBA also provides provisions for compliance within Sections 501 and 521 to protect the financial information held by the industry. This protection is on behalf of the consumers. GLBA generally applies to financial institutions or any organization "significantly engaged" in financial activities. Examples include banks and securities firms. More examples are firms dealing with mortgages, insurance, tax preparation, debt collection, and much more. The FTC maintains and enforces GLBA.

To protect personally identifiable information, GLBA divides privacy requirements into three principal parts:

- **Financial Privacy Rule**—The Financial Privacy Rule governs the collection and disclosure of customers' personal financial information.
- **Safeguards Rule**—The Safeguards Rule requires financial institutions to develop, maintain, and implement policies. These policies should tell how they will protect customer information.

Pretexting

Pretexting is a method of social engineering. It is more about human interaction than about technology. For pretexting to succeed, you must manipulate others to divulge sensitive information. The root of pretexting is pretext or a situation or reason that is deceptive or false. For example, investigators often use pretexting—at least in the movies! It typically involves some type of con or clever ruse.

Consider, for example, how to guess a password. You might use some programmatic mechanism to guess a password. Now consider how much easier it is to ask someone for the password, presumably under a pretext. This is one example of why companies so often reiterate that they will never ask you for your password. A famous recent example involved Hewlett-Packard (HP). At the time, contracted private investigators determined the source of an information leak. To do so, the investigators operated under a pretext. They impersonated HP board members or journalists from popular news outlets to obtain phone records.

There are countless examples of why pretexting occurs. The GLBA pretexting provision protects consumers from evildoers trying to obtain personal financial information under false pretenses. Identity theft is the greatest risk to consumers should their information be compromised.

- **Pretexting provisions**—The pretexting provisions protect consumers. This protection is from both individuals and organizations that obtain personal financial information under false pretenses.

The Financial Privacy Rule requires financial institutions to provide notices to their customers. The notices explain their privacy policies, specifically covering the information collection and sharing practices of the company. Consumers are also given control over limiting the sharing of their information or opting out. If the financial institution changes its policy, it must provide another notice to the consumer.

The Safeguards Rule requires financial institutions to develop an information security policy to consider the nature and sensitivity of the information they handle. The plan must include and the company must comply with the following:

- Designate at least one employee to coordinate an information security program.
- Assess the risks to customer information within each pertinent area of the company's operation. Evaluate the effectiveness of the current safeguards and risk controls.
- Implement a safeguard program. Regularly monitor and test it.
- Choose service providers that can maintain appropriate safeguards, and govern their handling of customer information.
- Evaluate and adjust the security program given events and changes in the firm's operations.

Likely, most organizations will protect against pretexting as part of their information security program. The best defense against pretexting is not technical, but rather awareness and training. Training is for both employees and customers. The pretexting provision makes it illegal to do the following:

- Make a false, fictitious, or fraudulent statement or representation to obtain customer information from the financial institution or its customers.
- Use forged, counterfeit, lost, or stolen documents to obtain customer information from the financial institution or its customers.

Health Insurance Portability and Accountability Act

U.S. Congress enacted the **Health Insurance Portability and Accountability Act (HIPAA)** in 1996. The primary purpose of the statute is twofold. First, it helps citizens maintain their health insurance coverage. Second, it improves the efficiency and effectiveness of the American health care system. It does so by combating waste, fraud, and abuse in both health insurance and the delivery of healthcare. The U.S. Department of Health and Human Services (HHS) is responsible for publishing requirements and for enforcing HIPAA laws. However, the Office of Civil Rights, a subagency of HHS, administers and enforces the Privacy Rule and Security Rule of HIPAA. These laws are divided across five titles, which include the following:

- Title I, Health Care Access, Portability, and Renewability
- Title II, Preventing Health Care Fraud and Abuse, Administrative Simplification; Medical Liability Reform
- Title III, Tax-Related Health Provisions
- Title IV, Application and Enforcement of Group Health Plan Requirements
- Title V, Revenue Offsets

Given the sensitive nature of one's personal health records, this regulation is usually taken very seriously and affects the following:

- Health care providers—Doctors, hospitals, clinics, and so on
- Heath plans—Those that pay the cost for the medical care such as insurance companies
- Health care clearinghouse—Those that process and facilitate billing

The last major update to the HIPAA rules was the HIPAA Omnibus Rule changes in 2013. While the fundamental requirements (referred to as *Safeguards*) in the act did not change, a number of details within each of the title's requirements under fine tuning:

- Performing a gap analysis to determine what policies and procedures must be revisited in light of the Omnibus Rules
- Revising privacy and security policies and procedures
- Revising breach notification policies, procedure
- Amending notices of privacy practices based on the new rules

- Enhancing training of the workforce and promoting more ongoing awareness
- Ensuring end-user training on proper handling of data is performed prior to granting access
- Updating risk analysis to reflect vulnerabilities such as mobile devices

Much of the focus around HIPAA is within the first two titles. Title I offers protection of health insurance coverage without regard to preexisting conditions to those, for example, who lose or change their jobs. Title II provides requirements for the privacy and security of health information. This is often referred to as administrative simplification. The broader law calls for the following:

- Standardization of electronic data—patient, administrative, and financial—as well as the use of unique health identifiers
- Security standards and controls to protect the confidentiality and integrity of individually identifiable health information

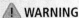

WARNING

Several proposed changes in HIPAA are expected in 2022 and beyond. One of the changes would increase the right to access health information for individuals, known as the Right of Access. This would include information stored electronically. During the pandemic, many caregivers could not access medical information for older adults in their families. This was particularly challenging during medical emergencies.

As a result, the HHS has provided five rules regarding Title II of HIPAA. These rules include the Privacy Rule, the Transactions and Code Sets Rule, the Security Rule, the Unique Identifiers Rule, and the Enforcement Rule. These five rules affect information technology operations within organizations. Specifically, the Privacy Rule and Security Rule affect information security. HIPAA is primarily concerned with **protected health information (PHI)**. PHI is individually identifiable health information. PHI relates to the physical or mental health of an individual. It can also relate to the delivery of health care to an individual as well as payment for the delivery of health care.

The Privacy Rule went into effect in 2003. It regulates the use and disclosure of PHI by covered entities. Covered entities, for example, include health care providers, health plans, and health care clearinghouses. In many ways, the Privacy Rule drives the Security Rule. Under the law, covered entities are obligated to do the following:

- Provide information to patients about their privacy rights and how the information can be used.
- Adopt clear privacy procedures.
- Train employees on privacy procedures.
- Designate someone to be responsible for overseeing that privacy procedures are adopted and followed.

The Security Rule followed the Privacy Rule. Unlike the Privacy Rule, however, the Security Rule applies just to electronic PHI (ePHI). The Security Rule provides for the **confidentiality**, **integrity**, and **availability** of ePHI, and contains three broad safeguards:

- Administrative safeguards
- Technical safeguards
- Physical safeguards

Each of the preceding safeguards consists of various standards. All are required or addressable. Required rules must be implemented, but addressable standards provide flexibility. This way, an organization can decide how to reasonably and appropriately meet the standard. Bear in mind, however, that addressable does not mean optional.

Administrative safeguards primarily consist of policies and procedures. They govern the security measures used to protect ePHI. **Table 2-1** provides a summary of the administrative safeguards, including the required and addressable standards.

Physical safeguards include the policies, procedures, and physical controls put in place. These controls and documentation protect the information systems and physical

TABLE 2-1 HIPAA administrative safeguards and implementation specifications.

SAFEGUARD	IMPLEMENTATION SPECIFICATION
Security management process	Risk analysis Risk management Sanction policy Information system activity review
Assigned security responsibility	Not applicable
Workforce security	Authorization and/or supervision Workforce clearance procedure Termination procedures
Information access management	Isolating health care clearinghouse function Access authorization Access establishment and modification
Security awareness and training	Security reminders Protection from malicious software Logon monitoring Password management
Security incident procedures	Response and reporting
Contingency plan	Data backup plan Disaster recovery plan Emergency mode operation plan Testing and revision procedures Applications and data criticality analysis
Evaluation	Not applicable
Business associate contracts and other arrangements	Written contract or other arrangement

structures from unauthorized access. The same goes for natural disasters and other environmental hazards. The physical safeguards include the four standards shown in **Table 2-2**, along with the implementation specifications.

Technical safeguards consist of the policies, procedures, and controls put in place. These safeguards protect ePHI and prevent unauthorized access. **Table 2-3** lists the five safeguards and corresponding implementation specifications.

Although covered entities must comply with the previously listed safeguards and implementation specifications, there isn't a safeguard listed that should surprise organizations. In fact, most of these safeguards are addressed through best practices for any sensitive information.

TABLE 2-2 HIPAA physical safeguards and implementation specifications.	
SAFEGUARD	**IMPLEMENTATION SPECIFICATION**
Facility access controls	Contingency operations Facility security plan Access control and validation procedures Maintenance records
Workstation use	Not applicable
Workstation security	Not applicable
Device and media controls	Disposal Media reuse Accountability Data backup and storage

TABLE 2-3 HIPAA technical safeguards and implementation specifications.	
SAFEGUARD	**IMPLEMENTATION SPECIFICATION**
Access control	Contingency operations Facility security plan Access control and validation procedures Maintenance records
Audit controls	Not applicable
Integrity	Mechanisms to authenticate ePHI
Person or entity authentication	Not applicable
Transmission security	Integrity controls Encryption

Children's Internet Protection Act

The **Children's Internet Protection Act (CIPA)** is a federal law introduced as part of a spending bill that passed Congress in 2000. The FCC maintains and enforces CIPA. This act addresses concerns about children's access to explicit content (such as pornography) online at schools and libraries by requiring the use of Internet filters as a condition of receiving federal funds. CIPA is a result of previous failed attempts at restricting indecent content. The Communications Decency Act and the Child Online Protection Act faced Supreme Court challenges over the U.S. First Amendment because the act violated the right of free speech contained within the Constitution.

CIPA does not provide for any additional funds for the purchase of mechanisms to protect children from explicit content. Instead, conditions are attached to grants and the use of E-Rate discounts. *E-Rate* is a program that makes Internet access more affordable for schools and libraries.

CIPA requires schools and libraries to certify compliance to implement an Internet safety policy and "technology protection measures," which means having technology in place that blocks or filters Internet access that is either obscene, harmful to minors, or represents child pornography. This requirement includes implementing a safety policy and controls that address the following:

- Access by minors to "inappropriate matter" on the Internet
- The safety and security of minors when using electronic communication such as email, chat rooms, and instant messaging
- Unauthorized access and unlawful activities by minors
- Unauthorized disclosure, use, and dissemination of personal information regarding minors
- Measures restricting minors' access to harmful materials

Before implementing the policy and controls, however, the law also requires schools or libraries to first provide public notice and to hold a public hearing to address the proposed Internet safety policy.

You might have noticed that the term *inappropriate matter* could be considered vague and controversial. As a result, the act is clear in stating that the government may not establish the criteria for making such a determination. The act states that the determination is made at the local level by the school board, local educational agency, or library.

Finally, schools and libraries must comply with one more step before they can receive the E-Rate. They must certify they have an Internet safety policy in place meeting the preceding requirements. Noncompliance with the law occurs if there is a failure to submit for certification. In this case, the institution will not be eligible for services at a discounted rate. In addition, failure to ensure the use of the computers in accordance with a certification will be required to reimburse all funds and discounts for the certification period.

Children's Online Privacy Protection Act

Like CIPA, the **Children's Online Privacy Protection Act (COPPA)** is a U.S. federal law designed to protect children. COPPA is maintained and enforced by the FTC. COPPA requires websites and other online services aimed at children less than 13 years of age to comply with specific requirements of the law.

In 2013, the FTC implemented new provisions that provide additional protections to keep pace with the changes in technology. The FTC also introduced a six-step plan to understand if an organization is required to comply with COPPA, and if so, how to be compliant. The six steps are as follows:

1. Determine if your company is a website or online service that collects personal information from children under 13.
2. Post a privacy policy that complies with COPPA.
3. Notify parents directly before collecting personal information from their children.
4. Get parents' verifiable consent before collecting information from their children.
5. Honor parents' ongoing rights with respect to information collected from their children.
6. Implement exceptions to COPPA's verifiable parental consent requirement.

With Step 1, an organization will likely need to consult the law and to understand precisely how terms are defined. For example, what does it mean to *collect*, or what exactly is considered *personal information?* Online services are obliged to comply with COPPA if asking for information that would even imply a child is less than 13 years of age—for example, "Do you now attend elementary school?"

After it is determined that COPPA applies, the next step requires the creation of a privacy policy. COPPA requires that the privacy policy list all operators who are collecting information. In addition, it must list an operator who will respond to any and all queries from parents. Next, the privacy policy must contain a complete description of the personal information that is collected and for what purposes. Finally, the policy must state the rights afforded to parents. For example, this must include a notice that parents have the right to review the information collected on their child and even provide direction that the collected data be deleted.

Except under limited classes of information, COPPA requires that parents be notified before data is collected from their children. The rule provides for very specific requirements that must be met with regard to such notice. Once notification requirements are met in Step 3, Step 4 requires verifiable consent. While the means of providing such consent is left up to the requesting organization, the rule does provide several examples of acceptable methods. One simple example is a signed consent form via fax, mail, or electronic scan. Another is the entry of a credit or debit card number when coupled with a financial transaction.

The final two steps require continual obligations upon the entity complying with COPPA. With Step 5, parents may ask to review, revoke, or delete the child's information at any time. Such requests must be honored by the complying organization. At the same time, the organization must take necessary precautions, such as taking reasonable measures to ensure that parents are in fact who they say they are. The final step provides rules around the need to protect the confidentiality and integrity of the information collected as well as ensure that adequate retention and disposal practices are maintained.

California Consumer Privacy Act

The number of state laws related to cybersecurity are too numerous to outline. The emerging laws tend to focus on privacy and contain many of the core principles found in the California Consumers Privacy Act (CCPA), which was implemented in January 2020.

The law allows consumers the right to find out who has access to their personal data. Consumers can stop data from being sold or transferred to third parties through an opt-out function that must be prominently posted or request that companies delete their data.

Table 2-4 outlines key concepts embedded in the CCPA and many states' privacy laws:

The CCPA was one of the first state laws to significantly expand the definition of personal information. The law recognized the increased importance and impact on an individual's personal identity over the Internet. The CCPA's list of data elements that constitute "personal information" includes the following:

- Identifiers, such as a real name, alias, postal address, unique personal identifier, online identifier, IP address, email address, account name, Social Security number, driver's license number, passport number, or other similar identifiers
- Commercial information, including records of personal property, products or services purchased, obtained or considered, or other purchasing or consuming histories or tendencies
- Biometric information such as fingerprints, facial recognition files
- Internet or other electronic network activity information, including, but not limited to browsing history, search history, and information regarding a consumer's interaction with a website, application, or advertisement
- Geolocation data
- Audio, voiceprints, electronic, visual, thermal, olfactory, or similar information
- Professional or employment-related information
- Education information, defined as information that is not publicly available as defined in the **Family Educational Rights and Privacy Act (FERPA)** (20 U.S.C. §1232g, 34 C.F.R. Part 99) which protects education records and the student's

TABLE 2-4 Key privacy concepts.	
CONCEPT	**OBJECTIVE**
Full disclosure	The idea is that an individual should know what information about them is being collected. They should be told how that information is being used.
Limited use of personal data	The idea is that only the data needed for the transaction should be collected. Do not collect more information than you need to provide the product or service.
Opt-in/opt-out	The practice of asking permission on how personal information can be used beyond its original purpose, such as a real-estate company asking permission of someone who sold their home if their information can be shared with a moving company. The difference between opting in and opting out generally refers to clicking a box on a webpage. In an opt-in process, unless the consumer clicks the "Yes" box, no additional service is offered. In an opt-out process, consumers are automatically enrolled in a service unless they click the "No" box or deselect the "Yes" box.
Data privacy	Expectations on how your personal information should be protected and limits place on how the data should be shared.
Informed consent	The idea that you are of legal age, capable, have the needed facts, and absent undue pressure can make an informed judgment.
Public interest	The idea is that an organization has an obligation to the general public beyond its self-interest. Although a vague term, it's not unusual for regulators to look at the impact a company has on the industry or the economy in general.

identification including disclosure of ay part of the student's Social Security number.

- Inferences are drawn from any of the information identified in this subdivision to create a profile about a consumer reflecting the consumer's preferences, characteristics, or the like

Payment Card Industry Data Security Standard

Payment Card Industry Data Security Standard (PCI DSS) is a worldwide information security standard that describes how to protect credit card information. If you accept Visa, MasterCard, or American Express, you are required to follow PCI DSS. These card companies formed the **Payment Card Industry Security Standards Council (PCI SSC)** to create the standard. The Payment Card Industry (PCI) Data Security Standard (DSS) was released in 2006. The standard applies to everyone who stores, processes, or exchanges cardholder information.

The standard requires an organization to have specific PCI DSS security policies and controls in place. The organization must also have these controls validated. If you are a small merchant, you can perform a self-assessment questionnaire. Large-volume merchants must obtain their validation through a **Qualified Security Assessor (QSA)**. Failing to validate, or failing the validation, can result in fines from the credit card companies. In extreme cases of noncompliance, you may be prevented from handling credit cards. Taking credit cards away could put you out of business.

The PCI DSS is an information security framework, so it has lots of technical requirements. Two, in particular, have been a challenge for organizations to implement: network segmentation and encryption. PCI strongly encourages isolating credit card systems at a network layer. For many open network designs and shared systems, this is a challenge. Without network segmentation, the standard talks about the need that all systems on that segment to be brought up to PCI DSS level standards. This could also be expensive. The second major challenge is encrypting data at rest. As discussed in previous chapters, encrypting data in transit is common over the Internet and public networks. Encrypting data at rest, however, can be technically challenging and at times not feasible.

There are six control objectives within the PCI DSS standard. To be compliant, you need to include these control objectives in your security policies and controls:

- Build and maintain a secure network—Refers to having specific firewall, system password, and other security network layer controls.
- Protect cardholder data—Specifies how cardholder data are stored and protected. Also sets rules on the encryption of the data.
- Maintain a vulnerability management program—Specifies how to maintain secure systems and applications, including the required use of antivirus software.
- Implement strong access control measures—Refers to restricting access to cardholder data on a need-to-know basis. It requires physical controls are in place and requires individuals to have unique IDs when accessing cardholder data.
- Regularly monitor and test networks—Requires access to cardholder data be monitored. Also requires periodic penetration testing of the network.
- Maintain an information security policy—Requires that security policies reflect the PCI DSS requirements. Requires these policies be kept current and an awareness program be implemented.

> **FYI**
>
> Compliance with PCI DSS is required for merchants and credit card processors. Enforcement of the PCI DSS requirements is through contractual obligations. Noncompliance can result in a merchant not being allowed to accept credit cards. The PCI Security Standards Council also provides guidance for software developers of payment application systems to ensure products used to accept credit card payments are secure.

PCI DSS is unlike most regulatory laws in one way. It is very specific with regard to requirements and expectations. The requirements generally follow security best practices and use the 12 high-level requirements, aligned across six goals, as shown in **Table 2-5.** Each requirement listed in the table consists of various subrequirements. Also

TABLE 2-5   Goals and high-level requirements for PCI DSS.

GOALS	HIGH-LEVEL REQUIREMENTS
Build and maintain a secure network.	1. Install and maintain a firewall configuration to protect cardholder data. 2. Do not use vendor-supplied defaults for system passwords and other security parameters.
Protect cardholder data.	3. Protect stored cardholder data. 4. Encrypt transmission of cardholder data across open, public networks.
Maintain a vulnerability management program.	5. Use and regularly update antivirus software or programs. 6. Develop and maintain secure systems and applications.
Implement strong access control measures.	7. Restrict access to cardholder data on a need-to-know basis. 8. Assign a unique ID to each person with computer access. 9. Restrict physical access to cardholder data.
Regularly monitor and test networks.	10. Track and monitor all access to network resources and cardholder data. 11. Regularly test security systems and processes.
Maintain an information security policy.	12. Maintain a policy that addresses information security for employees and contractors.

included are procedures for testing. These must be documented as either being in place or not in place.

Consider requirement 8, for example. It requires a unique ID to be assigned to each person with computer access. Within the security standard, this requirement consists of 21 subrequirements. Many of them are very specific:

- Incorporate two-factor authentication for remote access.
- Set first-time passwords to a unique value and change immediately after first use.
- Remove or disable inactive accounts at least every 90 days.
- Require a minimum password length of at least seven characters.

Since PCI DSS started, the Security Council periodically releases supplemental documents. These documents can be found on the Security Council website at https://www .pcisecuritystandards.org/minisite/en/pci-dss-v3-0.php.

CHAPTER SUMMARY

A common truth is that these laws recognize the power of information. The more personal the data, the more powerful the information. The power comes from the impact that personal information has on our lives. With the power of personal information comes the ability to influence everything from buying choices to political beliefs. It influences what type job we can have, car we drive, home we live, and it determines the quality of medical care we receive. The misuse and abuse of this information is equally powerful to make our lives miserable. Stealing a person's identity is a major problem. It can take years of effort to restore your credit. We've all hear stories of millions of credit cards stolen each year. While slow to react, the government does respond to these headlines and public pressure. Although compliance with regulations can touch many different groups within an organization, IT departments are increasingly discovering they need to stay abreast of the latest regulations as IT continues to be pervasive throughout organizations. It might seem overwhelming to keep up with the requirements of all the existing regulations, not to mention new ones. However, sound governance, risk-management, and compliance program within organizations using a well-defined framework can make the process much more efficient and effective.

KEY CONCEPTS AND TERMS

Acts of Congress	Family Educational Rights and Privacy Act (FERPA)	Payment Card Industry Data Security Standards (PCI DSS)
Availability		
Certification and accreditation (C&A)	Federal Information Security Management Act of 2002 (FISMA)	Pretexting
Children's Internet Protection Act (CIPA)		Protected health information (PHI)
Children's Online Privacy Protection Act (COPPA)	Gramm-Leach-Bliley Act (GLBA)	Public Company Accounting Oversight Board (PCAOB)
Confidentiality	Health Insurance Portability and Accountability Act (HIPAA)	
Cybersecurity	Integrity	Qualified Security Assessor (QSA)
E-Government Act of 2002	National Institute of Standards and Technology (NIST)	Regulatory agencies

CHAPTER 2 ASSESSMENT

1. Which of the following acknowledges the importance of sound information security practices and controls in the interest of national security?

A. FISMA
B. GLBA
C. HIPAA
D. FACTA
E. FERPA

2. What organization was tasked to develop standards to apply to federal information systems using a risk-based approach?

A. Public Entity Risk Institute
B. International Organization for Standardization
C. National Institute of Standards and Technology
D. International Standards Organization
E. American National Standards Institute

3. Pretexting is a technical method of intercepting passwords embedded in text messages.

A. True
B. False

4. Which of the following organizations was tasked to develop and prescribe standards and guidelines that apply to federal information systems?

A. NIST
B. FISMA
C. Congress
D. PCI SSC
E. U.S. Department of the Navy

5. What section of SOX requires management and the external auditor to report on the accuracy of internal controls over financial reporting?

A. Section 301
B. Section 404
C. Section 802
D. Section 1107

6. SOX explicitly addresses the IT security controls required to ensure accurate financial reporting.

A. True
B. False

7. Which of the following was established to have oversight of public accounting firms and is responsible for defining the process of SOX compliance audits?

A. COSO
B. Enron
C. PCAOB
D. Sarbanes-Oxley
E. None of the above

8. Which of the following is *not* one of the titles within SOX?

A. Corporate Responsibility
B. Enhanced Financial Disclosures
C. Analyst Conflicts of Interest
D. Studies and Reports
E. Auditor Conflicts of Interest

9. Which one of the following is *not* considered a principal part of the GLBA?

A. Financial Privacy Rule
B. Pretexting provisions
C. Safeguards Rule
D. Information Security Rule

10. Which regulatory department is responsible for the enforcement of HIPAA laws?

A. HHS
B. FDA
C. U.S Department of Agriculture
D. U.S. EPA
E. FTC

11. Which one of the following is *not* one of the safeguards provided within the HIPAA Security Rule?

A. Administrative
B. Operational
C. Technical
D. Physical

12. In accordance with CIPA, who determines what is considered inappropriate material?

A. FCC
B. U.S. Department of Education
C. The local communities
D. U.S. Department of the Interior Library
E. State governments

13. The Family Educational Rights and Privacy Act prohibits the use of Social Security numbers as directory information, even the use of the just the last four digits of a SSN.

A. True
B. False

14. PCI DSS is a legislative act enacted by Congress to ensure that merchants meet baseline security requirements for how they store, process, and transmit payment card data.

A. True
B. False

15. To comply with the Red Flags Rule, financial institutions and creditors must do which of the following?

A. Identify red flags for covered accounts.
B. Detect red flags.
C. Respond to detected red flags.
D. Update the program periodically.
E. All of the above
F. Answers B and C only

16. Having a photograph or physical description on an identification that is not consistent with the applicant or consumer presenting the identification is an example of what type of red flag category?

A. Alerts, notifications, or other warnings received from consumer reporting agencies or service providers.
B. The presentation of suspicious documents
C. The presentation of suspicious personal identifying information
D. The unusual use of or other suspicious activity related to a covered account

17. Regulatory compliance laws do *not* exist at what different level?

A. Local
B. State
C. Federal
D. International.

18. The Family Educational Rights and Privacy Act (FERPA) of 1974 is a U.S. federal law that protects the privacy of student education records and allows parents certain access rights to the student's educational records, even when a student turns 18 and attends college.

A. True
B. False

19. Which of the following does *not* deal with the HIPAA administrative safeguard of the security management process?

A. Risk analysis and management
B. Sanction policy
C. Facility security plan
D. Information system activity review

20. Which of the following does *not* deal with the addressable HIPAA administrative safeguard of workforce security?

A. Authorization and/or supervision
B. Workforce clearance procedure
C. Termination procedures
D. Contingency operations
E. This law attempts to limit children's exposure to sexual material.

What Is the Scope of an IT Compliance Audit?

T HE SCOPE OF AN information technology (IT) audit can vary depending on the specific risk and processes being examined, such as a network audit compared to an application audit. Nonetheless, there are common scope elements to all IT compliance audits, which include an examination of the related policies, adherence to those policies, and adequacy of vulnerability assessments.

A compliance review can determine if policies are being followed. The vulnerability assessment is used to measure the effectiveness of the policies. If everyone follows the policies, then the number of vulnerabilities declines. If the number of vulnerabilities does not decline, the fault typically lies with either individuals not adhering to policy or poorly designed policies. Vulnerability assessments need to be aligned with business goals. Additionally, the level of enforcement needs to align with the level of risk the organization is willing to accept.

The IT environment is vast and must be broken down into auditable chunks or domains. This chapter explores what is required to achieve and sustain compliance across different domains within the IT environment.

Chapter 3 Topics

This chapter covers the following topics and concepts:

- What your organization must do to be in compliance
- What you are auditing within the IT infrastructure
- What your organization must do to maintain IT compliance
- What are the different domains within the IT infrastructure

Chapter 3 Goals

When you complete this chapter, you will be able to:

- Understand what organizations need to do to achieve and maintain compliance
- Explain why protecting privacy data is important for achieving compliance
- Understand the process for selecting security controls
- Compare the different domains of IT infrastructure

What Must Your Organization Do to Be in Compliance?

Organizations typically are judged to be in compliance through adherence to internal policies. In other words, policies are not a strict legal interpretation of the law. Security policies are interpretations of legal requirements that lead to compliance.

A law is any rule prescribed under the authority of a government entity. A regulatory agency may be granted the authority under the law to establish regulations. These regulations inherit their authority from the original law.

Consider the distinction between laws, regulations, and security policies as follows:

- Laws establish the legal thresholds.
- Regulatory requirements establish what an organization has to do to meet the legal thresholds.
- Security policies establish how the organization achieves the regulatory requirements while meeting business goals.

Let's look at an example in the security world that relates to the interpretation of information security regulations. For example, the Gramm-Leach-Bliley Act (GLBA) was intended to ensure the security and confidentiality of customer information. GLBA Section 501(b) requires that the board or its designated committee adequately oversee the financial institution's information security program. What does "adequately oversee" mean? The Federal Deposit Insurance Corporation (FDIC) has issued a regulatory ruling that the organization's board must receive a formal report at least annually. Many organizations interpret that to be a formal report to the audit committee by both the Chief Information Security Officer (CISO) and Chief Audit Executive (CAE). The point is that organizations can achieve regulatory compliance in different ways. Often you write policies to achieve regulatory requirements. Most of the time, you do not write policy to the specific language of the law.

Just because a policy was violated does not mean it was a violation of the law. Often, simply violating a policy is not a violation of the law. The legal interpretation of statutes is a different skill set than policy interpretation. Often, the legal threshold to violate a law is high. It considers circumstance and intent. Only a court or regulatory body can determine if there are sufficient grounds for determining a violation of the law.

Although it is important to remain aware of the current laws and regulations, they should not be your sole driver. There are many risks to the business that are not addressed by laws and regulations. Regulations are written to address a specific area of concern that may have been a result of a public incident or class-action suit. Although ensuring adherence to regulations is a high priority, there is no substitute for common sense. The key point is that law always trumps policies with the regulators and the courts. But keep in mind that laws and regulations do not cover all risks. Additionally, laws and regulations can have conflicting requirements. That is why this balancing of these business goals and regulator mandates are baked into policies.

Policy and compliance are not just about technical measures, however. They must also consider nontechnical methods. There is no definitive answer or solution an organization can purchase that will provide it with compliance. Each organization must determine what is appropriate for it. To do this, an organization must consider current laws and industry standards along with the organization's mission.

Organizational **policies** provide general statements that address the operational goals of an organization. The role of information technology is to help accelerate the business. At the same time, consider security and compliance with laws and regulations to safeguard data. Specifically, IT and IT security policies provide the same high-level directives. They are also concerned, however, with protecting the confidentiality, integrity, and availability of information and information systems. Specifically, this includes sensitive intellectual property of the organization and data that are commonly protected under privacy laws, such as personal information about individuals.

Complying with an organization's internal policy requires standards. Internal **standards** describe mandatory processes or objectives that align with the goal of the policies. Establishing both policies and standards is critical for ensuring the success of the organization as well as compliance with the myriad regulations with which organizations must comply.

A good starting place is with a solid organizational governance framework. This framework considers the applicable laws and regulations and then sets the high-level requirements to secure and control the IT infrastructure. Frameworks such as Control Objectives for Information and Related Technology (COBIT) provide a blueprint for implementing high-level controls by defining control objectives within an organization. Further, control standards such as ISO/IEC 27002 and NIST 800-53 provide more technical requirements on how security controls should be designed and implemented.

When policies and control frameworks are in place, organizations can start implementing specific controls. These additional controls can further address risks to the organization. Perhaps one of the greatest challenges is determining what specific controls to apply. Always consider what is reasonable and appropriate for your organization. Too often, organizations spend too much time and money implementing controls that go beyond the requirements. This can even have the negative result of impeding the mission of the organization. On the other hand, many organizations may get compliance tunnel vision. That is, they lose sight of really addressing risk and are concerned only with being compliant.

Finally, consider that organizations are often required to comply with many different regulations. Many of these may have overlapping goals and intent. Therefore, you want to avoid chasing each one individually. By having sound policies in place and a framework for the application of controls, you will be able to map existing controls to each regulation, including future regulations. Thereafter, organizations perform a **gap analysis** to identify anything that is missing. A gap analysis is a comparison between the desired outcome and the actual outcome. From that gap analysis, the organization can address the gaps separately.

Although compliance with internal policies and compliance with legal requirements should be closely tied together, each of these can be divided into two high-level control objectives. In fact, they are included as control objectives within ISO/IEC 27002:

- Compliance with legal and regulatory requirements
- Compliance with security policies and standards and technical compliance

 WARNING

If your organization uses penetration tests and vulnerability assessments to check technical compliance, be careful. These could have a negative effect on the systems (for example, unconstraint penetration testing can cause business disruptions and unintended system outages).

Compliance with legal requirements includes controls such as identifying all applicable legislation, respecting intellectual property rights, ensuring proper use of cryptographic controls, preventing misuse of information-processing facilities, and protecting organizational records as well as data and privacy of personal information. Compliance with security policies and achieving technical compliance includes controls for complying with security policies and standards and for technical compliance audits.

Business View on Compliance

Businesses are taking an increased interest in how information risks are being managed and reduced. Security policies are not considered solely a technology issue anymore. The business also wants the security policies to reflect how they want information handled. You can look at the security policies collectively as a business statement of commitment to protect its information and customers. Good security policies keep the business healthy. Some of the basic concerns the business will have with implementing such a policy will include the following:

 WARNING

Publishing policy statements related to legal and regulatory issues are highly sensitive topics. Be sure to have your legal department review draft policy wording. Also, find out how they want working copies of policies labeled.

- Cost—Cost of implementing and maintaining controls
- Impact—Impact to customers
- Regulatory—Ability to legally defend

Policies are only effective if they are enforced. One thing management dislikes are surprises. Finding out later that security policies are too costly or impact the customers is not acceptable. To avoid this, management needs to be an important partner in implementing IT policies.

Protecting and Securing Privacy Data

In general, it is understood that privacy data must be protected. What is not so clear, however, is what constitutes privacy data. Some jurisdictions are very broad in their definition of privacy data, while other jurisdictions may narrowly define it. Generally, it's best to use the most comprehensive definition for an organization's industry, region, and regulatory mandates. For example, California Consumer Privacy Act has a comprehensive definition of privacy data elements. Depending on the environment in which an organization operates, privacy can take on different meanings. The American Institute of Certified Public Accountants defines **privacy management** as "the process of protecting the rights and obligations of individuals and organizations with respect to the collection, use, disclosure, and retention of personal information." Thus, privacy is about the personal information that might be used to identify an individual. Examples include the following:

- Name
- Social Security number (SSN)
- Home address
- Email address
- Physical characteristics

Personal information can also be considered sensitive. Consider, for example, sensitive financial or health information. When combined with personal information, this information becomes personal *and* sensitive. For example, a person's name by itself is not sensitive. Simply knowing there's a person who is called John Smith has no value. Combining the name with other information make the information sensitive such as John Smith has a social security number of x can put the person at risk for identity theft. As a result, the protection of this data becomes increasingly important when you consider the risks posed to this data, such as inadequate access controls, improper use, or unauthorized disclosure, to name a few.

For both individuals and organizations, the collection of personal data provides many benefits. Organizations, for example, benefit from increased market intelligence and competitive advantage, whereas individuals benefit from things such as personalized services and targeted offerings. On the other hand, individuals might be subject to spam and **identity theft** if that data are not protected properly. (Identity theft is the theft of someone's personal information for unauthorized use.) Organizations also are subject to litigation, negative publicity, and even financial loss.

Privacy data can be protected using numerous methods. For example, organizations can do the following:

- Develop appropriate privacy policies.
- Establish the position of a **privacy officer**. This is a senior-level management position within an organization responsible for handling privacy laws and their impact on the organization.

- Conduct training and awareness around data handling, identity theft, and **social engineering**. Social engineering involves manipulating people into divulging information.
- Consider adequate controls around data retention and data destruction.
- Conduct regular risk assessments of access controls.
- Limit data to only that which is required.
- Consider security technologies such as encryption.

Privacy laws and regulations vary not just by industry, but also by areas in which business is conducted. In North America alone, there are many laws concerning privacy. Popular examples include the following:

TIP

An auditor might want to conduct a social engineering assessment in which he or she impersonates an executive to obtain personal or sensitive data simply by asking for it.

- **Health Insurance Portability and Accountability Act (HIPAA)**—The Privacy Rule within Title II of this act is concerned with the security and privacy of health data.
- **GLBA**—The Financial Privacy Rule within the act is concerned with the collection and disclosure of personal financial information.
- **Children's Online Privacy Protection Act (COPPA)**—This act contains provisions for websites collecting personal information from children under 13 years of age.
- **National Do Not Call Registry**—This registry provides consumers with the choice to not receive telemarketing calls at home.
  - **California Consumer Privacy Act (CCPA) of 2020**
  - **NYDFS Cybersecurity Regulation** (23 NYCRR 500) of 2017
- **Electronic Communications Privacy Act of 2000**—This act regulates and protects the privacy of email and other electronic communications.
- **The Fair Credit Reporting Act**—This act regulates the use of consumer credit information.

As a result, IT compliance audits must consider privacy data and the application of an appropriate privacy control framework within organizations. First, consider the laws and regulations across multiple boundaries in which business is conducted. Further, the coordination between both general counsel and IT is necessary to understand both the legal and security repercussions.

Finally, organizations should consider a privacy audit. Most audits are concerned with the privacy oversight, privacy policies, and privacy controls within an organization. A privacy audit focuses on the following:

- Which privacy laws are applicable to the organization?
- Are the organizational responsibilities defined and assigned (for example, for the privacy officer and the legal department who is responsible for notifying regulators in the event of a privacy breach)?

- Are policies and procedures for creating, storing, and managing privacy data applied and followed?
- Are specific controls implemented, and are compliance tasks being followed? For example, is privacy data encrypted? Are there privacy statements and an opt-out mechanism on the organization's website?

Designing and Implementing Proper Security Controls

Information security is largely about managing risk. That means IT controls are implemented depending on the risk they are designed to manage. Although the focus is on mitigating risk by implementing appropriate security controls, there are other ways to deal with risk. Risk can also be avoided, transferred, or accepted. For example, driving a vehicle poses many risks. Consider the risk of loss due to theft or an accident. Most people choose to transfer the risk by purchasing insurance. Others might accept the risk by not purchasing insurance. Still, others might avoid the risk altogether by choosing not to drive.

Every day, you make personal decisions that consider controls regarding risk. Being human naturally makes you vulnerable to many different threats, which can have a tremendous impact on you. Many people wear a seat belt while driving, for example, to mitigate the risk of injury during an accident. Now think about how you might choose to protect your family while at home. Door locks are a good place to start. Door locks are also a relatively simple control. Yet some people have alarm systems, whereas others don't. The same concept applies to the threat of an assailant with a gun. Why doesn't everyone wear a bulletproof vest?

Managing risks involves making trade-offs. A solid understanding of the risks and proper consideration of the trade-offs results in the controls you select for your personal security and the protection of information. It is necessary to properly assess and prioritize risk.

The process of selecting security controls needs to be part of an overall framework for risk management. For example, the following activities consider the implementation of controls within the context of such a framework:

> **NOTE**
>
> Assessing and prioritizing risk doesn't just provide security. It also prevents wasted time and money on unnecessary controls that might have a negative impact on the goals and missions of the organization.

1. **Discover and classify data and information systems**—First, consider the confidentiality, integrity, and availability of the data and information systems. Next, examine the potential impact on the organization should confidentiality, integrity, or availability being compromised.

2. **Select security controls**—After you consider the impact, select appropriate security controls based on the risk to the systems.

3. **Implement security controls**—After selecting controls, put the controls in place to ensure risks are reduced to an appropriate level.

4. **Assess security controls**—Evaluate the effectiveness of the controls. The assessment provides the necessary information to ensure they are implemented correctly and meet the security requirements.

5. **Authorize the controls**—After considering the system in relation to the assessment of the controls, determine whether the risk that remains, the residual risk, is at an acceptable level.

6. **Monitor the controls**—Once controls are set, put a system of continuous monitoring in place. Changes within the organization or the information system, for example, might result in the need to update the security controls. In addition, an event involving the identification of a new threat or an event resulting in a breach will require an immediate assessment and possibly a change to the applied security controls.

COBIT is a popular and widely used control framework for IT in general. A high-level control objective with COBIT as related to the IT process is to "ensure systems security." These objectives have many common industry-accepted IT processes, including the following:

- Management of IT security
- Security plan
- Identity management
- User account management
- Security testing, surveillance, and monitoring
- Security incident definition
- Protection of security technology
- Cryptographic key management
- Malicious software, prevention, detection, and correction
- Network security
- Exchange of sensitive data

Although this framework provides a sound overall foundation of control objectives, other frameworks or standards provide more detailed guidance. Selecting security controls is best approached by first adhering to a common set of basic or baseline controls. Next, you might need to apply additional controls that are specific to the system or application. Finally, you might need to apply **compensating controls**. Compensating controls are necessary when a baseline security control cannot be implemented, for example.

> **NOTE**
>
> The 15 Critical Controls may frequently change based on the current environment. For the latest guidance, see *http://www. sans.org/critical-security-controls*.

Some common control baselines from the National Institute for Standards and Technology (NIST) are listed in Table 3-1. Controls described in the table are from NIST Standard 800-53. The controls are categorized by a high-level control family and include various controls that apply to each group. Within each family, the policy and procedures are always considered. In another example, SANS (SysAdmin, Auditing, Network, Security) Institute created a list of 15 Critical Controls primarily addressing the technical control area. Many people are more comfortable with the 20 **Critical Security Controls** than with other more comprehensive frameworks. This is largely by design. The list is intended to be "real world" and to provide actionable guidance that considers those controls that provide the largest security gains based on existing threats and vulnerabilities. The following list represents the 15 Critical Security Controls as of Version 8:

- Control 01: Inventory and Control of Enterprise Assets
- Control 02: Inventory and Control of Software Assets
- Control 03: Data Protection
- Control 04: Secure Configuration of Enterprise Assets and Software
- Control 05: Account Management
- Control 06: Access Control Management
- Control 07: Continuous Vulnerability Management
- Control 08: Audit Log Management
- Control 09: Email and Web Browser Protections
- Control 10: Malware Defenses
- Control 11: Data Recovery
- Control 12: Network Infrastructure Management
- Control 13: Network Monitoring and Defense
- Control 14: Security Awareness and Skills Training
- Control 15: Service Provider Management

Stop for a moment, review the 15 Critical Security Controls, and compare them with the controls listed in **Table 3-1**. How different are they? Is it possible to map many of the controls to controls of the other? Interestingly, the 15 Critical Security Controls map to about one-third of the NIST controls, to address the most critical controls based on an attack-based analysis. This basic control document was created based on the most prevalent types of attack. Again, these controls aren't meant to replace a more comprehensive set such as that provided by NIST. Rather, these 15 Critical Security Controls provide simpler "quick wins." **Table 3-2** contains a sampling of the first five types of attacks considered when developing the Critical Security Controls. Each attack type is followed by the most related Critical Security Controls. The complete list contains more than 23 attack types.

Choosing Between Automated, Manual, and Hybrid Controls

Policy enforcement can be accomplished through automated or manual controls. The time and effort involved in manual policy management can make automated tools an attractive option. Automated controls are cost-efficient for the large volume of work that needs to be performed consistently.

Automated control is configured into a device to enforce a policy requirement. Here's a shortlist of several common automated controls:

- Authentication methods
- Authorization methods

TABLE 3-1 Family of security control baselines and corresponding examples.

CONTROLS FAMILY	CONTROL EXAMPLES
Access Control	Account Management; Separation of Duties; Least Privilege
Awareness and Training	Security Awareness; Security Training; Training Records
Audit and Accountability	Audit of Record Retention; Auditable Events
Security Assessment and Authorization	Plan of Action and Milestones; Security Authorization
Configuration Management	Baseline Configuration; Configuration Change Control
Contingency Planning	Contingency Training; Alternate Storage Site
Identification and Authentication	Identifier Management; Cryptographic Module Authentication
Incident Response	Incident Handling; Incident Monitoring; Incident Reporting
Maintenance	Controlled Maintenance; Maintenance Tools
Media Protection	Media Access; Media Marking; Media Storage
Physical and Environmental Protection	Physical Access Controls; Visitor Control; Fire Protection
Planning	System Security Plan; Privacy Impact Assessment
Personal Security	Personnel Screening; Personnel Termination
Risk Assessment	Security Categorization; Vulnerability Scanning
System and Services Acquisition	Allocation of Resources; Security Engineering Principles
System and Communications Protection	Denial of Service Protection; Boundary Protection
System and Information Integrity	Malicious Code Protection; Spam Protection; Error Handling
Program Management	Enterprise Architecture; Risk Management Strategy

TABLE 3-2   Summary of attacks correlated to the Critical Security Controls.

ATTACK SUMMARY	CRITICAL SECURITY CONTROL
Attackers continually scan for new, unprotected systems, including test or experimental systems, and exploit such systems to gain control of them.	1
Attackers distribute hostile content on Internet-accessible (and sometimes internal) websites that exploit unpatched and improperly secured client software running on victim machines.	2, 3
Attackers continually scan for vulnerable software and exploit it to gain control of target machines.	2, 3, 4, 5
Attackers use infected or compromised machines to identify and exploit other vulnerable machines across an internal network.	2, 4, 10
Attackers exploit weak default configurations of systems that are more geared for ease of use than security.	3, 5, 6, 10

- Data encryption
- Logging events
- Data segmentation
- Network segmentation

The number of automated controls is limited only by the technology's capability. Continued improvement in technology allows for more automation. The biggest challenge isn't automation but deployment cost and integration across the IT infrastructure.

Consider an example where a policy says that users must change their passwords every 30 days. A central authentication server exists within the environment. The challenge is how to configure every device to use the authentication server. The IT environment can have thousands of devices. Each may have to be configured. Once configured, these devices have to be monitored to ensure the configuration is not changed. As new devices are added, the same configuration has to be applied to every device from servers to smart appliances. The configuration of an automated control may be simple. Applying it consistently across thousands of devices becomes a major challenge. The problem gets more complicated as the number of automated controls increases. The diversity of the technology in the environment can make supporting automated controls more complex.

Many commercial products come with enterprise management software to solve this automation challenge. Central policy management software is designed specifically for this purpose. These types of applications create policy rules on a central server. These rules are then sent to the various devices via an agent or agent-less architecture.

Automated policy management tools take security policies and implement them as configuration updates. Once the device is configured, the automated control enforces the policy. The enforcement can be a preventative or detective control. Either way, the control is automated. The control either prevents an event that is outside policy, or it detects that an event occurred. Our example of a policy that requires a password to be changed every 30 days is typically preventative control. The central authentication server forces users to change their passwords at the end of 30 days.

Policy management tools also correlate large amounts of data. They can discover devices on the network. They can track which device has the policies applied. These tools can also monitor policy violations. The tool can identify devices that do not have the policy applied. These tools identify existing configurations to compare with the desired policy state. Deviation from policies can be automatically corrected. This is a powerful tool. Auditors and regulators often request extracts from the policy management tools. This extract can help them assess the level of policy compliance.

TIP

Many administrator tools can support policy management. You can use administrator tools as the first step in auditing policy management.

Not all controls can or should be automated. Manual controls are appropriate for low-volume work. It's also appropriate for work that requires human judgment. Examples of manuals controls are as follows:

- Background checks
- Log reviews
- Access rights reviews
- Attestations

In each of these cases, volumes are low, and human judgment is important to the process. It is important that manual processes are clear. This means that both the step is clear and the criteria for the judgment are clear.

Let's walk through background checks as manual control. The process should be clear as to how to collect the information for the background check. The criteria should also be defined. For many jobs, minor traffic violations are acceptable. For other jobs, such as commercial drivers, any traffic violation may be considered unacceptable. A clearly defined security policy ensures everyone is treated equally on background checks. This can avoid legal problems.

A human can review logs for unusual activity that is difficult to automate. For example, when a programmer is granted elevated rights to fix a production problem, logs are often reviewed. The logs are reviewed to determine if the programmer performed an activity that exceeded the scope of the fix. For instance, the log review may change if the programmer changes account data in a database. These types of changes to fix an application may be unusual and require management follow-up.

Access rights include a review by the business to ensure adequate segregation of duties. This type of review is manual and requires knowledge of how the business operates. Based on this knowledge, a reasonable balance is struck between operational efficiency and reducing risks.

An "attestation" is a formal management verification. Management is attesting that a condition exists. Some regulations require management to attest that security policies and controls are in place. For example, SOX requires this type of attestation from senior management.

When someone makes an attestation, they are personally liable for the accuracy of the statement. This is a way the law holds management accountable to ensure appropriate controls are put in place. Making a false statement is often a crime. However, making a statement you believe is true that later turns out to be false may be defendable. How defendable depends on the information on which you based the statement. It's not if you knew, but whether you should have known. In other words, simply asking someone if the controls are in place is not sufficient.

Controls are rarely purely manual or automated. In many cases, they are a hybrid containing both automated and manual. For example, access rights reviews may be automated to send a generated list of access to be sent to a manager for a manual review. In this case, there are elements of both reducing the cost of generating the access list through automation and leveraging manual processes to yield the human judgment on the appropriateness of the access given the user's role.

What Are You Auditing Within the IT Infrastructure?

Across the infrastructure, an audit should focus primarily on the following three objectives:

- Examine the existence of relevant and appropriate security policies and procedures.
- Verify the existence of controls supporting the policies.
- Verify the effective implementation and ongoing monitoring of the controls.

Examining risk and IT controls throughout the IT infrastructure can be complex given the breadth of components across organizations. There are, however, a lot of similarities between different IT departments. It is helpful to define and, if necessary, break up the scope of the audit into manageable areas or domains of security responsibility. **Figure 3-1** illustrates these seven domains, which include the following:

- **User Domain**—The end users of the systems, including how they authenticate into the systems.
- **Workstation Domain**—The end users' operating environment.
- **LAN Domain**—The equipment that makes up the **local area network (LAN)**. A LAN is a computer network for communications between systems covering a small physical area.
- **LAN-to-WAN Domain**—The bridge between the LAN and the **wide-area network (WAN)**. A WAN is a network that covers a large area, often connecting multiple LANs.

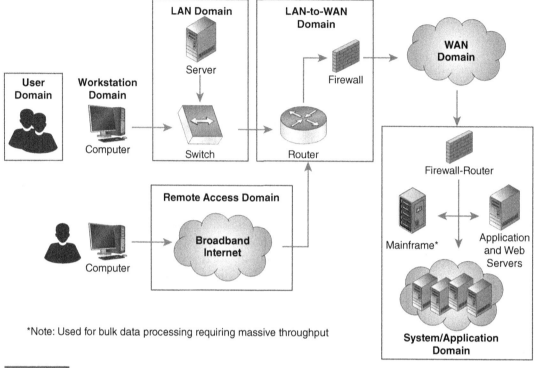

FIGURE 3-1

The seven domains of a Typical IT infrastructure.

- **WAN Domain**—The equipment and activities outside of the LAN and beyond the LAN-to-WAN Domain.
- **Remote Access Domain**—The access infrastructure for users accessing remote systems.
- **System/Application Domain**—Systems on the network that provide the applications and software for the users.

Within these seven domains, IT consists of hardware, software, network communications, protocols, applications, and data. Additionally, each domain is implemented within a physical space and includes people interacting with logical and physical aspects of the system. Breaking the audit into domains helps to define clear boundaries and determines the extent by which interconnected systems will be examined. An attacker needs to exploit a vulnerability in only one domain; however, each domain needs to be examined carefully. It only takes an exploit in one domain to weaken the others.

Although it is possible to separate these domains logically, there are many similarities concerning what is audited. For example, the following questions apply across all domains:

- Are there adequate policies and procedures in place?
- Are operating system security systems following standards and best practices?
- Are auditing logs configured, and are they being reviewed?
- Are appropriate authentication mechanisms in place?
- Are access control lists in place and configured correctly?
- Are systems patched from known vulnerabilities?
- Are disaster recovery and failover plans in place?
- What change control processes are in place, and are they followed?

This list represents only a small sample of questions to be asked and areas to be assessed. What is important to understand is that although each domain has its own unique characteristics, there are many overlapping requirements and controls.

User Domain

The User Domain covers the end users of information systems. An audit of the User Domain should be considered for anyone accessing the organization's information systems, including not just employees but nonemployees as well, such as contractors and consultants. This domain considers the roles and responsibilities of the users. It should examine all policies that relate to them—specifically, access policies.

The policies that apply might include the following:

- Acceptable use policy
- System access policy
- Internet access policy
- Email policy

Additionally, the User Domain includes the method by which the user authenticates to resources. Depending on the organization's policy, users can authenticate in several ways. Regardless of the method used, the intent is to ensure that users are indeed who they claim to be.

Policies must account for different roles within an organization. To illustrate this point, for purposes of discussion in this chapter we focus on six basic user roles as follows:

- Employees —These are regular staff employees of the organization.
- System administrator—These are employees who work in the IT department and provide administrative support to the systems and databases.
- Security personnel—These individuals are responsible for designing and implementing a security program within an organization.
- Contractors—These are temporary workers who can be assigned to any role.
- Guests and general public—This is a class or group of users who assess a specific set of applications.
- Auditors—These are individuals who evaluate controls for design and effectiveness.

We will discuss users' unique business requirements for access to information and how access rights are assigned to ensure segregation of duties. Later in this chapter, we align these unique user types to specific security policy examples. **Table 3-3** summarizes a high-level mapping of users to their individual needs for access.

> **NOTE**
People are often the weakest link in IT security. You could have the strongest technical and physical controls, but if personnel doesn't understand the value of security, none of those controls will matter. Consider the simple example of users who write down their passwords. Often, users post these passwords right on the system itself. Users also visit risky websites and unknowingly download malicious software.

Workstation Domain

The Workstation Domain refers to any computing device used by end users. This device is usually a desktop or laptop computer. However, a "workstation" can be any device that accesses data. This includes browsers on a mobile device, such as a smartphone or an Internet-attached device, and includes the following:

- Desktop computers
- Laptop computers
- Printers

TABLE 3-3 Typical Domain User's need for access.

TYPE OF USER	NEED FOR ACCESS	TYPICAL ACCESS RIGHTS
Employees	Need to access specific applications in the production environment	Access is limited to specific applications and information.
System Administrators	Need to access systems and databases to support applications	Access is broad and unlimited in context to the role. For example, database administrators may have unlimited access to the database but not the operating system.
Security Personnel	Need to protect networks, systems, and applications, and information	Access is provided to set permissions, review logs, monitor activity, and respond to incidents.
Contractors	Temporary workers needing the same access as a full-time worker in the same role	Access is the same as a full-time worker.
Guest and General Public	Need to access specific application functions	Access is assigned to a type of user and not to the individual.
Auditors	Need to review and assess controls	Access often includes unlimited read access to logs and configuration settings.

- Scanners
- Handheld computers and mobile devices
- Modems
- Wireless access points

Each of these devices should be authorized to access and connect to the organizational network and information resources. Thereafter, an audit of this domain would also ensure proper procedures and controls around maintaining the system hardware and software. Any desktop operating system, for example, should comply with the standards defined by the organization. The audit would take into consideration those security controls already applied. Standard operating systems and patch levels are typically mandated as well as specific configuration controls and the presence of anti-malware, desktop firewalls, and other security controls.

A Malicious Code Protection standard, for example, describes controls for preventing malicious software from infecting a workstation. An example of control statements in a Malicious Code Protection standard would be as follows:

- Anti-malware software will be used on all devices connected to the organization's network. IT staff shall be responsible to ensure that all devices have an approved version and release of anti-malware software installed and that a mechanism is in place to keep malware definitions appropriately current.
- In order to prevent malicious code propagation, no executable software, regardless of the source, may knowingly be installed on devices connected to the organization's networks without prior IT staff approval.
- IT staff will verify that software is free of malicious code before it is installed onto a device.
- Users must not intentionally disable anti-malware software unless directed to do so by IT staff.
- Software and data coming from any device connected to the organization's network that is distributed to another organization or customer shall be checked using the latest malware definitions and found to be free of malicious code prior to distribution.
- If symptoms of malicious code are detected, users shall immediately alert their agency staff.
- Users must not try to eradicate malicious code without the assistance and direction of IT staff. Procedures shall be established and relayed to users for handling malicious code contamination incidents.

LAN Domain

The LAN Domain refers to the organization's LAN infrastructure. A LAN allows two or more computers to connect within a small physical area. The small area could be a home, office, or a group of buildings. LANs provide each computer on the network access to centralized resources, such as file servers and printers. In addition, they provide an easy method by which all the computers can be administered. Various other elements comprise the LAN Domain, including the physical connections required, such as the wiring, and networking equipment, such as hubs and switches. An audit of the LAN Domain can examine various elements, such as the following:

- Logon mechanisms and controls for access to the LAN
- Hardening and configuration of LAN systems
- Backup procedures for servers
- The power supply for the network

> **NOTE**
>
> Many organizations don't allow the use of hubs within a LAN. Although switches are more expensive, they provide greater benefits and increased security. However, an attacker can benefit greatly from an internal network port because few companies protect against rogue or unrecognized devices on their LAN.

Each device on the network must be protected or else all devices can be at risk. A LAN is generally considered a trusted zone. Communications across a LAN are not usually protected as thoroughly as they might be if they were sent outside the LAN. A malicious person, for example, might be able to capture data going across the network quite easily. This is more easily done if hubs are used instead of switches. The attacker could simply plug into any network port in the building and capture valuable data. On the other hand, switches would require an attacker to have physical access to the switch. To prevent this, switches must be placed in secured rooms or secured closets.

LAN-to-WAN Domain

While a LAN typically covers a smaller defined geographical area, a WAN provides for long-distance communication to extend a network across a wider geographic area. Thus, a WAN can connect multiple LANs together. The transition from a LAN to a WAN typically involves equipment such as a router or a firewall. A *router* is used to forward data between different networks. A *firewall* is another common component. A firewall is placed between networks and is designed to permit authorized access while blocking everything else.

The WAN Domain is considered an untrusted zone. It might be made up of components outside the direct control of the organization and is often more accessible by attackers. The area between the trusted and untrusted zone, the LAN-to-WAN Domain, is protected with one or more firewalls. This is also called the boundary, or edge.

The public side of the boundary is often connected to the Internet and has public Internet Protocol (IP) addresses. These IP addresses are accessible from anywhere in the world. Attackers constantly probe public IP addresses looking for open ports and vulnerabilities. A high level of security is required to keep the LAN-to-WAN Domain secure.

An audit is critical to ensure that the environment is controlled correctly to prevent unauthorized access. Many components and controls work together to provide security. Organizations should carefully manage the configurations of all devices in this domain, such as firewalls, routers, and intrusion detection systems.

A Firewall Controls standard, for example, describes how LAN firewalls should handle application traffic. This kind of traffic includes web, email, and telnet traffic. The standard should also describe how the firewall should be managed and updated. The following are examples of statements from a typical Firewall Control standard: The default policy for the firewall for handling inbound traffic must block all packets and connections unless the traffic type and connections have been specifically permitted.

The firewall standard, for example, may block the following types of traffic:

- Inbound traffic from a nonauthenticated source system with a destination address of the firewall system itself. This type of packet normally represents some type of probe or attack against the firewall. One common exception to this rule would be in the event the firewall system accepts delivery of inbound email (SMTP on port 25). In this event, the firewall must allow inbound connections to itself, but only on port 25.
- Inbound traffic with a source address indicating that the packet originated on a network behind the firewall. This type of packet likely represents some type of spoofing attempt.
- Inbound traffic containing ICMP (Internet Control Message Protocol) traffic. Since ICMP can be used to map the networks behind certain types of firewalls, ICMP must not be passed in from the Internet or any untrusted external network.

Reproduced from Wack, John, Ken Cutler, and Jamie Pole. 2002. "Guidelines on Firewalls and Firewall Policy: Recommendations of the National Institute of Standards and Technology." National Institute of Standard sand Technology. https://www.usmd.edu/usm/adminfinance/itcc/firewallpolicynis.pdf

WAN Domain

The WAN Domain provides end-to-end connectivity between LANs. Like the LAN-to-WAN Domain, this environment includes routers, firewalls, and intrusion detection systems, but it also has many more telecommunications components. Examples include channel service unit/data service unit, codecs, and backbone circuits.

For most private businesses, the WAN is the Internet. A business may, however, lease semiprivate lines from telecommunications companies. These lines are semiprivate because they are rarely leased by only a single company. Instead, they are shared with other unknown companies. Again, the Internet is an untrusted zone. Any host on the Internet with a public IP address is at significant risk of attack, and you should expect any host on the Internet to be attacked even if that just means it is scanned for open ports and vulnerabilities. A significant amount of security is required to keep hosts in the WAN Domain safe. WAN audits help ensure the WAN is operating and configured as expected and is conforming to corresponding policies and standards.

Control standards for the LAN-to-WAN Domain address webpage content and access controls, Internet **user proxy** controls, **demilitarized zone (DMZ)** architecture controls, and more.

> **NOTE**
>
> When applied to computer technology, a DMZ is an area that exists between trusted and untrusted network segments. A DMZ provides improved levels of security while controlling external access to information and resources.

Remote Access Domain

The Remote Access Domain refers to the technology that controls how end users connect to an organization's LAN remotely. An example is someone who needs to connect to the office network from their home or on the road. The Remote Access Domain is made up of authorized users who access organization resources remotely. Access most often occurs over unsecured transports such as the Internet. Other unsecured transports include dial-up via a modem. Mobile workers often need access to the private LAN while traveling or working from home, for example. Mobile workers are granted this access using remote access solutions, such as a virtual private network (VPN), can create an encrypted communications tunnel over a public network such as the Internet. Because the Internet is largely untrusted, remote access might represent a significant risk. Attackers can access unprotected connections. They might try to break into the remote access servers as well. Using a VPN is an example of a control to reduce the risk. VPNs, however, have their vulnerabilities. For example, how does a user authenticate with the VPN? An attacker can gain access via the secured encrypted tunnel back to the corporate data just by knowing or guessing the credentials of the authorized user.

An audit should carefully consider the governing policies and procedures as well as the type of access provided.

---

technical TIP

A common control applied to VPN authentication requires the use of two-factor authentication. Two-factor authentication requires, for example, something the user knows and something the user has. This typically means a user is provided with a physical token that generates a new token code every minute. To authenticate, the user would provide his or her password or personal identification number (PIN) as well as the token code. An ATM card used at an automatic teller machine to get cash uses a similar process. The user inserts the card and provides a PIN. The user requires possession of one item and knowledge of the other.

---

technical TIP

You should lock down or configure a server using the specific security requirements needed by the hosted application. Shutting down unnecessary services or software is a great first step in keeping a system secure. In addition, each application might require a new set of security measures or controls. An email server requires one set of controls, whereas a database server requires a different set.

For example, a VPN control standard may describe the security requirements for VPN and other remote access connections to the organization's network. The following are examples of control statements you might find in this standard:

- Approved users (employees and authorized vendors) may use the VPN services.

- VPN use is to be controlled using either a one-time password authentication such as a token device or a public/private key system with a strong passphrase as described in the Multifactor Authentication to VPN Standard.

- When actively connected to the corporate network, VPNs will force all traffic to and from the computer over the VPN tunnel: all other traffic will be dropped.

- Dual (split) tunneling is NOT permitted; only one network connection is allowed.

- VPN gateways will be set up and managed by the organization's network operational groups.

- All computers connected to the organization's internal networks via VPN or any other technology must use the most up-to-date anti-virus software that is the corporate standard (provide URL to this software); this includes personal computers.

- VPN users will be automatically disconnected from the organization's network after 30 minutes of inactivity. The user must then log on again to reconnect to the network.

- The VPN concentrator is limited to an absolute connection time of 24 hours.

- Users of computers that are not organization-owned equipment must configure the equipment to comply with the organization's VPN and network policies.

- Only InfoSec-approved VPN clients may be used.

> **NOTE**
> Environments utilizing split tunneling allow end users to bypass certain devices, including proxy servers designed to block and track Internet usage. Additionally, a hacker who compromises an employee's home network through the split tunnel could potentially access the corporate system.

System/Application Domain

The System/Application Domain is made up of the many systems and software applications that users access. This, for example, includes mainframes, application servers, web servers, proprietary software, and applications. Mail servers send and receive email. Database servers host data that are accessed by users, applications, or other servers. Domain Name System (DNS) servers provide name-to-IP address resolution for clients. Knowledge within this domain can be very specialized. Operators may focus on one specific aspect, such as mail servers, and be quite familiar with associated security ramifications. On the other hand, that same person might know very little about databases.

Like the desktop operating system, server operating systems should be hardened to authorized baselines and configured according to policies and standards with the appropriate controls.

An Information Classification standard, for example, helps employees determine the classification of information that's generated, accessed, transmitted, and stored by the organization. This type of control standard also helps you identify procedures to protect the confidentiality, integrity, and availability of organizational data based on its classification. Information classification is also essential for complying with local and federal regulations regarding privacy and confidentiality of information. The following are example control statements in an information classification standard:

- All employees and contractors share in the responsibility for ensuring that the organization's information assets receive an appropriate level of protection by observing this Information Classification policy.
- Company managers or information "owners" shall be responsible for assigning classifications to information assets according to the standard information classification system presented.
- Where practicable, the information category shall be embedded in the information itself.
- All company associates shall be guided by the information category in their security-related handling of company information.

Maintaining IT Compliance

Simply achieving compliance is not enough. Compliance is an ongoing process that should be treated as a continuous function within the organization. Change is constantly occurring. The following are primary examples of why organizations must maintain IT compliance as an ongoing program:

- Organizations are dynamic, growing environments. As they adapt and grow, things change and compliance must be assessed against the changes.
- Threats evolve. Threats to organizations, like organizations themselves, constantly change and adapt. Organizations must respond and adjust appropriately to these threats.
- Laws, regulations, and industry standards continue to evolve, and new ones are introduced. Organizations are required to exercise due diligence. These efforts evolve as due care rises. What was good enough one day might not be enough the next.
- Many regulations require annual audits, ongoing reporting, and regular assessments against the environment.

Maintaining compliance requires a well-defined programmatic approach that involves processes and technology. This program needs to be monitored on an ongoing basis. At a minimum, the program should include the following:

- Regular assessment of selected security controls
- Configuration and control management processes
- Change management processes
- Annual audit of the security environment

Conducting Periodic Security Assessments

Regular security assessments should be part of the ongoing security strategy for any organization. Security assessments provide valuable metrics for maintaining compliance. In general, an assessment should address people, operations, applications, and the infrastructure throughout the organization. Because security assessments are conducted more often than, for example, an annual security audit, the purpose and the scope of a **risk assessment** can vary widely. Generally, a security assessment is grouped into different types:

- **High-level security assessment**—Provides an overall view of the information systems and is useful when examining across a broader scope
- **Comprehensive security assessment**—Provides a more targeted, concise, and technical review of information systems; involves control reviews and identification of vulnerabilities
- **Preproduction security assessment**—Used for new systems prior to being placed in production; may also be used for systems after having undergone a significant change

In addition to undergoing an initial security assessment, organizations should also determine how often they conduct assessments thereafter. Some of the considerations that should factor into the decision for ongoing assessments include the following:

- Expected benefits
- Scheduling requirements
- Applicable regulations and industry standards
- System and data classification

High-impact systems—for example, systems that process or store sensitive information—might require more frequent assessment than those that have a lesser impact. Also, consider when the last assessment was completed, as even a system with a moderate or low impact can present issues if the system has not been assessed in a long time. Often, the ongoing assessment process is driven by an organization's requirement to demonstrate compliance with regulations or standards.

Performing an Annual Security Compliance Audit

The regular security assessment should be supplemented with annual security audits. Although annual audits of specific functions are required for many organizations, an annual internal audit provides the organization with an independent review of the adequacy and effectiveness of IT security's internal controls. An audit should never be thought of as a one-time event.

In fact, as with security assessments, organizations have embraced the idea of continuous auditing. An audit completed less than once a year can offer only a narrow scope of the evaluation. This results in not providing real value for the organization.

Organizations with an internal audit function are in the best position to implement audits that are more frequent or to put in place a continuous audit program.

Defining Proper Security Controls

The environments of controls are made up largely of a basic set of principles that apply across the various domains. These basic principles are embedded throughout security operations and administration management. These include the following:

- Defined roles and responsibilities
- Configuration and change management
- Environments for development test and production
- Segregation of duties
- Identity and authentication
- Principle of least privilege
- Monitoring, measuring, and reporting
- Appropriate documentation

When a basic control environment is in place, organizations can begin implementing additional controls to continue reducing risk to acceptable levels. An important aspect of maintaining compliance is defining and adjusting proper security controls. Although there are many different guiding documents for control standards, organizations must be careful of which specific controls they implement and how they put those controls into place.

Selecting and maintaining the right controls requires consideration of completed risk assessments. This risk assessment must address real threats while considering the trade-off between risk and benefit. If you start by implementing controls properly along with proper documentation, then maintaining them shouldn't be as difficult. On the other hand, it might be easier to become complacent. As a result, organizations might not document the changes to controls and the implementation of new controls after a basic set is in place.

Creating an IT Security Policy Framework

IT security typically falls within an established IT policy framework. To maintain compliance, however, organizations should create a framework for IT security. A policy framework provides for a structured approach for outlining requirements that must be met. The framework can be thought of as a pyramid, as shown in **Figure 3-2**.

The framework starts on the top with very clear and concise objectives or requirements and then continues downward, exposing further details and additional guidance. At the topmost level is the policy. The policy regulates conduct through a general statement of beliefs, goals, and objectives. Next, standards support the policies. The standards are mandated activities or rules. Next, a **guideline** further supports the standard as well as the policy. Guidelines provide general statements of guidance but are not mandatory. Here is an example of these three components:

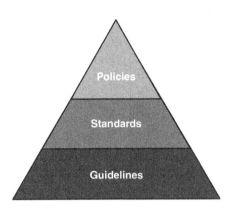

FIGURE 3-2

A policy framework.

- **Policy**—Users are required to use strong authentication when accessing company systems.
- **Standard**—Users are required to use two-factor authentication when accessing the remote network, combining a physical one-time token code with a PIN.
- **Guideline**—Always keep your token within your possession and be aware of your surroundings when entering your PIN.

In addition to these three items, a **procedure** can also be part of the framework. A procedure provides step-by-step instructions that support the policy by outlining how the standards and guidelines are put into practice.

Implementing Security Operations and Administration Management

Information technology has become a big part of how organizations operate and enables customers, partners, and suppliers to stay connected. This requires the organization to implement and evolve its security and operations management functions to handle rapid change in accordance with stated policies. This added complexity makes it even more challenging to ensure that systems within the organization comply with security policies and standards. Consider that unauthorized changes are prevalent and new vulnerabilities appear daily. In addition, mistakes are bound to happen with the configuration and deployment of new systems. Auditing tools, industry standards, and frameworks provide solid foundations on which to base security operations and administration management.

Configuration and Change Management

Although **configuration and change management** isn't typically considered a function of IT security, it is very much related because of its implications with regard to IT security. Configuration and change management is a process of controlling systems throughout their life cycle to make sure they are operating as intended in accordance with security policies and standards. Additionally, configuration and change management involve the identification, control, logging, and auditing of all changes made across the infrastructure.

Change management is typically founded upon baseline configurations defined for systems. Subsequently, it ensures that authorized changes to the system do not affect their security. Additionally, change and configuration management provides a method for tracking unauthorized changes. Changes that are not authorized can negatively affect the system's security posture. Thus, a process for change and configuration management ensures that changes are requested, evaluated, and authorized. The following represents the high-level process:

1. **Identify and request a change**—A need for a change is recognized and a formal request is submitted to a decision-making group.
2. **Evaluate change request**—An impact assessment is done to determine operational or security effects the change may have on the system or related systems.
3. **Decision response**—A decision typically results in the request either being approved or denied.
4. **Implement approved change**—If the request is approved, the change can be implemented in the production environment.
5. **Monitor change**—Administrators ensure the system operates as intended as a result of the change.

A review board usually manages this five-step process. A committee of employees from multiple disciplines within the organization makes up this board.

CHAPTER SUMMARY

It is everyone's responsibility to adhere to security policies and report noncompliance. This is accomplished by the collective action of many leaders. Compliance starts with executive support. This support goes beyond receiving permission to implement IT policies. Executive support also means personal commitment by the managers to use their position and skills to influence the adoption of policies of their teams.

While the law requires audits, organizations find it more necessary to conduct regular assessments. Regular assessments help ensure that audits will be more successful as well as ensure the confidentiality, integrity, and availability of information and information systems. The protection of privacy data needs to be considered in addition to just the protection of intellectual property. Audits and assessments usually begin based on a framework. When a foundation is in place, companies are finding it easier and more effective to conduct regular audits and assessments.

This chapter examined the scoping of IT infrastructure audits and the relationship among laws, regulations, and policies. We discussed the difference between a law and policy. We examined different methods of assessing adherence to policies. We examined the strengths and weaknesses of automated and manual controls. Finally, the chapter examined the policy frameworks.

KEY CONCEPTS AND TERMS

Compensating controls
Configuration and change
  management
Critical Security Controls
Demilitarized zone (DMZ)
Gap analysis
Guideline
Identity theft
LAN Domain

LAN-to-WAN Domain
Local area network (LAN)
Policies
Privacy management
Privacy officer
Procedure
Remote Access Domain
Risk assessment

Social engineering
Standards
System/Application Domain
User Domain
User proxy
WAN Domain
Wide-area network (WAN)
Workstation Domain

CHAPTER 3 ASSESSMENT

1. After mapping existing controls to new regulations, an organization needs to conduct a(n) _____ analysis.

2. Which of the following best describes the rights and obligations of individuals and organizations with respect to the collection, use, disclosure, and retention of personal information?

A. Security management
B. Compliance management
C. Privacy management
D. Personal management
E. Collection management

3. The process of selecting security controls is considered within the context of risk management.

A. True
B. False

4. If a baseline security control cannot be implemented, which of the following should be considered?

A. Compensating control
B. Baseline security standard revision
C. Policy revision
D. None of the above

5. Account management and separation of duties are examples of what type of controls?

A. Audit and accountability
B. Access control
C. Security assessment and authorization
D. Personal security

6. Which one of the following is *not* one of the seven domains of a typical IT infrastructure?

A. User Domain
B. Workstation Domain
C. LAN-to-LAN Domain
D. WAN Domain
E. Remote Access Domain

7. Which of the following policies would apply to the User Domain concerning the seven domains of a typical IT infrastructure?

A. Acceptable use policy
B. Internet access policy
C. Security incident policy
D. Firewall policy
E. Answers A and B
F. Answers B and D

8. Mitigating a risk from an IT security perspective is about reducing the risk to zero.

   A. True
   B. False

9. Which of the following is an example of why an ongoing IT compliance program is important?

   A. Organizations are dynamic, growing environments.
   B. Threats evolve.
   C. Laws and regulations evolve.
   D. All of the above

10. Policies, standards, and guidelines are part of the policy _____.

11. Which one of the following is *not* part of the change management process?

   A. Identify and request
   B. Evaluate change request
   C. Decision response
   D. Implement unapproved change
   E. Monitor change

12. What can be done to manage risk? (Select three.)

   A. Accept
   B. Transfer
   C. Avoid
   D. Migrate

13. Regarding the seven domains of IT infrastructure, the Workstation Domain includes which of the following? (Select three.)

   A. Desktop computers
   B. Laptop computers
   C. Remote access systems
   D. Email servers
   E. Handheld devices

14. Adequate controls over privacy data helps prevent _____ theft.

15. Which of these is *not* an effective method used by organizations to protect privacy data?

   A. Develop appropriate privacy policies.
   B. Conduct irregular risk assessments of access controls.
   C. Establish the position of a privacy officer.
   D. Limit data to only what is required.

16. Personal information, such as a person's name by itself, can be considered sensitive information

   A. True
   B. False

17. Which of these domains of security are responsible for the end users' operating environment?

   A. User Domain
   B. Workstation Domain
   C. LAN Domain
   D. LAN-to-WAN Domain

18. Which of these domains of security are responsible for the systems on the network that provide the applications and software for the users?

   A. LAN Domain
   B. WAN Domain
   C. Remote Access Domain
   D. Application Domain

19. A WAN typically covers communication to a smaller defined geographical area.

   A. True
   B. False

20. Which of the following components of an IT policy framework would require users to use two-factor authentication when accessing the remote network—usually combining a physical one-time token code with a PIN?

   A. Policy
   B. Standard
   C. Guideline

PART TWO

Auditing for Compliance: Frameworks, Tools, and Techniques

Auditing Standards and Frameworks

ONDUCTING AUDITS AND ASSESSMENTS is a way of measuring an organization's adherence to common industry practices. Why is that important? Imagine yourself in front of a regulator or your boss and trying to explain your opinion on the completeness and accuracy of the IT infrastructure control environment. Standards and frameworks are the yardsticks by which an opinion can be formed. These standards and frameworks are the columniations of knowledge and experience of experts across many industries. They represent a path to ensure adherence to many laws, rules, and regulations. In short, close adoption of industry norms through the appropriate standards and frameworks reduces risks and threats to an organization. Equally important, in the event of a data breach or major technology failure, demonstrated compliance to commonly accepted standards and frameworks could provide a defensible position with the regulators.

Organizations should adopt and enhance industry-accepted practices for governance, security, and compliance. Choosing from guiding control standards and frameworks is an ideal start. This chapter explores the importance of such standards and frameworks. This chapter also introduces several popular frameworks and standards in use today. There are still many more. Regardless, all have a common theme of putting in place sensible practices within organizations.

Chapter 4 Topics

This chapter covers the following topics and concepts:

- Why frameworks are important for compliance auditing
- Why standards are important in compliance auditing
- How standards and frameworks differ
- What NIST 800-53 provides
- How the Institute of Internal Auditors (IIA) standards and guidance are important
- How to develop a hybrid auditing framework or approach

Chapter 4 Goals

When you complete this chapter, you will be able to:

- Understand the importance of using a framework for audits
- Describe various strategies for using standards and frameworks for compliance auditing
- Understand IIA and how it relates to auditing
- Describe the key parts and importance of Control Objectives for Information and Related Technology (COBIT)
- Understand the importance and benefits of a Service Organization Control (SOC) engagement
- Describe the key ISO/IEC standards that relate to information security
- Describe the National Institute of Standards and Technology (NIST) 800-53 and 800-53A standards
- Understand the need for hybrid auditing approaches

Difference Between Standards and Frameworks

The terms *standard* and *framework* have distinct differences and should not be used interchangeably. A standard is typically more rigid than a framework. A standard will typically outline a specific way of achieving a **control objective**. For example, a standard may say an application must use a complex password of at least eight characters.

A framework tends to provide broad guidance and allows flexibility on how to achieve the control objectives. A framework is designed to be applied across multiple situations and allows for more judgment. Part of the intent of a framework is to ensure that all core risk topics are considered and appropriately applied. For example, a framework may say that administrative accounts must have elevated authentication and be closely monitored.

Notice the contrast between a standard and a framework. The framework requires administrative accounts to enhance authentication but does not specify the "how." This may mean the use of complex passwords as in the example of the standard or it may result in the use of multifactor authentication. As such, standards typically list a set of controls that are prescriptive and must be followed exactly, while frameworks tend to focus more on required outcomes leaving it up to the organization to determine the best method to implement.

Other terms you will come across as an auditor include policy, standards, procedures, guidelines, and baselines. For the purpose of this chapter, we will discuss standards and

TABLE 4-1 Description of standards, procedures, guidelines, and baselines.	
TITLE	**DESCRIPTION**
IT Policy	A set of rules on how technology assets within an organization should be used and operated. Additionally, a policy defines core roles and responsibilities.
Standards	Mandatory actions, explicit rules, or controls that are designed to support and conform to a policy. A standard should make a policy more meaningful and effective by including accepted specifications for hardware, software, or behavior. Standards should always point to the policy to which they relate.
Procedures	Written steps to execute policies through specific, prescribed actions; this is the how in relation to a policy. Procedures tend to be more detailed than policies. They identify the method and state, in a series of steps, exactly how to accomplish an intended task, achieve a desired business or functional outcome, and execute a policy.
Guidelines	An outline for a statement of conduct. This is an additional (optional) document in support of policies, standards, and procedures and provides general guidance on what to do in particular circumstances. Guidelines are not requirements to be met but are strongly recommended.
Baselines	Platform-specific rules that are accepted across the industry as providing the most effective approach to a specific implementation.

frameworks in detail. However, it is important to understand the basic content of each of these documents, which provide differing levels of guidance and rules. **Table 4-1** are examples of common documents which provide varying levels of guidance.

Think of standards and framework as complementary pair in which a framework provides structure and standards provides the rules within the confine of the framework. Consider the roadway system as a framework with the traffic rules being the standard by which we operate the car.

Why Frameworks Are Important for Auditing

In general, a **framework** is a conceptual set of rules and ideas that provide structure to a complex set of situations. Although a framework may be rigid in its skeleton, the idea is to provide flexibility. The framework includes distinct components, such as an introduction, learning objectives, headings, and a summary. Yet the authors have flexibility as long as they are within the confines of this framework.

Information technology (IT) environments are different from one to the next. Despite many similarities, each environment is different. Each company, for example, has different objectives. They have different ways of achieving goals. They have different risk profiles. IT departments exist to help support and drive the business. As long as no two organizations are exactly alike, neither will two IT departments be exactly alike.

An auditor must deal with multiple types of organizations. As a result, each audit is different. The size of the audit varies. The resources needed for the audit vary. The steps carried out for each audit also vary. A framework, however, provides a consistent system of controls to which IT departments can adhere. This system of controls also provides an auditor with a consistent approach for conducting audits.

Controls tend to be either descriptive or prescriptive. A **descriptive control** framework provides for governance at a higher level. These control frameworks are important in helping to align IT with business or enterprise goals. The challenge is that they don't provide a prescribed method for turning these objectives into action. A **prescriptive control** framework approach helps standardize IT operations and tasks, while still allowing for flexibility. Organizations often apply both approaches together within IT, and audits tend to make use of both.

A more governing and descriptive type of framework may dictate a control objective that each IT organization should ensure systems security. Such an approach typically provides additional controls, such as ensuring network security or ensuring identity management. A major component of ensuring network security involves using firewalls. How each organization actually applies this varies. What if there is not a local area network–to–wide area network (LAN-to-WAN) connection? In this case, there may not be a firewall at any border; there may only be firewalls between internal network segments. One company might use a software firewall. Another might use hardware. There are also different types of firewalls. An administrator might use an Application Layer firewall in one situation and a Network Layer firewall in another. For the auditor, the control objective stays the same, yet the audit procedure may vary because of the differences.

The Importance of Using Standards in Compliance Auditing

There is no shortage of frameworks and standards for IT departments and auditors to rely on. There are many different standards from varying organizations, each with its own strengths and weaknesses. However, they all have the same common goal of establishing prudent and good practices around IT control. Many organizations find that they need to use a blend of standards to accomplish their goals. Auditors tend to focus or specialize on particular standards, yet many organizations may seek an audit or assessment against a particular standard. Many organizations, in the beginning, look to their peers and to auditors for what framework and standards they should be using. It is important, however, to consider the needs of the specific organization.

While trying to determine a specific standard to which to adhere, it is helpful to consider the high-level differences among them. Consider the following attributes that vary among different standards and frameworks:

- **Depth and breadth**—Some go far and wide, whereas others are narrow and deep. Guiding principles that cover a wide range might be most suitable to your organization. Alternatively, more prescriptive guidance around describing and assessing actual controls might be helpful.

- **Flexibility**—One standard might apply across the entire organization, whereas another might be limited to a specific department or team.

- **Reasoning**—Some standards provide stronger guidance about why they make a particular statement around controls. Sometimes, the reasoning can be important, as those put in place and auditing controls understand how and why they apply.

- **Prioritization**—Although each organization determines acceptable risk, some standards can provide guidance for focusing on certain areas over others.

- **Industry acceptance**—Some standards are generally accepted more than others. Acceptance also varies by industry.

Standards and frameworks are closely tied to the previous discussion of policies and standards. A framework should offer IT organizations a method for establishing an approach to managing IT risks. The use of a framework combined with an analysis of risk helps guide the development of appropriate written policies and standards within the organization. A high-level control from a framework might state, for example, that systems should be protected from unauthorized access. As a result, an organization develops several policies that pertain to enforcing authorized access to its systems. One such policy states that individuals are assigned unique user names and passwords for the system. In turn, a standard may dictate specific parameters—for example, usernames must follow the format of first initial preceded by last name and be at least eight alpha-numeric characters. Finally, a procedure indicates how to apply the requirements on a particular system.

Clearly documented policies, standards, and procedures provide auditors with an obvious path upon which to base their audits. An unclearly documented policy structure makes the auditor's and auditee's jobs much more difficult. Audits go more smoothly when both parties work from closely aligned frameworks and accepted practices. If, for example, an auditor discovers a lack of clear policies, a standard provides a solid baseline on which to base the findings. For example, an audit deficiency that states that password security should "be stronger" is less powerful than one that states that password requirements aren't up to a specific standard or best practice.

Auditing against standards works best when the auditor and the organization agree on a specific standard. Organizations first select frameworks most appropriate to their business. Then it is the auditor's job to evaluate whether the company-selected standard is reasonable. The auditor must assess against the standard. This is one reason why most companies go with recognized and mature standards. The following are some key recommendations when selecting a standard:

- **Select a standard that can be followed**—This allows the standards to be more easily put in place. It also allows others within the organization and auditors to embrace the standards.

- **Employ the standard**—This reduces liability for having selected a specific standard that is not actually put into place.

- **Select a flexible standard**—This provides the organization the ability to remain responsive to changing business environments and consider its own risk profile.

In the next sections, you'll learn about different frameworks and standards. Standards are relevant to the individuals and groups within the organization. **Figure 4-1** illustrates the hierarchy of governance and

> **⚠ WARNING**
>
> A standard control framework provides a strong foundation for an internal policy structure. However, failure to act on or meet what has been stated in an internal policy may result in an audit deficiency.

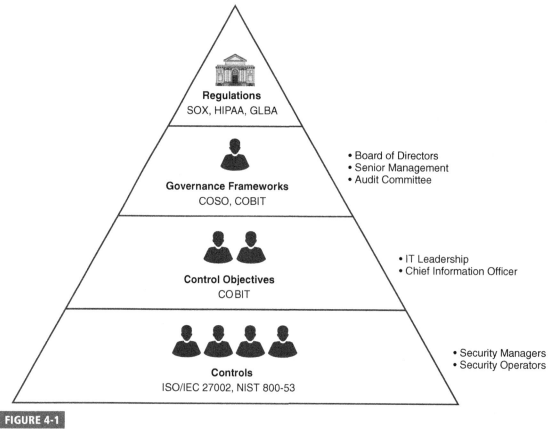

Regulations
SOX, HIPAA, GLBA

- Board of Directors
- Senior Management
- Audit Committee

Governance Frameworks
COSO, COBIT

- IT Leadership
- Chief Information Officer

Control Objectives
COBIT

- Security Managers
- Security Operators

Controls
ISO/IEC 27002, NIST 800-53

FIGURE 4-1

The hierarchy of standards and personnel.

controls. The diagram includes sample standards as well as the people to which they apply.

Following are the high-level steps an organization may take to apply the use of standards:

1. Educate personnel, beginning with senior management.
2. Choose the standards that the organization will follow.
3. Put the people in place and provide the needed resources to apply and meet the standard.
4. Confirm the standards are being met by using an internal audit and outside resources as needed.

Institute of Internal Auditors

The **Institute of Internal Auditors (IIA)** provides internal auditors with standards and guidance on how to perform an audit. The IIA standards are not technology-audit specific and can be applied to any audit or assessment such as accounting or business audits.

The IIA standards are important as they establish core principles the auditor must follow. These principles and supporting standards ensure the highest professionalism from the auditor:

- Demonstrates integrity
- Demonstrates competence and due professional care
- Is objective and free from undue influence (independent)
- Aligns with the strategies, objectives, and risks of the organization
- Is appropriately positioned and adequately resourced
- Demonstrates quality and continuous improvement
- Communicates effectively
- Provides risk-based assurance
- Is insightful, proactive, and future-focused
- Promotes organizational improvement

The standards include a code of ethics that set professional requirements outlined in an International Professional Practices Framework. All IIA members and certified internal auditors are required to conform to the standards and code of ethics.

 TIP

It is important that non-IIA members follow IIA standards as many regulators assess an auditor's performance based on these standards.

The internal audit function assures your board of directors, audit committee, and other stakeholders that risks are appropriately and reasonably controlled. The IIA standards assure that the audits and assessments are performed to the highest standards possible. In sum, the IIA standards provide the auditor function with credibility.

The IIA standard provides useful guidance on how to avoid conflicts of interest. For example, suppose an auditor is asked to provide advice on how to control a specific risk for an application under development. An auditor with broad risk knowledge would potentially have valuable insights to offer, yet once given, should that same auditor be allowed to audit that application? In other words, by giving advice would could an auditor be expected to fairly audit his or her work?! IIA standard 1130 provides such guidance as follows:

> The internal audit activity may provide assurance services where it had previously performed consulting services, provided the nature of the consulting did not impair objectivity and provided individual objectivity is managed when assigning resources to the engagement.

The conflict of interest is just one of many situations auditors may find themselves in. This specific example is given to illustrate the power of having clear standards that can help auditors understand the rules and expectations of their role. Care should always be taken during the audit planning process to ensure the situation could not be perceived as an impairment of independence or objectivity.

> **NOTE**
>
> Several organizations establish standards for performing audits. Auditors should review the standards and frameworks that are commonly used within their specific industry, organization, and audit discipline. For example, the **Committee of Sponsoring Organizations (COSO)** has established many financial and risk management standards for auditing financial systems and relevant to detecting fraud. We will not go in-depth on COSO standards as this book is focused on IT infrastructure audit topics in which other standards and frameworks are more relevant.

COBIT

While the IIA standards set clear audit standards and frameworks, they lack specific details on how to audit and assess technology. The Control Objectives for Information and Related Technology (COBIT) is a global standard and IT management framework developed by the ISACA to help businesses develop, organize and implement, manage, and audit the organization's IT environment.

COBIT offers an IT-specific framework and is an excellent supplement to COSO and adheres to IIA guidance. COBIT provides corporate management, IT management, and auditors with an accepted set of processes and controls to develop IT governance and control within an organization. Specifically, COBIT allows IT management to develop clear policies and apply good practices. COBIT even considers other standards as it seeks to be the overarching IT governance framework. COBIT is business-focused, process-oriented, controls-based, and measurement-driven. COBIT considers risk and stays close to the business by focusing on the benefits associated with IT. COBIT helps to align IT with the business or enterprise requirements by doing the following:

- Mapping controls to key business requirements
- Classifying IT activities into a process model
- Identifying the key IT resources to be controlled
- Defining the framework for control objectives

By providing enterprise-focused alignment, management can better understand what IT does. In addition, COBIT provides additional benefits:

- Clear accountability and responsibility
- Acceptance from third parties, auditors, and regulators
- Fulfillment of COSO requirements concerning the IT control environment

COBIT serves as a valuable framework across different groups. For example, management can use COBIT to assess the performance of IT processes by comparing enterprise goals against the IT-related goals. Both types of goals are provided within COBIT. Those implementing COBIT as well as auditors can leverage the control requirements and assigned responsibilities from within COBIT.

COBIT 2019 is an IT management framework to help organizations develop, organize, and implement strategies related to the common practices of information management and governance. The performance management system allows more flexibility when using maturity and capability measurements. The core principles contained within COBIT 2019 are listed below and on the next page. Each of these principles should be embedded in various IT controls and processes that an auditor can exam.

What Is ISACA?

ISACA was once an acronym for Information Systems Audit and Control Association. Today, ISACA goes only by the acronym in an effort to appeal to a broader range of groups. In the late 1960s, ISACA was formed by a group of like-minded individuals seeking guidance on the auditing of computer systems. This group was initially known as the EDP Auditors Association.

At the time of this writing, ISACA has more than 220 membership chapters in more than 180 countries, with more than 140,000 members. ISACA is behind several globally recognized professional certifications for information systems auditors and IT security and governance professionals. ISACA also publishes a technical journal and hosts conferences worldwide. ISACA, along with its affiliated IT Governance Institute, provides several valuable resources to IT professionals. For students, ISACA offers a student membership program geared to those considering a career in IT.

Before looking at the framework in-depth, let's first explore some of the principles of COBIT 2019, as follows:

1. Provide Stakeholder Value
2. Holistic Approach
3. Dynamic Governance System

4. Governance Distinct from Management
5. Tailored to Enterprise Needs
6. End-to-End Governance System

Provide Stakeholder Value

The principle to "provide stakeholder value" largely addresses two important ideas:

- IT functions exist to help an organization achieve its goals while minimizing risks. Technology for technology's sake is meaningless. In other words, using technology to achieve an organization's goal provides stakeholder value. So who is the stakeholder? In this context, a stakeholder is anyone with a vested interest in the organization's success. For example, a customer holding an insurance policy is a stakeholder because they rely on the health of the company to pay out on claims when needed. A shareholder is a stakeholder because they hope the company will make a profit. Management is a stakeholder because they rely on IT systems to accurately implement their business objectives.

- Value that is created must be done so in a way that also considers risk and the appropriate use of resources. Therefore, the enterprise goals must be aligned properly to IT resources.

To help with this alignment, consider the following when implementing IT systems:

- Benefits realization
- Risk optimization
- Resource optimization

Based on the needs, you can then map enterprise goals to determine which goals are primary or secondary. COBIT 2019 provides 17 sample goals across the following four dimensions:

- Financial
- Customer
- Internal
- Learning and growth

For example, the following are the five sample enterprise goals in the internal dimension:

- Optimization of business process functionality
- Optimization of business process costs
- Managed business change programs
- Operational and staff productivity
- Compliance with internal policies

Finally, these IT-related goals cascade down to what is known as *enabler goals*. Enablers are things such as processes or people. The enablers influence the outcomes and help accomplish goals.

Holistic Approach

The principle of a holistic approach refers to the importance of looking at how all the IT processes and components come together. Components can be defined in various ways. At a high level, consider the following components and how they come together to deliver IT services:

- Principles, policies, and frameworks
- Processes
- Organizational structures
- Culture, ethics, and behavior
- Information
- Services, infrastructure, and applications
- People, skills, and competencies

Finally, a performance-management component is baked into this. Based on metrics, this determines if using the enablers is having a positive outcome.

Dynamic Governance System

The principle of dynamic governance is a simple and powerful concept that focuses on change. Change is said to be the one constant in IT. Think about how the Internet itself has enabled change. The remote work environment was a key enabler during the 2020 pandemic to connect workers to the office. The Internet allows us to talk with individuals around the world to exchange ideas and information and to buy products and services. It has increased competition and made certain products, once rare, now affordable. We've automated factories as well as improved safety systems in ordinary products, such as computerized alarm systems to prevent anyone from breaking into our homes. Common place in our work environments is an array of applications that give instant access to knowledge that would have been difficult or impossible to gain previously. This is not just accessing information but allowing us to collaborate and create new bodies of knowledge through commonplace applications like email, spreadsheets, personal databases, and word processing software.

Dynamic governance is the recognition that business requirements, technology, and risks are under constant changes. Consequently, IT governance must be dynamic and adjust to the constantly changing landscape.

> **NOTE**
>
> It is important to periodically measure performance outcomes to assess the effectiveness of governance processes and systems. When there is a misalignment, meaning when governance effectiveness declines, it is a good indicator that change in the governance process or system may be needed.

Governance Distinct from Management

The principle that "governance [is] distinct from management." COBIT makes a strong statement on the differences between governance and management. This is because they differ greatly and each ultimately serves a different purpose. According to COBIT 2019, governance ensures that stakeholder needs, conditions, and options are evaluated to determine balanced, agreed-on enterprise objectives to be achieved; setting direction through prioritization and decision-making; and then monitoring performance and compliance against agreed-on direction and objectives.

On the other hand, management runs day-to-day activities. Management builds, runs, and monitors activities in alignment with the direction set by the governance body to achieve the enterprise objectives. Governance and management are complementary disciplines. Governance guides management and the collective activities of management to achieve organizational goals. As a result, governance tends to take a longer view of outcomes, while management tends to take a more tactical view with a focus on execution. Both are critical to an organization's success. Plenty of resources are available to enable and implement COBIT 2019 and these principles. These principles are included in the ISACA's *COBIT 2019 Implementation* professional guide.

Tailored to Enterprise Needs

The principle of "tailored to enterprise needs" goes back to the idea *that one size does not fit all!* All organizations are unique and often have different goals, objectives, and measurements of success. For example, an emerging technology start-up company may be willing to take on more risks to break into a new market. But a health care company must minimize risks that could result in harm to their patients.

 NOTE

The **risk appetite** refers to understanding the level of risk-taking by the business. This approach understands the business, its processes, and its goals and then determines the overall prioritization and funding needed to mitigate risks. The risk appetite often represents the amount of risk reduction the business is willing to fund.

As a framework, COBIT covers IT governance requirements for many industries. The key is to understand a framework that establishes broad requirements that must be tailored to each company's needs. We tailor by setting the risk appetite of the company through a deep understanding of risks and competing drivers, and as a result, IT priorities can be set.

Not all business risks can be eliminated, but they can be reduced. Often through technology, the business can balance several competing drivers. Some of these drivers include the following:

- Keep costs low while keeping customer satisfaction high
- Meet legal obligations

End-to-End Governance System

The principle of "end-to-end governance" means not to look at technology over-sight in isolation. It is this collective view of the process steps and its reliance on technology that provides the best view of risk. If you look at technology in isolation, you can lose business context. For instance, assume you are assessing customer privacy based on regulatory mandates. If you follow the process, you can identify risks during the hand-off between the business rules on handling customer data and how technology systems enforce those rules by limiting access. Both require effective governance. Looking at both governance processes as an end-to-end process provides a holistic view as described previously.

Service Organization Control Reports

These days, most organizations outsource some function of their infrastructure to a third-party business. Imagine you are the owner of a company. Deciding to put your company's sensitive data in someone else's hands is a difficult decision to make. You'll likely want to ensure that certain controls are in place before you take on such a risk. The functions provided by the third-party businesses are going to affect the user organization's records. This could be your customer's health or financial information, for example.

As a result, service organizations find it important to instill trust and confidence in their customers. The service organization has a vested interest in helping its customers understand that adequate controls and processes are in place. **Service Organization Control (SOC) reports** provide such assurance. The Auditing Standards Board of the American Institute of Certified Public Accountants (AICPA) issues and maintains these auditing standards. The primary stakeholders for SOC reports include the following:

- **User entities**—The user entities, or organizations that rely on a service provider, benefit from SOC reports because they mitigate the risk associated with outsourcing services.
- **Service organizations**—The service organizations want to earn and keep the business of the user entities. SOC reports provide user entities with confidence and the assurance of trust.
- **Auditors**—Auditors from both the service-organization side and the user-entity side must understand the framework and standards for performing SOC engagements.

The Sarbanes-Oxley Act (SOX) has placed increased importance on SOC assessments. A goal of SOX is to maintain investor and public confidence through the accuracy and reliability of financial reporting. SOX essentially mandates the establishment of adequate internal controls. Consider that many organizations outsource all sorts of activities that could have implications on SOX. These activities include payroll functions, for example, which are commonly outsourced. SOX ensures that adequate controls are in place is required regardless of whether that data are stored and processed in-house or by an external party.

FYI

Although some service organizations may find a SOC engagement to be expensive and difficult, they might find they have little choice. This is because SOX Section 404 requires management to certify financial controls, even if they have been outsourced to a third party. Because a SOC 1 report can fulfill this obligation, organizations are demanding it from those to whom they outsource their operations.

SOC reports take the form of three different engagements, which produce three different reports. The following are the three types of engagements and associated SOC reports:

- **SOC 1, Report on Controls at a Service Organization Relevant to User Entities' Internal Controls over Financial Reporting**—These reports are based on Statement on Standards for Attestation Engagements No. 16 (SSAE 16). This has replaced what was commonly known as Statement on Auditing Standards (SAS) No. 70, or SAS 70. This report is intended to assure organizations (user entities) that rely on the service provider. Auditors of the user entities employ these reports in performing financial audits. There are two types of SOC 1 reports— Type 1 and Type 2. A Type 1 report includes the auditor's assessment of whether the description of the service organization's system is fair as of a specific date. A Type 2 report is similar but also reports on the effectiveness of the controls through a specific period.

- **SOC 2, Report on Controls at Service Organization Relevant to Security, Availability, Processing Integrity, Confidentiality, or Privacy**—A SOC 2 report was specifically created to address the wide and growing use of technology and cloud-based providers. As the name of the report implies, the SOC 2 considers the security, availability, integrity, confidentiality, and integrity of the service organization's system and data. As with SOC 1, there are two types of SOC 2 reports: Type 1 and Type 2. A Type 1 report provides management's description of the organization's systems and the suitability of controls. A Type 2 report does the same but also includes management's assessment of the controls' effectiveness.

- **SOC 3, Trust Services Report for Service Organizations**—SOC 3 is similar to SOC 2 but may be more appropriate for a service provider when the provider's customers don't have the need or knowledge to use the details provided by SOC 2. Unlike SOC 1 or SOC 2 reports, which are intended for specific audiences or restricted, SOC 3 reports can be freely distributed.

 WARNING

User organizations should not view a SOC report as a "rubber stamp" of approval for information security controls based on recommended practices. The audit is an assessment of financial controls related to the service organization's stated objectives. User organizations should examine each report carefully.

Table 4-2, adapted from the AICPA's "SOC Reports Information for CPAs," provides a comparison between the three different SOC types. Further, the AICPA website (*http://www .aicpa.org*) provides comprehensive information and valuable SOC guides and publications.

Although SOC 1 reports have effectively replaced SAS 70 reports since about 2010, they continued to be called SAS 70 reports even many years later. If that wasn't confusing enough, the SOC 1 report is also commonly referred to as SSAE 16, which again is the standard on which the SOC 1 brand is based. Finally, it's important to point out that a SOC 1 report, as was the original intent of the SAS 70, is strictly related to internal controls over financial reporting. This need is largely AICPA's intent behind the SOC 2. In the absence of any true relationship of internal

TABLE 4-2 Comparison of SOC reports.			
	SOC 1 REPORT	**SOC 2 REPORT**	**SOC 3 REPORT**
Controls affected	Financial	Security, availability, processing integrity confidentiality, or privacy	Security, availability, processing integrity, confidentiality, or privacy
Associated attestation standard	AT 801, Reporting on Controls at a Service Organization (Based on SSAE 16)	AT 101, Attestation Engagements	AT 101, Attestation Engagements
Guidance and aids	*AICPA Guide*, "Service Organizations: Reporting on Controls at a Service Organization Relevant to User Entities' Internal Control Over Financial Reporting Guide"	*AICPA Guide*, "Reporting on Controls at a Service Organization Relevant to Security, Availability, Processing Integrity, Confidentiality, or Privacy"	*AICPA Technical Practice Aid*, "Trust Services Principles, Criteria, and Illustrations"
Contents of report	Description of system and the auditor's opinion of the controls. A description of the auditor's test of the controls and results in a Type 2 report.	Description of system and the auditor's opinion of the controls. A description of the auditor's test of the controls and results in a Type 2 report.	Auditor's opinion of whether effective controls of the system have been maintained.

Source: American Institute of CPAs

controls over financial reporting, a SOC 2 would be most appropriate for user entities that deal with many IT providers—and specifically the growing cloud service providers. Thus far, however, the trend has still been focused on SOC 1 compliance. While SOC 1 and its predecessor are well understood and accepted, the others have yet to fully mature.

ISO/IEC Standards

The **International Organization for Standardization (ISO)** is a nongovernment group that brings both the private and public sectors together and creates solutions for business and society. New

> **NOTE**
>
> Many organizations place reliance on the SOC report to ensure vendors and third-party processors have an effective control that can be relied upon to process the company's data.

standards are created by industries or the ISO itself. When a particular industry identifies a specific need, it informs a technical committee within the ISO to get standards developed. If a committee does not exist, a new one may be set up. To be accepted, though, the members of the ISO technical committee must establish majority support and a global relevance must be set. The technical committees within ISO are composed of experts from specific industries such as technology and business. Additionally, other entities such as laboratories, government agencies, consumer organizations, and academia may join the committee experts.

ISO/IEC 27000 is a series of standards and related terms that guide on matters of information security. This includes implementing, designing, and auditing an **information security management system (ISMS)**. An ISMS describes the policies, standards, and programs related to information security. These standards were established by the ISO and **International Electrotechnical Commission (IEC)**. Other popular series include ISO 9000 and ISO 14000, which deal with quality management and environmental management, respectively. The technical committee directly responsible for the ISO 27000 series is ISO/IEC JTC1 (Joint Technical Committee 1) SC 27 (Subcommittee 27). This nomenclature is especially useful when browsing the standards catalog at the ISO website. The ISO/IEC JTC1 is the joint committee responsible for IT. Within these are several subcommittees. Subcommittee 27 defines IT security techniques. Other subcommittees include SC 37 for biometrics and SC 35 for user interfaces. Within just ISO/IEC JTC 1/SC 27 there are well over 100 published standards. The focus here is on the ISO 27000 series and specifically the first three standards.

Table 4-3 lists the published ISO/IEC standards in the ISMS family of standards. The next two sections provide details on ISO/IEC 27001 and 27002. Both of these standards focus on information security systems and processes and are complementary to each other.

FYI

It is common in speech as well as in print to find these standards preceded only by "ISO" rather than "ISO/IEC" used throughout this chapter. The 27000 series is also called the ISMS family of standards and is often shortened to ISO27k.

> **NOTE**
>
> ISO/IEC 27001 is not a control standard. It focuses on management and processes and relies upon other standards such as ISO/IEC 27002. ISO/IEC 27002 focuses on specific controls to make ISO/IEC 27001 possible.

ISO/IEC 27001 Standard

ISO/IEC 27001 is a worldwide standard formally known as "ISO/IEC 27001:2013—Information Technology—Security Techniques—Information Security Management Systems—Requirements." It was originally established in October 2005 as ISO/IEC 27001:2005 and replaced British Standards Institute Security Management Standard BS7799-2.

ISO/IEC 27001 is the best-known specification in the ISMS family of standards. It contains accepted

77777777

TABLE 4-3 ISO/IEC 27000 ISMS family of standards.

TYPE OF STANDARD	PUBLISHED STANDARD	DESCRIPTION
Vocabulary	27000	Information security management systems—overview and vocabulary
Requirement	27001	Information security management systems—requirements
	27006	Requirements for bodies providing audit and certification of information security management systems
Guideline	27002	Code of practice for information security controls
	27003	Information security management system implementation guidance
	27004	Information security management— measurement
	27005	Information security risk management
	27007	Guidelines for information security management systems auditing
	27008	Guidelines for auditors on information security controls
	27013	Guidance on the integrated implementation of ISO/IEC 27001 and ISO/IEC 20000-1
	27014	Governance of information security
	27016	Information security management— organizational economics
Sector-specific guideline	27010	Information security management for inter-sector and inter-organizational communications

(Continues)

TABLE 4-3 ISO/IEC 27000 ISMS family of standards.		*(continued)*
TYPE OF STANDARD	**PUBLISHED STANDARD**	**DESCRIPTION**
	27011	Information security management guidelines for telecommunications organizations based on ISO/IEC 27002
	27015	Information security management guidelines for financial services
	27018	Code of practice for protection of personally identifiable information (PII) in public clouds acting as PII processors
	27019	Information security management guidelines based on ISO/IEC 27002 for process control systems specific to the energy utility industry
	27779	Information security management in health using ISO/IEC 27002
Control-specific guideline	27031	Guidelines for information and communication technology readiness for business continuity
	27032	Guidelines for cybersecurity
	27033	Network security—multipart
	27034	Application security—multipart
	27035	Information security incident management
	27036	Information security for supplier relationships—multipart
	27037	Guidelines for identification, collection, acquisition, and preservation of digital evidence
	27038	Specification for digital redaction
	27039	Selection, deployment, and operations of intrusion detection systems (IDSes)
	27040	Storage security

good practices and provides an accepted baseline against which IT auditors can audit. It specifies the auditable requirements for establishing, applying, operating, maintaining, reviewing, monitoring, and improving a control framework based on an organization's information security risk. Such risk applies to the information structure within the organization. This includes, for example, management responsibility and documentation. It also applies across all departments, such as human resources, facilities, and operations. It looks at the entire organization and its information assets and walks through a process to determine the associated risks. The process calculates the risk and impact to the organization. Then, it considers the steps needed to remove, reduce, or accept the risk.

The requirements established in ISO/IEC 27001 cover all styles of organizations, such as large enterprises to small and medium-sized businesses. This also includes federal agencies and not-for-profit organizations. Although ISO does not perform certifications, it is common for organizations to assert that a product or system is certified to an ISO standard. This may be done by an accredited certification body. Many organizations choose to not become certified, yet still implement the standard. Becoming certified does often lend credibility, but it is certainly not required. Organizations will still benefit from the good practices either way. Further, certification makes it clear that the organization has done the following:

- Performed due diligence
- Ensured that information controls meet the organization's needs on an ongoing basis
- Considered risks associated with the organization

According to the ISO organization, ISO/IEC 27001:

> !WARNING
>
> Unlike many other standards and frameworks, the ISO standards are not free of charge. ISO charges fees for the standards, and ISO maintains a prohibitive copyright stance.

...specifies the requirements for establishing, implementing, maintaining, and continually improving an information security management system within the context of the organization. It also includes requirements for the assessment and treatment of information security risks tailored to the needs of the organization. The requirements set out in ISO/IEC 27001:2013 are generic and are intended to be applicable to all organizations, regardless of type, size, or nature.

In other words, ISO/IEC 27001 provides the high-level framework upon which an organization can implement an ISMS. Optionally, the specification serves as the framework by which accredited auditing organizations may conduct a formal assessment for the purpose of certification.

The contents of ISO/IEC 27001 is made up of the following sections and annex:

- **Introduction**—This section briefly summarizes the intent of the standard, which is to establish a continuous process for an ISMS.
- **Scope**—This section specifies that ISMS applies to all organizations.
- **Normative references**—This section provides references to other documentation that plays a major role in implementing the standard.

- **Terms and definitions**—This section simply references ISO/IEC 27000, which defines the vocabulary.
- **Context of the organization**—This section lists the internal and external factors that influence the goals of the ISMS.
- **Leadership**—This section emphasizes the need to establish and communicate management responsibility.
- **Planning**—This section explains the need to establish information security objectives, along with how those objectives will be achieved.
- **Support**—This section outlines the required support and documentation needed.
- **Operation**—This section details the requirements for assessing the efficiency and effectiveness of the ISMS.

> **NOTE**
>
> ISO/IEC 27001 certification is not a one-time exercise. To maintain the certification, organizations must undergo ongoing review and monitoring of the ISMS.

- **Performance evaluation**—This section discusses the opportunity to make improvements through monitoring and measuring controls, processes, and management.
- **Improvement**—This section addresses the need for issues to be identified and quantified so corrective action can be applied.
- **Annex A**—This provides a listing of controls and control objectives, which are related to those found in ISO/IEC 27002.

PDCA

Plan-do-check-act (PDCA) is a significant ongoing approach for continuous improvement. While the latest version of ISO/IEC 27001 no longer directly incorporates the PDCA model, it was a well-known fixture in ISO/IEC 27001:2005. PDCA also is known by other names, including the Shewhart cycle, Deming cycle, or Deming wheel. This approach is popular in varying situations focused on continuous improvement. It is also applied when defining a repetitive work process.

Although not invented by Dr. W. Edwards Deming, he certainly popularized its use. Deming, often called the father of quality management, is known for his work in quality improvement. He is credited with having been the driving force behind Japan's reputation for quality products. He later had a profound impact in the United States.

The four steps within PDCA are conceptually simple. Deming called this four-step process the *Shewhart cycle* after Walter A. Shewhart, an accomplished statistician. The key principle of the PDCA is iteration. With each cycle completed, the knowledge about the underlying system being studied improves. Repeating the process brings perfection closer.

While the PDCA model has been removed from the latest version, the ideas still exist. In fact, the sections for planning, support, operation, performance evaluation, and improvement within ISO/IEC 27001:2013 demonstrate that the PDCA model is still very much alive.

FYI

ISO/IEC 27002 came from a UK government document originally published in 1995. The original document was republished as British Standard (BS) 7799. This was later republished by the ISO in 2000 as ISO 17799. This standard was updated in 2005 and finally renamed to bring it within the 27000 series of information security standards. The final document today is ISO/IEC 27002.

ISO/IEC 27002 Standard

ISO/IEC 27002 is formally known as "ISO/IEC 27002:2013 Information Technology—Security Techniques—Code of Practice for Information Security Management." Whereas ISO 27001 formally defines mandatory requirements for an ISMS, ISO/IEC 27002 provides suitable information security controls within the ISMS. ISO/IEC 27002 is merely a code of practice or guideline rather than a certification standard. Thus, organizations are free to select and put in place other controls as they see fit. While at the core, ISO/IEC 27001 provides suitable controls for use within an ISMS, it is often used within a context outside of a formal ISMS. It also serves a couple of other purposes. For example, organizations use ISO/IEC 27001 as a generic framework for commonly accepted controls or as a baseline for developing controls.

Eighteen sections make up ISO/IEC 27002. The introduction and the first four sections provide introductory material, whereas the rest of the sections provide the core recommendations and controls. Sections 5 through 18 provide the following framework:

- Overview of organizational goals being addressed
- List of practical controls
- Guidance for how to put each of the controls in place
- Additional information, including cross-references within the standards and other standards

The preceding framework applies to the key sections within the documents, which are summarized in the following list:

- **Information Security Policies**—Covers management guidance and the need to have a documented information security policy and review process
- **Organization of Information Security**—Covers the organization of information security as related to the internal organization parties and mobile devices and teleworking
- **Human Resource Security**—Covers employment of employees and those associated with an organization regarding pre-employment checks, dismissal, and change of employment

- **Asset Management**—Covers the discovery and classification of assets and information, including how to handle media
- **Access Control**—Covers business requirements, user controls, and responsibilities, application-level controls, and access controls for networks and operating systems
- **Cryptography**—Covers cryptographic controls, including both the policy on the use of cryptography and key management
- **Physical and Environmental Security**—Covers secure facilities and equipment security
- **Operations Security**—Covers the largest range of areas, including operational procedures such as change and capacity management; malware, backup, operational software controls, and vulnerability management; and audit, logging, and monitoring
- **Communications Security**—Covers network security management and information transfer
- **Systems Acquisition, Development, and Maintenance**—Covers systems development and acquisition, including security requirements of systems, correct processing applications, and test data
- **Supplier Relationships**—Covers information security and managing aspects related to third parties or suppliers
- **Information Security Incident Management**—Covers information security incident management, including reporting of events and security weaknesses and improvements
- **Information Security Aspects of Business Continuity Management**—Covers protecting critical processes from disruption
- **Compliance**—Covers complying with legal requirements, security policies, standards, and technical compliance, and considerations for information systems audits or reviews

Each of the preceding key topics in ISO 27002 comprises many individual controls detailed in the standard. This standard provides wide coverage across the information security domain and is quite specific in the prescription of controls. As a result, the security community has embraced it widely.

▶ **NOTE**

The National Institute of Standards and Technology (NIST) works with the public and private sectors to establish relationships between NIST's security controls and those provided by ISO 27002, for example.

NIST 800-53

NIST 800-53 provides a comprehensive catalog of security controls. **NIST 800-53A** provides a framework for assessing the adequacy of in-place controls. Although both are targeted to the federal government, many organizations appreciate the depth and prescriptive nature of the NIST standards. As a result, they are widely used outside of government, even if used as a complement to other standards such as ISO/IEC 27002. NIST 800-53 addresses a wide range of controls. The controls consider multiple aspects, including management, technical, and operational. The catalog of controls is grouped into 17 families of controls, which include the following:

- Access Control
- Awareness and Training
- Audit and Accountability
- Configuration Management
- Contingency Planning
- Identification and Authentication
- Incident Response
- Maintenance
- Media Protection
- Physical and Environmental Protection
- Planning
- Personnel Security
- Risk Assessment
- Security Assessment and Authorization
- System and Services Acquisition
- System and Communication Protection
- System and Information Integrity

The framework for each of the preceding families of controls is composed of the following elements:

- **Control**—A descriptive statement of the security measure put in place to provide reasonable assurance the process or function is working as expected
- **Supplemental guidance**—Additional guidance for consideration
- **Control enhancements**—Information on augmenting the control with additional functionality or increased security
- **References**—A listing of related federal laws, executive orders, directives, policies, standards, and guidelines related to the control
- **Priority and baseline allocation**—A listing of codes used for prioritizing decisions during security control implementation and control enhancements for systems of varying degrees of impact

This standard discusses in detail the process for conducting assessments. This includes topics on preparing for the assessment, developing the plans, conducting the assessment, and follow-on reporting, analysis, and other activities.

Cybersecurity Framework

In 2014, NIST released the first version of what is known as the **Cybersecurity Framework**. This framework is a result of President Barak Obama's Executive Order 13636, "Improving Critical Infrastructure Cybersecurity," issued in 2013. The development of the framework is a result of collaboration between both government and private-sector participants, given the vested interests and associated stakeholders. The current version is NIST 800-53, Revision 5, which was published on September 23, 2020.

The purpose of the Cybersecurity Framework is to provide a voluntary structure for reducing the risks to critical infrastructure. The first version considers various other standards and best practices, and "provides a common language and mechanism for organizations" to do the following five key items:

- Describe their existing cybersecurity stance.
- Describe their ideal end state for cybersecurity.
- Prioritize areas for improvement as related to managing risk.
- Measure progress toward the ideal end state.
- Encourage communication among the various stakeholders.

The Cybersecurity Framework is made up of three components:

- The Framework Core
- The Framework Profile
- The Framework Implementation Tiers

The Framework Core is a matrix of activities and associated references. The framework includes various categories across five different functions. These functions are as follows:

- Identify
- Protect
- Detect
- Respond
- Recover

For each of the categories or subcategories across one of the aforementioned functions, references are included. References draw on existing standards, guidelines, and best practices. The framework includes an example for the Protect function. Within the Protect function are various categories, such as Data Security and Access Control. For example, ISO/IEC 27001 provides control A.8.3.3 for physical media transfer. This control serves as an informative reference to the Data Security subcategory and specifically addresses the subcategory "Data during transportation/transmission is protected to achieve confidentiality, integrity, and availability goals."

The Framework Profile provides the primary mechanism to improve the security posture by comparing the existing state or profile with the ideal end state or target profile.

Finally, the Framework Implementation Tiers define four levels, which describe how an organization manages risk. The following are the tiers in order from least mature to most:

- **Tier 1**—Partial
- **Tier 2**—Risk informed
- **Tier 3**—Risk informed and repeatable
- **Tier 4**—Adaptive

Various frameworks, and especially the Cybersecurity Framework, consider that organizations may use or reference multiple frameworks and standards. The Cybersecurity Framework is purposely designed to supplement these other programs. Further, it can be used by organizations just starting out or to improve existing programs.

CHAPTER SUMMARY

There are many IT frameworks to choose from. There are frameworks promoted by government agencies, universities, corporations, global commissions, vendors, industry groups, associations, and individuals. So how do you know which to choose? There's no simple answer. The selection will depend on your industry as well as your management's view of risk and any bias within your organization. You should focus on selecting those standards that are widely accepted.

Equally important is to look at audit standards and frameworks as a measure of success. Essentially, frameworks help you define what "good" looks like. If a framework is a measure, consider who will be judging that success such as a regulator. If you are in the banking industry, for example, NIST is often used to assess the completeness of the information security program. Thus selecting NIST as a framework in that case not only helps establish the information security program but also helps in evidencing to regulators the completeness of the program.

The chapter examined the difference between standards and frameworks and the importance of auditing. We explored several major IT frameworks such as NIST, COBIT, and ISO. Additionally, we examined the foundational professional standards established by the IIA as a useful resource for all auditors.

KEY CONCEPTS AND TERMS

Committee of Sponsoring
   Organizations (COSO)
Control objectives
Cybersecurity Framework
Descriptive control
Framework
Information security
   management system (ISMS)
Institute of Internal
   Auditors (IIA)

International Electrotechnical
   Commission (IEC)
International Organization for
   Standardization (ISO)
ISACA
ISO/IEC 27001
ISO/IEC 27002
NIST 800-53
NIST 800-53A

Plan-do-check-act (PDCA)
Prescriptive control
Risk appetite
Service Organization Control
   (SOC) reports
Statement on Standards for
   Attestation Engagements No.
   16 (SSAE 16)

CHAPTER 4 ASSESSMENT

1. A(n) _____ is a conceptual set of rules and ideas that provide structure to a complex and challenging situation.

2. Frameworks differ from each other in that they might offer varying levels of depth and breadth.

   A. True
   B. False

3. Avoiding the need for audits is one reason organizations develop clearly documented policies, standards, and procedures.

   A. True
   B. False

4. Which of the following should organizations do when selecting a standard? (Select three.)

   A. Select a standard that can be followed.
   B. Employ the selected standard.
   C. Select a flexible standard.
   D. Select a standard that other organizations in the same geographic location are using.

5. A standard and a policy are exactly the same.

   A. True
   B. False

6. Responding to business requirements in alignment with the business strategy is an example of an IT _____.

7. Which one of the following is *not* true of COBIT?

   A. It is business focused.
   B. It is security centered.
   C. It is process oriented.
   D. It is controls based.
   E. It is measurement driven.

8. Which one of the following is *not* one of the four domains of COBIT?

   A. Plan and Organize
   B. Implement and Support
   C. Acquire and Implement
   D. Deliver and Support
   E. Monitor and Evaluate

9. SSAE 16 Type 1 includes everything in a SSAE 16 Type 2 report, but it adds a detailed testing of the controls over a specific time frame.

   A. True
   B. False

10. Organizations may be audited for both ISO/IEC 27001 and ISO/IEC 27002 and receive a formal certification for each.

   A. True
   B. False

11. ISO/IEC 27002 is a code of _____ for information security management.

12. The key difference between a framework and standard is?

    A. A framework provide broad control objectives

    B. A standard define how the control objective is to be achieved

    C. A framework is designed to cover multiple situations

    D. All of the above

13. NIST is a framework that applies only to government funded systems.

    A. True

    B. False

14. Which of these is a listing of codes used for prioritizing decisions during security control implementation and control enhancements for systems of varying degrees of impact?

    A. Supplemental guidance

    B. Control enhancements

    C. References

    D. Priority and baseline allocation

15. The Framework Core is a matrix of activities and associated references that uses various categories across five different functions including which of the following? (Pick three.)

    A. Identify

    B. Protect

    C. Refer

    D. Respond

16. Which of the following components of IT governance deals with ensuring the proper management of IT resources and that they are used responsibly?

    A. Strategic alignment

    B. Resource management

    C. Risk management

    D. Performance measurement

17. ISO/IEC 27002 certification is not a one-time process but needs to be continuously updated.

    A. True

    B. False

18. ISO/IEC 27002, formally known as "ISO/IEC 27002:2013 Information Technology—Security Techniques—Code of Practice for Information Security Management" is made up of 16 sections of code.

    A. True

    B. False

4

Auditing Standards and Frameworks

Planning an IT Infrastructure Audit for Compliance

AUDIT PLANNING SHOULD NOT be overlooked. Placing importance in the audit planning process ensures that auditors are able to effectively evaluate the relevant risks associated with the business. An effective audit plan will evaluate the risk to be covered, as well as, the approach to evaluating the risk. The audit plan ensures adequate staff with the right skill sets are available, that audit tools and technology are available, and which audit processes will be used to ensure completeness of results. What goes into the planning process directly affects the quality of the outcome. The planning stage is the first step and takes place before any of the detailed audit work begins. A proper plan ensures that resources are focused on the right areas and that potential problems are identified early. Although each audit will vary, the plan and approach to each audit follow similar characteristics. Despite the best plans, however, circumstances do change, and plans need to be adjusted. As a result, flexibility must be considered. Significant errors, suspected fraud, and misrepresentation can all have a considerable effect on the initial plan. Regardless, proper planning helps ensure an effective and timely audit.

Chapter 5 Topics

This chapter covers the following topics and concepts:

- How to define the scope, objectives, goals, and frequency of an audit
- What risks to cover in the engagement
- How to assess IT security
- How to obtain information, documentation, and resources
- How to map the security policy framework definitions to the seven domains of IT infrastructure
- How to identify and test monitoring requirements

- How to identify critical security control points that must be verified throughout the IT infrastructure
- How to build a project plan

Chapter 5 Goals

When you complete this chapter, you will be able to:

- Define the scope and frequency of an audit
- Identify the key requirements for an audit
- Understand the importance of risk management in assessing security controls
- Identify the information and resources needed for an IT audit
- Relate the IT security policy framework to the seven domains of IT infrastructure
- Understand why monitoring requirements help with an IT audit
- Identify security control points
- Differentiate between the project management tasks of an IT audit

Defining the Scope, Objectives, Goals, and Frequency of an Audit

The scope, objectives, goals, and frequency of audits are based on a risk. The goal of the planning phase of an audit is to define an audit universe and then identify the risk that puts the organization's goals in jeopardy. An **audit universe** is defined as the collection or grouping of auditable areas, units, or entities grouped of logically separate areas to ensure full coverage of risks. For example, to cover all of the IT infrastructures we can logically separate the information technology (IT) operations versus the information security (IS) functions. Both are needed to ensure data are appropriately processed and applications are protected to support the business's goals. Consequently, an auditable entity or grouping can be organizationally or functionally aligned.

Once the auditable entities and groups are defined, the next step is to determine the risks associated with each grouping. For example, cutting-edge high-tech firms are highly reliant on skilled teams of developers, while a retail store may be reliant on older technologies. Both situations come with different risks and, thus, may have a different set of priorities when it comes to auditing.

To determine the risks associated with each auditable entity, a detailed assessment and analysis should be performed. Typically, these assessments and analyses are performed annually as part of the audit planning cycle. **Audit cycles** are how often do you audit or assess an auditable entity. This is important because rarely there are enough time and resources to do a complete audit in one year. Consequently, if you have an audit cycle of a designated amount of time—say five years—you would then be able to break up operations audits into five parts and at the end of five years have complete coverage for that auditable entity. There is no specific rule on how short or long these cycles can be; however, generally three to five years is the accepted norm. It is important to note that these cycles are not rigid; if a higher risk is identified within a cycle, you would audit that more frequently. For example, on the five-year cycle, if you audited the data backups two years ago but recently determined an elevated risk with the increase in ransom attack, it may be still necessary to re-audit your backups based on the increased risk.

Assessments are a very important process to determine the risks and thus drive the audit frequency. While risks will not a complete scope, they drive the need to audit and will be the starting point for scope discussion. Specifically, if you know what risks are driving the need to have an audit, then the scope at a minimum will cover all the risks identified.

The detailed assessments and analysis of risk should include a review of the following:

- IS threats and vulnerabilities
- Operational dependencies and efficiencies
- Legal and regulatory requirements
- Business goals and objectives

Depending on the risk, the frequency of audits varies. Critical systems controls might need to be monitored more often than noncritical controls. In more high-risk situations, automated or continual audit tests might be considered.

Before performing an audit, the auditor should first define the **audit scope**. The scope includes the area or areas to be reviewed as well as the time frame to complete. Experienced auditors know it's just as important to define what will be audited as it is to define what will not be audited. Risk often drives these decisions to include or exclude areas of concern. Most importantly, the higher risks should be covered. Risks need to align to likelihood. If you have a seemingly slightly higher risk item but the likelihood is very low compared to a slightly lower risk item with a much higher likelihood, typically the one with a higher likelihood would take priority. If the scope is not clearly defined, **scope creep** occurs, likely increasing the auditor's workload. Scope creep is a term common to projects where the plans or goals expand beyond what was originally intended.

The **audit objective** or the goal of the audit is to ensure the identified risks are appropriately being managed by the organization. Both scope and objective are closely related. For the audit to be effective, the scope must consider the objectives of the audit. Defining scope requires the identification of the relevant deployed controls that will mitigate the risks identified. Time is another consideration dependent upon the objective. The depth and breadth of an audit usually determines the time frame required to meet the objectives.

When defining the scope, the auditor should consider the controls and processes across the auditable entities of IT infrastructure. This includes relevant resources such as the following:

- Data
- Applications

- Technology
- Facilities
- Personnel

Auditors need to ensure the scope is sufficient to achieve the stated audit objectives. Restrictions placed on the scope could seriously affect the ability to achieve the stated objective. Examples of restrictions that an organization may place on an auditor that could have such a negative impact include the following:

- Not providing enough resources
- Limiting the time frame
- Preventing the discovery of audit evidence
- Restricting audit procedures
- Withholding relevant historical records or information about past incidents

Planned audit activities also have a defined rate of occurrence, known as the **audit frequency**. There are two approaches to determine audit frequency. Audits can occur on an annual basis or every two or three years, depending on regulatory requirements

---

Project Management

An audit is a project. As with any project, proper planning is necessary. Auditors should be familiar with the Project Management Institute (PMI), which has created a standard named *A Guide to the Project Management Body of Knowledge (PMBOK)*. This guide provides a well-known and applied framework for managing successful projects.

A project, such as an audit, has three important characteristics. First, a project is temporary. This means it has an identified start and end date. Unlike operations or a program, a project lasts for a finite time period. Second, a project is unique and produces unique results. At the end of the project, a deliverable is produced. Although projects might be similar, the process, resources, constraints, and risks, for example, will differ. Finally, a project is progressively elaborated. Because each project is unique, the process is more dynamic. Projects will occur in separate steps. As the process continues, the next phase becomes clearer.

Projects require someone to manage them. This position is often given the title of project manager. Large projects and even audits might have a dedicated project manager. Other times, the person managing the project might be the project expert. Project management requires the management of three competing needs to achieve the project objectives. Known as the *triple constraint*, these include scope, cost, and time. Consider, for example, a project with a large scope, but with little time and cost. More than likely, quality will be compromised. A project manager must be aware of all three constraints at the start of and throughout the project.

and the determined risk. IT audits also are known for not following a predefined frequency, but instead using a continuous risk-assessment process. This is more appropriate given the fast-paced change in technology as well as the threats and vulnerabilities related to IT.

Identifying Critical Requirements for the Audit

The risk assessment will influence the critical requirements for an IT audit. Overall, there are various types of IT audits. In addition to infrastructure audits for compliance, other examples include audits specific to IT processes, such as governance and software development. Another example includes integrated audits, where financial controls are the focus.

Auditing IT infrastructure for compliance incorporates the evaluation of various types of controls. IT organizations today are concerned with controls relating to both security and privacy. Traditionally, privacy and information security activities are separate activities. The two, however, have become more interrelated, and coordination between the two has become a priority for many organizations. Two major factors contributing to this are regulatory issues and the rapid growth and widespread use of the Internet. As a result, both privacy and information security are converging, specifically around compliance issues.

Implementing Security Controls

Before an evaluation of controls can begin, the auditor must first identify the critical controls. To do so, the auditor must consider the audit scope and objective along with the risk assessment. Documentation and any preliminary interviews also help to identify the requirements.

Controls can be classified into different groups to aid in understanding how they fit into the overall security of a system. **Table 5-1** illustrates the different dimensions of control classifications. Understanding the classifications provides auditors with a foundation to identify and assess critical controls.

A high-level classification of controls for IT systems includes general and application controls. General controls are also known as infrastructure controls. These types of controls apply broadly to all system components across an organization. Application controls apply to individual application systems. Types of application controls include various transaction controls, such as input, processing, and output controls.

Three IT security controls groupings that are covered by the National Institute of Standards and Technology (NIST) include management, operational, and technical controls. The following list provides a description and examples of each of these:

- **Management controls**—These controls are typically governed by management as part of the overall security program. Examples include the following:
  - Security policy
  - Security program management
  - Risk assessment
  - Security and planning in the system development life cycle
  - System and services acquisition

TABLE 5-1 NIST 800-53 R5 Cybersecurity and Data Protection Program (CDPP)			
CONTROL GROUPING	**POLICY #**	**NIS 800-53 R5 CONTROL FAMILY**	**IDENTIFIER**
Management	1	Assessment, Authorization, and Monitoring	CA
Management	2	Planning	PL
Management	3	Program Management	PM
Management	4	Risk Assessment	RA
Management	5	System and Services Acquisition	SA
Management	6	Supply Chain Risk Management	SR
Operational	7	Awareness and Training	AT
Operational	8	Contingency Planning	CP
Operational	9	Incident Response	IR
Operational	10	Media Protection	MP
Operational	11	Personnel Security	PS
Operational	12	Physical and Environmental Protection	PE
Operational	13	Personally Identifiable Information (PII) Processing and Transparency	PT
Technical	14	Access Control	AC
Technical	15	Audit and Accountability	AU
Technical	16	Configuration Management	CM
Technical	17	Identification and Authentication	IA
Technical	18	Maintenance	MA
Technical	19	System and Communication Protection	SC
Technical	20	System and Information Integrity	SI

Data from NIST 800-53 R5 Cybersecurity & Data Protection Program.

- **Operational controls**—These controls are implemented by people rather than systems. These controls are often interrelated with both management and technical controls. Examples include the following:
  - Personnel and user issues
  - Contingency and disaster planning
  - Incident response and handling

- Awareness, training, and education
- Physical and environmental security
- **Technical controls**—These controls are performed by the IT systems. Examples include the following:
  - Identification and authorization
  - Logical access control
  - System Communications
  - Cryptography

Control functions can be further classified as one of the following three types:

- Preventative controls describe any control that's designed to stop unwanted or unauthorized activity from occurring. A few examples include physical controls such as fences, locks, and alarm systems.
- Detective controls describe any controls to detect and alert to unwanted or unauthorized activity in progress or after it has occurred. A detective control does not prevent the event but alerts you to the event. Physical examples include alarms or notifications from a physical sensor (door alarms, fire alarms) that alert guards or police. An audit log reviewed regularly could be considered a detective control.

> **NOTE**
>
> Antivirus software is a common control that spans all three controls. It can prevent a system from getting a virus in the first place. It can detect if a virus is on the system. Finally, it can react and correct the situation by removing or quarantining the virus.

- Corrective controls include any measures taken to repair damage or restore resources and capabilities following an unauthorized or unwanted activity. Examples could be restoring corrupted files from a backup server.

Protecting Data Privacy

Audits of IT infrastructure relating to security are common. However, due to recent legislation regarding the need to protect personally identifiable information, audits specific to privacy are more commonplace than before. ISACA defines privacy within the context of information systems as "adherence to trust and obligation in relation to any information relating to an identified or identifiable individual (data subject). Management is responsible to comply with privacy in accordance with its privacy policy or applicable privacy laws and regulations."

Privacy audits go beyond traditional IT audits in that the entire information life-cycle process needs to be considered. This includes not just the controls relating to how it was gathered and secured, but also how it is collected, used, and retained. Specifically, privacy audits address the following three concerns:

- What type of personal information is processed and stored?
- Where is it stored?
- How is it managed?

A privacy audit should consider what privacy laws are applicable to the organization. Auditors should consider who has responsibility for privacy within the organization. This includes the roles of legal counsel and whether a **chief privacy officer (CPO)** role is established. (The CPO is a senior-level position responsible for the overall management of an organization's privacy program.) Finally, the policies and procedures specific to privacy should be examined. **Table 5-2** provides examples of privacy principles that can be implemented through privacy controls and processes.

TABLE 5-2 The Generally Accepted Privacy Principles.	
PRINCIPLE	**DESCRIPTION**
Management	The entity defines, documents, communicates, and assigns accountability for its privacy policies and procedures.
Notice	The entity provides notice about its privacy policies and procedures and identifies the purposes for which personal information is collected, used, retained, and disclosed.
Choice of consent	The entity describes the choices available to the individual and obtains implicit or explicit consent with respect to the collection, use, and disclosure of personal information.
Collection	The entity collects personal information only for the purposes identified in the notice.
Use and retention	The entity limits the use of personal information to the purposes identified in the notice and for which the individual has provided implicit or explicit consent. The entity retains personal information for only as long as is necessary to fulfill the stated purposes.
Access	The entity provides individuals with access to their personal information for review and update.
Disclosure to third parties	The entity discloses personal information to third parties only for the purposes identified in the notice and with the implicit or explicit consent of the individual.
Security for privacy	The entity protects personal information against unauthorized access.
Quality	The entity maintains accurate, complete, and relevant personal information for the purposes identified in the notice.
Monitoring and enforcement	The entity monitors compliance with its privacy policies and procedures and has procedures to address privacy-related complaints and disputes.

Assessing IT Security

Examining IT security is a key component of auditing IT infrastructure for compliance. An audit can help identify fraud, ineffective IT practices, improper use of resources, and inadequate security. Assessing IT security is largely about ensuring that adequate controls are in place. Controls cost money, however. The selection and implementation of controls must be a result of a consideration of risk.

Suppose you want to build a fence to protect a cow. Building the fence will cost money. Exactly how much money it will cost might depend upon the quality and size of the fence. How much might you be willing to spend? Of course, you should first understand why you want to protect the cow. How valuable is this cow to you? What are you protecting the cow from? Let's assume the cow has some type of value to you—otherwise, there would be little reason to spend money on protecting the cow. Is a fence the only solution? Could you tie the cow to a tree instead? If you decide to build the fence, is it strong enough? Is it high enough? Now suppose you decide to have the security of your fence assessed. What you *don't* need is for the auditor to come by and tell you what you already know—that you have a fence in place. Rather, what would be useful is a determination of the lack of controls, the ineffectiveness of controls, or even the use of unnecessary controls. If your cow turns out to be a bull, for example, perhaps that fence won't be so effective. Is the fence effective against someone determined to steal the cow? To understand these issues, consider the following:

- Is a control even required?
- How much effort or money should be spent on a control?
- Is the control effective?

Understanding the answers to these questions requires thought about risk. This is why risk management needs to be a key part of organizations and any audit.

Risk Management

Managing and understanding risk is a key operating component of any organization. Risk is about uncertainty. Yet, there will always be uncertainties across organizations. Uncertainty presents both challenges and opportunities for companies. Risk management provides a method for dealing with uncertainty. This includes identifying which ones to accept and which ones to control. The Committee of Sponsoring Organizations (COSO) of the Treadway Commission, which provides a framework for **enterprise risk management (ERM)**, identifies the following key components of ERM:

- Aligning risk appetite and strategy—This helps the organization manage the uncertainty by considering the goals of the organization.
- Enhancing risk response decisions—This improves the organization's ability to make decisions about how to better manage risk.
- Reducing operational surprises and losses—This enhances the organization's ability to identify potential events or threats and react appropriately.

- Identifying and managing multiple and cross-enterprise risks—This helps the organization consider related risks from across the organization and provides a unified response across the varying risks.
- Seizing opportunities—This helps the organization recognize events from which new opportunities can be pursued.
- Improving deployment of capital—This improves how organizations divide their financial resources to enhance performance and profitability.

How do you implement risk management? For risk management to be effective, it must be systematic, structured, collaborative, and cross-organizational. Risk management relies on each business unit to contribute to a larger and holistic view of risk. For risk management to be effective, there must be a common set of processes each business unit can execute against. At the very least, the following risk management processes need to be implemented across the organization.

1. Risk Identification

Risk identification is the process of documenting potential risks and then categorizing the actual risks the business faces. The totality of potential and actual risks is sometimes referred to as the risk universe. The risk universe is used to prioritize the risk an organization is willing to accept. Those risks an organization is not willing to accept then become risks to remediate or mitigate.

2. Risk Assessment

Understanding the likelihood and potential impact of a risk to the organization is essential to establishing prioritization for acceptance or remediation. For example, if the impact on the organization is small, it may not make sense to spend a lot to remediate the risk. An organization might divide risks into "high, moderate, or low," depending on their potential for disruption. The exact categorization method is less important than the recognition that some risks present a more pressing threat than others. Risk analysis helps businesses to prioritize mitigation.

3. Risk Mitigation

Risk mitigation is the implementation of your response to the risk assessment. It is the action organization takes to reduce exposure and minimize impact. Following our previous example, the implementation might involve as simple as creating security awareness training. Alternatively, higher risks may involve the deployment of new preventative controls.

 NOTE

It's important to understand that risk management is not a one-off event; it's a process that recurs throughout the year.

4. Risk Monitoring

Risks are not static; they change over time and controls can fail. Risk monitoring is the process of "monitoring" the risk to ensure controls are working effectively, processes are operating within risk tolerance, and new risks are not introduced.

Threat Versus Vulnerability Versus Risk

The terms threat, vulnerability, and risk are too often used interchangeably. There are distinct differences and care should be used when applying them. A common set of definitions is as follows:

- A **threat** is anything that can exploit a vulnerability, intentionally or accidentally that can lead to an adverse impact on the organization. For example, a hurricane might wipe out your data center.
- A **vulnerability** is a weakness or control gap that can be exploited by threats, such as locating your data center in a building that cannot withstand high winds.
- A **risk** is a potential for loss, damage, or impact to the organization as a result of the vulnerability occurring due to the threat. For example, if a hurricane occurs and the data center building collapsed, what would be the impact on the organization?

The key component of risk management includes a risk assessment. Planning an audit of IT infrastructure depends on this assessment. The audit plan should be prepared only after a risk assessment is complete. The key reason for this is that the audit will focus on those areas with the highest risk.

There are several methodologies for assessing risk specific to IT environments. NIST 800-30, "Guide for Conducting Risk Assessments," is one such example. This guide provides a practical nine-step process as follows:

- System characterization—Identify and understand the systems and their operating environment.
- Threat identification—Identify potential methods or situations that could exploit a weakness.
- Vulnerability identification—Identify flaws or weaknesses that can be triggered or exploited, which might result in a breach.
- Control analysis—Analyze controls to reduce the likelihood of a threat successfully exploiting a vulnerability.
- Likelihood determination—Determine the likelihood of an attack by considering the motivation and capability of the threat source along with the nature of the vulnerability in relation to the current controls.
- Impact analysis—Determine the impact of a successful attack on a vulnerability by a threat. Consider the mission of a system, data criticality, and data sensitivity.
- Risk determination—Consider the likelihood, magnitude of impact, and adequacy of controls as an equation of risk.
- Control recommendations—Consider controls to reduce the level of risk to an acceptable level.
- Results documentation—Document to manage the observations on threats and vulnerabilities as well as risks overall and recommended controls.

Evaluating risk requires looking at the different parts of the risk equation. Effective risk management starts with identifying the IT assets and their value. Next, organizations need to identify the threats and vulnerabilities to these assets. An analysis or assessment of both threats and vulnerabilities is a key part of the risk-management process. Next, organizations need to identify the likelihood each threat will exploit a vulnerability. Finally, organizations need to consider the impact of the risk. Risks should then be prioritized. This enables organizations to give attention to the most severe. Different methodologies are available, which provide clear frameworks for evaluating risk.

Part of the risk-assessment process requires an examination of those activities that represent danger. Threats to IT are numerous and can affect the loss of confidentiality, integrity, and availability in a number of ways. Analyzing the potential threats requires the identification of all possible threats first. This is called **threat identification**.

All the threats in **Table 5-3** represent varying degrees of potential risks if they are accompanied by vulnerabilities. Each organization will identify its unique threats. Even businesses with multiple locations will have threats specific to that location. To really understand threats, think about your own personal situation. What threats are common to you and where you live? Do these threats change as you travel? What threats exist based on your lifestyle and goals?

You need to consider likelihood when examining threats. Using the example of a hurricane earlier in this section, it is safe to say that the threat of a hurricane affecting the state of Iowa does not exist. The threat of a tornado, however, does exist. As a result, organizations should develop a threat classification mechanism. A simple example may include a classification of low, medium, and high:

- Low—No previous history of the threat, and the threat is not likely to occur

- Medium—Some history of the threat, and the threat might occur

- High—Substantial history of the threat, and the threat is likely to occur

> **NOTE**
>
> Threats don't pertain to all organizations equally. This is part of what makes threat identification a difficult task. Consider organizations that place their application in the cloud; they would have less risk from potential hurricanes than those that maintain their own data center. Major cloud service providers typically place their data centers in hardened facilities located in regions to reduce hurricane threats. Information about threats such as natural disasters is readily available and easily obtained through private and governmental resources. The threats that are more difficult to identify are those that pertain specifically to the organization. Table 5-3 provides examples of various adversarial threat sources. The table includes a list of threats, motivations, and methods that might be used to carry out an attack. The methods are also known as **threat actions**.

Vulnerability Analysis

After performing a threat analysis, you need to identify weaknesses or flaws. Specifically, you need to identify vulnerabilities that can be exploited by the previously identified threats. This is known as **vulnerability analysis**. There are many ways to identify vulnerabilities, such as the following:

TABLE 5-3 Examples of threats, motivations, and threat actions.

THREAT	MOTIVATION	THREAT ACTION
Cracker	Challenge Ego	Social engineering System intrusion
Criminal	Monetary gain Destruction of information	Computer crime Fraudulent act Information bribery
Terrorist	Destruction Exploitation Revenge	Bomb System penetration System tampering
Espionage	Competitive advantage Economic espionage	Economic exploitation Information theft Social engineering
Insiders	Curiosity Ego Revenge Unintentional errors	System bugs System sabotage Unauthorized access Computer abuse

- Vulnerability lists and databases published by industry organizations
- Security advisories
- Software and security analysis using automated tools

 TIP

The MITRE Corporation catalogs vulnerabilities in the Common Vulnerabilities and Exposures (CVE), which includes tens of thousands of items.

It is important to consider threats relative to vulnerabilities. Think about operating system patches issued by Microsoft or Apple. Typically, these fix potential vulnerabilities, which were previously unknown and have since been discovered. In most cases, these vulnerabilities affect a particular piece of the system. Say, for example, Microsoft issues a patch to fix a vulnerability for a particular service of the operating system. However, what if you don't use this service or the service is turned off? In this case, the vulnerability is not really vulnerable. What if the particular system you use does not and will never be connected to the Internet? In this case, the threat in question does not exist. This is why it is important to pair threats with vulnerabilities. Threats are matched with existing vulnerabilities to further understand the risk. Finally, likelihood and impact must be considered. What is the likelihood that a particular threat can exploit a specific vulnerability? If that occurs, what would be the impact?

Consideration of all these elements involves trade-offs. For example, you can do many things to remove or reduce specific threats and vulnerabilities in your personal life, but you might choose not to. You might even choose not to apply specific controls that can reduce the risks. Many of these decisions are based on your goals and personal trade-offs. As you consider these concepts, think about the following:

- Why do some people live in areas with higher crime rates?
- Why doesn't everyone wear a bulletproof vest?
- Why do you ride in or drive vehicles when there are approximately 40,000 vehicle deaths per year in the United States?
- Why do some people spend more money on home security systems than others?

Risk Assessment Analysis: Defining an Acceptable Security Baseline Definition

Given the previous inputs, the final step is to determine the level of risk. When pairing threats and vulnerabilities, risk is determined primarily by three functions:

- The likelihood of a threat to exploit a given vulnerability
- The impact on the organization if that threat against the vulnerability is achieved
- The sufficiency of controls to either eliminate or reduce the risk

At this point, matrixes and other mechanisms are useful for qualitatively understanding risk. Such matrixes typically categorize the impact and likelihood of threats as low, medium, or high. The product of this results in a risk being low, medium, or high.

An alternative approach is to analyze impact and likelihood *quantitatively*. Such matrixes might use percentage values or a numerical count instead of defining what is high versus medium. Quantitative risk analysis, while more accurate and objective, can also be more time-consuming and expensive.

Applying controls to a system helps eliminate or reduce the risks. In many cases, the goal is not to eliminate the risk. Rather, what's important is to reduce the risk to an acceptable level. Applying controls is a direct result of the risk-assessment process combined with an analysis of the trade-offs. Several examples of the trade-offs include the following:

- Cost—Are the costs of a control justified by the reduction of risk?
- Operational impact—Does the control have an adverse effect on system performance?
- Feasibility—Is the control technically feasible? Will the control be feasible for end users?

> **NOTE**
> The best security is layered. This means the information system is composed of multiple controls operating at different layers. This is similar to a castle and its location high on a hill surrounded by a moat, a series of walls, and then locks and guards.

An effective risk-assessment process helps establish known good baselines for IT systems. A **baseline** is the system in a known good state, with the applied minimum controls relative to the accepted risk. Baselines provide a solid and simple method from which to audit a system. Comparing a system against a baseline can help identify nonexistent controls that should be applied as well as controls that have been removed or disabled. Additionally, a baseline audit can help identify a system that has been compromised or otherwise altered.

An information system may have security controls at different layers in the system. For example, an operating system or network component typically provides an identification and authentication capability. An application may also provide its own identification and authentication capability, rendering an additional level of protection for the overall information system. As organizations select and specify security controls, they should consider components at all layers in the information system to provide effective security architecture and privacy.

In addition to the results of the risk assessment, numerous best-practice baselines exist to help organizations select appropriate security controls. These include the many documented standards from NIST. Several of these are introduced later in this chapter.

Obtaining Information, Documentation, and Resources

The Control Objectives for Information and Related Technology (COBIT) framework provides a good starting point for auditors to assess IT controls. Before beginning an audit, however, the auditor needs to first gather information from people and relevant documentation as well as identify required resources. The information the auditor needs before performing an audit includes the following:

- An understanding of the organization and what its business requirements and goals are
- Knowledge of how the security program is currently in place
- Industry best practices for the type of organization and systems

Documentation related to business structure, configuration, and even previous audits should be gathered and reviewed. In many cases, auditors will need to request further documentation during the course of the audit. At any point, if the auditor is not given adequate documentation, the auditor should notify the responsible personnel.

In addition to understanding the regulatory and industry requirements to which the organization must adhere, auditors should have a much larger understanding of the business. General knowledge about the business can be gained by gathering information on business and reporting cycles, key business processes, and key personnel to interview. Strategic objectives of an organization reveal details about the organization in the future and how this will affect its information systems. In addition, information about the operational objectives for internal control provides relevant information with regard to the current state of the organization.

An organization's written policies are among the most important documents for an auditor. They provide a guideline from which to check the environment for gaps. More specifically, the auditor can determine whether the organization is stating it is doing something that it is not.

Many other types of documentation should be gathered depending upon the scope of the audit across the seven domains of IT infrastructure. Examples include the following:

- Administrative documentation
- System documentation
- Procedural documentation

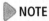
NOTE

Documentation is a good sign that an organization has a sound security program in place. Other documents should include standards, procedures, previous audit reports, risk assessments, and network diagrams.

- Network architecture diagrams
- Vendor support access documents and agreements

Existing IT Security Policy Framework Definition

The results of an audit will reflect how well an organization is adhering to its security policy. However, risk management must be considered. How well an organization adheres to its own policy when combined with an assessment risk helps to identify any gaps.

Security controls are essential to measuring policy compliance. Every control must include one or more security policies. However, security policies will not contain security controls. This is because as technology changes, security controls often change. However, often the related security policy itself will not change. Policies are effective when they are well understood by employees and are clearly enforced. If policies change too frequently, they become confusing and difficult to understand.

By separating security controls from security policy, the business can focus on achieving goals independent of the technology. The result is that the business can focus on employee behavior from a business perspective. The security control can focus on system behavior from a technology perspective. Auditing security policies can ensure requirements are not overly prescriptive and become not achievable.

Frameworks exist to help with risk-management programs, security programs, and policy creation. International Organization for Standardization/International Electrotechnical Commission (ISO/IEC) 27002, for example, provides a structured way for organizations to determine their IT security policy. Accounting and audit firms traditionally had their own interpretations of security standards. They, however, have been increasing the use of existing frameworks for benchmarks. It is important for the auditor to know upon what framework an organization has based its policy. This knowledge allows better alignment between the organization's policy and the audit. Most internal audits, to ensure compliance across the IT infrastructure, will align with the comparable framework.

Many organizations now have taken steps to implement a security policy framework. However, there are still many instances in which the policy is not actually being enforced. Additionally, information security policies are living documents. Business environments change. Technologies change. Risks change. As a result, companies with existing policy frameworks might discover that their policies are outdated. The IT security policy must be managed as an ongoing program to evolve with changing requirements and ensure adherence.

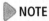
NOTE

An IT audit doesn't just assess adherence to the security policy; it also uncovers situations in which the policy needs to be refined.

Finally, policies are fundamental to the organization's actions. The policies drive the behavior of the people within an organization and even the technologies acquired. One of executive management's responsibilities is to set goals. Management further supports these goals with a set of objectives. These objectives are communicated throughout the organization by policies. This applies not just to IT security policies but also to policies across the organization. The policies set the standards, which help drive the business to achieve its goals. An organization's policies are quite important if they are expected to drive actions and behaviors from the top down. Therefore, high-level policies should be approved and signed by executive management.

> **TIP**
>
> It is a good practice to have executive management approve and sign each high-level policy and provide a statement about the importance of the policy and how it helps support the objectives and goals of the organization.

Configuration Documentation for IT Infrastructure

The auditor will gather documents related to the configuration of the systems being audited. Although a single system component is possibly made up of thousands of configuration elements, the following are examples of items the auditor should gather from documentation:

- Host name
- Internet Protocol (IP) addresses
- Operating system
- Patch level
- Hardware specifications
- Installed software
- Protocols
- Service configuration
- User accounts
- Password settings
- Audit log settings

Applications that reside on the computer systems might also have their own configuration documents. These should be gathered as well. Finally, network documentation is required for the network segments pertaining to the applications and systems being audited.

Many organizations will have standard configuration documents for role-specific systems. Examples include the configurations for the following:

- Firewalls
- Web servers
- Mail servers
- Domain Name System (DNS) servers
- File Transfer Protocol (FTP) servers

Interviews with Key IT Support and Management Personnel: Identifying and Planning

Interviews play an important role in both the information-gathering process and during the audit. Interviews with IT management, for example, can reveal expectations about the organization to the auditor. Interviewing IT support personnel can reveal pertinent information that might not otherwise be discovered. These interviews can also provide greater focus in areas that need it. For example, personnel doing the daily work can help identify weak controls and broken processes.

Properly conducted interviews might even reveal more serious violations, such as fraud. Effective interviews often result in employees offering information about fraud and other serious activities, even when hotlines and other reporting processes exist. These conversations should be an interview, however, and not an interrogation. A friendly and nonthreatening environment fosters openness and honesty with those being questioned. The **Institute of Internal Auditors (IIA)** defines the audit interview as "a specialized form of communication used to gain information and assist in evaluation."

Although interviews play a key role throughout the audit, they help to further define the scope during the planning phase. Individual interviews alone might be reason enough to expand the scope. Interviews looked at collectively can provide the auditor with more information. Taken together, these interviews might reveal patterns. Interviews can aggregate enough data to reveal new information. Reasons to expand the scope from the initial interviews can vary, but common examples include the following:

- Lack of controls
- Override of controls
- Fraudulent activity

Some of the most valuable information for audits will be a result of the interview. Therefore, the interview and how well it is performed can make a difference in the outcome of the audit. A simple framework for conducting effective interviews is composed of the following six steps:

- Preparing
- Scheduling
- Opening
- Conducting
- Closing
- Recording

Preparing for the interview is essential. It is important to be cognizant of others' time and of the job functions they must continue to accomplish even during an ongoing audit. The auditor should prepare a list of questions or at least go into the meeting knowing exactly what it is he or she hopes to achieve or learn. Additionally, an auditor should think like a psychologist. Be aware of the positions and the personalities of those being interviewed. Preparation and scheduling can happen in parallel. It is important, however, to ensure that enough time is given for preparation. When scheduling, the auditor should try to remain as flexible as possible.

The next two steps constitute the actual interview. The opening sets the tone for the remainder of the interview. Opening with a positive tone and clear expectations, combined with thorough preparation, makes conducting the interview much easier. This leads us into the next step, which is asking the questions. At this point, however, it is not enough to have well-thought-out questions. The auditor must be adept at listening as well. The auditor should understand the reporting hierarchy and how management might influence the interviewee's responses. Closing the interview occurs after the auditor has asked all the required questions or when time is up. The interview should ideally end politely and on an upbeat note. The auditor should thank the interviewee for his or her time and suggest an agreed-upon protocol should the auditor require anything else. This leads into the final step of recording. Taking notes is certainly acceptable during the interview process, but it can be disruptive to the interview flow. Even if notes are taken, after the interview, the auditor should immediately review the notes and organize them as needed.

NIST Standards and Methodologies

NIST 800-53 provides a catalog of security controls and a framework to assess the controls. As with the ISO/IEC frameworks, many organizations base their policies on NIST. NIST provides many more standards, including low-level documentation that has proven useful for internal auditing and assessments.

The Computer Security Division (CSD) of NIST provides several popular publications. All of their publications reflect their research on IT security issues. The publications they provide include the following:

- Special Publications—The 800 series publications, sometimes called **Special Publications**, provide general-interest documents for the IT security community. NIST also publishes the 500 series of Special Publications, which covers IT.

- NIST Internal Reports (NISTIR)—The NIST Internal Reports (NISTIR) are publications that describe niche technical research.

- Information Technology Laboratory (ITL) Bulletins—The **Information Technology Laboratory (ITL) Bulletins** are publications that provide an in-depth look at timely topics of importance.

- Federal Information Processing Standards (FIPS)—The **Federal Information Processing Standards (FIPS)** are standards documents published by NIST and approved by the secretary of commerce.

Of these four different document types, the Special Publications from NIST are more likely to be used for audits and assessments. The publications are known for their depth and prescriptive stance. In addition to the two standards listed at the beginning of this section, the following are examples of other NIST Special Publications:

- SP 800-50, "Building an Information Technology Security Awareness and Training Program"

- SP 800-57, "Recommendation for Key Management"
- SP 800-58, "Security Considerations for Voice Over IP Systems"
- SP 800-61, "Computer Security Incident Handling Guide"
- SP 800-68, "Guide to Securing Microsoft Windows XP Systems for IT Professionals"
- SP 800-70, "National Checklist Program for IT Products—Guidelines for Checklist Users and Developers"
- SP 800-95, "Guide to Secure Web Services"
- SP 800-115, "Technical Guide to Information Security Testing and Assessment"
- SP 800-123, "Guide to General Server Security"

The preceding list provides several examples of the many different publications from NIST. SP 800-70 defines the National Checklist Program (NCP). The NCP is a government repository of available security checklists or baseline configurations for operating systems and applications.

Mapping the IT Security Policy Framework Definitions to the Seven Domains of a Typical IT Infrastructure

The IT security policy framework includes policies, standards, and guidelines. Each of these includes technology, processes, and personnel. The seven domains of a typical IT infrastructure need to be mapped into the framework. The seven domains of a typical IT infrastructure are as follows:

- User Domain
- Workstation Domain
- LAN Domain
- LAN-to-WAN Domain

> **technical TIP**
>
> It is helpful to map the infrastructure against the control objectives for the audit. This can provide a clear scope and ensure that every necessary element is addressed against the control objectives. A challenge for auditors is considering the components or pieces of the IT infrastructure that relate to a key issue. Consider the common example of financial reporting. It is not just the application controls that need to be assessed. Even a single financial reporting system may rely on many supporting technologies across the various domains of IT infrastructure. As a result, it is important when developing an audit plan to have a complete picture of all processes and technology across the infrastructure. A security policy framework can help with scope planning by defining boundaries. It also ensures the consideration of all relevant pieces such as interconnected systems to achieve the audit objective. Mapping the security policy framework to the seven domains of IT infrastructure helps define appropriate boundaries for the audit.

- WAN Domain
- Remote Access Domain
- System/Application Domain

In some cases, policies might be very specific to only a single domain. For example, the User Domain maps specifically to human resources security. This encompasses controls relating to items such as pre-employment background checks and information security awareness and training. The seven domains also map across various high-level areas. Examples include access control and operations management.

Standards further help align the seven domains to the security policy. This includes, for example, access control requirements for networks, users, applications, and operating systems. Just as IT infrastructure needs to be organized within a policy framework, the infrastructure needs to be considered within the framework used for an audit.

The **IT universe** includes all the auditable resources or components within an organization. Naturally, the seven domains of typical IT infrastructure are a large part of this IT universe. The IT universe may be defined as one or more domains of IT infrastructure or even a portion of a single domain. In addition, the IT universe may describe specific entities, locations, functions, or processes within the organization.

Identifying and Testing Monitoring Requirements

Perhaps one of the most important and beneficial elements of an IT security program for auditors is monitoring. All frameworks include a control objective for regularly assessing and monitoring IT systems and controls. For example, COBIT places a heavy emphasis on monitoring, as defined by the key areas within the framework. COBIT states that continuous monitoring and evaluation of the control environment helps provide answers to the following questions:

- Is IT performance measured to detect problems before it is too late?
- Does management ensure that internal controls are effective and efficient?
- Can IT performance be linked back to business goals?
- Are adequate confidentiality, integrity, and availability controls in place for information security?

Auditors are trying to answer the same questions. Therefore, auditors should identify the tools already put in place by organizations that they can leverage to help answer these questions. Of course, one of the objectives of most audits, regardless of the IT domain being audited, is to identify and test monitoring requirements. Although organizations might have monitoring solutions in place, it doesn't necessarily mean that they are monitoring the right things.

In addition, many companies might be monitoring the right things but might not have a process in place to make the data actionable. Computer logs provide a perfect example. Are logs being generated? Is the correct information being captured? Is that information being maintained correctly? Are system analysts examining the log data? After analysts examine the data, are any actions taken to deal with identified problems? Depending upon the maturity of the organization, many systems manage these events and information and even provide ways to correlate and make this data more manageable and actionable.

Identifying and testing whether an organization has implemented a sound program for monitoring provides a lot of the information required by an auditor. Consider the following control objectives suggested by COBIT:

- Monitor, evaluate, and assess performance and conformance
- Monitor, evaluate, and assess the system of internal control
- Evaluate and assess compliance with external requirements

The outputs provided from these objectives are a valuable resource to auditors. Except in situations where these controls are nonexistent, auditors can derive usable data regardless of maturity.

Identifying Critical Security Control Points That Must Be Verified Throughout the IT Infrastructure

Adequate controls should be in place to meet high-level defined control objectives. The organizational risk assessment plays an important role in identifying high-risk areas. Areas identified as being the riskiest should be assessed as often as possible. Levels of risk across the IT infrastructure vary across organizations. This is a result of differing objectives and risk appetites. Regardless, most organizations do share common critical controls.

Security controls are the cornerstone of a well-defined security program. The security controls prevent or detect a security breach. Security controls allow businesses to resume operations after a major security incident. However, an organization can apply so many security controls that it becomes a problem for the customers. When a security control cannot distinguish between acceptable behavior and unacceptable behavior to support the customer, then the business is impacted.

IS policy provides business meaning to security controls. This relationship between security controls and security policy ensures that competing priorities stay in balance. This relationship also ensures that the business risks and requirements are considered in building security controls.

Critical Security Controls (CSC) is a term to describe a minimum set of recommended IS controls that should be implemented to safeguard the IT environment and customer data. These recommendations on what constitutes the CSC can have small variations between professional organization and frameworks.

 TIP

The Critical Security Controls for Effective Cyber Defense provide an appendix that maps the top 20 critical security controls to specific controls in NIST SP 800-53.

NIST Special Publication 800-53, unlike the Critical Security Controls, provides a comprehensive library of security controls. The Critical Security Controls, on the other hand, only provide a subset but are focused more on what's believed to be the most important controls. Keep in mind that this is only a generalization. After the critical controls are addressed, further controls can be considered from the NIST document, for example.

Building a Project Plan

Having the appropriate people assigned to perform an audit is critical. This affects the effectiveness and efficiency of the audit. Consider that IT professionals could not possibly be experts across all seven domains of the IT infrastructure. Thus, it is not feasible to expect an auditor to be able to perform an adequate audit across all areas. Depending on the scope of an audit, appropriate resources must be obtained to perform the audit.

Other helpful resources include tools to support the IT auditing process. Various tools are available to assist in developing and managing the project plan and associated elements, such as tasks, deliverables, and timelines. The IIA lists several types of tools that can facilitate an audit:

> **NOTE**
>
> Although resources and budgets can be tight, organizations need to ensure adequate auditing resources. The Public Company Accounting Oversight Board (PCAOB) Auditing Standard No. 2 states that "an ineffective control environment was a significant deficiency and a strong indicator that a material weakness exists."

- Electronic work papers—This provides a document management system to help centralize and provide workflow management of the audit process.
- Project management software—This includes mechanisms for managing any project, including auditing projects. These software packages help track progress to established milestones. Project management software helps define the timeline of the plan and for reporting the status.
- Flowcharting software—This provides a way to visually document processes.
- Open issue tracking software—This allows for easy tracking of audit deficiencies and areas that still need to be addressed. In many cases, this function can be integrated or included with a document management system.
- Audit department website—Internal auditing departments typically have an intranet-based solution that provides for collaboration and communication. Even external auditors benefit from maintaining secure Internet-based portals that provide the same functions.

The previous list of tools is useful for the overall management of the audit. During the course of an audit, however, auditors will likely use additional tools to aid in the efficiency and effectiveness of carrying out the audit. Various programs and utilities can help automate tests during the course of the audit. From a planning perspective, it's important to understand that identification of such tools should be included as part of the planning process.

CHAPTER SUMMARY

Developing an audit plan is a necessary step before conducting the actual audit and reporting findings. Identifying and prioritizing risks is a key component of the audit plan. This provides the necessary information to make informed decisions about the scope and objectives of an audit and what resources will be required. Performing key tasks such as aligning the scope with the objectives and gathering all pertinent information beforehand makes the process of testing controls much easier. The auditor's ability to conduct the audit and report on the results will be a direct reflection on the approved plan.

The chapter examined key audit components and how they work collectively to build toward a successful audit, such as scope, objectives, and frequency of an audit. We discussed frameworks and privacy principles. Additionally, we reviewed the basics of an information security audit.

KEY CONCEPTS AND TERMS

Audit cycle
Audit frequency
Audit objective
Audit scope
Audit universe
Baseline
Chief privacy officer (CPO)
Critical Security Controls (CSC)

Enterprise risk management (ERM)
Federal Information Processing Standards (FIPS)
Information Technology Laboratory (ITL) Bulletins
Institute of Internal Auditors (IIA)

IT universe
Risk
Scope creep
Special Publications
Threat
Threat actions
Threat identification
Vulnerability
Vulnerability analysis

CHAPTER 5 ASSESSMENT

1. Which one of the following can an audit help identify?

A. Fraud
B. Ineffective IT practices
C. Improper use of resources
D. Inadequate security
E. All of the above

2. Which of the following is the discipline of managing and understanding uncertainty?

A. Audit management
B. Metrology
C. Risk management
D. Cryptology

3. Threat is synonymous with risk and can be used interchangeably.

A. True
B. False

4. Which of the following is *not* an example of a technical controls performed by the IT systems?

A. Identification and authorization
B. Computer support and operations
C. Audit trails
D. Cryptography

5. Which of the following is the best example of a potential vulnerability to an IT system?

A. Hacker
B. Terrorist
C. Unpatched operating system
D. None of the above

6. The results of a risk assessment help define the audit objectives.

A. True
B. False

7. When applying controls, which of the following is *not* an example of what needs to be considered when examining the trade-offs?

A. Feasibility
B. Cost
C. Operational impact
D. Due diligence

8. Which of the following is *not* an example of operational controls?

A. Personnel and user issues
B. Incident response and handling
C. Logical access
D. Physical and environmental security

9. Which of the following defines the goals for an audit?

A. Audit objective
B. Audit scope
C. Audit frequency
D. Audit report

10. Which of the following is *not* a category of IT security controls defined by NIST?

A. Physical controls
B. Management controls
C. Operational controls
D. Technical controls

11. Which of the following documents should be included in the gathering process of an IT audit?

A. Policies and procedures
B. Previous audit reports
C. Network diagrams
D. Answers A and C only
E. Answers A, B, and C

12. Only security operations personnel need to follow IT security policies.

A. True
B. False

13. Fraudulent activity uncovered during interviews would be a reason to expand the scope of an audit.

A. True
B. False

14. Which of the following describes all the auditable components within an organization?

A. Cosmos domains of IT
B. Domains of applications
C. IT universe
D. Universal audit

15. Which one of the following is *not* an example of an audit facilitating tool defined by the IIA?

A. Project management software
B. Flowcharting software
C. Electronic work papers
D. Presentation software

16. What is an important characteristic of a project such as an audit?

A. The project is continuous and ongoing.
B. The project is standard and produces standard results.
C. The project will occur in separate steps, getting progressively elaborate.

17. Of the following four different document types, which is *most* likely to be used for audits and assessments because of their depth and prescriptive stance?

A. Special Publications
B. NIST Internal Reports (NISTIR)
C. Information Technology Laboratory (ITL) Bulletins
D. Federal Information Processing Standards (FIPS)

18. Which type of tool includes mechanisms for managing any project, including auditing projects, by helping track progress to established milestones?

A. Electronic work papers
B. Project management software
C. Flowcharting software
D. Open issue tracking software

Conducting an IT Infrastructure Audit for Compliance

AFTER THE AUDIT TEAM completes an auditing plan and that plan is approved, the audit team can scope audits to assess the information technology (IT) infrastructure for compliance. Testing for compliance is centered on the presence of adequate controls or countermeasures in the planned scope of the IT infrastructure. This includes verifying that policies are put in place and appropriately followed.

Audits are not just about testing controls. Effective governance, management oversight, and adherence to policies drive a risk culture that mitigates risk exposure. IT policies are more than simple business requirements that translate into technology controls. Policies, and how they are enforced, reflect the business perception of risk. Policies can reduce business risks by setting the "tone at the top" and promoting a risk-aware culture. Tone at the top refers to senior management's stated commitment. In this case, it is senior management's stated commitment to supporting the policies. It's more than just words. It's the actions senior management takes to implement and enforce these policies. This tone by management and the resulting risk-aware culture can build trust with the customer and the auditors.

The actual execution of an audit can vary widely based on the scope and objectives of the plan. Several methods, frameworks, and automated tools are available to assist in the process. The choices made will depend on the areas being assessed and the depth and breadth at which controls need to be examined.

Chapter 6 Topics

This chapter covers the following topics and concepts:

- What minimum acceptable level of risk and appropriate security baselines are
- How to identify documented policies, standards, procedures, and guidelines
- How to perform a security assessment for the entire IT infrastructure and individual domains
- How to incorporate the security assessment into the overall audit validating compliance process
- How to use audit tools to organize data capture
- Which automated audit reporting tools and methodologies are available
- How to review baselines
- How to verify and validate proper configuration and implementation of security controls and countermeasures
- What problems may arise when conducting an IT infrastructure audit

Chapter 6 Goals

When you complete this chapter, you will be able to:

- Understand how to conduct an audit of IT infrastructure
- Recognize strategies to manage risk and provide baseline configurations to control risk
- Understand why conducting a gap analysis is important
- Recognize when it is necessary to conduct an audit using a layered approach
- Evaluate different methods and techniques for performing an IT security assessment
- Understand how a security assessment fits into the audit process
- Identify different types of tools used in an audit
- Recognize the value of monitoring and configuration management to the audit process
- Articulate a methodology for testing security controls
- Identify common issues that might hamper the audit efforts
- Understand safeguards necessary for security operations and administration roles

Identifying the Minimum Acceptable Level of Risk and Appropriate Security Baseline Definitions

For an organization to develop security baselines, it must select proper controls. However, the decision to apply or not apply controls is based on risk. Specifically, the controls put in place manage the identified risks. As a result, a risk assessment needs to be completed first.

It might seem easiest to apply a wide range of controls based on different recommendations. Remember, however, that there are costs associated with these controls. For example, you can take many different steps to secure your home and minimize risks. Most people consider door locks as necessary. Beyond that, there is no universal rule of home security to which everyone adheres. Even door locks are available in varying strengths. Consider other measures a homeowner might take. Examples include bars on the windows, storm shutters, insurance, burglar alarms, smoke detectors, carbon monoxide detectors, cameras, safes, watchdogs, outdoor lighting, fences, and even weapons. These examples of home controls are similar to IT controls in that there is a cost

---

Risk Management Approach

Most frameworks (such as Control Objectives for Information and Related Technology [COBIT], National Institute of Standards and Technology [NIST], and International Organization for Standardization [ISO]) require controls that identify and manage risk. While these frameworks all have unique approaches, they do have the following common characteristics:

- Risk-based management
- Align the businesses risk appetite
- Reduce operation disruption and losses

A framework that risk-based management determines to deploy is based on the highest risk to the organization's objectives. This includes considering business objectives, legal obligations, and the organization's values.

Align the business' risk appetite refers to understanding the tolerance for taking risks by the business. Inherent in this approach is understanding the business, its processes, and goals. Then the overall capital needs to mitigate identified risks is determined. The risk appetite is represented by the amount of risk the business is not willing to fund. In other words, it how much risk and potential problems the business is willing to accept.

Reducing operation disruption & losses are the core goals of these frameworks over the long term. The frameworks will reduce surprises and ensure risks are systematically identified and reduced, eliminated, or accepted.

Each of the frameworks establishes a path from requirements to control. In other words, once a risk is identified, specific controls can be applied to mitigate or reduce the threat. The ability to operationalize a framework is critical to its success.

associated with each of them. Depending on the type or mission of the business, the cost justifications vary. The controls are based on the level of risk the organization faces.

Security controls follow three unique design types:

- Preventive
- Detective
- Corrective

Preventive Security Control

A **preventive control**, also sometimes called "preventative control," stops incidents or breaches immediately. As the name implies, it's designed to prevent an incident from occurring. A firewall ideally would stop a hacker from getting inside the organization's network. This kind of control is an automated control.

Automated control has logic in software to decide what action to take. With an automated control, no human decisions are needed to prevent an incident from occurring. The human decisions occurred when the security control was designed.

Detective Security Control

A **detective control** does not prevent incidents or breaches immediately. Just as a burglar alarm might call the police, a security control alerts an organization that an incident might have occurred. When you review a credit card statement, your review is a detective control. You review the statement for unauthorized charges. The process of reviewing the statement did not prevent the unauthorized charge from occurring. The review, however, triggers corrective action if needed.

A detective control is considered a manual control. A manual control relies on a human to decide what action to take. Still, manual controls can have automated components. For example, a system administrator could automatically receive a cell phone text when the number of invalid login attempts reaches some threshold on a server. The administrator still needs to take some manual action.

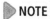 **NOTE**

The distinction between automated and manual controls is if a human decision is required to take action. If so, the control is considered manual. Conversely, if no human decision is required to take action, the control is considered automated.

Corrective Security Control

A **corrective control** does not prevent incidents or breaches immediately. A corrective security control limits the impact on the business by correcting the vulnerability. How quickly the business can restore its operations determines the effectiveness of the control.

For example, backing up files to be able to restore data after a system crash is a corrective security control. A corrective control is either automated or manual. For instance, you may automatically mirror (create exact copies of) files and then restore them in the event of hard drive failure. This is an automated control. If a human is required to decide when to restore the backup, that is a manual control.

Remember that IT is not completely independent. IT exists to support the business. Understanding the minimum level of acceptable risk and implementing baseline controls depend on IT being aligned with the objectives of the business.

Organization-Wide

Establishing a baseline based on a control framework needs to be relative to the **risk appetite** of the organization. The

> **⚠ WARNING**
> Effectively managing risks is a complex task. Be careful not to focus only on risk management and lose sight of the organizational goals.

Committee of Sponsoring Organizations (COSO) defines risk appetite as "the degree of risk, on a broad based level, that an organization is willing to accept in pursuit of value." Management considers the organization's risk appetite first in evaluating strategic alternatives, then in setting objectives aligned with the selected strategy, and in developing mechanisms to manage the related risks. Risk appetite is a broad-based look at the amount of risk an organization is willing to take to achieve its objectives. This should not be confused with **risk tolerance**. Risk tolerance is about the ranges of acceptance for specific risks. Identifying levels of risk tolerance allows the organization to stay within its defined appetite for risk.

IT supports the enterprise risk management (ERM) strategy in a few ways:

- ERM depends on accurate and timely information. Information systems process and store this information. Maintaining the integrity and availability of the data is needed. As a result, adequate controls need to be placed on systems.

- The IT environment supports not only the ERM function but also all other operations of the business. As a result, the IT environment and associated controls need to be aligned with the organization.

In addition to looking at individual controls, an auditor will ensure the IT environment is aligned with the organization's risk appetite. Additionally, the auditor will assess the organizational alignment among the various risk functions, which is sometimes referred to as the **three lines of defense**.

The first line of defense is the business unit (BU). The business deals with controlling risk on day-to-day business. It identifies risk within the business, assesses the impact, and mitigates the risk whenever possible. The business is expected to follow policies and implement the ERM program. The business will develop both short- and long-term strategies for reducing its risk within the BU. The BU would own the risk. Meaning, they are directly accountable to ensure the risk is mitigated or reduced.

The second line of defense is the ERM program. This team is responsible for managing risk at an enterprise level. The team provides guidance and advice to the first line. They align policies and ensure the risk management program aligns with company goals. The team has oversight and management roles of risk committees and risk initiatives.

The second line is responsible for engaging the business to develop a risk strategy and gauging the risk appetite of the organization. They have an obligation to report to the board material noncompliance and excessive risks that put the organization's goal at jeopardy.

The third line of defense is the independent auditor. The auditor's role is to provide the board and executive management independent assurance that the controls and risk function is designed and working well. Additionally, auditors serve as advisors to the first and second lines of defense in risk matters. The third line must keep its independence but does have an important role to provide input on risk strategies and directions.

There are several views on how closely involved the third line of defense can be in advising leadership without losing its independence. Their concern is if the third line of defense advises on a course of action, can they now audit and develop a truly independent opinion on its success? Many audit organizations develop rules of engagement to avoid conflict. There are also several views on whether their external auditors are the fourth line of defense or part of the third line.

This model demonstrates how organizational roles can be used to create a separation of duties within the risk functions. In the ideal world, the first line of defense would self-assess and identify all the risks. It's not realistic to expect such precision. What is not caught in the first line, the second line should catch. What the first and second lines do not catch, the third line should catch. At this point, while risks still exist in the environment, these risks should not be significant and should be manageable. Consequently, a regulator determination that an organization is not in compliance with regulation would also lead to questions about the effectiveness of the organization's three lines of defense.

Seven Domains of a Typical IT Infrastructure

After considering the organization's risk appetite and tolerance, further consideration of the following is needed:

- The value and importance of data
- Risks to the IT infrastructure
- The level of expected quality of service

The seven domains of a typical IT infrastructure are composed of people, processes, and technology. This includes employees, partners, and customers interacting with data and using software and applications across a hardware infrastructure. Looking across the seven domains of a typical IT infrastructure can reveal immediate vulnerabilities. For example, domains consisting of remote access, wide-area networks (WANs), and cloud computing environments all reveal potential rogue Internet connectivity. Gathering the appropriate documents can provide an immediate view into the domains and inventory of the IT infrastructure.

Mitigating risk within the IT infrastructure includes the application of controls. Again, the risks that organizations want to minimize are based on the value of the assets coupled with how a vulnerability being exploited by a threat would affect the confidentiality, integrity, and availability of the data

> **NOTE**
> Most businesses today rely on the Internet as a facilitator for accomplishing their goals. The Internet is a prime example of an IT component that has a clear benefit for the organization but also introduces risk. As a result, basic security controls are applied to protect the organization from numerous threats.

and associated systems. Reducing the risk depends on what controls are available, how much they cost, and if they are cost efficient. As a result of this analysis, organizations typically take a risk-based approach. A more detailed look at these strategies includes the following:

- **Accept the risk**—Do nothing and manage the consequences if the risk is realized.
- **Avoid the risk**—Seek alternatives or don't participate in the risky activity.
- **Share the risk**—Transfer or divide the risk with other parties.
- **Control the risk**—Apply mechanisms or countermeasures to minimize the effects of the risk.

Figure 6-1 provides a simple illustration of components of risk and how the preceding strategies might be applied. The approach an organization takes needs to consider the risk appetite of the organization. The risk might be so great, for example, that avoidance might be the best solution.

Business Liability Insurance

Business liability insurance is a way of sharing the risk as it lowers the financial loss to the business in the event of an incident. Even when a business has well-defined security policies, problems can still occur. Business liability insurance will pay the business for losses within the limits of the policy.

Business liability insurance can be issued to both organizations and individuals. For example, a computer engineer performing consulting services could obtain professional liability insurance. Such a policy would cover any successful claims that they were negligent or made errors during the performance of their professional services. The same type of coverage would apply to large companies facing claims that their product or services were negligent or in error.

An important benefit of this insurance coverage is the payment of legal fees. Even when found innocent, the legal costs can be substantial. These policies do have set limits,

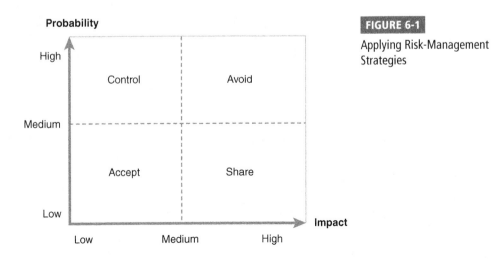

FIGURE 6-1

Applying Risk-Management Strategies

conditions, and requirements that the policyholder must meet. These policies also have exclusions such as illegal acts that void the policy. Overall these insurance policies are another good tool to further reduce the risk beyond the effort taken by the company to manage business risk.

Controlling Risk

Compensating controls are alternative measures put in place to mitigate a risk in lieu of implementing a control requirement or best practice. Suppose you don't want to spend the money on anti-virus software and choose to accept the risks. You might take a compensating measure, such as not opening file attachments or only visiting reputable websites. Often, layering compensating controls is necessary. In addition to changing your habits, you might also back up your data regularly.

Armed with an understanding of risks within the IT infrastructure, the risk-mitigation strategies will be factored into the appropriate security baseline. An audit of the **baseline controls** will determine the following:

- Are the controls effective at reducing the targeted risk?
- Do the controls incorporate a mix of preventive, detective, and corrective controls?
- How are the controls monitored and audited in case of failure or breach?

The term *baseline control* comes from the configuration management function. Configuration management describes activities that lead and standardize configurations. A configuration represents controls applied to any IT infrastructure device or software. According to the Institute of Electrical and Electronics Engineers (IEEE), a baseline, also called a reference configuration, is: "A specification or product that has been formally reviewed and agreed to by responsible management, that thereafter serves as the basis for further development, and can be changed only through formal change control procedures."

For example, a firewall baseline may determine which ports should or should not be open depending on the business need. Baselines are product-specific. For example, a baseline for Microsoft SQL database versus Oracle database may both disable the default account but will achieve that requirement using different product settings.

Baselines are important because they simplify the audit process. An auditor would first verify the baseline is compliant with policy and industry norms. Once the baseline is verified, the auditor would then verify the baseline has been applied consistently across the IT infrastructure. For example, let's assume an organization hosts 200 database servers of the same type. Potentially an auditor needs only to check the baseline configuration to meet policy requirements once. Then test if the same configuration was applied to the 200 servers. Any unauthorized deviation from the baseline would be considered noncompliance.

Gap Analysis for the Seven Domains

A gap analysis is an examination of the current state of controls against the desired state of controls, as illustrated in **Figure 6-2**. The difference between the two indicates the

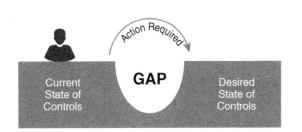

FIGURE 6-2

Control Gap Analysis

required action. The ongoing risk-assessment process determines the desired state. Thus, once a gap is closed, it does not necessarily stay that way. The results of a gap analysis determine the absence of baseline controls. Moreover, a gap analysis is ideally used once a baseline is established. It further defines the need for additional controls or enhancements to existing controls.

Analyzing gaps requires attention to the type of system and its value or criticality. Depending on the criticality of the system, different baselines may apply. The National Institute of Standards and Technology (NIST) provides baseline control recommendations across three different types of information systems: low impact, moderate impact, and high impact. NIST provides different baseline controls for different classifications. For example, users accessing low-impact systems might be required to identify themselves with a unique user name and authenticate with a password. This would meet a baseline requirement of an information system uniquely identifying and authenticating users.

Gap Analysis of Service Providers

Many organizations use and continue to expand their use of external service providers for operational, IT, and even IT security functions. The concept of a gap analysis can also be applied to these service providers. First, organizations should assess the security controls of any third party to which they outsource any of their IT or business functions. This might involve verifying the service provider has completed an SOC 1 audit. Organizations should also review the specific controls in place at the service provider. It is not unusual to find that a service provider's controls aren't up to the standards of its client organization.

As a result, organizations can take several approaches. For example, they might decide that the use of the service isn't worth the risk. They might look for another provider that can support the required security controls. Other possibilities include negotiating with the service provider or examining contractual obligations of the service provider. Finally, an organization might employ further compensating controls within the organization if it continues to use the services and if the service provider cannot support the additional controls.

> **FYI**
>
> Multifactor authentication is analogous to using an automatic teller machine. Withdrawing money requires a personal identification number (PIN) and a physical card. Neither component by itself is sufficient. Information systems typically rely on a combination of two or more components for authentication. Typically, this includes something held, such as a card or a token that provides one-time passwords, along with something known, such as a password or PIN. Something inherent might also be included in the authentication process, including biometric features such as a fingerprint.

> **TIP**
>
> Reviewing third-party contracts will indicate the level of controls they are obligated to implement. It's common practice in many organizations to provide third-party service providers a version of the internal security policies. In this case, contract language typically reads that the third-party's internal control will meet or exceed those controls of the organization.

Consider an example from NIST 800-53 for monitoring physical access in an information system environment. The control states that the organization should do the following:

- Monitor physical access to the facility where the information system resides to detect and respond to physical security incidents.
- Review physical access logs.
- Coordinate results of reviews and investigations with the organization's incident response capability.

The previous points represent the baseline control for all systems regardless of the impact level. NIST further provides two more control enhancements for monitoring physical access. These are as follows:

- The organization monitors physical intrusion alarms and surveillance equipment.
- The organization employs automated mechanisms to recognize potential intrusions and initiate designated response actions.

Systems designated as moderate impact would require not only the original baseline control but also the first control from the previous two items. The high-impact system baseline control would require the original baseline control and both controls from the previous list. If an organization had broadly implemented the original baseline controls but not the others, a gap analysis would reveal whether the control enhancements were necessary. As a result, the organization would clearly understand where it currently stands with regard to monitoring physical access. It would also understand where it needs to be and have clear guidance on what it needs to do to fill the gap.

Identifying All Documented IT Security Policies, Standards, Procedures, and Guidelines

The organizational security policy framework is the foundation for the management of information security. This foundation provides internal direction and support as well as providing direction for assessments and audits. The quality of the entire information security program depends on the policies in place. Fortunately, policies can be one of the least expensive controls. Unfortunately, they are often the most difficult to implement effectively. In fact, the first control objective within the International Organization for Standardization/International Electrotechnical Commission (ISO/IEC) 27002 standard states that management should set a clear policy direction by implementing and reviewing the security policy document. The policies provide reference documents for auditors and provide the statement of management intent throughout the organization. As a result, the policy framework, which also includes standards, procedures, and guidelines, will help guide the organization and audits.

Although frameworks such as ISO/IEC 27002 provide guidance for policy development, the scope and maturity of policies vary widely across organizations. It is not uncommon to find companies that lack any type of policy framework at all. Only slightly better are organizations that have a basic or boilerplate policy in place. In these situations, audit and compliance groups are valuable resources to help review the proposed policies, making sure they are realistic, in line with business objectives, and enforceable.

During the audit preparation, the governing policy document should have already been reviewed. During the course of the audit, however, this policy will help identify the standards, procedures, and guidelines needed to effectively understand and assess the IT environment. Although explicit audits against the documented policies and supporting documents are common, the existence and extent of such documentation should always be considered regardless of the type of audit. In other words, the auditor should always identify and evaluate policies, standards, and procedures. Even though ISO/IEC 27002 has a control objective dedicated to security policies, it references individual policies, standards, and procedures throughout all the other controls as well.

The IT infrastructure audit requires the auditor to rely heavily on the documented policy framework. This helps identify the gaps for improvements to the policy as well as fulfill the responsibilities to evaluate adequate controls. Ultimately, the goal is to gain assurance around the strategic view and use of IT controls. Realizing this goal is built on the security policy framework.

Conducting the Audit in a Layered Fashion

The auditor should conduct the audit according to the scope of the plan. This includes auditing the systems included in the plan within the specified time frame. Categorizing the audit into recognizable chunks by domains helps keep the audit focused with minimal reference to other systems. Although the scope may be defined to a specific domain, the auditor needs to recognize the various system inputs, processes, and outputs. This ensures that other domains are covered as needed.

A layered audit approach across the domains of the IT infrastructure will be necessary when systems span the domains. This is especially evident in audits of a particular process. An external audit over financial reporting controls is a perfect example. A company's financial system can span multiple domains and even include third-party providers such as payroll service providers. This means the auditor has to verify the controls considering the process and the infrastructure that the process uses.

Two types of testing are available to an auditor: specifically, a test of design and test of operating effectiveness.

The testing of design is used to determine whether the controls operated as designed would achieve the risk reduction goal. At this point, the audit does not determine if the control is deployed. The question is, "If the control was deployed, would it reduce the risk appropriately and achieve the control objective?" The auditor can test design through interviews, observation of the company's operations, and inspection of relevant documentation. Walkthroughs that include these procedures ordinarily are sufficient to evaluate design effectiveness.

The testing of operating effectiveness is used to determine whether the control is operating as designed and whether the person performing the control possesses the necessary authority and competence to perform the control effectively. This test ensures the control is fully deployed and is achieving the control objectives.

These should be viewed as two separate audit tests. First the auditor tests the design and then tests for operational effectiveness. In the case where a control fails design, then the auditor should not test for operating effectiveness. In other words, if the design of the control is flawed, then regardless of if it's deployed or not, the control will not achieve its goal and reduce risk.

Performing a Security Assessment for the Entire IT Infrastructure and Individual Domains

Various tools are used to perform a security assessment. The assessment may target the entire IT infrastructure, a single domain of the IT infrastructure, or anything in between. All assessments should follow a plan and be performed with a disciplined approach. There are different approaches to identify security weaknesses within an organization. Some of the approaches include the following:

- **Network scan**—This provides an automated method for discovering host systems on a network. Although a **network scan** doesn't necessarily discover all vulnerabilities, it does determine which systems are active on the network and what services they offer or what ports are available. A network scan provides valuable information pertaining to the environment. A network scan can also provide an adversary with a footprint from which he or she can later conduct a more targeted attack. For this reason, network scans are an important part of defining the assessment process and understanding what an attacker might discover and target.

- **Vulnerability scan**—This provides the fundamental process for managing vulnerabilities. A **vulnerability scan** is an automated method for testing a system's services and applications for known security holes. Most vulnerability scans also provide reports on the identified holes along with additional information for improving security. Unlike a network scan, which looks more broadly for available systems, a vulnerability scan is targeted to specific systems. Vulnerability scans can be conducted across the entire infrastructure or specific components within the individual domains, such as the following:

- Operating systems
- Web servers
- Mail servers
- Databases
- File Transfer Protocol (FTP) servers
- Firewalls
- Load-balancing servers
- Switches and hubs
- Wireless access points

- **Penetration test**—A **penetration test** is most often associated with a security assessment. A penetration test, also known as a pen test, is an active, hands-on assessment that uses methods similar to what a real-world attacker might use. A penetration test goes beyond simply looking for vulnerabilities. When vulnerabilities are identified, a penetration test attempts to actually exploit the vulnerability. The test helps determine how practical or viable specific attacks might be. This includes understanding what the impact might be of a successful attack.

The technical skill set required to conduct a security assessment depends on the scope of the assessment and the types of tools or techniques used. Knowledge of basic security principles and technical fundamentals, such as understanding **Transmission Control Protocol/Internet Protocol (TCP/IP)**, is helpful. TCP/IP is the basic protocol, or language, of modern networks and the Internet.

All three of the preceding methods may be used independently or may be used together as part of the overall plan. It is common, for example, for a network scan to precede a penetration test. Both network scans and vulnerability scans are more easily automated on a regular basis than a penetration test. Penetration tests require more planning and coordination.

There are several popular frameworks for conducting comprehensive security assessments. Three examples are as follows:

> ⚠️ **WARNING**
> Network and vulnerability scans and penetration testing can impact performance on the network. Consequently, rather than performing these assessments, the auditors will review the result of the IT team performance. This approach promotes proactive assessment by the first line and reduces the likelihood that the audit will negatively impact the business systems.

- **Open Source Security Testing Methodology Manual (OSSTMM)**—A method that takes a scientific approach to security testing, the **Open Source Security Testing Methodology Manual (OSSTMM)** is made up of five sections called channels, and each channel includes various modules.
- **Information Systems Security Assessment Framework (ISSAF)**—A method for evaluating networks, systems, and applications, the **Information Systems Security**

Assessment Framework (ISSAF) is divided into a three-phase approach, which includes a nine-step assessment process.

- **NIST 800-115**—A guide to the basic technical testing and examination functions of conducting an information security assessment, **NIST 800-115** is composed of seven major sections and several appendixes.

Regardless of the method chosen, each uses similar techniques for conducting a security assessment. The remainder of this section uses the NIST methodology as a guide. NIST breaks the assessment down across three different types of primary techniques:

- Review techniques
- Target identification and analysis techniques
- Target vulnerability validation techniques

Review techniques involve examining the components across the domains of IT infrastructure. Reviewing is a passive process, using noninvasive techniques, and has minimal impact on the systems. **Table 6-1** provides examples of specific review techniques.

TABLE 6-1   Summary of major capabilities of review techniques.

TECHNIQUE	CAPABILITIES	SKILL SET
Document review	Examines policies and procedures for accuracy and completeness	General knowledge of information security and information policies
Log review	Provides data on system use, changes, and configuration Might reveal potential problems and deviations from policies and standards	Knowledge of log events and ability to interpret log data Ability to use automated logging and log correlation tools
Ruleset review	Exposes holes in security controls based on rulesets	Knowledge of ruleset formats Ability to correlate and analyze rulesets from different devices and different vendors
Network sniffing	Monitors network traffic to capture information such as active systems, operating systems, communication protocols, and services Exposes unencrypted communications	Knowledge of TCP/IP and networking Ability to interpret and analyze network traffic Ability to deploy and use network-sniffing tools
File integrity checking	Identifies changes to important files and can identify unwanted files that might be malicious	General file system knowledge Ability to use file integrity checking tools and interpret the results

along with the capabilities of the technique and the specific skill set required to use the technique.

After performing a document review, the next step involves the use of target identification and analysis techniques. The goal is to identify active devices along with their available ports and services and look for possible vulnerabilities. The information collected sets the stage for the next step of trying to exploit and validate the vulnerabilities. **Table 6-2** provides examples of the techniques involved, along with the capabilities of the technique and the specific skill set required to use the technique.

Finally, with the information from the previous phase, potential vulnerabilities are probed further. The techniques shown in **Table 6-3** are used to exploit the vulnerability.

An organization may use all the preceding techniques as part of an overall security assessment or selected parts. Additionally, the techniques can be used across the IT infrastructure, or they may focus on only specific domains. This depends on the objectives

TABLE 6-2 Summary of major capabilities of target identification and analysis techniques.

TECHNIQUE	CAPABILITIES	SKILL SET
Network discovery	Discovers active devices on the network Identifies communication paths and facilitates determination of network architectures	General TCP/IP and networking knowledge Ability to use both passive and active network discovery tools
Network port and service identification	Discovers active devices on the network Discovers open ports and associated service/applications	General TCP/IP and networking knowledge Knowledge of ports and protocols Ability to use port-scanning tools Ability to interpret results from tools
Vulnerability scanning	Identifies hosts and open ports Identifies known vulnerabilities Provides advice on mitigating discovered vulnerabilities	General TCP/IP and networking knowledge Knowledge of ports, protocols, services, and vulnerabilities Ability to use automated vulnerability-scanning tools and interpret the results
Wireless scanning	Identifies unauthorized wireless devices on the network Discovers wireless signals outside an organization Detects potential backdoors and other security violations	General knowledge of computing and wireless transmissions, protocols, services, and architecture Ability to use automated wireless scanning and sniffing tools

TABLE 6-3	Summary of major capabilities of target vulnerability validation techniques.	
TECHNIQUE	**CAPABILITIES**	**SKILL SET**
Password cracking	Identifies weak passwords and password settings	Knowledge of secure password composition and how operating systems maintain passwords Ability to use automated cracking tools
Penetration testing	Tests security using the same methods and tools that attackers use Verifies vulnerabilities Demonstrates how vulnerabilities can be exploited iteratively to gain access to internal systems	Extensive knowledge of TCP/IP, networking, and operating systems knowledge Advanced knowledge of network and system vulnerabilities and exploits Knowledge of techniques to evade security detection
Social engineering	Allows testing user awareness and if proper procedures are followed	Ability to influence and persuade people Ability to remain calm under pressure

of the assessment, which must consider available time and resources.

Incorporating the Security Assessment into the Overall Audit Validating Compliance Process

The section "Performing a Security Assessment for the Entire IT Infrastructure and Individual Domains" listed some security assessment techniques. These techniques help determine the feasibility of a successful attack against organizational resources. A security assessment is a component of a full IT security audit. Despite the technically focused nature of security assessment methods such as penetration testing and vulnerability assessments, they are not substitutes for an internal audit of IT security. An audit should also include a risk assessment and pay particular attention to internal controls.

The overall process of validating compliance should take a more holistic view. A penetration test, for example, might reveal only a limited number of vulnerabilities that are actually exploited, thus ignoring other vulnerabilities. As a result, these tools and methods should complement the overall audit process.

ISACA produces a series of auditing standards, guidelines, and procedures for information systems auditors. ISACA guidance includes an approach to assess the existing system and infrastructure environment through analysis of the audits performed across the COBIT framework. Several types of information are often collected:

- Security requirements and objectives
- System or network architecture and infrastructure, such as a network diagram showing how assets are configured and interconnected
- Information available to the public or accessible from the organization's website
- Physical assets, such as hardware, including those in the data center, network, and communication components and peripherals (e.g., desktop, laptop, PDAs)
- Operating systems, such as PC and server operating systems, and network management systems
- Data repositories, such as database management systems and files
- A listing of all applications
- Network details, such as supported protocols and network services offered
- Security systems in use, such as access control mechanisms, change control, antivirus, spam control, and network monitoring
- Security components deployed, such as firewalls and intrusion detection systems
- Processes, such as a business process, computer operation process, network operation process, and application operation process
- Identification and authentication mechanisms
- Government laws and regulations pertaining to minimum security control requirements
- Documented or informal policies, procedures, and guidelines

A holistic view of the IT infrastructure cannot be produced through a single audit. Rather it's an accumulation of audits over time. The ISACA guidance provides a framework for organizing the collected audit material into a single comprehensive opinion of the overall health of the IT infrastructure.

In many situations, an information systems auditor might not have the skills necessary to perform a security assessment. Additionally, there might be other limitations or constraints that prevent the auditor from performing such a technical analysis. In such situations, the auditor might consider using the work of other experts. The expert can be internal or external to the organization as long as independence and objectivity are preserved. Examples of experts provided by ISACA include the following:

- An information system auditor from an external accounting firm
- A management consultant
- An IT expert or expert in the area of audit who has been appointed by top management or by the information systems audit team

The auditor should determine that the expert's work is relevant to the audit objectives. The auditor should also obtain a letter indicating that he or she has the right to access the results from the work of others. Before incorporating the results of an assessment into the audit, the auditor should review all supporting documents and reports. This includes determining that the assessment supports the audit objectives. If necessary, the auditor should conduct additional testing for supporting audit evidence if it is not covered in the assessment.

Using Audit Tools to Organize Data Capture

> **NOTE**
>
> Publications and documents sometimes use the acronym CAAT instead of CAATT. In general, the term can describe both tools and techniques. In addition, it is not uncommon to see the acronym use the term *aided* rather than *assisted*. Best to think about CAATT as a class of tools build specifically to aid auditors.

Auditors can increase their productivity through the use of **computer-assisted audit tools and techniques (CAATT)**. These tools and techniques are simply computer applications that auditors use to assist them in their job functions. With these tools, auditors can perform tests that otherwise might be difficult or even impossible to do manually. This includes analyzing large amounts of data or increasing the coverage of the audit.

Although there are many specialized audit-specific tools available, even an office spreadsheet application is considered a CAATT. The tools and techniques include general audit software, audit expert systems, utility software, and even simple queries and scripts. CAATTs are used for many different functions, including the following:

- Testing transactions in applications
- Reviewing procedures
- Testing system and application controls for compliance
- Conducting automated vulnerability assessments
- Performing penetration testing

During the course of an audit, one of the objectives of the auditor is to produce evidence. Much of the process will still be manual. The use of CAATTs, however, allows for the production of much more evidence than what would be possible manually. Before using an automated or computer-based tool, the auditor should first be familiar with the tool and have the necessary knowledge and skills required to use it. The auditor should also take necessary steps to be successful and to limit the risk of using such tools during the process. Examples include the following:

- Establish any related resource requirements. This includes making sure the needed IT facilities, equipment, data, and personnel are available and accessible.
- Understand the type of data to be examined. This includes how much data, what type of data, and the format of the data.

CHAPTER 6 | Conducting an IT Infrastructure Audit for Compliance · **147**

6

Conducting an IT
Infrastructure Audit
for Compliance

Using Automated Audit Reporting Tools and Methodologies

Many organizations use automated audit reporting tools. Most systems, for example, are capable of producing many different types of audit logs. These logs detail various types of activity throughout the system, including security data. Examples include the following:

- Failed authentication attempts
- Technical policy changes
- Account changes
- Privileged use

Traditionally, the challenge is managing the voluminous amount of data generated by these systems. This problem is further compounded considering the number and different types of systems across an organization. The components within the seven domains of typical IT infrastructure, for example, are all capable of producing audit trails or log data. Making matters more difficult is the fact that an event generated in one domain may likely contribute to other events being generated in the other domains. Yet by maintaining a silo approach to storing and managing this data, correlation of events is not easy and might be impossible.

Fortunately, automated solutions are available and in use by many organizations. These solutions aggregate all of this data centrally and provide mechanisms to correlate, alert, and report upon this data. These solutions can provide meaningful data from otherwise huge amounts of raw log data. From an organizational perspective, automated audit reporting tools or information and event management help simplify compliance, improve security, and optimize IT operations. Specific examples include the following:

- Meeting compliance regulations requiring the retention and review of audit records
- Identifying security incidents, such as policy violations and fraudulent activity
- Diagnosing and preventing operational problems
- Conducting forensic analysis
- Establishing operational, security, and performance baselines and being able to identify new trends and problems
- Reporting on historical data

Event Correlation

Event logs can provide valuable information. Fortunately, nearly every type of system is capable of generating log data. Furthermore, some systems can bring all of these disparate logs together into a single location. Unfortunately, this creates a mountain of log data, which can be so overwhelming that eventually it all just gets ignored.

Event correlation enables organizations to better manage the vast amounts of data. Correlation of events provides a more effective means to mitigate threats and vulnerabilities as well as respond more quickly to incidents. A terminated employee account, for example, can be associated with an attempt to log on to a system with that same account. Individually, these data would not generate any alerts, but when combined, they become valuable information. In another example, multiple rules can be tied together. Consider the following example, which would detect a sequence and pattern of activity within the environment indicative of malicious code:

1. Suppose an IP address attempts connection to network 10 times and is denied 9 times
2. The same IP address triggers an IDS server event within the network
3. Correlating the two event triggers an security operations alert with the attack vector map indicating the firewall as point of origin.

Table 6-4 provides a sample set of taxonomy for data collected and associated sample events. Security operations should regularly review the data, from which meaningful information can be abstracted. Additionally, operations should leverage programmatic alerts and correlation rules to help identify suspicious activity.

TABLE 6-4   Types of log data and information the data might reveal.

DATA CATEGORY	COMMON EVENTS	SUSPICIOUS ACTIVITIES REVEALED
Computer performance	Resource usage, errors, availability, shutdowns, and restarts	Unauthorized use, compromised systems, denial of service (DoS) attacks
Network performance	Traffic load, errors, network interface status, network scans	DoS and distributed denial of service (DDoS) attacks, information-gathering activities as a precursor to actual attack
Users	Logon and logoff data, privilege use and modifications, failed system access attempts	Brute-force attacks on passwords, compromised accounts, privilege abuse
Applications	Application-specific events depending on type, such as web servers, firewalls, databases, remote access servers, and Domain Name Servers (DNS)	Attempts to exploit vulnerabilities, brute-force attacks, information-gathering activities as a precursor to actual attack, DoS attacks
File system	Access to data, changes to access control lists, changes to file properties, file additions, and file deletions	System compromise, privilege abuse

Audit and logging systems need to be maintained to perform an efficient analysis of events. Whereas a single failed logon, for example, might not be a cause for concern, many rapid failed logon attempts should be. Maintaining and managing audit logs through the use of these systems also provides the organization with a great mechanism to respond to audit requests. This, of course, provides an auditor with a trove of available data to support the evidence-gathering process. Auditors can take, for example, a representative sampling of logs from the various systems across the IT infrastructure to ensure that automatically audited events comply with the stated policies and procedures.

Reviewing Configurations and Implementations

Managing the configuration of information systems is traditionally a function of IT operations. Configuration management, however, has a direct impact on information security and compliance. As a result, **security configuration management (SCM)** pertains more specifically to the configuration items that are directly related to controls or settings that represent significant risk if not managed properly. This includes the controllable parameters for hardware and software. Configuration management as a program is made up of several pieces, such as the following:

- **Configuration change control board**—A group of personnel responsible for governing configurations and configuration changes
- **Baseline configuration management**—The plan for establishing the basic standard of system configurations and the management of configuration items
- **Configuration change control**—A process for managing changes to the configuration standards defined for information systems
- **Configuration monitoring and auditing**—A process for identifying current configurations and testing configurations against established baselines

The configuration includes the specifics on a system's settings. Auditors can review the implementation of configuration items to ensure that prescriptive controls are put in place. The configuration can then be compared with standards and procedures. This task is difficult, however, in the absence of the previously mentioned components of a configuration management program. Even with a change control process in place, systems undergo unauthorized and untracked changes. These changes can directly affect the security of the systems. In addition to unauthorized changes, monitoring helps identify the following:

- **Misconfigurations**—This ensures that authorized changes are correctly put in place and remain in place.
- **Vulnerabilities**—These include missing system patches as well as configuration items related to a missing patch to determine and prioritize risk.
- **Unauthorized systems and software**—These include systems not managed by a configuration monitoring solution as well as software not authorized for use on the managed system.

What makes configuration management especially useful for auditors is that most of the data about the systems is contained in a **configuration management database (CMDB)**. The CMDB provides a central repository from which reports can be run. Thus, everything about all the systems at a particular point in time is stored in a database. Examples of configuration items include the following:

- Operating system type
- Service pack level
- Security patches
- Software installed
- Users
- Device drivers
- Hardware configuration
- Service and port status
- Access permissions
- Authentication controls
- Audit settings
- Protocols

Many configuration monitoring and auditing solutions are capable of providing predefined templates from which the configuration items can be assessed. Many of these templates are based on industry-recommended practices such as those from NIST. In addition, organizations can configure auditing templates to align with their own internal policies and standards. The following are sample templates that can be programmatically run to assess parameters specific to the template:

- **Operating system**—This includes audit templates for each version of the operating system across UNIX, Linux, Mac OS, and Windows, for example.
- **Database**—This includes audit templates for different types of databases that verify the database security and configuration parameters.
- **Application**—This includes audit templates to assess applications for expected configurations.
- **Network device**—This includes templates to verify appropriate settings across the network infrastructure, such as routers, switches, and firewalls.
- **Best practice documents**—This includes templates to be run across different parts of the infrastructure to test for compliance based on recommended practices from organizations such as NIST and the Center for Internet Security (CIS).
- **Regulations and standards**—This includes templates specifically targeted to assess against regulations such as the Health Insurance Portability and Accountability Act (HIPAA) or industry standards like PCI DSS.

When systems aren't compared against acceptable baselines, the systems could be configured inconsistently in a number of different ways. Configuration management and the use of monitoring tools ensure that systems stay configured as originally intended. This makes systems easier to troubleshoot and maintain and makes them more secure.

Auditing Change Management

The one constant in information technology is "change." Organizations are constantly being pressed to innovate and often turn to technology to drive improvements. Add to this the constant need to upgrade the security of the IT infrastructure to keep pace with cybersecurity threats can be overwhelming. Change must be thoughtful, well tested, and authorized to ensure the reliability of the systems.

An audit of the change management environment should assess how the balancing of the competing interests is achieved through change managements policies and processes. An audit should assess the following in all changes:

- Authorization
- Testing
- Documentation
- Monitoring
- Meets control objectives

Strong change management means system upgrades are tested, scheduled within upgrade windows, and have the capability to be uninstalled (sometimes referred to as "rolled back") if needed. An audit should review the results of major network or system upgrades that could have significant enterprise impact.

This audit includes determining the quality of the information generated by the change management program and assessing whether it is enough to manage the change management process. Additionally, change management performance metrics should be assessed for their existence, effectiveness, monitoring activities, and responses to any program deviations.

An audit of change management should review the previously listed risk indicators as a good measure of the likelihood that controls are or are not effective. Auditing IT processes can be very productive. Good business results happen due to the quality of the processes used to produce them. Reviewing the policies and procedures and related processes that have been implemented will help determine if IT investments will be productive and how changes are implemented in a controlled manner.

Verifying and Validating Proper Configuration and the Implementation of Security Controls and Countermeasures

Auditing security controls across the IT infrastructure involves testing the controls or countermeasures using available documents, interviews, and personal observation.

This section provides an overview of testing and validating controls based upon NIST SP800-53A, which provides an approach to assessing security controls. Regardless of the exact methods used, however, the principles are the same.

Each control to be tested should have an accompanying assessment objective. The objective provides the foundation or high-level statement to determine the effectiveness of the control. Based on this, one or more assessment objectives are validated using a specific method. Such methods include examination, interviews, and testing. Using these methods against particular assessment objects will produce the results, which is a determination of the effectiveness of the controls. The assessment objects vary and include different types of elements. Three broad categories of objects include the following:

- **Specification objects**—These include documents such as policies, procedures, plans, and architectural designs.
- **Mechanism objects**—These are the specific hardware and software countermeasures installed and configured.
- **Activity objects**—These are the security-related actions involving IT personnel.

The effort required to assess controls will vary not just across the objectives. The auditor should also consider impact levels, or the sensitivity and importance of the information systems. The effort is directly related to the depth and breadth of the assessment. NIST's assessment framework uses the terms depth and coverage and also defines their associated values. A summary of these definitions is as follows:

- **Depth**—This addresses the thoroughness and level of detail in the examination, interview, and testing process.
- **Coverage**—This addresses the breadth of the examination, interview, and testing process of objects.

Depth and coverage each have three different values. The values that address depth are generalized, focused, or detailed. The values that address coverage are representative, specific, and comprehensive. Representative coverage makes use of a limited sample of assessment objects. Further, the goal is to determine that a security control is put in place and that there aren't obvious faults. More specific coverage builds on this by increasing the scope to achieve greater confidence that the control is not only put in place correctly with no obvious faults, but it is also operating as intended. Finally, comprehensive coverage uses a much larger sample of assessment objects to achieve the results of representative and specific coverage. It also ensures the control is operating on an ongoing basis that is continually improved.

The varying levels of depth have the same relative expectations. This includes making sure controls are put in place and free of obvious errors. It also includes making sure the controls are consistently operating as intended and are supported by continual improvement. Interviews and document reviews at a general level include high-level discussions and examination. A more focused assessment asks questions in greater depth and requires a more detailed analysis of documents. Finally, a detailed assessment includes asking deep, probing questions and performing thorough analysis of documents across a greater body of evidence.

In addition to interviews and document reviews, testing depth uses methodologies that require varying degrees of knowledge about the environment being tested. This ranges from having no knowledge of the infrastructure or implementation of a control to having considerable and extensive knowledge of both the infrastructure and details about the control.

Based on the tests of each control, an unbiased and factual determination is made as to the effectiveness of the control. The control should either satisfy or not satisfy the expected state. In some situations, the auditor will not be able to determine how effective a control is because of lack of information or an inability to test. In situations where the objectives of the control are not fulfilled, the auditor needs to understand and document how the control differs from what is expected. In addition, the auditor should note how these findings affect confidentiality, integrity, and availability.

Continuous Improvement

Continuous improvement could be viewed as the "we found a better way" or "lessons learned." As employees find new ways to improve, it's considered as a potential improvement. One hopes the driver to find a better way was not a system crash or breach. In those cases, you are typically dealing with lessons learned from the incident. Either way, you can think of it as the "suggestion box." Employees identify needed changes and write a suggestion. The suggestion is either accepted or rejected. If accepted, it enters the formal reengineering process.

Identifying Common Problems When Conducting an IT Infrastructure Audit

The most common problem encountered during an audit is a lack of communication. If management doesn't understand the scope and purpose of your audit program, they will not provide full support. This will result in their team giving you minimal support. Worst, when pressed, you risk creating a hostile environment between the audit and the IT teams. Effective communications are essential to building trust and being perceived as a value-add partner.

Avoid technobabble and terms that need to be defined. Be clear with presenting risk in clear understandable terms. Practical examples are important. If a risk sounds so unlikely and has minimal impact, the audit finding may be technically correct but would be viewed as adding little to no value. Remember that an audit report ultimately goes to management, not the technical IT staff. Leadership needs to understand what the auditor found and why the auditor thinks it is important.

An audit should be an opportunity to build relationships within all levels of the IT and chief information security officer originations. Make friends with IT and security staff. Understandably, these folks can feel threatened and get a little defensive when an auditor is seen as assessing the quality of their work. Ultimately they should be the experts on the technology, and an auditor is an expert on potential risks. An effective audit should combine these skills to form an opinion for leadership. Disagreements are expected but should be navigated through respect and professional dialogue.

Effective planning and a well-defined scope are essential. Scope creep refers to the expansion of scope after the audit has started. Sometimes this cannot be avoided. For example, suppose you auditing the access management function and determining a potential regular compliance issue. You may choose to expand the scope to include the second-line risk function. Scope creep should always be avoided when possible. When not possible, it should only be used to exam a significant noncompliance issue, and the expanded scope are should be narrowly focused to resolve that specific compliance issue raised. Audits that are full of shame and blame are demeaning and unproductive.

I think it's easy—and tempting—to write your audit assessment with a scathing or accusatory tone, thinking that if you fill the report with enough high severity findings you will get management motivated to start remediating things. Instead, what often happens is the IT/security staff (the ones responsible for making things better) get reprimanded for your findings, their team morale takes a hit, and everybody suffers audit fatigue from your thousand-page report.

Instead of focusing on reprimands, focus on remediation. At the end of the day, most companies know they have issues, and they're looking to you for help and guidance. One item to include with the audit deliverables is a security objectives that offers remediation guidance for each identified risk, along with the expected time. That way, clients can couple the detailed audit report with their proposed management action plan and essentially have a playbook they can follow to improve the control environment That's what we as consultants and auditors want for our clients and organizations, and that's why we got into the audit profession in the first place, right?

NIST defines several areas of potential challenges when conducting security testing and assessments. All these areas could potentially apply to an audit as well. These areas include the following:

- **Time and resources**—A solid plan is critical to maximizing the use of available time and resources. Both are sometimes underestimated for many different reasons. For example, systems might not be testable during normal business hours. Often, there is only a small window of opportunity each day. Because technology evolves so quickly, assessors and auditors might find that they don't have the requisite skill set to adequately perform specific actions.

- **Resistance**—IT personnel might be resistant to an assessment or an audit for many reasons. Operationally, IT personnel might have concerns about outages. On a personal level, individuals might be defensive and fearful for their jobs or fearful of being reprimanded.

- **Temporary behavior**—Users and operators might adjust the processes and systems for which they are responsible before an audit or an assessment to comply with policies. Upon completion of the audit, however, systems and behaviors often return to the state prior to the audit or assessment.

- **Immediate response**—As weaknesses or audit deficiencies are uncovered, there might be a desire to immediately address the issue. Although generally acceptable and encouraged, changes need to adhere to the organization's policies and change management procedures.

- **Changing technology**—Technology and the tools used to assess it are constantly evolving. As a result, auditors need to be committed to ongoing information technology education, including the use of new tools and techniques.

- **Operational impact**—There is always the possibility that tests might inadvertently disrupt the systems being tested. To limit any negative impact, the assessor or auditor should maintain proper documentation, including a detailed list of actions being performed.

Validating Security Operations and Administration Roles, Responsibilities, and Accountabilities Throughout the IT Infrastructure

There are many different roles for security operations and administration across the IT infrastructure. Security operations and administration are responsible for implementing the policy framework to protect the confidentiality, integrity, and availability of the company's information and supporting technologies. The foundation of these operations is first based on assigning, identifying, and classifying the information and information systems, and then implementing and maintaining the appropriate controls to protect the information and infrastructure.

The tasks include managing authentication and access controls, security hardware, and security software. Security operations and administration personnel are directly involved in the implementation and administration of controls designed to allow access only to those authorized. They also maintain the systems that prevent fraud, violations, and other malicious and even unintentional breaches of confidentiality, integrity, and availability.

Those assigned to protect assets are not above committing irregular or illegal acts. In fact, without proper controls in place, such activities are easier to perform. This includes fraud, theft, suppression of information, and other legal violations. Examples of safeguards that need to be verified include the following:

> **NOTE**
>
> Security operations and administration personnel need to be held accountable for their responsibilities. Because of the important responsibilities of the security and administration staff, additional safeguards need to be in place to prevent inappropriate use and misconduct.

- **Security operation policies**—Policies form the foundation for holding staff accountable. Policies define the behaviors that must be complied with by security and administration personnel. Periodically testing the staff on the organization's policies helps increase accountability.

- **Assignment of responsibilities**—Those assigned with security and administration roles need to have clear expectations and responsibilities. This helps foster and enforce accountability within the individual roles.

- **Maintenance procedures**—These provide clear guidance for the security operations and administration staff in the performance of their duties to prevent misconfigurations and errors.

- **Segregation of duties**—Segregation of duties (SOD) divides roles and responsibilities so a single individual or group can't undermine a critical process. From an IT perspective, this includes, for example, separating testing, development, and production environments to prevent unauthorized changes. Another example includes preventing the person who approves configuration changes from being the person who implements them. Segregation of duties is also referred to as *separation of duties* or *separation of responsibilities*.

- **Rotation of duties**—The safeguard of **rotation of duties** rotates employees into different functions and helps mitigate collusion to circumvent what segregation of duties helps prevent.

- **Least privilege**—The safeguard of **least privilege** involves users having access only to what they need to perform their duties.

- **Mandatory vacation**—For sensitive positions, a contiguous one-week vacation should be required. This reduces the opportunity for an employee to commit unethical or illegal acts. It allows others to fill in to support the position and verify the work being performed.

- **Screening**—Employees responsible for managing security and sensitive data within an organization should be carefully screened prior to employment. This includes background checks, for example, to ensure the individuals are suited for the position.

- **Training and awareness**—A continuous program of training is necessary to ensure employees understand the responsibilities associated with their duties and are adequately prepared to perform them effectively.

Security operations and administration personnel need to be held accountable. Strong accountability also serves the goal of preventing fraud and inappropriate use.

Separation of Duties

A foundational component of internal control is the segregation of duties (SOD) for high-risk transactions. The underlying SOD concept is that no individual should be able to execute a high-risk transaction and conceal errors or fraud in the normal course of their duties.

The layered security approach can be a SOD, which means to have two or more layers of independent controls to reduce risk. The approach leverages the redundancy of the layers so if one layer fails to catch the risk or threat, the next layer should. By its nature the more layers, the better the risk and threat reduction. However, the more layers, the more burdensome and expensive the process becomes. So there needs to be a balance between cost and return in risk reduction.

A key area where SOD is applied is in the management of access controls for administrative rights of operating systems (known as the "root" level access). If these accounts are accessed by unauthorized users the impact on the organization is high. Typical SOD controls for these accounts may include the following:

- Keeping the group of administrators small and well managed
- Unlocking elevated permissions only when needed
- Prohibiting administrators from reviewing business content files and folders, such as client files

CHAPTER SUMMARY

You learned in this chapter how important an infrastructure audit is to ensure compliance with U.S. laws. An organization needs to build trust with its customers, shareholders, and the public. You also learned the importance of communications and scoping an audit well. The chapter examined a number of scope items to include in an infrastructure audit. Sometimes regulations are built out of pressures and public headlines when something goes wrong. The chapter examined the pressures and motivations of both the regulators and the IT teams. We discussed potential problems that an audit may come across in performing the engagement.

An audit will provide comfort over the design and control effectiveness of the IT infrastructure. A holistic view of the IT infrastructure can be produced through an accumulation of audits over time. The chapter discussed both manual and automated controls that can be brought into a holistic view of the health of the IT infrastructure control environment.

KEY CONCEPTS AND TERMS

Baseline controls

Computer-assisted audit tools and techniques (CAATT)

Configuration management database (CMDB)

Corrective control

Detective control

Information Systems Security Assessment Framework (ISSAF)

Least privilege

Network scan

NIST 800-115

Open Source Security Testing Methodology Manual (OSSTMM)

Penetration test

Preventive control

Risk appetite

Risk tolerance

Rotation of duties

Security configuration management (SCM)

Segregation of duties (SOD)

Three lines of defense

Transmission Control Protocol/ Internet Protocol (TCP/IP)

Vulnerability scan

CHAPTER 6 ASSESSMENT

1. The decision to apply or not apply controls is based on risk.

   A. True
   B. False

2. Which one of the following is the best example of avoiding risk?

   A. The IT department decides to install an antivirus device at its network border.
   B. The IT department outsources its vulnerability management program to a third party.
   C. The IT department disables the ability for end users to use portable storage devices.
   D. The IT department installs data loss prevention software on all end users' workstations.

3. Which of the following is an examination of the current state of controls against the desired state of controls?

   A. Control objective
   B. Gap analysis
   C. Baseline analysis
   D. Log review

4. The purpose of a network scan is to identify as many vulnerabilities as possible.

   A. True
   B. False

5. A(n) _____ is an assessment method that uses methods similar to what a real-world attacker might use.

6. Which one of the following is *not* an example of a review technique?

   A. Password cracking
   B. File integrity checking
   C. Log review
   D. Network sniffing

7. If required, an auditor is justified in the use of security assessment techniques such as penetration testing and vulnerability analysis and may consider using the work of other experts.

   A. True
   B. False

8. What does CAATT stand for?

   A. Computer Assisted Audit Tools and Techniques
   B. Computer Aided Assessment Tools and Techniques
   C. Compliance Auditing Assisted Tactical Techniques
   D. Compliance Assisted Audit Tactical Tools

9. Which of the following are examples of information provided by audit logs?

   A. Failed authentication attempts
   B. Account changes
   C. Privileged use
   D. All of the above

10. Which of the following benefits does an automated security information and event management log solution provide?

   A. Diagnosing and preventing operational problems
   B. Assigning appropriate responsibilities to security operations
   C. Management of a configuration change control board
   D. All of the above

11. A configuration _____ database provides a central repository of configuration items.

12. Which one of the following best describes an assessment objective for a control?

   A. A high-level statement to determine the effectiveness of a control
   B. A detailed statement on what activities need to occur to implement a control
   C. A definition of responsibilities to be assigned to security operations for the management of a control
   D. A statement about the required depth or coverage required to test a control

13. Which one of the following is *not* an example of a level of depth required to assess a control?

   A. Comprehensive
   B. Generalized
   C. Focused
   D. Detailed

14. Which of the following best describes documents such as policies, procedures, plans, and architectural designs?

   A. Specification objects
   B. Mechanism objects
   C. Activity objects
   D. Configuration objects

15. Preventing a user who approves a configuration change from being the person who implements the change is an example of which of the following?

   A. Rotation of duties
   B. Least privilege
   C. Segregation of duties
   D. Dual control

16. What type of framework focus determines which controls to deploy based on the highest risk to the organization's objectives?

   A. Risk-based management
   B. Align the businesses risk appetite
   C. Reduce operation disruption and losses

17. What type of framework focus will reduce surprises and ensure risks are systematically identified and reduced, eliminated, or accepted?

   A. Risk-based management
   B. Align the businesses risk appetite
   C. Reduce operation disruption and losses

18. True or False. The distinction between automated and manual controls is if a human decision is required to take action.

   A. True
   B. False

19. Of the following security controls, which unique design type is a manual control that does not avert an incident from happening but rather alerts an organization about the breach?

   A. Preventive
   B. Detective
   C. Corrective

20. Business liability insurance can only be issued to organizations and not individuals.

   A. True
   B. False

Writing the IT Infrastructure Audit Report

COMMUNICATION OF AUDIT RESULTS typically includes the publication of an audit report. The exact format to use will vary greatly depending on the organization, industry norms, and standards set by the audit department leadership. A vast number of templates and industry examples are available to choose from. Regardless of the format selected, audit reports should contain at a minimum the following:

- The scope, including the time period to which the opinion pertains
- The overall opinion of the auditor
- A summary of the information that supports the opinion
- The risk, framework, or other criteria used as a basis for the overall opinion
- Any individual observations or gaps that need to be remediated to reduce the risk, including the impact on the organization's goals if timely remediation is not taken

It is important to keep in mind that the target audience for the audit report is senior management. The audit report is the opportunity to make a persuasive argument that moves management into action. The risk and impact to the organization if action is not taken must be clear and concise. In many ways, the report reflects on the competence and helps build credibility of the auditor. The report must be clear, concise, timely, and persuasive.

In this chapter, we will discuss the key elements to be included in an audit report. The chapter will also discuss a thoughtful approach to building an audit report.

Chapter 7 Topics

This chapter covers the following topics and concepts:

- Anatomy of an audit report
- Audit report ratings
- Audit report opinion
- What a summary of findings comprises
- What the IT security assessment results include
- How to report on the implementation of IT security controls and frameworks
- How to analyze gaps in IT security controls and countermeasures
- How to assess compliance throughout the IT infrastructure
- What to include in compliance recommendations

Chapter 7 Goals

When you complete this chapter, you will be able to:

- Write a proper executive summary
- Understand audit findings and their importance to the audit report
- Understand the gap analysis and its importance to the audit report
- Identify the risk components part of an IT security assessment and audit report
- Understand how IT security controls identified in the IT audit report relate to the security policy framework and protection of privacy data
- Identify key areas from which a gap analysis should be documented
- Understand how to report on a compliance assessment
- Understand how to craft meaningful compliance recommendations

Anatomy of an Audit Report

We will use a simplified audit report format to drive our discussion on audit content. The exact audit report template will vary by an organization's industry, needs, and type of audit being documented. Often a professional practices group within the internal audit department will set strict standards on the format and content to be used. These strict standards help to maintain consistency across audits and will address any regulatory requirements for the particular industry.

A simplified audit report format will include three report sections, as follows:

1. Executive summary
2. Background
3. Findings and issues

The **executive summary** section will contain the overall opinion, judgment, or conclusion reached. Audit reports are an assessment of the overall health of the control environment being assessed. The executive summary is a holistic view considering all the controls within the environment being assessed. The executive summary is not used to showcase how an audit was performed but to quickly capture the conclusion of the auditor.

Getting the right tone is essential. Remember that an executive summary is a persuasive argument to motivate leadership into corrective action. If the tone of the audit report does not substantially match leadership perception of risk, then the auditor's findings may be ignored.

All controls within an environment would rarely fail an audit assessment. It is important to put the risk in its proper context. Equally importantly, take the time to give credit for the control environment that is working effectively. When possible use precise data measurement to size the risk to leadership. Let's consider the tone of these two statements:

- 10% of the transactions failed to process which could lead to [impact statement]
- 90% of the transactions were properly processed [impact statement]

This is the art of creating a persuasive argument that comes with experience. Putting the risk in the correct context through the creation of a balanced story sets the right tone. In both examples the impact statement is important to help management understand the impact if correction action is not taken. It can be a subtle difference in wording and tone that goes a long way in building partnership and credibility. A subtle difference can help an auditee's mindset shift from a perception that the audit is criticizing their work to the audit is trying to improve the control environment and build upon their success.

The reasons for an unfavorable overall opinion must be stated. Auditing is said to be about contrast. An audit often will contrast the target state with the current state, for example, testing if the current deployed control is compliant with current policies or industry framework. In this example, the gaps between what is deployed control and the policy are the reason for the unfavorable opinion.

A strong reference target state for your opinion will make the audit report more persuasive. Examples of a strong reference target state are internal policies, regulatory requirements,

TIP

A good rule of thumb is that an executive summary should be no more than one page. The auditor will have documents (often called "workpapers") that detail all the activity performed by the auditor. Workpapers tend to be very detailed, including what data was collected, who was involved in the data collection, test steps performed, and much more. The executive summary should contain the MINIMUM supporting material needed to support the opinion. A mistake made by some new auditors is to try to put too much information in the executive summary in an attempt to build credibility and showcase the thoroughness of the audit.

industry norms, known information security vulnerabilities, and business objectives. Clear and concise evidence on control gaps against these authoritative sources adds to the credibility and persuasiveness of the audits.

When an overall opinion is issued, it must take into account the strategies, objectives, and risks of the organization. The opinion must be based on reliable, relevant, and evidenced information. The formulation of such opinions requires consideration of the following considerations:

- Impact of noncompliance—the urgency of remediation
- Opinion is objective, fair, impartial, and unbiased
- Opinion is balanced and considers mitigating and compensating controls
- Clear and concise—can the risk be explained in business terms avoiding unnecessary technical language

The **background** section will contain more structured data than the executive summary. Think of the background more like an appendix in a book. It contains supplemental material that can be useful for readers who are not familiar with the subject or the audit engagement details.

The background section contains the details on the following:

- **Scope**—This details the processes and controls that were examined during an audit. For example, An audit may review access management (AM) control environments
- **Scope exclusions**—This covers any processes and controls that were excluded from the scope, for example, if AM for vendors were excluded.
- **Time period**—This refers to the point in time under audit examination, for example, AM control environment as it exists from January 2021 to December 2021.
- **Control environment**—This is a high-level description of the control environment.

The control environment description would help any reader who is not familiar with the business or processes being assessed. This could include a description of the accountable business units, past regulatory issues, and recent technology changes and migrations.

The background section intends to put the audit reports' observations and opinions in context. Let's suppose a business just built a brand new data center and a number of the processes are not fully working. This may be considered less significant given the industry and management's expectation on a burn-in period needed to get operations fully functional. Conversely, an existing data center facility with a stellar track record of performance begins to have processing failures. In the latter example, management may consider the processing failures and noncompliance gaps more concerning.

The **finding and issue** section will contain the individual observations that elevate to audit findings. Each audit finding would detail the observations and include an opinion on the root cause. Audit issues with high impact on the organization are usually referenced in the executive summary. The underlining detail and description of the finding would be in the finding and issue section.

This section would describe in detail the rationale of the noncompliance, any reference authoritative sources used, and the root cause of the failure. Achieving clarity and precision in audit observations is essential to understanding what went wrong and must be clear about the impact to the organization if the issue is not remediated. The construction of the audit issue must be precise and clear such that management can action remediation.

The root cause is critical to get right for the management's remediation to be effective. The root cause is what leads to the defect and noncompliance. For example, if someone failed to take action, was it due to training or poor management oversight or a design flaw within an application? Understanding the root cause of an audit issue will allow management to formulate an action plan to permanently fix the defect.

Evidence highlighted in the audit issue gives substantiation to your professional audit opinion. An audit must assess the nature, competence, sufficiency, and evaluation of the audit evidence to determine its accuracy. An audit finding must be relevant and the evidence must be reliable. Consider the old saying, "all poodles are dogs, but not all dogs are poodles." Be sure the evidence being presented in your audit issue is directly relevant to the conclusion and opinion being asserted.

> **NOTE**
>
> Not all observations elevate to audit findings. Traditionally audit findings are observations that have a more significant impact on an organization or represent a systemic failure. For example, let's assume a background check is performed for all new hires and an email notification is sent to the manager once completed. An audit was performed of this process and based on hundreds of background checks that were all completed as required by policy. However, in one instance, the manager is notified by phone, not email. The one deviation would be verbally discussed with the process owner, noted in the auditor's workpapers, but would most likely not rise to an audit finding in the report.

Audit Report Ratings

An audit report rating is typically assigned to the overall opinion, reflecting whether that control environment is adequately reducing the risk to the organization. The audit report rating is typically found on the same page or header as the executive summary. There is no one standard format for an audit report rating used. Like the report format itself, the rating scale will depend on the organization and industry norms.

Regardless of the rating scale used, the audit rating will reflect the overall opinion on the health of the controls being assessed. The rating scale is simplified to provide management a quick snapshot of the audit's overall opinion. An example of the rating scale for an audit report is as follows:

- **Satisfactory**—The control environment is substantially compliant with policies and industry norms.
- **Needs improvement**—The control environment is partially compliant with policies and has pockets of noncompliance that need to be remediated.
- **Ineffective**—The control environment is substantially noncompliant with policies and industry norms and requires urgent remediation to become compliant with policies.

> **NOTE**
>
> Some audit reports may not have a rating. For example, suppose an audit is assessing a project that is building a new customer portal. Much of this audit work may be considered advisory in nature, meaning the auditor may provide an opinion on controls not yet deployed. These types of audit engagements often do not have a rating. They are considered advisory in nature and provide management advice on what controls and risks should be considered as part of a future state.

Notice in our example that these audit report ratings are on the overall health of the control environment. The rating does not reflect a specific control but should be a holistic opinion on the collection of controls. This is where art versus science comes in determining the overall health of a control environment. To illustrate, let's consider a situation where 9 out of 10 controls passed the audit examination and were found to be compliant. Is passing 90% of the time satisfactory, needs improvement, or ineffective? Depends on the impact on the organization. For example, let's assume a piece of factory machinery must be checked for safety before every shift and the supervisor initials the check. There is a substantial difference between the supervisor forgetting to initial and forgetting to perform the safety check.

Audit Report Opinion

An audit report is an opinion on the health of the control environment. It is important to distinguish the difference between an audit report rating and opinion. While these terms are often used interchangeably, there are significant differences. For discussion, consider a report rating for an information technology (IT) infrastructure audit as the overall conclusion of an auditor and a report opinion is the level of confidence in the evidence supporting the report rating.

An unqualified or "clean" opinion is what is generally assumed when reading an internal audit report. The unqualified opinion simply means that the auditor is confident that sufficient evidence exists to support the report rating.

> **NOTE**
>
> External financial audits also use some of these same terms. While these same terms may be used, they may have very different meanings in a financial or regulatory context. For example, external financial audits may have four types of audit report opinions, i.e., unqualified opinion, a qualified opinion, an adverse opinion, and a disclaimer of opinion.

The key takeaway is that any time an auditor's opinion is not unqualified, the reason must be stated as part of the executive summary. When evidence is not available to make an unqualified opinion, the auditor can choose to simply stop the audit and not issue a report or issue the report with an explanation. For example, let's assume a major application is being released in the next 60 days and management has asked the audit to do an assessment. The auditor may have insufficient time to do a review of all the controls. Nonetheless, of the controls tested, the auditor may have sufficient evidence to issue a qualified audit opinion on the likely success of the application rollout. The qualification on the evidence available should be clearly expressed and included as part of the report rating.

Summary of Findings

An audit **finding** is a documented conclusion of a control or process. It involves noncompliance to policies and industry norms. The objective of the audit determines how findings need to be documented. As findings are discovered, further investigation might be required to satisfy the objectives, which will be summarized in the final report. The following four elements constitute a finding:

- **Criteria**—This identifies the expected or desired state. This provides the context for evaluating the evidence collected by the auditor and the subsequent procedures the auditor performs. The criteria might be based, for example, on regulations, policies, standards, and external frameworks.
- **Condition**—This identifies the situation within the IT environment that exists.
- **Cause**—This identifies the reason for the gap between the circumstance and the criteria. The cause also provides a starting point from which the auditor can make a recommendation to correct the situation.
- **Consequence**—This identifies the effect or potential impact on the IT landscape based on the contrast between the circumstance and the desired state. Essentially, this includes consequences that might occur as a result of this difference. It might also reveal negative consequences that have already been occurring.
- **Corrective action** —This identifies what management action is required to remediate the related risks.

Within each of the different areas of IT, audit findings can get very specific. A summary of findings across the seven domains of a typical IT infrastructure should be broader. To provide this in a meaningful, yet concise, way requires an analysis of the gaps. This includes a measure of where the organization is and where it would like to be. This requires a complete understanding of the systems across the IT domains as well as the level of control the enterprise needs. Factors that affect the level of control may include regulatory requirements and risk analysis. An auditor might also compare the organization with industry peers and the organization's practices with other recommended practices.

Management action plans and appropriate follow-up are critical to closing the process. Recommendations provide the action that management should take to deal with deficiencies. It is the documented action plan, however, that provides the guidance for correcting those deficiencies. This includes assigning responsibility for each recommendation and assigning deadlines. Agreed-upon actions should be documented within the recommendations if this information is provided by management prior to the final report.

As part of the document-gathering process of an audit, the auditor should consider previous audit results and past recommendations. Likewise, documented results and recommendations will be examined with the next audit. This provides a process for continual awareness of changing environments and constant improvement.

IT Security Assessment Results: Risk, Threats, and Vulnerabilities

Any existing security assessment should include details about risk as part of the workpapers. Details include full documentation of the identified threats, vulnerabilities, and resulting risks. The findings inform management of the resulting risk to the environment. This information provides management with the data necessary to make informed decisions to manage risk. The results will help drive how resources are allocated to address potential uncertainties.

The key components of the assessment should include the following:

- **Introduction**—This provides the purpose and scope of the assessment. This includes the systems, personnel, locations, and other details about the assessed environment.

- **Approach**—This describes the methods taken. This includes those involved as part of the assessment and the techniques and tools used to collect information. A description of the risk scale or matrix used should also be discussed.

- **System characterization**—This provides details about the infrastructure systems. This includes the hardware, software, data, interfaces, and associated users. A discussion of existing technical, management, and operational controls may be included.

- **Threat statement**—This is a complete outline of potential threat sources and associated activities.

- **Assessment results**—This provides details on vulnerabilities and threats—specifically, the pairing of threats with vulnerabilities that can be exploited.

- **Summary**—This provides a concise review of the observations as well as risk levels. This may include any recommendations.

The assessment should describe the approach in detail. This includes the methodology used and details about the approach and definitions. A good practice is to use an established approach to assessing risks. **Table 7-1, Table 7-2, Table 7-3,** and **Table 7-4** are adapted from NIST SP 800-30, "Risk Management Guide for Information Technology Systems."

TABLE 7-1   Likelihood determination ratings and descriptions.

LIKELIHOOD LEVEL	WEIGHT FACTOR	DESCRIPTION
High	1.0	The threat source is highly motivated, and sufficiently capable and controls to prevent the vulnerability from being exercised are ineffective.
Medium	0.5	The threat source is motivated and capable, but controls are in place that may impede successful exercise of the vulnerability.
Low	0.1	The threat source lacks motivation or capability, or controls are in place to prevent or at least significantly impede the vulnerability from being exercised.

TABLE 7-2 Impact levels and descriptions.		
MAGNITUDE OF IMPACT	**WEIGHT FACTOR**	**IMPACT DESCRIPTION**
High	100	Exercise of the vulnerability may result in a highly costly loss of major tangible assets or resources. Exercise of the vulnerability may significantly violate, harm, or impede an entity's mission, reputation, or interest. Exercise of the vulnerability may result in human death or serious injury.
Medium	50	Exercise of the vulnerability may result in the costly loss of tangible assets or resources. Exercise of the vulnerability may violate, harm, or impede an entity's mission, reputation, or interest. Exercise of the vulnerability may result in human injury.
Low	10	Exercise of the vulnerability may result in the loss of some tangible assets or resources. Exercise of the vulnerability may noticeably affect an entity's mission, reputation, or interest.

TABLE 7-3 Resulting risks as a product of impact and threat likelihood.			
THREAT LIKELIHOOD	**IMPACT LEVEL**		
	LOW (10)	**MEDIUM (50)**	**HIGH (100)**
High (1.0)	Low $10 \times 1.0 = 10$	Medium $50 \times 1.0 = 50$	High $100 \times 1.0 = 100$
Medium (0.5)	Low $10 \times 0.5 = 5$	Medium $50 \times 0.5 = 25$	Medium $100 \times 0.5 = 50$
Low (0.1)	Low $10 \times 0.1 = 1$	Low $50 \times 0.1 = 5$	Low $100 \times 0.1 = 10$

Table 7-1 provides the definitions for determining the likelihood of a threat. The assessment should then describe the next step to determine the impact that would result from a vulnerability being exploited. Table 7-3 provides the impact levels and associated definitions. Next, the report should provide a determination of the resulting risk. The

TABLE 7-4	Risk level descriptions.
RISK LEVEL	**RISK DESCRIPTION**
High	If an observation or finding is evaluated as a high risk, there is a strong need for corrective measures. An existing system may continue to operate, but a corrective action plan must be put in place as soon as possible.
Medium	If an observation is rated as medium risk, corrective actions are needed, and a plan must be developed to incorporate these actions within a reasonable period of time.
Low	If an observation is described as low risk, management must determine whether corrective actions are still required or decide to accept the risk.

resulting risk is based on the threat likelihood and the impact the threat would have if successful. Table 7-4 provides the method to determine risk. It is based on multiplying the likelihood of a threat occurring by the impact the threat might have.

Risk level can be assigned to each audit finding. The risk level can be based on the resulting product of threat likelihood multiplied by the impact level provides a rating of risk. In this example, it would be categorized as low, medium, or high. **Table 7-5** provides the description of the resulting rating. This also includes actions that must be taken as a result.

The results of the assessment should include a pairing of identified vulnerabilities with associated threats. For each pair, the report includes a brief description of the threat and vulnerability. It should also give a description of existing controls in place to reduce the risk. The results from the previous tables should also be included as summary items. This includes the threat likelihood rating, risk impact rating, and overall risk rating.

The following is an example of a vulnerability/threat pair analysis: "Weak passwords are vulnerable to hackers." These passwords are more easily guessed or cracked by automated programs. The existing control enforces passwords to be alphanumeric and at least five characters long. The likelihood, impact, and risk rating are all medium. As a result of the risk, a recommended control such as increasing password complexity or length should be documented.

Reporting on Implementation of IT Security Controls and Frameworks

We discussed the importance of frameworks. Many IT organizations have adopted the use of different frameworks. An IT shop may deploy controls based on ISO versus NIST versus COBIT. Even within NIST, is it NIST CSF or NIST 800-53? How do we convey our findings in the context of a framework? Fortunately, there is no shortage of framework mapping. For example, NIST.gov (n.d.) has a framework mapping in the format of an Excel spreadsheet.

TABLE 7-5	NIT CSF Cybersecurity Framework mapping for ID.AM-1.		
FUNCTION	**CATEGORY**	**SUBCATEGORY**	**REFERENCES**
IDENTIFY	Asset Management (ID. AM): The data, personnel, devices, systems, and facilities that enable the organization to achieve business purposes are identified and managed consistent with their relative importance to business objectives and the organization's risk strategy.	ID.AM-1: Physical devices and systems within the organization are inventoried	• CCS CSC 1 • CCS CSC 1 • COBIT 5 BAI09.01, BAI09.02 • ISA 62443-2-1:2009 4.2.3.4 • ISA 62443-3-3:2013 SR 7.8 · ISO/IEC 27001:2013 A.8.1.1, A.8.1.2 • NIST SP 800-53 Rev. 4 CM-8

These mappings, especially in the format of Excel, can be easily modified as assessment checklists. Let's look at a portion of the NIST Cybersecurity Framework (CSF) spreadsheet previously mentioned as illustrated in Table 7-5.

This spreadsheet can help an auditor in multiple ways. When gaps are identified the findings can be put into context the IT teams can understand. For example, an audit test for completeness and accuracy of an IT inventory can be reported as either a NIST CSF ID.AM-1 failure or a NIST SP 800-53 CM-8 failure.

The audit report would not get into this level of detail in the executive summary. The reporting at this level within the audit findings section may be important to the subject matter expected (SME) within the IT teams.

Another benefit of these types of framework mappings is to ensure an auditor testing is complete and comprehensive. Additionally, columns can be easily added to ensure that all the relevant controls within the audit's scope are covered. For example, an audit scope to cover access management could forget to include related inventories as required by NIST CSF ID.AM-1. Having such checklists as a method of communicating and verifying scope coverage can be a valuable tool.

In many industries, the NIST CSF is commonly used. The framework is logically structured and designed to help communicate risk across the enterprise. The fact that the NIST CSF is a dominant standard adds significant weight to communication with leadership. These NIST CSF functions are unique categories and subcategories that outline the IT security requirements that must be adhered to. Consequently, regulatory expect evidence of compliance in the organization's use and handling of data.

> **NOTE**
> Mapping audit results to each function, category, and subcategory correspond directly to the NIST CSF, further improving uniformity across organizations as they strengthen capabilities such as their data privacy and cybersecurity operations.

Per Documented IT Security Policy Framework

Are controls put in place as stated in the IT security policy framework? Control frameworks such as those from COBIT, NIST, and the International Organization for Standardization (ISO) are useful here. They provide an effective means to assess and document an organization's implementation of controls. This process is quite effective, especially when the organization's framework is based on a well-known external framework.

The organization might have mappings of its controls to well-known frameworks. If available, auditors may use these mappings but should verify them first. This should be included in the final report. In addition, it provides the method for conducting the analysis of any gaps. These gaps should also be documented. Documenting the gap analysis is discussed in the next section.

Privacy Data

Frameworks mentioned earlier include controls. These controls are essential to protecting privacy data. An audit may be concerned with assessing the protection of privacy data. Alternatively, it may be concerned with compliance with privacy laws. In both cases, the audit should report specifically on established privacy principles. Refer to the Generally Accepted Privacy Principles (GAPP) if necessary. Also noteworthy are the organization's current implementation, related controls, and associated risks. **Table 7-6** provides examples of related risks relevant to each privacy principle.

The risks to the organization for each of the privacy principles should be clearly documented in the audit report. In recent years, IT security personnel have had to be more

TABLE 7-6 Generally Accepted Privacy Principles and associated risks.

PRIVACY PRINCIPLE	RISK
Management	Lack of accountability can result in inadequate privacy protection as well as noncompliance with legislation.
Notice	If individuals cannot obtain the privacy policies, they may deny consent to use personal information.
Choice and consent	If consent is not obtained prior to collecting personal information, the organization can suffer reputational risk and loss of customer trust.
Collection	Collecting more information than is needed can result in increased retention and security costs and introduce additional liability.
Use and retention	Personal information could be prematurely destroyed, resulting in information not being available to make important decisions.

(Continues)

TABLE 7-6 Generally Accepted Privacy Principles and associated risks.   *(continued)*

PRIVACY PRINCIPLE	RISK
Access	Individuals unable to access their information might not be able to correct inaccurate information. This could result in a negative decision being made about the individual, resulting in legal liability.
Disclosure to third parties	Providing data to third parties with inadequate controls could affect customer retention and result in identity theft.
Security for privacy	Inadequate security controls could result in the unauthorized use of privacy data, causing harm to individuals.
Quality	Basing business decisions on inaccurate personal information could result in lost profits.
Monitoring and enforcement	Customer satisfaction and retention might be jeopardized if customer inquiries or complaints are not adequately addressed as a result of an ineffective monitoring process.

aware of privacy implications. The implications are due to the growing number of privacy regulations. IT controls for privacy go beyond just securing data to prevent improper use. Most IT frameworks address privacy to a certain extent. In addition, both the IIA and ISACA publish guidelines. These guidelines establish common privacy controls and audit processes.

IT Security Controls and Countermeasure Gap Analysis

A gap analysis means comparing and contrasting the "as is" to the "to be." For security controls, this involves comparing the present state of controls with a desired state of controls. Well-known frameworks help organizations set up a desired state. This process also helps better manage operational risk. This includes adherence to regulatory and industry requirements to protect sensitive systems and information as well as privacy data.

At a minimum, common baseline security controls should be in place. Any gaps to the following types of controls should be clearly documented:

- **Information security policies**—This provides direction for the entire organization regarding goals, risks, and applicable laws and regulations.
- **Information security responsibilities**—This defines how staff will execute the policies, assign responsibilities, and promote accountability.
- **Information security awareness, education, and training**—This defines the program to provide initial and ongoing security education across the organization.
- **Correct processing in applications**—This prevents errors and unauthorized misuse of applications.

- **Vulnerability management**—This reduces the risk of known vulnerabilities being exploited.
- **Business continuity management**—This provides methods to continue critical operations in spite of business interruptions.
- **Security incident management**—This ensures security-related events are communicated and acted upon to allow corrective action to be taken by security staff.

 NOTE

It is important to contrast your security control environment with peers' organizations. Information security is an area that can be overengineered. At times cybersecurity threats can seem endless and overwhelming. Understanding how peers and the industry perceive these threats can help the organization rightsize solutions.

⚠ **WARNING**

You should get legal counsel during the process of a gap analysis regarding regulatory requirements. Legal requirements vary from state to state and across different countries. Organizations that operate within a single country may still have to meet certain requirements based on the flow of information to other countries.

The report should clearly identify any major gaps. The report should also provide supporting documentation as to the overall implementation of controls, which includes noting any gaps. A simple approach could include, for example, a spreadsheet with a list of controls and columns to identify a control that is in place, partially in place, or not in place. Another common method is to use a percentage. **Table 7-7** provides an example of identifying gaps for security incident management controls management based on ISO/IEC 27002.

Compliance Requirement

Proper security controls are essential to maintaining and safeguarding the IT environment, which exists to help drive the organization's goals. You can group compliance broadly into two categories: compliance with internal policies and standards and compliance with regulatory and industry requirements. Controls explicit to compliance should be included as part of a policy to ensure adherence with applicable legislation and internal governance.

At a minimum, organizations should have a program to manage compliance with internal policies and standards. Specifically, this includes identifying areas of noncompliance and methods for correction. Additionally, technical controls should be in place to ensure systems are compliant with standards. This would also include a program for

TABLE 7-7 Sample gap analysis of security incident management controls.

CONTROL	COMPLETION STATUS
Report information security events as quickly as possible.	100%
Report security weaknesses in systems and services.	50%
Establish incident response responsibilities and procedures.	100%
Learn from your information security incidents.	0%
Collect evidence to support your actions.	25%

penetration testing and vulnerability assessments. In addition, the organization should have a documented control program in place. This program should manage the audit requirements of information systems.

The final report should identify how the report and associated audit and assessment activities fit into the organization's control. Next, it should include the current state of compliance with legal requirements and compare this with where the organization needs to be.

Has the organization identified all legal, regulatory, and industry-specific requirements? Without these key controls, it will be difficult for the organization to implement and enforce further controls. Additionally, the organization should document the gaps for the following requirements:

- **Respecting intellectual property rights (IPRs)**—Organizations, regardless of size, depend on proprietary software and other intangible assets. Examples of intellectual property include those items protected by copyrights, trademarks, patents, and trade secrets. **Intellectual property rights (IPRs)** are the exclusive privilege to intangible assets.

- **Protecting and retaining organizational records**—Laws and regulations set time periods for which organizations must hold and protect specific types of data.

- **Protecting personal information**—Numerous laws have been enacted to protect the collection, processing, and storage of personal information.

- **Preventing users from using systems for unauthorized purposes**—Because of legislation that provides protection against computer misuses, organizations are required to meet requirements for security monitoring access notification.

- **Managing the proper use and import or export of cryptographic controls**—Although laws have been relaxed in recent years, there are legal restrictions on the export of cryptographic technology to rogue states or terrorist organizations. In fact, strong cryptography for many years was considered munitions and was part of a list that included items such as firearms, tanks, chemical agents, and nuclear weapons.

Compliance Assessment Throughout the IT Infrastructure

The results of a compliance assessment should clearly address whether specific requirements are met. For example, consider the following:

- **Compliant**—This indicates that there is enough credible evidence to show that a particular requirement has been met.

- **Noncompliant**—This indicates that enough credible evidence was collected to show that policies were not adequately followed.

- **Not determined**—This indicates that not enough evidence was collected to make an appropriate compliance determination.

The testing procedures used should be documented. This should also include comments regarding the determination. For example, consider compliance with the Payment Card Industry Data Security Standard (PCI DSS). PCI DSS requires that vendor-supplied

TABLE 7-8 A sample documented PCI DSS compliance test result.			
PCI DSS REQUIREMENT	**TESTING PROCEDURES**	**STATUS**	**COMMENTS**
Do not use vendor-supplied defaults for system passwords and other security parameters.	Attempted to log on to a sample of selected critical systems using the default vendor-supplied accounts and passwords taken from vendor documentation	Compliant	The point-of-sale systems do not support vendor-supplied default pass-words.

default passwords be changed before installing a system on the network. The report would include this along with the other requirements followed by the corresponding testing procedures and results. **Table 7-8** provides an example of the documented results for this requirement.

Presenting Compliance Recommendations

Audit reports should be persuasive arguments for management to take action to reduce risks. When presenting audit reports and recommendations, it's an opportunity to put a voice and answer questions that management may have. Over 2,000 years ago, Aristotle identified three methods to master the art of persuasion, which still apply today:

- **Ethos**—Establishing credibility, character, and show you are committed to the welfare of others, and you will gain trust.
- **Logos**—Use data, evidence, and facts to support your point of view.
- **Pathos**—Wrap your big idea in a story that will elicit an emotional reaction.

These methods work well for auditors. Present your findings in an (ethos) way that builds on the successes already established within IT such as reference well established industry standards. Present your findings based on (logos) data and clear and convincing evidence such as the use of data analytics. Finally, present your findings through a risk (pathos) story that management can easily relate to and instinctively want to take action to correct to correct such as the impact if action is not taken.

Additionally, compare your idea to something familiar and used for example. It will help you clarify your argument on the business impact making the abstract risk more concrete. Be brief and allow the audit report to speak for itself. Do not read but summarize the report. Keep the big ideas and explain them in as few words as possible. People have a limited attention span, so talk about your strongest points first.

Audits sometimes reveal major risks or compliance gaps. In those cases, the final reports may include recommendations supported by the audit findings. The recommended actions should be logically tied to a finding for which the problem has also been identified. A recommendation is more valuable to the organization when it is specific, sensible, cost-effective, and actionable.

CHAPTER SUMMARY

This chapter discussed the importance of the audit report as a persuasive augment to control risks. The impact is imperative for management to take corrective action. The writing style can be positive and build on the IT successes through control enhancements. The writing style can make to ensure corrective action is complete and timely. The content of a report can not only informs readers but motivates them.

In summary, the chapter highlighted the following key concepts:

- Keep the executive summary short and concise

  Tailor the report to our stakeholders' needs. If you overwhelm the readers with too much information, the report will have less impact.

- Keep the message simple in business terms, not technobabble

  Big ideas are best expressed in small words, never small ideas in big words. Our writing is most persuasive when we use clear, direct, and familiar language. This does not mean "dumbing down" our reports. It means clear concise thought with compelling evidence explained in plain language.

- Make your best ideas stand out by highlighting the biggest impact findings first

  We need to make it easy for busy executives to read, absorb, and take action. Prioritize the report leading with the strongest risk and high impact findings.

- Consider the implications

  We all try to be unbiased, but it is easy to overlook the implication of our words. Audit reports by their nature can come across as criticisms. The tone needs to be fair, objective, and supportive of the efforts and accomplishments of the IT teams. When readers buy into our ideas, corrective action is more likely to be effective.

KEY CONCEPTS AND TERMS

Background	**Finding**	**Intellectual property rights (IPRs)**
Executive summary	**Finding and issue**	

CHAPTER 7 ASSESSMENT

1. Which of the following is *not* a purpose of the audit report?

A. Provide an action plan for auditors to implement controls.
B. Communicate the results.
C. Prevent misunderstanding of the results.
D. Facilitate follow-up corrective action.

2. An abstract of an audit report provides a brief review intended for senior-level management who might not have the time to read and understand the entire report.

A. True
B. False

3. An executive summary should never be more than one page long.

A. True
B. False

4. Which of the following best describes an audit finding?

A. The procedures used to find IT controls
B. A documented conclusion that identifies deficiencies
C. A verbal recommendation to improve controls
D. The auditor's fee

5. There may be times where an audit report should not have a formal rating.

A. True
B. Fale

6. Which one of the following is the product of the likelihood of a threat occurring and the impact the threat could have?

A. Occurrence
B. Risk
C. Vulnerability
D. Likelihood of impact

7. Which one of the following is *not* a privacy principle as identified by GAPP?

A. Secrecy
B. Choice and consent
C. Collection
D. Use and retention
E. Disclosure to third parties

8. Which of the following best describes a business that is found to have unlicensed software installed throughout the environment?

A. They have violated export restrictions on cryptographic software.
B. They are not adequately protecting personal information.
C. They have violated intellectual property rights.
D. Answers B and C

9. Which of the following best describes when compliance of a control cannot be determined due to a lack of collected evidence?

A. Not determined
B. Not applicable
C. Compliant
D. Answers A and B

10. The final audit report includes recommended actions, which should be associated with which of the following?

A. Findings
B. Vulnerabilities
C. Threats
D. None of the above

11. Which section of a simplified audit report will include a quick overview of the conclusion an auditor makes?

A. Executive summary
B. Background
C. Findings and issues

12. In the background section of the audit report, what part will help the reader understand the business or process being assessed?

   A. Scope
   B. Scope exclusions
   C. Time period
   D. Control environment

13. Not all observations elevate to audit findings in the report if the organization is notified by alternative means.

   A. True
   B. False

14. Since an audit report is an opinion on the health of the control environment, an audit report rating and opinion are the exact same thing.

   A. True
   B. False

15. Which of these key components of a security risk assessment provides details about the infrastructure systems, including the hardware, software, data, interfaces, and associated users?

   A. Approach
   B. System characterization
   C. Assessment results
   D. Summary

Compliance Within the User Domain

T HE MORE USERS ON a system, the more valuable the services become. This telecommunication concept is called Metcalfe's law. If there were only two telephones on the system, the value of the network would be very limited. At any given time only two people could talk. But add millions of phones, and suddenly the value of the system increases exponentially. This exponential factor is also true when it comes to information security risks. As the number of people accessing your network increases so does the number of risks. As the population of users on your network rises so does the need to access information and the complexity of the security that must be provided. Inevitably, this complexity of information security controls leads to gaps in the protection of the information through the intentional and unintentional actions of users.

Effective audits can identify these gaps and noncompliance controls. In this chapter, we will examine different types and elements to be included in a User Domain audit. We will discuss user access needs and how those needs lead to risks that must be controlled and audited.

Chapter 8 Topics

This chapter covers the following topics and concepts:

- How User Domains relate to business drivers
- Which items are commonly found in the User Domain
- What separation of duties means
- What least privilege is
- What need to know is
- What confidentiality agreements are

- What employee background checks are
- How acknowledgment of responsibilities and accountabilities relate to compliance
- How security awareness and training for new employees relate to compliance
- What information systems security accountability is
- Organization's right to monitor user actions and traffic
- What best practices for User Domain compliance are

Chapter 8 Goals

When you complete this chapter, you will be able to:

- Identify business drivers
- Compare how items found in the User Domain contribute to compliance
- Describe methods of ensuring compliance in the User Domain
- Summarize best practices for User Domain compliance

User Domain Business Drivers

People have an advantage over automated controls in dealing with the unexpected. This is especially true when dealing with changing customer needs. Automated controls can only mitigate risks that have been clearly identified and encoded in their software. Consequently, the User Domain will always have more unpredictable risks that must be addressed.

While people are essential in implementing effective security policies, they are also the weakest link. Unlike automated security controls, people can let their guard down. Automated controls never sleep or take vacations and work relentlessly 24 hours a day. People on the other hand can simply have a bad day, be distracted, and may not have information security at the top of their minds. Another unknown is the skill level between people. Also, people are inconsistent and leave at the end of their shift. Offices may end their standard work week on a Friday. These offices may reopen on Monday, or even Tuesday when Monday is a holiday. These long weekends are a prime time frame for weaknesses in information security to be exploited by an insider.

Three areas of human weakness are a driver of noncompliance and potential security risks: social engineering, human mistakes, and insider threat.

Social Engineering

Social engineering is a term referring to manipulating or "tricking" a person into weakening the security of an organization. Social engineering comes in many forms. One form is simply having a hacker befriend an employee. The more intimate the relationship, the more likely the employee will reveal knowledge that can be used to compromise security. Another successful method is pretending to be from the information technology (IT) department. This is sometimes called "pretexting." The hacker calls an employee and tries to convince the employee to reveal information, such as the employee's ID and password. The hacker might ask the employee to check a website, claiming to be having trouble accessing the site. No information is being asked for. Simply checking if the employee is having the same problem. Unknown to the employee, accessing the website loads malware to take over the employee's machine.

Many different techniques fall under social engineering, but they all rely on tricking the employee into a noncompliant action. A hacker uses social engineering because it is much easier than breaking through automated controls, which can take weeks, months, or years. The results can be uncertain. You may never be able to bypass the automated controls. If you do bypass the controls, you still may not be able to access the information you want. Randomly calling employees and posing as an IT department employee, or customer service needing urgent help, can be accomplished within a few hours. It only takes one individual letting down their guard to be successful.

Human Mistakes

The one characteristic we all share is that we make mistakes. Sometimes in our life, we make an error due to carelessness, a lack of knowledge, or simply an oversight. We may perceive a threat that does not exist. Or miss a real threat that is right in front of us. Several studies indicate that human error and mistakes account for the vast majority of cybersecurity breaches. For example, Kaspersky's IT security economics in 2019 report tells us that "inappropriate IT resource use by employees" is the most common cause of a data breach. The UK Information Commissioner's Office (ICO) study of 2019 security data breaches concluded that 90% were caused by human error.

Carelessness can be as simple as leaving your password on the keyboard with a sticky note or failure to read warning messages that pop-up and still click "Okay." Carelessness can occur because an employee is untrained or does not perceive information security as important. These careless employees are prime targets of hackers who develop malicious code.

Technology often outpaces an employees' skills. It's not uncommon to find an employee feels that just as they acquired a solid understanding of a system or application, it's upgraded or replaced. Too much change in an organization is unsettling at best, and at worst, it can lead to portions of your workforce being inadequately trained. An untrained worker can unknowingly create a security weakness through omission. Failing to log off can leave the system exposed.

Another weakness is that people can be intimidated into weakening security controls. This can happen when a supervisor or an executive asks an employee to take shortcuts or bypass normal control procedures. The employee feels compelled to follow the instructions of individuals in power. The lack of leadership support for security policies is one reason security implementations fail.

Insiders

One significant threat to information security comes from the insider. The term "insider" refers to an employee, consultant, contractor, or vendor. The insider may even be the IT technical people who designed the system, application, or security that is being hacked. The insider knows the organization and may know the countermeasures and the applications. If insiders are from the IT department, they may know what is logged, what is checked and not checked, and may even have access to local accounts shared between administrators. As a result of this knowledge, they have a greater likelihood of bypassing the security controls and hiding their tracks. Hackers can hide their tracks by deleting or altering logs and time stamps.

Employees with a long history with the organization may pose a greater risk. These employees may be in a position of trust. These individuals have a sense of how the organization will respond to incidents and can tailor their attacks accordingly.

The motivation of an insider is not always greed. An individual may feel disgruntled for a variety of reasons, from feeling mistreated to being passed over for some reward or promotion. They may have some disappointment in their life outside work. The insider may simply have a sense of entitlement, "taking" the rewards they feel they have earned.

A Verizon 2021 Data Breach Investigations report suggests that insiders are responsible for around 22% of security incidents.

Anatomy of a User Domain

The User Domain is the part in the IT infrastructure that formalizes how information flows in and out of computer systems. This domain defines components you need to control to ensure your environment is compliant with applicable requirements. **Figure 8-1** shows the User domain in the context of the seven domains in the IT infrastructure.

User Domain controls are designed to help ensure compliance by placing limits on acceptable user actions. A User Domain control is any mechanism that interacts with a

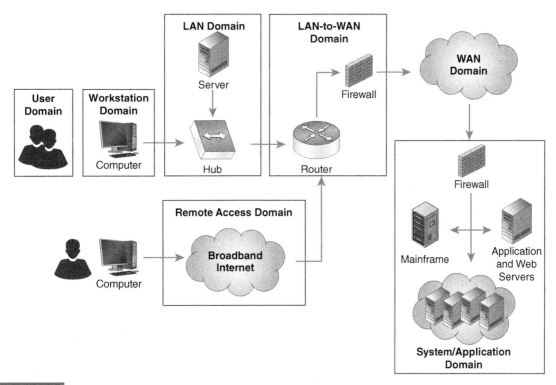

FIGURE 8-1

The User Domain Within the Seven Domains of a Typical IT Infrastructure

user and reacts when a user's actions meet certain conditions. The overall purpose of User Domain controls is to restrict user behavior to approved, or compliant, behavior. The User Domain consists of a variety of types of users. Each user type has unique access needs. As the different types of users in the domain grow so does the security complexity. At a minimum, each type of user has unique business needs and, thus, will require unique rights to access certain information.

By limiting what users can do, compliance-related security controls restrict users to appropriate actions. These restrictions can include limits on what users can access and what actions they can perform. Although limiting users to meet compliance requirements might be desirable or even necessary, it can make it more difficult to complete required business functions. One of the difficulties of ensuring security in the User Domain is designing secure controls that still allow and promote necessary business functions.

It is important that you implement compliance requirements in a way that minimizes the impact on **business drivers**. Business drivers are the components, including people, information, and conditions, that support business objectives. Any negative impact on business drivers can also have a negative impact on your organization's ability to satisfy business objectives. Carefully research the impact on business drivers before you implement any compliance controls.

Compliance requirements dictate how your organization conducts its activities. Whether the compliance requirement comes from legislation, regulation, industry requirements, or even your organization's standards, the result is focus. In most cases, your organization can control activities to ensure compliance in multiple ways. Always consider alternative controls to achieve the result that compliance requires. You will find that some controls are less costly and less intrusive than others. Do not just accept the first control that does the job. Often, other controls are just as good but intrude less on your organization's activities.

You can meet many compliance requirements using one of several controls. If one control has a negative impact on business drivers, consider another control. You can often justify eliminating one control if another control will achieve the same goal (see **Figure 8-2**).

FIGURE 8-2
Alternative Controls

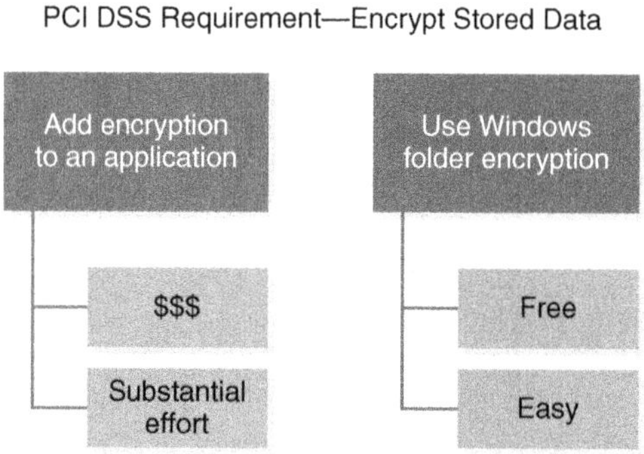

PCI DSS Requirement—Encrypt Stored Data

Protecting Data Privacy

Most organizations are composed of many different departments and lines of business. An employee may be full time or part time. An employee may be in a customer-facing role or a back-office corporate function. Regardless of their job in the organization, they will have access to information that needs to be protected.

Each of these users must understand their role and the proper handling of sensitive and private information. Knowing who is accessing the organization's information and ensuring these individuals are well educated is essential to the success of implementing security policies. These core requirements, employee authentication, and education must be outlined in security policies. Employee access must be managed throughout the life of an employee's career with the organization. There is always pressure to grant and extend user access so a user can be as productive as possible. There is little tolerance by some executives to wait weeks for access to be set up after an employee joins an organization. Often there is a need to extend the user's access in response to changing business needs. While there's significant pressure to grant employees new access rights, the same pressure may not exist to remove access.

An audit should verify that these pressures do not result in shortcuts that could put customers and sensitive data at risk. For example, Health Insurance Portability and

Accountability Act (HIPAA) regulation requires all users to be properly trained on how to handle health information. Making sure records reflect the user received training prior to being granted access is one method to assess the effectiveness of this control.

Implementing Proper Security Controls for the User Domain

It takes careful planning in any domain to develop multiple layers of proper security controls. Control layers should complement other layers and work together to avoid exposing a single point of failure. In the User Domain, an **acceptable use policy (AUP)** for each type of user serves as a training guide and direction document for other controls. Simply put, the AUP is a statement of which actions are acceptable and which ones are not.

The AUP is not the only security control for the User Domain, but it is an important one. Solid User Domain controls help ensure compliance with your organization's security policy. As you design controls, make sure you develop multiple layers to protect each resource. Your goal should be to force an attacker to defeat several controls to compromise a resource. That way, no single control failure exposes a resource to an attack. But before you can design solid controls, you need to explore components commonly found in the User Domain.

Items Commonly Found in the User Domain

The User Domain contains several common items or components. You should consider each component when evaluating activities for compliance. People and documentation are the most common items in the User Domain. Each of these two broad categories includes several smaller types of items with unique characteristics. The following are different types of people in the User Domain:

- **Employees**—This group has the greatest stake in the organization. Most long-term employees feel a greater sense of responsibility toward their employer than shorter term personnel do. Employees generally have more privileges and access to organization resources. Although you can trust most employees, an unethical employee can cause substantial damage because of access to information and knowledge of the organization.

- **Contractors**—Contractors may bring specialized skills to an organization, but they also pose potential risks. Because contractors may have access to sensitive information, you must monitor them and give them only enough access to do their jobs. Contractors may be less loyal to the organization than employees are due to contractors' limited employment. All these reasons present contractors as a greater risk for security violations.

- **Guests/third parties**—Other parties might have no duties related to sensitive information but might still have access to an organization's network. Many organizations commonly provide Internet access to visitors. You should use strict controls to ensure guests do not have access to any sensitive information.

Figure 8-3 illustrates items commonly found in the User Domain.

The User Domain contains more than just people. People who are resources for an organization must have formal directions for how they carry out activities. These activities should support the meeting of business goals. You need a collection of documents that outlines activities that support business activities to determine whether an action is acceptable or unacceptable. The User Domain also needs documented policies to direct the actions of people. The following are distinct types of documentation in the User Domain that affect compliance:

- **Human resources (HR) manuals**—HR acquires and manages an organization's personnel. Personnel management includes security awareness and education. Because many security incidents involve users, it is important to provide written documentation of an organization's policies and procedures. HR manuals provide information on how people within an organization should conduct themselves in any situation.

- **IT asset AUPs**—AUPs provide guidance for personnel on the proper use of resources. They also define what constitutes improper use. An IT asset AUP covers the use of all IT assets, such as computers, wireless access points, networks, and printers.

- **Internet AUPs**—Internet AUPs define proper and improper use of an organization's Internet access.

- **Email AUPs**—Email AUPs define proper and improper use of an organization's email capability.

A solid basis for compliant activity requires a well-organized User Domain with clear roles and expectations. In the following sections, you will learn about important concepts to build a secure environment of compliant behavior.

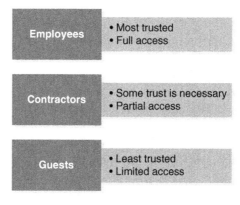

FIGURE 8-3

Common Documentation Items In the User Domain

Employees
- Most trusted
- Full access

Contractors
- Some trust is necessary
- Partial access

Guests
- Least trusted
- Limited access

Separation of Duties

A common theme in compliance requirements is to reduce the ability of any one element to compromise data security. In the User Domain, this means that no single person should have the ability to bypass security controls that protect data. Each computer user's role should limit the scope of permitted actions.

Most computer systems restrict access to deny unauthorized users. The first step in gaining access to data is to identify yourself to the information system and authenticate your identity. This process commonly involves providing a user ID and a password. Once you are identified and authenticated, the operating system grants authority in the form of permissions and rights. These permissions and rights are defined by your assigned roles. You can only accomplish what your assigned roles allow.

The concept of **separation of duties** requires that users from at least two distinct roles be required to accomplish any business-critical task. This means that users from at least two roles must collude to compromise data security. Although collusion is still possible, it is far less likely than if a single user could gain exclusive access to sensitive data without anyone else looking. Going further, separation of duties helps avoid conflicts of interest. For example, the role of administering a system should not be the same role that audits that system for potential compliance violations. **Table 8-1** contains some examples of separation of duties in IT environments. **Figure 8-4** illustrates separation of duties in an IT environment.

TABLE 8-1 Examples of separation of duties in an IT environment.

ROLE RESTRICTION	DESCRIPTION
Only grant limited access for external personnel to the computer and files they need for the current project.	External personnel can help complete projects but should have limited access to resources. This restriction helps reduce the number of people who have access to each part of a system and reduces the opportunities for data compromise.
Prohibit all access to production environments for developers.	Developers have the ability to write programs that access sensitive data and should not have the ability to bypass configuration-management controls. Configuration-management controls require a separate role to promote software from development to production.
Do not allow general administrative users to create backups of critical data.	It is easy to create backups on media that fit in a pocket. Create a role for backup operators and only allow a small number of individuals to create backups.

FIGURE 8-4

Separation of Duties

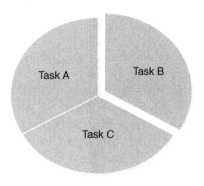

• Separate critical business processes into units of work
• A different person performs each unit of work

The problem is that excessive access rights represent a serious security risk. As an individual changes role, that person's access rights must be adjusted. Prior access rights that are no longer needed must be removed. New access rights must be properly approved and granted. This change is for the employee's protection as much as it is for the organization. When a security incident occurs, one of the first steps is to identify who may have had access. This is accomplished by reviewing individuals' access rights. Employees can avoid suspicion when they have no access to affected systems, applications, and information. Removing unneeded access also reduces security vulnerabilities. In the event an employee's ID and password are compromised, hacked access rights would be contained within the employee's current role. Consider the following example:

> In a bank, a teller may be able to initiate the process of sending money between banks from one account to another. This is an important service needed to provide commercial customers. Before the money is sent, however, the bank manager must approve the transfer. This dual control creates a separation of duties to reduce fraud. If the manager was once a teller and retained access to transfer rights, then there is a serious security risk. The employee in this scenario could start and approve the transfer of money.

technical TIP

You can define User Domain roles at the operating system level to limit what users can and cannot do. One method of access control uses operating system groups to define access permissions for objects, such as files, folders, and printers.

Least Privilege

The first step in implementing separation of duties is to remove unnecessary user privileges. Any unnecessary privilege provides an opportunity for a user to violate the AUP and perform unauthorized data access. It makes sense to use access controls to prevent unauthorized data access. The process of allowing only the level of access your users require might be tedious, but it is necessary to secure sensitive data.

The ultimate goal is to define access control where each user has the permissions to carry out assigned tasks and nothing else. This is the principle of least privilege. User permissions beyond what is required to carry out necessary tasks are excessive and potentially unsecure.

Security policies must make clear that individuals must only have the security rights appropriate for their job. The security policies also outline the required processes needed to ensure that when new rights are assigned, the leader approving the new access understands the risks involved. Removing prior access that is no longer needed accomplishes the following:

- Reduces the overall security risk to the organization
- Maintains segregation of duties
- Simplifies investigation of incidents

Putting least privilege into practice can be challenging. Organizations with many users often use roles, or groups, to define access permissions. Administrators define roles that represent small tasks, such as "accounts receivable user" and "accounts receivable manager," and grant specific permissions to each role. Individual user accounts can belong to one or more roles and inherit the permissions from each of the role definitions.

> **⚠ WARNING**
>
> Do not confuse least privilege with need to know. Need to know is a concept and is not a term used in context to access rights. Need to know refers to understanding what an employee needs to know to perform their job function or job role. While similar, least privilege is granting the minimal level of access to perform a task. For example, assume you have a catalog of prices for your sales force that contains both consumer and commercial pricing. Under least privilege, you may want to limit access to these prices only to the sales department. However, further limiting access by salesperson depending on their customer may not make sense even though an individual salesperson may not have a need to know the pricing for every product.

System Administrators

Applying least privilege to system administrators can be challenging. System administrators often need unlimited rights on specific systems. They are employees, and as such, the same concerns and issues for employees will apply to system administrators. By the nature of their roles, they will need the highest rights to be able to install, configure, and repair systems, such as operating systems and databases. The access right is often referred to as elevated privileges. With this access come enormous responsibilities to protect the information on those systems and to protect their credentials. A systems administrator's credentials are a prime target for hackers. If they can compromise an administrator's ID and password, for example, they may have unlimited access to install malware.

If, by the nature of the role, access rights are broad, then controlling or limiting access can be a challenge. One mitigating risk is monitoring and logging the system administrator's activity. The system administrator should only be using broad access rights in the performance of specific duties. Let's consider database administrators. They will need access to the database to apply patches, resolve issues, and configure applications. Yet they normally will not need to access customer personal information stored within the database. Logging their activity is a means to verify that they are not abusing their access rights. Logs could record if they granted themselves access beyond the scope of their roles or accessed information that was not part of their duties. While you may not be able to prevent a system administrator from accessing customer information, logs can be used as a detective control. A detective control can only report that a violation may have occurred while a preventative control will both detect and prevent a potential violation

But if system administrators have such broad rights, couldn't they just turn off the logs? Yes, they typically can. However, the act of turning off or altering logs can be detected. Many systems write an entry when the log service is started and stopped. Additionally, logs can be sent to a log server. A log server is a separate platform used to collect logs from platforms throughout the network. Access to these log servers can be further restricted. Analyzing logs can help you detect gaps in logs, which are an indication the log service was turned off. Analyzing logs can also help detect if they have been altered. Knowing that their activity is being monitored can be a deterrent to system administrators.

There's also a widely accepted approach that states system administrators' access rights should be limited to their daily tasks, such as monitoring. This approach would elevate systems administrator rights through a separate process when they need to install, configure, upgrade, or resolve an issue on the system. The approach assumes that tasks associated with the elevated rights occur so infrequently that the additional process is not burdensome. Some system administrators resist this approach. Having unfettered access does make their job easier. This approach to elevate system administrator rights through a separate process has become a leading practice in a number of highly regulatory industries. The financial services industry, for example, has widely accepted this approach. Adopting this approach over granting elevated rights to their normal credentials has some key advantages:

1. It reduces the overall security risk to the organization. In the event the system administrator's credentials are compromised, access would be limited.

2. It dramatically reduces the volume of logs to review to detect if administrators abuse their access rights.

3. It improves the alignment and understanding between technical tasks and business requirements.

Typically, this approach records the business reason for the elevated rights being granted. This answers the question as to "why" the security administrator would be accessing certain files. This information can also be used to identify patterns of control weaknesses.

   The process for capturing business requirements and elevating privilege is well established. The process of granting elevated rights to correct a critical failure is often called a "firecall-ID" or "break glass" process. A firecall-ID process provides emergency access to unprivileged users. The name implies the urgency behind granting access to resolve the problem quickly. During a firecall-ID process, the issue or problem would be defined in what's called a trouble ticket. The trouble ticket would then be assigned to someone to fix the problem along with the elevated permissions needed. The individual then completes the work and closes the ticket. When the ticket closes, access is removed.

Confidentiality Agreements

Employees who work with sensitive information can be both a great asset and a great risk. A person who understands the inner workings of your organization can protect sensitive information or defeat your security controls. Someone who knows your organization could make violations difficult to detect. Contractors who have access to sensitive information can be just as dangerous. How should your organization protect sensitive information from insiders? The answer is to implement a defense-in-depth strategy. Solid access controls and the principle of least privilege are both important, but neither is enough.

   Some information leaks occur because of simple ignorance or carelessness. If workers don't know that information is sensitive, they might treat it with less care. When hiring personnel, you should communicate your organization's security policy clearly. The employee or contractor **confidentiality agreement** is a document that accomplishes this. Another name for this document is a **non-disclosure agreement (NDA)**.

   A confidentiality agreement is a legally binding document. By signing this document, each party agrees to keep certain types of information confidential. A confidentiality agreement is a necessary part of any relationship that involves sensitive information.

   Confidentiality agreements allow organizations to disclose sensitive information to a small number of parties without concern that an information leak might cause harm. For example, these agreements allow organizations to share specifications of unreleased products to business partners. Sharing this type of information allows business partners to develop companion products before the release of original products. Most major software vendors, such as Microsoft and Apple, do this to allow their development partners to write software for new operating systems before the release date. The confidentiality agreement protects the operating system vendor by prohibiting partners from releasing information about the new product.

> **WARNING**
>
> Binding confidentiality agreements should define time frames for the agreement. Confidentiality agreements are not valid forever. A good agreement specifies a date range within which parties must make disclosures and a date range within which disclosure restrictions are in force. A lack of either period could invalidate the agreement.

Another important feature of a confidentiality agreement is that it can protect patent rights. Publicly disclosing an invention can result in forfeiting any patent rights. An organization must keep information about the invention confidential until filing a patent application. Confidentiality agreements with anyone who has access to confidential information can protect your organization from a damaging public disclosure.

A confidentiality agreement defines the types of information parties can and cannot disclose. A confidentiality agreement also specifies how parties may use confidential information. The agreement defines expected behavior and the consequences of violating the agreement. A well-written confidentiality agreement lowers the risk of disclosing confidential information.

Employee Background Checks

Many organizations perform a **background check** on prospective employees before hiring them. The purpose of a background check is to uncover any evidence of past behavior that might indicate a prospect is a security risk. In reality, all personnel are security risks because they must be trusted with sensitive information. A background check can uncover information that indicates a person might be an undue security risk.

Background checks can vary in depth. For example, a background check might simply verify a Social Security number as authentic and belonging to the applicant. Or a background check might involve conducting a police criminal check and reviewing a prospective employee's complete history. Each organization sets the scope of background checks. The job description and the organization's desire to use a prospect's history to predict future actions affect the scope of the investigation. You can conduct background checks using internal resources or by engaging external specialists. External resources can reduce your ongoing expense and may provide higher-quality information due to the use of specialists. However, external resources who conduct background checks operate under additional restrictions.

 TIP

Background checks are typically performed at time of hire. Many organizations only perform background checks once. Depending on the user's role, a more frequent background check may be warranted, such as in the case of system administrators.

Although background checks are important and might provide interesting insight into a person's background, you must perform them with care. The **Fair Credit Reporting Act (FCRA)** requires that you obtain permission from the subject of a background check before you begin the investigation. In addition, if you decide not to extend an offer due to information contained in the background check report, you must provide the reason and the contact information for the investigating organization. You must also give the prospect the opportunity to dispute any negative information in the report. This safeguard helps prevent incorrect information from harming an unsuspecting individual.

Background checks can reveal quite a lot about a prospective employee. A prospect with prior criminal history might not be a suitable candidate for a role that allows access to very sensitive information. Knowing the background of prospective employees is a crucial step in granting authorization to sensitive information. Although a background check won't catch every potential attacker, it can help identify some of the high-risk candidates.

Acknowledgment of Responsibilities and Accountabilities

Auditing is the process of examining systems to verify they are in compliance with defined policies. In short, auditing ensures that activities comply with policy. This process provides value only when it objectively reviews evidence of actions. An auditor who overlooks any evidence of noncompliance isn't effective. Because of the potential of negative findings, it is important that all parties engaged in auditing activities understand their responsibilities to the audit process.

Do not view auditing simply as a search for problems. Auditing is an opportunity to identify noncompliance issues before they escalate and possibly cause damage. This positive attitude toward auditing must start with upper management, who should share it with all affected parties. If upper management does not fully support the efforts of auditors, it is unlikely anyone else will.

Upper management can influence the quality of the audit process by assigning responsibilities and accountabilities. Every employee bears some responsibility in the IT security audit process. Every agent of your organization must maintain the security of your information. Because the IT security auditing process verifies compliance with security policies, all employees bear responsibility for carrying out your policies.

Each task in the audit process has one or more people who are responsible or accountable for that task. Many organizations use a **RACI matrix** to document tasks and personnel responsible for the assignments. RACI stands for responsible, accountable, consulted, and informed. To create a RACI matrix, do the following:

> 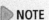 **NOTE**
>
> Repetitive auditing and taking action on the results of audits are proactive forms of continuous improvement. The general idea is that constantly adhering to policies results in higher quality output, not just fewer violations.

1. List tasks along one axis and personnel or roles along the other axis.
2. Assign a level or responsibility for each role and task.
3. Assign each person or role a level of responsibility and accountability for each task.

The entries in the matrix will contain one of the following:

- **R (Responsible)**—This is the person who actually performs the work to accomplish the task. It may be multiple people.
- **A (Accountable)**—This is the person who is accountable for the proper completion of the task. Only one person is accountable for each task. The Accountable is likely the Responsible's manager.
- **C (Consulted)**—This is the person who provides input that is helpful in completing a task. It may be multiple people.

TASK/ROLE	MANAGEMENT	PROJECT MANAGER	AUDITOR	USER
TABLE 8-2 Simple RACI matrix for an IT audit.				
Develop audit plan	A	R	C	I
Develop audit activities schedule	A	R	C	I
Conduct audit activities		A	R	C
Review audit results	A/R	R	R	C
Identify noncompliant elements	A	I	R	C
Develop plan to address noncompliant elements	A	R	C	I
Develop noncompliant mitigation activities schedule	A	R	C	C
Conduct noncompliant mitigation activities		A	R	R

- **I (Informed)**—This is the person who desires to be kept up to date on a task's progress. This may be multiple people.

Table 8-2 shows a simple RACI matrix for an IT audit.

The RACI matrix clarifies the responsibilities and accountabilities for a set of tasks. A RACI matrix provides upper management with a tool that communicates and conveys tasks. Without the acceptance of audit responsibilities and accountabilities, the auditing process might encounter resistance. Management and other employees might view the audit process as punitive.

Security Awareness and Training for New Employees

Security awareness is not just a good idea—it's the law! Many regulations require security policies and a security awareness program. Having a security awareness program is considered a must in most industries. Not having a well-defined security awareness program opens an organization to a number of legal liabilities and regulatory penalties. The following list highlights a few examples of regulations requiring a security awareness program:

- Federal Information System Security Managers' Act
- Health Insurance Portability and Accountability Act
- Gramm-Leach-Bliley Act and Sarbanes-Oxley Act

- Sarbanes-Oxley Act
- The Federal Information System Security Managers' Act (FISMA)
- NIST SP 800-53, Recommended Security Controls for Federal Information Systems
- The NIST Computer Security Handbook

This is just a sampling of federal laws that require a formal security awareness program. Many laws at the state level also require security awareness, such as most state privacy laws. These laws will outline the frequency and target audience of the training.

One of the key objectives of a security awareness program is to promote a risk-aware culture. This means keeping information security at top of employees' minds in their daily job. You want people to automatically and intuitively react to situations in a way that reflects the security policies' core principles. A security-aware culture is all about people acting in accordance with the organization's beliefs and priorities.

Communication of security policy through a security awareness program is vital. Even the best policy is of little use if no one is aware of it. Security awareness tries to change behavior. Security awareness consists of a series of campaigns aimed at improving understanding of security policies and of risks to the organization. Security awareness is not a one-time event. It's a campaign that strives to keep reinforcing the message in different ways. The message must be consistent in the manner in which it is delivered and commensurate with the level of expertise of the target audience.

Information Systems Security Accountability

Information security is everyone's responsibility. Most individuals want to do a good job if they know what the rules are. It's also difficult to hold individuals accountable if they have not been instructed as to what is and is not acceptable. That is the core reason behind a security awareness program. The basic benefits of a security awareness program are to inform workers of the following:

- Basic principles of information security
- Raise awareness of risk and threats
- Prepare them to deal with unexpected risks
- How to report suspicious activity, incidents, and breaches
- Help build a culture that is security and risk-aware

Incorporating Accountability into Annual Employee Performance Reviews

It is everyone's responsibility to adhere to security policies. This is accomplished by the collective action of many leaders. The enforcement starts with executive support. This support goes beyond receiving permission to implement security policies. Executive support also means personal commitment by the managers to use their position and skills to influence the direction of their teams.

Executive support is key to security policy enforcement. At some point in the enforcement process, you need to change workers' behaviors. This can require disciplinary action. Even taking workers aside and coaching them runs the risk of negatively impacting a department. It is important that you lay the foundation for such discussions in advance. Incorporating accountability for adherence to security policies is one method. You accomplish this through the executive of the department. This executive can send a clear message that there's zero tolerance for ignoring security policies. The executive must be clear that violations of policies will be taken seriously and noted in an individual's annual performance. This type of message establishes a tone at the top.

It's important to remember that the employees look to executive management for direction. The executive leaders are expected to lead by example. This means they follow the same policies as employees. The act of exempting themselves devalues the policy's importance. Executive management needs to take an active interest in key performance indicators and show continued support. They should be visible in approving a deviation from policies only when absolutely necessary.

Noncompliance with policies and any improper handling of data should be reflected in annual performance reviews. The performance review sends a powerful message about the importance of security policies, risk management, and the risk culture within the organization.

Organization's Right to Monitor User Actions and Traffic

The prevailing legal view is that employers have the right to monitor workers' activities on company computers. This right is not absolute. In other words, it's important that an organization acts in accordance with its policies and the law. The policies must be clear and concise. The COVID-19 pandemic in 2020 forced many users to work from home, using personal networks and potentially personal equipment. The interpretation of what can and cannot be monitored becomes blurred.

The controls in place to monitor user activity remotely from home networks and equipment should be reviewed by the organization's legal department annually. The laws on privacy and expectations on employees continue to evolve. Policies and related controls allowing such capability should be updated potentially more frequently than other policies. Having such updated policies reduces employees' argument that they perceived a right to privacy. It is always best that organizations put in writing their intent to monitor workers' activities when accessing company data regardless of the end-user device.

There are a number of good reasons to monitor workers' computer activities:

- Maintaining a productive workforce
- Detecting when security policies are not being followed
- Maintaining the security of sensitive data
- As a general deterrent of noncompliant behavior

When the lines between a worker's personal and professional life blur, the court rulings can become less clear. Some organizations, for example, allow personal smartphones to be used to send and receive company emails. Even when these devices have the same encryptions and other controls, it blurs the legal lines between work and personal life. Although this is done to reduce costs, it can quickly create legal entanglements.

There is little dispute that organizations can monitor employer-owned computers used during work hours through company accounts. There are typically three areas of monitoring employee actions that should be in the scope of an audit:

- Internet
- Email
- Computers.

The legal department needs to check state regulations. Certain states have specific regulations regarding employee monitoring. For example, Maryland, Illinois, and California require user consent. A few states like Connecticut and Delaware require the user to be given notice before the monitoring begins.

Being transparent about the monitoring and the reasoning behind the decision is important. Morale and productivity could be harmed if employees feel less trusted and micromanaged. The reality employers need to keep in mind is that the lines between work and personal life are often blurred. Leadership must have honest and open conversations with users on expected behavior. Finally, this expected behavior is in policy and part of the user's training.

Best Practices for User Domain Compliance

The best practice is a leading technique, methodology, or technology that through experience has proved to be very reliable. Best practices tend to produce consistent and quality results. The following brief list of best practices is focused on the user and should be considered in the audit scope. These best practices go a long way to protecting users and the organization. These basic best practices are as follows:

- **Attachments**—Never open an attachment from a source that is not trusted or known.
- **Encryption**—Always encrypt sensitive data that leaves the confines of a secure server. That means encrypting devices like laptops and backup tapes. It also means encrypting sensitive data in transit such as email remote access.
- **Layered defense**—This approach establishes overlapping layers of security as the best way to mitigate threats.
- **Least privilege**—The principle of least privilege is a concept that says that individuals should only have the access necessary to perform their responsibilities.
- **Patch management**—Be sure all network devices, including user desktops and laptops, have the latest security patches.
- **Unique identity**—All users accessing information must use unique credentials that identify who they are. The only exception is accessed by the public to an organization's publicly facing website.
- **Virus protection**—Virus and malware prevention must be installed on everyone's desktop and laptop.
- **Firecall-IDs**—Limit administrator and elevated privileges until needed.

The patch management is an essential part of a layered defense. Even when you do everything right, there may be a vulnerability in the operating system. An effective patch management program will mitigate many of these risks.

CHAPTER SUMMARY

The User Domain defines information system users and the actions they carry out. A critical factor of maintaining secure systems is ensuring users' compliance with policies and the organization's security goals. Because user actions result in handling private and sensitive information, it is necessary to control and monitor user actions. Systems must uniquely identify users and allow access only to information for which they are authorized. Auditing activities should examine all access decisions and the rules that govern such decisions for compliance. Defining limits within the User Domain and validating user activities provide important control.

In this chapter, we discuss limits that should be placed on the user. We discussed User Domain elements that should be considered in scope for an audit and the importance of training users and holding individuals accountable.

KEY CONCEPTS AND TERMS

Acceptable use policy (AUP)	Confidentiality agreement	RACI matrix
Background check	Fair Credit Reporting Act (FCRA)	Separation of duties
Business drivers	Non-disclosure agreement (NDA)	

CHAPTER 8 ASSESSMENT

1. Which type of control only reports that a violation has occurred?

   A. Preventive
   B. Detective
   C. Corrective
   D. Restorative

2. The term _____ defines the components, including people, information, and conditions, that support business objectives.

3. Which of the following types of policies defines prohibited actions?

   A. Access control policy
   B. Password usage policy
   C. Acceptable use policy
   D. Violation action policy

4. Which of the following terms ensures at least two people must perform a series of actions to complete a task?

   A. Separation of duties
   B. Least privilege
   C. Need to know
   D. User clearance

5. When using DAC, a subject must possess sufficient clearance as well as _____ to access an object.

6. Which of the following terms defines a strategy in which you grant access that allows a user to complete assigned tasks and nothing else?

   A. Separation of duties
   B. Least privilege
   C. Need to know
   D. User clearance

7. Which type of agreement can protect the ability to file a patent application?

A. Relinquish ownership agreement
B. Security clearance waiver
C. Background check agreement
D. Confidentiality agreement

8. What condition must exist for a background check to be governed by FCRA?

A. The investigation includes credit history.
B. The investigation is performed by a third party.
C. The investigation is performed by the prospective employer.
D. The investigation includes criminal history.

9. Which of the following best describes the purpose of auditing?

A. It finds the root causes of violation issues.
B. It assists investigators in identifying blame for violations.
C. It verifies that systems are operating in compliance.
D. It searches for hidden unacceptable use of IT resources.

10. Using a RACI matrix, which attribute refers to the party that actually carries out the work?

A. Responsible
B. Accountable
C. Consulted
D. Informed

11. Which department should take the lead in User Domain compliance accountability?

A. Information technology
B. Information security
C. Human resources
D. Security

12. A confidentiality agreement sets the expectations of each employee and sets job performance standards.

A. True
B. False

13. Which of the following is a series of individual tasks that users accomplish to comply with one or more goals?

A. Policy
B. Standard
C. Procedure
D. Guideline

14. Which of the following is a collection of requirements the users must meet?

A. Policy
B. Standard
C. Procedure
D. Guideline

15. Discretionary access control is based on roles and granted permissions.

A. True
B. False

16. Removing prior access that is no longer needed as a security policy will achieve what?

A. Reduces the overall security risk to the organization
B. Maintains segregation of duties
C. Simplifies investigation of incidents
D. All of the above

17. What type of security risk relies on human weakness to trick an employee into an act of noncompliance without their knowledge?

A. Social engineering
B. Human mistake
C. Insider threat

18. The goal of a security awareness program is to hold an individual accountable if they have not been instructed as to what is and is not acceptable with information security.

A. True
B. False

19. What type of documentation in the User Domain provides guidance for personnel on the proper use of resources?

A. IT asset AUPs
B. Internet AUPs
C. Email AUPs

20. One significant threat to information security comes from the, _____ , which refers to an employee, consultant, contractor, or vendor who knows the organization, may know the countermeasures and the applications.

Compliance Within the Workstation Domain

LOCKING YOUR FRONT DOOR but leaving your window open does not offer very good security. Let us assume you have good authentication and security on your network. You know who is signed into your network. If the workstation was breached, malicious software on the workstation can be used to access and extract sensitive and confidential data from the network. From the network's view, the user and workstation can look legitimate. This increases the importance of ensuring the workstation is compliant with policies and has appropriate security controls in place.

Examining risk from an infrastructure view means following data through the end-to-end environment. As we move through the technology infrastructure, we find similar risks and need to secure each point along the data flow. The Workstation Domain refers to any computing device used by end users. Most times when someone uses the term "workstation," they are talking about desktop or laptop computers. But it can be any end-user device that accesses information. For discussion purposes within this chapter when we use the term "workstation" we are referring to an end user's desktop or laptop computer.

An end user typically authenticates in the User Domain to access data and services on the workstation. Once you know who they are, then the end user is authorized by the workstation itself. Each workstation has an identity much like an end user. Not only can you restrict what data and services a user can access but can also restrict specific workstations.

This chapter will explore considerations in auditing workstations and common controls found in the workstation domain.

Chapter 9 Topics

This chapter covers the following topics and concepts:

- How compliance law requirements relate to business drivers
- Which devices and components are commonly found in the Workstation Domain
- The benefits of a central management system
- Importance of patch management
- How to maximize C-I-A
- How to manage workstation vulnerability
- How to ensure adherence to documented information technology (IT) security policies, standards, procedures, and guidelines
- What best practices for Workstation Domain compliance are

Chapter 9 Goals

When you complete this chapter, you will be able to:

- Identify compliance law requirements and business drivers
- Compare how devices and components found in the Workstation Domain contribute to compliance
- Explain the difference between a standard account and administrator account
- Describe methods of ensuring compliance in the Workstation Domain
- Summarize best practices for Workstation Domain compliance
- Explain the benefits of encrypting the hard drive of a laptop

Compliance Law Requirements and Business Drivers

Users typically access information from workstations. This is not always the case, especially as organizations are increasingly using mobile devices such as smartphones and tablets. But workstations are still the most common way for corporate users to view and modify your organization's information. Because workstations provide access to information, they become an attack vector for unauthorized users. It is important that you ensure all items in the Workstation Domain are compliant. **Figure 9-1** shows the Workstation Domain in the context of the seven domains in the IT infrastructure.

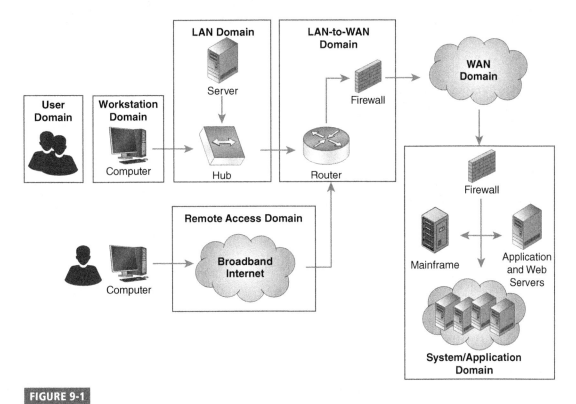

FIGURE 9-1

The Workstation Domain Within the Seven Domains of a Typical IT Infrastructure

The Workstation Domain defines the controls within the workstation itself, such as limiting who can install software on the workstation. It's not uncommon that workstations are shared by multiple end users. Workstation settings must be stable, and one end user cannot impact another. To achieve this, the end user often has limited rights on a workstation. Meaning, they can typically access the software that has been installed, have some rights to configure the software to their needs, but do not have unlimited rights to make any change that could impact another user. This also ensures that an end user does not inadvertently infect the workstation with a virus or malware. For example, in Microsoft Windows operating systems, two common accounts are encountered: **standard user account** and **administrator account**.

As the name implies, the standard user account allows the user to use installed software such as office applications like MS Excel and MS PowerPoint, web browsers, and email. A standard user is not allowed to install new software, or create, edit, or delete system files. System files are those files that are needed to keep the operating system of the workstation working properly. To make these types of changes, you need privileges that come with an administrator account.

Importance of Policies

Policies are one of the first places an auditor should start when auditing workstations. Policies will define the level of compliance required and the strength of the security controls to be deployed. Policies will often identify who is accountable for deploying workstations and, thus, point the auditor in the direction to obtain the supporting process documentation. It's rare that an organization installs a clean operating system and configures each machine from scratch for each newly purchased computer. Doing so would increase the likelihood of human errors, that could lead to expensive and dangerous as each workstation is potentially applying different levels of security controls.

As applications, technology, and the needs of your organization change over time, it's important to keep these workstation images up to date. This includes at a minimum an annual security review. This will ensure you know how all the systems are configured. If security software and policies are put into place based on how one set of computers is configured, the outlier computers can be more readily identified.

Security policies are good at outlining the rules for protecting the workstation. Let us consider a security policy that states "all data at rest that are stored outside the organization network must be encrypted." Would this typically apply to workstations behind locked doors in the nonpublic offices in the corporate headquarters? Probably not. Those corporate offices would be using the corporate network to connect those desktop computers. How about laptops? Yes! Because laptops are portable and can be used outside the corporate offices, the laptop's hard drive would need to be encrypted. With the increased use of mobile computing, it's common for sensitive data to leave the network. As a result, many companies that handle sensitive information encrypt employee laptop hard drives. That way, in the event the laptop is lost or stolen the sensitive data remain protected.

While not an exhaustive list, the following illustrates common workstation policies:

- Password complexity such as lengthy passwords
- Screen lock after a certain amount of idle time and requiring authentication to get back in
- USB port access restrictions limit the ability to copy company data to an unencrypted thumb drive
- Personal usage outlining many employees use their devices such as browsing nonwork websites
- Loss and theft to make sure employees have a clear process to follow if their work device gets lost or stolen.

Due Diligence

Paying attention to compliance can reduce liability in direct and indirect ways. You can think of it in terms of additional insurance. In the context of information security, the term **due diligence** means the ongoing attention and care an organization places on security and compliance. You can reduce your exposure to third-party liability by investing resources in establishing and maintaining compliance. Demonstrating aggressive compliance activities can reduce the liability potential if security incidents result in damages. In short, being compliant reduces risk and looks good in court.

Protecting Data Privacy

Many recent legislative and regulatory requirements extend the scope of threats to information to include all users. There is no assurance users will be compliant. Organizations need additional layers of controls to protect information because not all threats come from malicious users. Some threats come from simple ignorance. For example, procedural changes might prohibit users from transferring protected files to remote workstations. Properly trained users should not attempt to transfer files to remote workstations, but well-meaning users who are not aware of the new policy might unknowingly violate the policy. The proper way to handle this situation is to do the following:

- Ensure all users receive updated training.
- Place access controls in the Workstation Domain to prohibit inappropriate actions such as encrypting laptop hard drives.

You need both types of controls to secure information from all users.

Increased attention to security increases the need to hold employees accountable for security. Because employees generally have more access to information than other authorized users do, they have greater ability to affect the information's security. A greater ability to affect security means you need a greater scope of controls. The most common concern for information security that is reflected in most recent legislation is protecting information privacy. Although information integrity and availability are important, privacy is a primary concern of many regulations. All information system users are accountable for the privacy of the information they access. This puts a greater amount of responsibility and accountability on users.

A solid security strategy should include several types of controls to ensure user compliance. You've already seen some controls in the User Domain. The Workstation Domain is the domain that contains the devices and components to access information. Controlling activities in the Workstation Domain can provide an effective layer of information security. Workstation Domain controls should validate and support controls

9

Compliance Within the
Workstation Domain

in other domains. Although controls in the User Domain are important, you need additional controls to ensure compliance with your security policy and any additional security requirements. Controls in the Workstation Domain should work with controls in other domains to ensure a high level of overall compliance.

Implementing Proper Security Controls for the Workstation Domain

Computers prepared by major manufacturers come preloaded with software and user accounts with default passwords. It is not unusual to find preloaded software with known security vulnerabilities that have been common targets by hackers. Even seemingly common original equipment manufacturer (OEM) applications, firmware, and hardware drivers can make the new workstation already vulnerable.

Not properly configuring the workstation can be costly. If you have a workstation on which the system has been irreparably damaged by a virus or just an ill-timed power outage, restoring it to its OEM state may not solve the underlining security vulnerability. Especially, if you don't have spare computers properly imaged ready to go, this also means lost hours of productivity for the staff.

Workstation Domain controls are security controls that prohibit, validate, or detect user actions. Users initiate actions in the Workstation Domain that generally involve some stored information. In short, users generally access information using some type of workstation device. It makes sense to place controls at the workstation level to ensure information access is compliant. Proper controls in the Workstation Domain should work with other controls in all domains to enforce compliance without interrupting normal operation.

For example, the Payment Card Industry Data Security Standard (PCI DSS) prohibits merchants from storing the **card verification value (CVV)**. The CVV is a three- or four-digit number that card issuers print on each credit card. The CVV provides additional authentication when rendering payment for online transactions.

 NOTE

Your Workstation Domain controls should not just duplicate User Domain controls but should provide a second level of assurance.

One control to avoid storing the CVV is to remove any user prompts for the CVV. Although that complies with the PCI DSS data requirement, it also disables the merchant's ability to ask for the CVV to authenticate the transaction. You should not implement this control because it interrupts a necessary business function. Look for another control that balances security and business requirements.

Management Systems

Workstation security is often a matter of determining some basic security configuration rules and applying them consistently across your enterprise. Applying such security without disrupting the business is a concern. The days of sending a person to each desk to configure a workstation for most organizations are long past. Security policies can help establish a reliable patch management process that is automated. Security policies can specify the type and frequency of patches that need to be applied. The policies often require such patches to be tested in a lab setting before being applied to workstations. Changes are typically rolled out through management systems across the workstation population.

Workstations are typically managed by a central **management system** that can update software, apply patches, and update configuration as needed. These management systems have evolved and help apply workstation changes in a timely manner. These systems are capable of many functions:

- **Inventory**—Refers to tracking assets such as workstations and what software is installed
- **Patch management**—Refers to applying patches to workstation operating system and software
- **Help desk**—Refers to allowing help desk technical personnel to remotely access the workstation
- **Log**—Refers to capturing workstation logs for forensic and support purposes
- **Security**—Refers to ensuring security configurations are appropriately maintained

Devices and Components Commonly Found in the Workstation Domain

The Workstation Domain connects users to local resources. Remote users are covered in the Remote Access Domain. The Workstation Domain includes all local resources that support user functionality and allow users to interact with your information system. In some cases, Workstation Domain items collect and present information as well as process that information. In other cases, processing occurs in another domain. In either case, users use the Workstation Domain to interact with the rest of your environment, including your data. Each type of device or component in the Workstation Domain presents potential vulnerabilities and security challenges. It is important that you carefully consider each type of component when you design Workstation Domain controls. **Figure 9-2** shows the most common devices and components you'll find in the Workstation Domain.

Uninterruptible Power Supplies

An **uninterruptible power supply (UPS)** provides continuous usable power to one or more devices. The primary purpose of a UPS is an integrated battery that provides power to connected devices when the AC power fails. When the AC power fails or even falls below usable voltage, the UPS automatically switches to its battery to provide uninterrupted power to any devices connected to the UPS. This feature allows the connected devices to continue operating normally during power outages. Because the backup power depends on the UPS battery, the duration of the power is limited—generally around 30 minutes.

FIGURE 9-2

Devices and Components in the Workstation Domain

 NOTE

High-quality power strips often provide surge protection and are highly recommended for laptops.

Laptops typically do not need an external UPS given they can operate on an internal battery. Most UPS appliances also provide surge protection referred to as conditioned power. Meaning that any voltage surges are removed before providing power to devices. This surge-filtering capability protects connected devices from potential damage from high voltage.

Desktop Computers

Desktop computers have historically been the most common type of Workstation Domain device. That trend is rapidly giving way to laptops and mobile computing. Desktop computers are designed to be stationary and are often physically connected to an organization's network to share information and devices. Because they are commonly connected to other network resources, it is important to carefully control access to these computers.

Most desktop computers have substantial local processing power and are often used to locally create and manage data. Although this ability can reduce the workload on other domain devices, it can also lead to data leakage. Users who are comfortable working with information locally on a desktop computer might not be diligent about backing up the information or perhaps about protecting the information.

Desktop computers have grown in power and storage capacity in recent years to the degree that they rival the capabilities of some server computers. This increase in power encourages users to install more and more software on their desktop computers. Allowing unsupervised software installations can lead to desktop computers that are difficult to support or even dangerous to your organization. Many computer problems relate to conflicts among programs that are competing for resources. Allowing users to install unapproved programs increases the likelihood of conflicts with approved programs.

Desktop Computers and Privacy

Many users think of their desk environment and desktop computers as private areas. When conducting security assessments, it is a common practice to examine desktop environments for confidential information. Far too many users write their passwords on sticky notes and place them on or around the computer monitor. Another favorite place to "hide" passwords is under the keyboard. This common practice punctuates two warnings:

- Don't make compliance with your password policy so difficult that users have to write down their passwords.
- Pay attention to physical controls that keep unauthorized people away from authorized users' desks.

A lack of desktop computer control also increases the likelihood that users will unknowingly install malicious software. A desktop computer with malware is not only a threat to locally stored information but also to all other devices connected to your network. It is important to understand the risks of allowing too much user freedom and implement the appropriate controls to protect your organization.

Laptops/Tablets/Smartphones

Many companies, in an effort to save money, are allowing individuals to use their personal devices for work, such as accessing company email from their smartphone. While this may save money in the short term, it does open new risks to the company. This practice is often referred to as "Bring Your Own Device" (BYOD). If BYOD is permitted, policies must be clear on acceptable practices. There must be a clear distinction between what security controls are required for corporate devices at work versus personal devices for work. For example, Blackberry products include enterprise mobility software products that isolate company applications from personal applications on your mobile phone. Meaning, while you are using the phone for personal use, the phone cannot access any corporate application.

As computers shrink in size and grow in capabilities, several new classes of computers now rival the desktop as the most popular type of workstation. Laptop computers are typically larger, more powerful class of portable computers. Laptop computers can do everything a desktop computer can do while maintaining a small enough profile to be very portable. Most laptop computers fit easily into briefcase-size bags and backpacks.

 NOTE

Applying full disk **encryption** to laptops has emerged as a de facto standard in many industries. For laptops running the Microsoft Window operating system, the "bit locker" function that comes with Windows OS is commonly deployed to achieve hard drive encryption.

Tablet devices and smartphones have gained greater widespread capabilities and use. They are smaller and lighter than laptop computers. Their smaller size and lighter weight means that they have fewer hardware options and limited capabilities. Tablets and smartphones are designed to act as access devices to network devices and do not provide much local storage. Although they lack much local storage space, they still pose risks because of their support for network access.

As with desktop computers, it is important to control access to network resources and the ability to install unauthorized software. In fact, the need to control portable computers is more important than with desktop computers. The portable nature of laptops, tablets, and smartphones means these computers are transported and used at locations physically outside of your organization. In most cases, users connect portable computers to other networks when they are away from your organization's building. Connecting to unprotected networks can be extremely dangerous. Users can pick up infected programs when connected to other networks and then introduce them the next time they connect to your network. Your security policy should include specific standards for using portable computers to connect to your networks.

Local Printers

A local printer is any printer connected directly to a computer. Local printers are not shared by multiple users. Because these printers are not connected to your organization's network, they aren't controlled from a central location. This means local users can print anything they want. Allowing users to access local printers without any controls can lead to several types of issues, including the following:

- **Personal use of the organization's resources**—Users can print any files to local printers. This can include personal information that might violate the acceptable use policy.
- **Disclosure of private information**—Users can print files with little or no control over content. There is always the chance that printed documents could end up in the wrong person's hands.
- **Printer buffer access**—Most printers retain copies of recently printed documents. It is not difficult to get a printer to reprint previously printed documents. It can be difficult to control this behavior on local printers.

Minimize local printer use in your organization. Printers should generally be networked and managed from a central location in another IT domain.

Wireless Access Points

Wireless access points typically encrypt the traffic between the workstation and the network. The authentication of the workstation and encryption of the wireless traffic is an important security control. As stated earlier in the chapter, a workstation can have a unique identity just like the user of the workstation. This workstation identity can be used to restrict workstation access to the network. For example, you could limit the time of day when a workstation is allowed to access the network.

When considering vulnerabilities to the workstation, access control is important. The objective of access control is to make sure only authorized people can gain access to data and services. But that objective in a wireless environment is different from a wired local area network (LAN). Access control is even more important for wireless WLANs (wireless local area networks) than for regular systems and networks because of the ease of accessibility and broadcasting of the data.

Wireless access points can pose serious threats to organizations. At first glance, they do not seem too dangerous, but they can provide damaging backdoor entryways into your network. These devices do have a place in a secure environment but not in the Workstation Domain. Modems provide a connection to another computer or network and belong in another domain where you can control them in a way that protects your network. Wireless access points provide a wireless connection to the network or computer systems.

 WARNING

Dial-up modems provide a connection to another computer or network through a telephone connection. Historically they were used in some data centers for remote hardware support by vendors. Nowadays such remote hardware support is typically connected through an encrypted Internet tunnel. As a general rule, dial-up modems should not be permitted.

Fixed Hard Disk Drives

Virtually all general-purpose computers have at least one internal, fixed hard drive. Computers primarily use fixed hard drives to store the computer's operating system as well as application programs and data. Some leading-edge or special-purpose computers use solid state memory to store programs or information, but most of today's computers use hard disk drives. Disk drives store files that contain data, instructions, or both.

Privacy laws and regulations address both types of file contents. Compliance with different requirements often means restricting how you access certain types of information or how you must store information. For example, under the Health Insurance Portability and Accountability Act (HIPAA), you must protect all private medical information from unauthorized disclosure. That often means using centralized storage with carefully monitored access and storage controls. You implement centralized storage in another IT domain, not in the Workstation Domain. Continuing the example, assume you use your workstation to access private medical information. You decide to copy the information into a document and store it locally on your workstation while you edit the information. The decision to store the information locally potentially just violated HIPAA. The problem is that you have just placed private medical information in an area that unauthorized users can potentially access.

You must carefully control what devices in the Workstation Domain can do. The good news is that you do have some control when Workstation Domain devices reach across domains. Storing information from another domain is only one issue. You also need to control files stored on the hard disk that originate outside your organization's IT infrastructure. Outside programs and files often result from activity while you are connected to another network. In most cases, Internet access provides the inbound path for unwelcome files. Malicious files and software can infect unprotected computers and then spread to other computers and devices in your organization. Controls in the Workstation Domain for disk drive access can help prevent infections and protect the rest of your network.

Removable Storage Devices

One last category in the Workstation Domain includes devices you connect to computers as you need them. You use most of the devices in this category to store files to transport to another computer. These devices include the following:

- Removable hard disk drives
- Universal serial bus (USB) flash drives
- Removable CD-ROM and DVD drives
- Removable tape drives

There are other removable storage devices, but these are the most common. In fact, the most common devices are USB flash drives. These drives are compact, easily available, and can rival internal storage drives in terms of capacity.

Because you can transport removable media easily and connect it to other computers, it is important that you control the files you transfer both to and from any such devices. In general, you should control two types of transfers:

 TIP

Two common workstation controls for removable media would be to not permit access or to encrypt the device. For example, when a user inserts a thumb drive into the workstation, then access to the thumb drive will be denied. Alternatively, anytime data are written to the thumb drive, it is encrypted and can only be read by a company workstation.

- **Information you copy to a removable device to ensure you protect data privacy**—This type of control keeps you from divulging private information.
- **Data you copy from a removable device to block malicious code or data**— This type of control prevents the rest of your environment from introducing malicious code.

Understanding the devices and components in the Workstation Domain is the first step to establishing controls to secure this domain. The next step is to understand data and device access controls. You will learn about Workstation Domain access rights and controls in the next section.

Access Rights and Access Controls in the Workstation Domain

You learned in the previous sections how important it is to implement the correct controls in the Workstation Domain. Proper security controls limit access to objects based on a user's identity. Access control methods may be based on the permissions granted to a user or group, or they may be based on a user's security clearance. Either way, access rights start with knowing which user requests access to an object and what the user's identity permits him or her to do.

Most computers require you to log on before you can access any resources on the computer. Even systems set up to automatically log on are actually logging on to a predefined user account. The first step in logging on is to provide a user ID or username. Providing user credentials or claiming to be a specific user is called **identification**. Simply identifying yourself is not enough. If all you have to do is claim to be a user, anyone can claim to be a system administrator and gain permission to carry out potentially harmful actions. Operating systems require users to follow the identification step with authentication. **Authentication** is the process of providing additional credentials that match the user ID or username. Only the operating system and the real user should know the authentication credentials. The most common authentication credential is the password. Other options include security tokens and biometric characteristics. When you provide the correct user ID and authentication credentials, you are logged on to your user account.

As the operating system logs you on, it looks up security **authorization** information and grants you access permissions based on your identity. (Authorization refers to the access rights allowed.) There are two main approaches for authorizing users to access objects. Both approaches evaluate whether a user, also called a **subject**, has the permission to access some resource, also called an **object**. Access objects can be files, directories, printers, or any resource. There are other methods as well, but two methods are the most common ones you'll encounter.

The first access method uses **access control lists (ACLs)**, which are lists of access **permissions** that define what each user or security group can do to each object. Each object uses ACLs or permissions to define which users can access it. The object's **owner** can grant access permissions to any desired user or group. Because granting access is at the owner's discretion, this type of access control is called discretionary access control (DAC).

The second type of access control is not based on specific permissions but on the user's security clearance and the object's classification. Organizations that use this type of access control assign a specific classification to each object. Security classifications used by the U.S. government, for example, include Top Secret, Secret, Confidential, and Unclassified. Other governments and nongovernmental organizations use slightly different classifications, but most classification schemes are similar. Each user receives a security clearance that corresponds to one of the classifications in use. The operating system grants access to objects based on a user's security clearance and the requested object's classification. For example, a user with a Secret clearance can access Secret, Confidential, and Unclassified objects but cannot access Top Secret objects. Because there is no discretion involved in granting access, this access method is called mandatory access control (MAC).

Authentication Types

There are three main types of authentication credentials—**Type I (what you know)** , **Type II (what you have)**, and **Type III (what you are)**. The credentials are described as follows:

- **Type I authentication (what you know)**—This is information only a valid user knows. The most common examples of Type I authentication are a password or personal identification number (PIN).
- **Type II authentication (what you have)**—This is a physical object that contains identity information, such as a token, card, or other device.
- **Type III authentication (what you are)**—This is a physical characteristic (biometric), such as a fingerprint, handprint, or retina characteristic.

FYI

C-I-A stands for confidentiality, integrity, and availability. The term is also known as A-I-C (availability, integrity, and confidentiality). Some information systems security professionals refer to the tenets as the *C-I-A triad* to avoid confusion with the U.S. Central Intelligence Agency, commonly referred to as the CIA.

Type II authentication is generally stronger than Type I, and Type III is generally stronger than either Type I or Type II. You can make the authentication process even stronger by using more than one type at the same time. Using two types of authentication is called **two-factor authentication** and using more than two types is called **multifactor authentication**. Using more than a single authentication type strengthens the process by making it more difficult to impersonate a valid user.

Regardless of the access control method you use, the end result is the ability to restrict access to objects by user account. Access control methods enable you to define an access control strategy that allows you to define controls to support your security policy.

Maximizing C-I-A

IT auditors commonly look at risks in three aspects: operational risks, asset risks, and financial reporting risks. Operational risks are associated with the operations of the entity, especially regarding its information systems and underlying technologies. Asset risks are associated with the loss or damage to assets. Since data are valuable assets, they are included in that aspect of risk assessment. Financial reporting risks involve risks that could cause errors or fraud in the financial reporting data, especially those of material nature. When looking at these risks through the workstation lens, it is important to consider how the data are kept confidential and data integrity is maintained while the workstation services remain available.

The overall purpose of compliance requirements is to enforce the basic pillars or tenets of security. Although some compliance requirements might seem to be unnecessary, they all should work together to support the **C-I-A** properties of secure systems. As a review, here are the three tenets of information security:

- **Confidentiality**—Assurance that the information cannot be accessed or viewed by unauthorized users
- **Integrity**—Assurance that the information cannot be changed by unauthorized users
- **Availability**—Assurance that the information is available to authorized users in an acceptable time frame when the information is requested

Figure 9-3 shows the C-I-A triad.

Notice that a central theme of the C-I-A properties is the difference between authorized and unauthorized users. The identification, authentication, and authorization process you

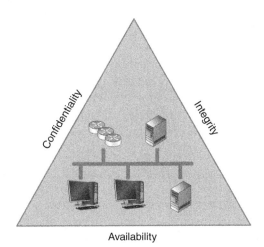

FIGURE 9-3

C-I-A Triad

learned about in the previous section provides the foundation for securing information in any domain. Maximizing the C-I-A properties is all about ensuring authorized users can access trusted data and unauthorized users cannot.

Maximizing Availability

Secure information serves the purpose for which it was created. Secure information must be available when the information is requested. This requirement means that information should be available during normal processing but also during and after unusual events. Unusual events include minor events, such as short-term power outages, up to major disruptions and disasters. Two fundamental areas in the Workstation Domain can affect availability:

- Surviving power outages
- Executing a solid backup and recovery strategy

You should address each area when you create Workstation Domain controls.

Surviving Power Outages

The easiest way to ensure your computers and devices can continue operating in the event of a power outage is by using a UPS. The first step in implementing the right UPS is to list each of the computers and devices you want to protect. Consider any supporting devices you'll need along with computers. For example, if you want to be able to stay online during a power outage, you'll need to ensure you connect any network access devices to the UPS as well. Once you have a list of all devices, add up the power requirements for all devices you'll attach to the UPS. Then search UPS manufacturers for a UPS that will satisfy your service and power requirements. An Internet search is a good place to start.

Backup and Recovery Strategy

A UPS is fine to keep your computers up and running when the power goes out for a few minutes, but what do you do in case of a disaster? What happens to the programs and data on your Workstation Domain computers if a fire in your office destroys the computers? Fire is only one type of disaster your computers might encounter. Information that burns up in a fire or is destroyed in a flood is not available when you need it. Because the information isn't available in this situation, it isn't very secure.

> **technical TIP**
>
> UPS devices come in many price ranges and provide varying levels of service. Lower-cost UPSs simply switch over to a battery when you lose full power. Higher-cost UPSs provide line conditioning and handle brownouts and blackouts in different ways. Higher-priced UPSs also tend to provide backup power for longer periods of time. Don't just shop for price—carefully examine the features on several different UPS models before purchasing one.

You must have a plan to periodically create secondary copies of your important information. This secondary copy is often called a backup. Creating a backup copy of information is important, but it is only one step in a plan to ensure availability. The real key to ensuring availability is to have a plan for restoring your information to the state in which it existed before a disaster. Your backup and recovery strategy should include the following:

- **Backup plan**—This plan creates frequent backup copies of important files. This plan includes identifying the files you need to back up, deciding on which backup utility to use, and setting a schedule for creating backups.
- **Safe media storage plan**—This plan protects your backup copies, including procedures for transporting backup media to a protected location. In most cases, you want to keep copies of your important information in remote locations to keep them safe from disasters that might affect your primary office. Consider keeping backup copies far enough away from your primary office that a disaster won't affect them. For example, a flood or earthquake can affect a large area. You may need to store backup copies far away, even in a different geographic region.
- **Restore plan**—This plan uses the backup media to restore your environment to working order. This is often the plan people overlook. You need backups, but you also need a plan that tells how to use the backups to rebuild a working system.

The most important aspect of ensuring availability is to plan for situations that might disrupt your organization's activities and know what to do in those instances. Plan ahead, and you won't likely be caught not knowing what to do when a disaster strikes.

Maximizing Integrity

The term **malware** refers to a collection of different types of software that share the goal of infiltrating a computer and making it do something. In many cases, malware does something undesired and operates without the explicit consent of the owner. This is not always the case, however. Some types of malware are downloaded and installed with the owner's full knowledge. Malware can be loosely divided into two main categories: programs that spread or infect and programs that hide.

Programs that spread or infect actively attempt to copy themselves to other computers. Their main purpose is to carry out instructions on new targets. Malware of this type includes the following:

- **Virus**—A software program that attaches itself to or copies itself into another program for the purpose of causing the computer to follow instructions that were not intended by the original program developer is called a **virus**.

- **Worm**—A self-contained program that replicates and sends copies of itself to other computers, generally across a network, is called a **worm**.

Other malware hides in the computer to carry out its instructions while avoiding detection. Malware that tends to hide includes the following:

- **Trojan horse**—Software that either hides or masquerades as a useful or benign program is called a **Trojan horse**.

- **Rootkit**—Software that modifies or replaces one or more existing programs to hide the fact that a computer has been compromised is called a **rootkit**.

- **Spyware**—Software that covertly collects information without the user's knowledge or permission is called **spyware**.

Understanding these five basic types of malware and how to protect your systems from them is important to a solid security plan. You install anti-malware software to protect Workstation Domain computers. There are many anti-malware software products from which you can choose. Carefully review suppliers and their products for costs, functionality, and support. The best place to look for specific anti-malware for your operating system is the Internet. Use an Internet search engine to search for "anti-virus software" and "anti-spyware software."

After you decide on one or more anti-malware products, you must develop procedures to ensure the products and their signature databases are kept up to date. With new viruses, worms, and Trojan horses being released every day, it is important that your software be kept current to recognize as many new threats as possible. Up-to-date anti-malware software can help make your Workstation Domain computers more secure and able to ensure information integrity.

Maximizing Confidentiality

Because Workstation Domain computers may store sensitive or private information, it is important to protect the information from disclosure to unauthorized users. Two methods are commonly used to protect information confidentiality. Access controls can help ensure that unauthorized users cannot access protected objects. The easiest way to deny access to anyone other than authorized users is through access permissions. If you grant read and write access only to authorized users, the operating system ensures the information's confidentiality. Regardless of your choice of access control methods, you can assign user accounts to enforce confidentiality.

There is a drawback to using operating system access controls. It is possible for an attacker with physical access to a computer to boot the computer using alternate boot media. Most Workstation Domain computers have USB ports and CD/DVD drives. Either of these can support booting. If you insert a bootable CD/DVD or USB drive, many computers will boot from the alternate devices instead of the internal disk drive.

Booting from alternate boot media makes it easy to access files directly from the disk. If you boot from a CD/DVD or USB drive, you can bypass the operating system access controls and access any files you want. So, operating system access controls don't fully protect the confidentiality of your information. To protect private information at all times, you need to protect it even when the operating system isn't running. Only encryption provides that much protection.

---

technical TIP

Whether a particular computer will boot from the CD/DVD drive or USB device before the internal disk drive depends on that computer's complementary metal-oxide semiconductor (CMOS) configuration. Most computers allow you to enter a setup mode to alter CMOS settings, including the device boot order, by pressing the Delete key, F2, or F11 early in the boot process. Specific keys and options differ between computer manufacturers.

TIP

Each operating system supports encryption a little differently and some need third-party software to encrypt folders or entire drives. Explore how your operating system supports encryption and how use it to secure private information.

Encrypting data makes them unreadable to everyone without the decryption key. You can encrypt all sensitive information and provide the decryption key only to authorized users. Attackers can still boot your computer using alternate media; however, they will see only encrypted files and will be unable to read their contents.

Workstation Vulnerability Management

A **zero-day vulnerability** is an unknown exploit for which there is no patch or fix available. At the heart of it, you may be one of the first to encounter the exploit. Consequently, zero-day vulnerability can create complicated problems well before anyone realizes something is wrong. There is no opportunity for detection because the vulnerability is unknown. An attack happens once that flaw, or software/hardware vulnerability, is exploited and attackers release malware before the vendor can create a patch or fix.

Once a patch is released, the exploit is no longer called a zero-day exploit. These attacks are rarely discovered right away. In fact, it often takes months and potentially years before the vendor learns of the vulnerability. Monitoring for anomalies within the workstation logs and help desk reports is an important part of workstation vulnerability management.

Because Workstation Domain computers and devices are commonplace and plentiful, they make good attack targets. Workstations generally are not located in areas that are as secure as devices in some other domains. They also exist in sufficient numbers that there is a high probability of finding vulnerable computers.

Although you can't make every computer and device totally secure, you can make them secure enough to frustrate all but the most determined attackers. In general, your computer environment doesn't have to be totally secure—just more secure than the attacker's next target. If you can get an attacker to give up and go on to another target, you have been successful.

Operating System Patch Management

One of the first attack activities is to identify a target machine's operating system and look for any known vulnerabilities. There are multiple methods attackers use to identify, or fingerprint, a target machine. **Fingerprinting** a computer means identifying the operating system and general configuration of a computer. Attackers will fingerprint a computer and use that information to identify known vulnerabilities for that operating system version.

> **TIP**
>
> Explore options for automatically acquiring and applying operating system patches. Automatic updates can reduce the administrative workload by ensuring the latest patches get installed on Workstation Domain computers.

It is important to keep your operating system up to date and patched. Applying the latest security patches eliminates many of the vulnerabilities attackers are looking for when planning attacks.

Application Software Patch Management

After fingerprinting, a computer attacker scans target computers for information on resident applications. Just like operating systems, applications may contain security vulnerabilities and provide attackers with an opportunity to compromise a computer. It is important to keep your applications as well as your operating system up-to-date.

Develop a plan to keep all applications up-to-date. Each application's provider may approach the update process differently. Some vendors provide automatic update notifications, and others report updates only when directly queried. Know the update policy for each of your vendors. Create procedures to ensure you update all applications with the latest security patches. Keeping applications current will reduce the number of vulnerabilities on your computers and make it harder for attackers to succeed.

Adherence to Documented IT Security Policies, Standards, Procedures, and Guidelines

Workstation Domain computers and devices are often the most visible components to users. The majority of users access an organization's applications and information using Workstation Domain computers. That means Workstation Domain computers and devices tend to interact with users a lot. Many security issues result from user errors and can be addressed with proper training. However, training can address only some of the security issues related to users. Eventually, an untrained, unmotivated, or careless user will violate security policy and will perform an action that causes a security incident. The incident might be large, or it might be very small and unimportant. Regardless, it is important to employ multiple layers of controls to ensure security does not rely on any single control. Even organizations with very effective training programs encounter problems that users create.

A solid security policy should define multiple layers of controls working together to keep your information secure. Your security policy should direct security activities and state standards that maintain compliance with legislation, regulations, and any other requirements. Following procedures and guidelines should always result in fulfilling your security policy as well as any other organizational policies.

FYI

How your organization implements its security policy can follow an auditing framework. For example, if the organization follows the Committee of Sponsoring Organizations (COSO) or Control Objectives for Information and Related Technology (COBIT) auditing framework, the process of implementing the security policy and guidelines can be more aligned to that framework. This helps an organization compare "apples to apples" while auditing. Similarly, if an organization relies on outsourced services, it can make use of auditing standard SSAE 16 to best assess the provider.

Periodically, an organization should assess its adherence. To accomplish this, an organization can perform a gap analysis to determine what holes might exist in how it enforces the security policy. Specifically, the organization can compare the present situation with the desired situation. Once identified, the gap between is used to create actionable tasks.

Procedures define the steps necessary to fulfill the intent of the security policy. The Workstation Domain procedures can cover many aspects of maintaining computers and devices but should include the following:

- Change password procedure
- Logon/logoff procedure
- Backup procedure, including handling backup media
- Recovery procedure
- Update operating system and application software procedure
- Maintain private data procedure
- Malware alert procedure
- Grant/deny object access procedure

Procedures provide the step-by-step instructions for fulfilling the security policy but cannot include every variable. Sometimes, you have to make decisions based on the information at hand. In these cases, guidelines can help you make decisions that still comply with your security policy and any other organizational policies. Workstation Domain guidelines can include the following:

- Strong password guideline
- Document-naming guideline
- Printer use guideline
- Software installation guideline
- Handling backup media guideline
- Internet use guideline

Use operating system controls whenever possible to enforce Workstation Domain policies. These controls will not fulfill all aspects of the security policy, but they will provide a solid foundation for ensuring your information's security. Controls you will find in most current operating systems include the following:

- General object access permissions
- Shared object access permissions
- Private object access permissions
- Printer permissions
- Audit logging settings
- Authentication requirements
- User rights

Taken together, policies, procedures, and guidelines provide the instructions and limits that enable your users to comply with your security policy when using components of the Workstation Domain. Even though you design and deploy controls to limit user actions, you still should deploy additional controls to detect noncompliant behavior. Use your operating system's access audit logging features to keep log files of interesting object access requests. Carefully consider which objects you want to audit. Auditing access requests for all objects will slow your computers down and waste disk space. Identify the objects that contain sensitive or private information and enable audit logging for those objects.

 NOTE

Reviewing audit logs will show how users are using Workstation Domain computers and devices. The audit process uses these log files to validate that usage complies with your security policy.

A second useful technique during an audit is to compare a snapshot, or baseline, of a computer or device as it currently appears with a baseline from a previous point in time. Any differences between baselines could indicate unintended changes and possible vulnerabilities. Your audit plan should include procedures to create periodic baselines that you can use to detect unwanted changes to your computers and devices. A baseline can contain many types of information, but should include the following:

- Users and settings
- Groups and members
- File list with access permissions
- Access control lists
- Configuration settings for important applications and services
- Installed application list
- Startup/shutdown and logon scripts or batch files
- Network adapters and configuration

You should include any other information that describes the configuration of a specific computer. One of the easiest ways to create baselines is to include the commands that list the desired information in a script or batch file. You can compare saved output from any baseline to see configuration changes between snapshots. Creating periodic baselines supports the overall audit process to ensure compliance with stated security goals.

Best Practices for Workstation Domain Compliance

Workstation Domain computers and devices provide local computing resources and often provide initial access into your organization's shared resources. It is important to maintain a secure Workstation Domain for the security of the locally stored information as well as to keep other domains secure. Allowing Workstation Domain components to be unsecure increases the vulnerability for other domains you access from workstations. There are many strategies for keeping the Workstation Domain secure. Each organization should customize its Workstation Domain policies, procedures, and guidelines for its specific set of requirements. Here are general guidelines and best practices to attain and maintain compliance with norms in various industries within the Workstation Domain:

- Require unique user accounts for each person. Do not allow multiple people to use the same user account.
  - Require user accounts to be domain accounts centrally managed versus using local machine accounts.
  - Limit user account privileges such as limiting who is an administrator on the workstation.
- Require strong passwords and train users on the importance of keeping passwords private. Require users to change passwords at a specified interval, such as every 90 days.
- If one person performs duties of several roles, create a unique user account for each role.
- If using DAC, assign object permissions for all shared objects to grant access only to necessary subjects.
- If using MAC, establish simple standards for assigning security classifications to objects.

- Create a backup schedule that minimizes the amount of work that would be lost if a disaster destroyed the computer just before the next backup.
- Document procedures for labeling, transporting, storing, and reusing backup media.
- Document the steps necessary to restore your system from a backup after data loss.
- Test your recovery procedure at least every six months.
- Test the power outage operation of your UPS at least monthly.
- Conduct informal monthly audits that include creating monthly baselines.
- Check for anti-malware software and signature database updates daily.
- Scan for operating system and application updates at least weekly.
- Audit users, groups, and access permissions/data classification at least quarterly.
  - Require full disk encryption for laptops and removable media.
  - Ensure machine images are updated with the current workstation security configurations.
  - Automatically backup data from the workstation.
  - Lock workstation screen after so many minutes of idle time.
  - Secure the workstation bios with a password.
  - Disable guest accounts.
  - Disable user account after so many invalid login attempts.
  - Ensure workstation security patches are applied on a timely basis, including malware detection signatures for virus scanning software.

Although this list of best practices is not exhaustive, it is a good foundation to keep Workstation Domain computers and devices secure.

CHAPTER SUMMARY

The ramifications of a breach of security are more severe for some businesses that are regulated. There is an expectation that leading practices are being applied to prevent such breaches. Security policies help identify those practices and ensure they are applied to protect the workstation, including ensuring that all workstations that access the network are patched and have virus scanning software installed. The business may not be aware of many of these basic common controls expected by regulators. The security policies ensure such controls are in place and thus help ensure regulatory compliance.

We learned in this chapter how important it is to break up the technology and vulnerabilities on a workstation into manageable parts. We examined why they exist, the related business concerns, and finally, how to mitigate common vulnerabilities and risks. We understand that security policies have to be aligned with the business. The chapter also examines the changing nature of workstation technologies such as wireless and handheld devices. We understand the importance of security policies keeping pace with these technology changes. We learned techniques to keep this workstation data protected and private.

KEY CONCEPTS AND TERMS

Access control lists (ACLs)
Administrator account
Authentication
Authorization
Card verification value (CVV)
C-I-A
Dial-up modems
Due diligence
Encryption
Fingerprinting
Identification
Malware
Management system
Multifactor authentication
Object
Owner
Permissions
Rootkit Standard user account
Subject
Trojan horse
Two-factor authentication
Type I (what you know)
Type II (what you have)
Type III (what you are)
Uninterruptible power supply (UPS)
Virus
Worm
Zero-day vulnerability

CHAPTER 9 ASSESSMENT

1. ________ means the ongoing attention and care an organization places on security and compliance.

2. PCI DSS allows merchants to store the CVV number.

A. True
B. False

3. Which of the following choices protect your system from users transferring private data files from a server to a workstation? (Select two.)

A. Increase the frequency of object access audits.
B. Deliver current security policy training.
C. Place access control to prohibit inappropriate actions.
D. Enable access auditing for all private data files.

4. Some attackers use the process of ________ to find modems that may be used to attack a computer.

5. Which security-related act requires organizations to protect all personal medical information?

A. HIPAA
B. GLBA
C. SOX
D. SCM

6. Always use a UPS device for desktop and laptop computers.

A. True
B. False

7. Vendors often publish patches to prevent a Zero-day vulnerability.

    A. True
    B. False

8. The _____ property of the C-I-A triad provides the assurance the information cannot be changed by unauthorized users.

9. What are the types of malware? (Select two.)

    A. Programs that actively spread or infect
    B. Programs that slow down data transfer
    C. Programs that cause damage
    D. Programs that hide

10. A(n) _____ is a type of malware that is a self-contained program that replicates and sends copies of itself to other computers.

11. Workstations are typically managed by a central _____ that can update software, apply patches, and update configuration as needed.

12. Dial-up modems for hardware support from vendors are a common practice and as a rule should be allowed.

    A. True
    B. False

13. Encrypting the laptop hard drive is a common control that ensures data are protected even if the device is stolen.

    A. True
    B. False

Compliance Within the LAN Domain

A LOCAL AREA NETWORK (LAN) has network devices that connect two or more computers. A LAN can be either simple or complex. If you have a wireless network device at home, you have a simple LAN. Let's say you have a home cable modem connected to a wireless device (usually called a wireless router). The wireless router creates a LAN, bridging the WAN (Internet) to your home.

Organizations often view LANs much like utilities, such as electricity, water, or gas. The organization expects the LAN to be always available and always have capacity. It's also thought of as a commodity that should be inexpensive to install and run. This puts tremendous pressure on LAN resources and technology teams. The constant demand for more resources and increased connectivity increases network complexity and can lead to intentional and unintentional control gaps. Intentional gaps in information security are simply risks that cannot be closed. These are risks the business must accept. Unintentional gaps are far more dangerous because they deal with the unexpected. Both intentional and unintentional gaps in information security or weaknesses can be exploited and can be identified in an audit.

Cybersecurity gaps are vulnerabilities that are prone to exploitation by cybercriminals trying to access your network. These gaps can exist in several places, including your physical surroundings, software, and hardware. Some vulnerabilities can be rectified with minimal effort and time, but detecting and solving most weaknesses will require a professional network audit.

A network audit helps gain visibility into any potential network issues, allowing them to be remediated before causing outages or impacting performance. In this chapter, we will review key LAN components that should be considered in the scope of a network (LAN) audit.

Chapter 10 Topics

This chapter covers the following topics and concepts:

- How LAN Domains relate to business drivers
- Which devices and components are commonly found in the LAN Domain
- What LAN traffic and performance monitoring and analysis are
- What LAN configuration and change management are
- Which LAN management tools and systems are commonly used
- How to maximize C-I-A
- How to manage patches
- How to ensure adherence to documented information technology (IT) security policies, standards, procedures, and guidelines
- What best practices for LAN Domain compliance are

Chapter 10 Goals

When you complete this chapter, you will be able to:

- Examine compliance law requirements and business drivers
- Compare how devices and components found in the LAN Domain contribute to compliance
- Describe methods of ensuring compliance in the LAN Domain
- Summarize best practices for LAN Domain compliance

LAN Domain Business Drivers

An organization has two main security concerns when it comes to information collected, stored, and processed: Is the information safe? Can you prevent confidential information from leaving the organization? These seem like easy questions but are complicated to answer. In part, these questions are answered through well-defined policies. Security policies ensure alignment to business requirements. When risks exist, security policies ensure a risk assessment is performed so that management can make a balanced decision.

Network auditing refers to the process of gathering, analyzing, and studying network data to assess the network's health. Network auditing gives businesses insight into how successful their network control, risk assessments, and management operations are, particularly regarding both internal policy and external compliance regulations.

Network auditing typically involves analyzing the following network components:

- Business products and goals
- Network risk assessments
- Control implementation
- Availability
- Security
- Management
- Performance

As part of network audits planning, a deep understanding of the business products and goals is essential to understanding if the right network resources are in place. An organization whose revenue is primarily built on having an Internet presence may have very different network needs than a business selling products at a retail store location.

A **denial-of-service (DoS)** attack occurs by flooding the targeted host on a network with traffic until the target host cannot respond or simply crashes. What does this mean for the user? Legitimate users like customers are unable to access information, products, and services. DoS attacks have many costs, such as reputation, inability to service customers, time and resources to restore services, systems, devices, or other network resources due to the actions of a malicious cyberthreat actor. Services affected may include email, websites, online accounts (e.g., banking), or other services that rely on the affected computer or network. A denial-of-service condition is accomplished by preventing access for legitimate users.

> **TIP**
>
> Audits are not just about identifying gaps. An audit also assesses how well a business self-identifies and remediates gaps. A review of risk assessments performed by the business will provide insight into how the business perceives risks and its capability to remediate them.

As LANs become increasingly useful to authorized users and attackers, it is more important than ever to ensure compliance to policies and industry norms within the LAN Domain. **Figure 10-1** shows the LAN Domain in the context of the seven domains in the IT infrastructure.

Organizations rely on networked resources more than ever in today's environments. LANs make it possible to share expensive resources, such as color printers and high-performance disk subsystems. LANs enable more efficiency in critical business functions by supporting faster information transfer and resource sharing. These benefits often result in direct cost reductions and productivity increases. Organizations rely on LAN resources to maintain cost-efficient operations. Protecting the LAN-based services directly affects costs and efficiency. A solid security policy that includes compliance with all appropriate requirements should support efficient and cost-effective operations. Implementing the controls necessary to support your security policy in the LAN Domain makes your organization more secure and more effective.

Data Leakage Protection

In this section, you will focus on the business concern of how to prevent confidential information from leaving the organization. Network capability plays a significant role as

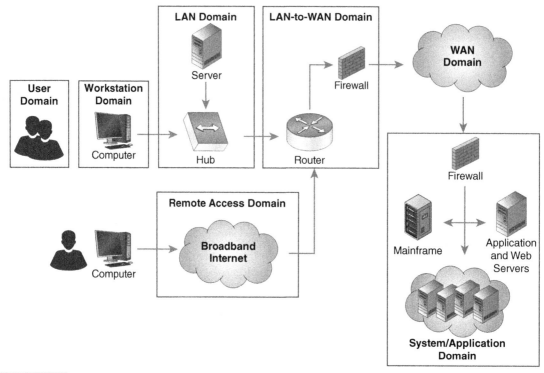

FIGURE 10-1

The LAN Domain within the seven domains of a typical IT infrastructure

do other domains such as User and System/Application. Data leakage protection (DLP) does overlap some with other domains.

Security policies define what's often called either a data loss protection (DLP) or a data leakage protection (DLP) program. Both terms refer to a formal program that reduces the likelihood of accidental or malicious loss of data leaving the network.

Company managers worry about secret business information ending up in competitors' hands. Managers must also protect customer privacy as required by law. A hacker does not have to be physically present to steal your business secrets, especially if the hacker is a disgruntled employee who might work in a data-sensitive area of the company. Your top salesperson might leave the company to work for a competitor and email your entire sales database to his home Internet account. These are not theoretical losses to a business. You must ensure that all of your potential data leaks, both physical and digital, are plugged.

The concept of DLP comes from the acknowledgment that data are often copied, change form, move, and are stored in many places. This sensitive data often leave the protection of application databases and end up in emails, spreadsheets, and personal workstation files. Business is most concerned about data that live outside the hardened protection of an application.

A typical DLP program provides several layers of defense to prevent confidential data from leaving the network, including the following examples:

- **Network device connectivity**—Limiting device connectivity also limits data flow.
- **Network monitoring and blocking**—Network traffic is monitored, and unusual data traffic leaving the network is blocked based on defined thresholds.
- **Classifying and tagging data**—Data labeled confident or sensitive can be more easily identified and blocked from leaving the network.
- **Encryption of end-user devices**—Data residing in end-user devices remain protected.
- **Communication monitoring and blocking**—Communication is monitored, and emailing confidential data, such as files, to a personal "Gmail" or "Hotmail" account is blocked.

Inventory

The DLP inventory component attempts to identify where sensitive data may be stored. This inventory includes both the network devices and the application. An inventory would include scanning workstations, email folders, and file servers. The process requires inspecting the content of files and determining if they contain sensitive information such as Social Security numbers. Once identified, data would be appropriately classified, and the access rights adjusted as needed. For example, this helps prevent private customer information from accidentally being stored in a public email folder.

"Flat" networks are a challenge at a network layer. These are networks with little to no segmentation. The result is virtually all network devices can talk to each other. This approach simplifies network management and reduces maintenance costs. The problem is it does not allow confidential and sensitive data to be isolated and protected. Worse yet, once the network is hacked, all devices on the network are potential targets. Understanding the network topography is an important part of the network audit.

Perimeter

The DLP perimeter component ensures that data are protected on every endpoint on your network, regardless of the operating system or type of device. It checks data as it moves, including writing data to non-network services and devices such as email, CDs, USB devices, instant messaging, and print.

When sensitive data are written to an unauthorized device, the technology can either stop and archive the file or send an alternate. It stops data loss initiated by malware and file-sharing that can hijack employee information.

You can also establish and manage security policies to regulate and restrict how your employees use and transfer sensitive data. It uses the same basic technology that is applied with the inventory component. It has the same limitations. Because you are dealing with data movement, you can add rules not often found in the inventory process, such as not permitting certain file types, such as database files, to be emailed.

Regardless of content, these rules can stop a hacker from sending a large volume of data outside the network.

Encryption of Mobile Devices

In many ways, mobile devices like phones are mobile external hard drives. It's the same information that can sit on a workstation or server. When an executive receives an email on an upcoming merger or a doctor about a patient, the information needs the same protection as if it were on a workstation or server. The information on mobile devices is subject to the same regulatory requirements. This means you must also apply the same level of controls, such as encryption. Mobile devices are physically outside your control. The hard drive of mobile devices can be removed and scanned. While physically removing the mobile drive cannot be prevented, encrypting it means the data are useless and only be accessed by an authorized user.

Implementing Proper Security Controls for the LAN Domain

A LAN in the business world is far more complex than a home network. The business LAN has many layers of controls. Let's look at two general types of LANs, flat and segmented networks.

As discussed, a flat network has little to no controls to limit network traffic. When a workstation connects to a flat network, the workstation can communicate with any other computer on the network. Think of a flat network as an ordinary neighborhood with each home representing a network device. Anyone can drive into the neighborhood and knock on any door. This does not mean whoever answers the door will let the visitor in. However, the visitor has the opportunity to talk their way in. In the case of flat networks, you can talk your way in by being authorized or by breaching a server, such as guessing the right ID and password combination. Flat networks are considered less secure than segmented networks because they rely on each computer (i.e., each home on the block) to withstand every possible type of breach. They are also less secure because every computer in the network can potentially see all the network traffic. This means a computer with a sniffer can monitor a sizable portion of the communication with a LAN.

A segmented network limits what and how computers can talk to each other. By using switches, routers, internal firewalls, and other devices, you can restrict network traffic. Continuing the analogy from the previous paragraph, think of a segmented network as a gated community. To access that neighborhood, you must first approach a gate with a guard. The guard opens the gate only for certain traffic to enter the community. Once inside, you can knock on any door. A segmented network acts as a guard, filtering out unauthorized network traffic. Many standards like Payment Card Industry Data Security Standard (PCI DSS) require network segmentation to further protect credit cardholder information.

Why do you want to segment a network? The basic idea is that by limiting certain types of traffic to a group of computers, you are eliminating a number of threats. For example, if you have a database server with sensitive information that by design should only receive database calls (such as Structured Query Language (SQL) traffic), why allow File Transfer Protocol (FTP) traffic? If the server is not properly configured, the FTP service could be used as a method to hack into the computer. By eliminating the FTP traffic, you have effectively eliminated that attack vector. You should still make sure the server is properly configured to prevent such an attack. However, you reduced the likelihood of a successful breach because the attacker must first breach the segment (i.e., get by the guard at the gate) and then breach the database server (i.e., break down the door). Security is never absolute, but segmenting your network creates layers of security that dramatically reduce the likelihood of a data breach.

> **NOTE**
> Attack Vect is a term commonly used to mean method or pathway used by an unauthorized user to access or penetrate the target host or system.

The following network devices are commonly found on LANs:

- Switch—A **switch** connects multiple devices within a LAN. A switch has ports that can filter traffic. You can set up rules that control what traffic can flow where. A switch can route traffic only to the port to which the system is connected. This reduces the amount of network traffic, thus reducing the chance that someone will intercept communication. The ability to configure a switch to control traffic is a real advantage to blocking potential hacks of the network.
- Router—A **router** connects LANs or a LAN and a WAN.
- Firewall—A firewall comprises software or hardware device that filters the traffic in and out of a LAN. Many firewalls can do deep-packet inspections in which the firewall examines the contents of the traffic as well as the type of traffic. A firewall can be used internally on the network to further protect segments and isolate sensitive and confidential data. Firewalls are most used to filter traffic between the public Internet WAN and the internal private LAN.

Devices and Components Commonly Found in the LAN Domain

The LAN Domain's primary responsibility is to provide your users with the ability to connect to and share resources. To meet this goal, the LAN Domain contains four main types of components. These components work together to allow users to share resources on the network and reduce the need for multiple dedicated resources, such as printers, file storage systems, and backup devices. The four main types of components in the LAN Domain are as follows:

- **Connection media**—This includes the adapters and wires (sometimes) that connect components together in the LAN Domain. Not all connection methods use wires. Wireless devices use radio waves to transmit data instead of wires. So connection media includes wireless adapters.
- **Networking devices**—The hardware devices, such as **hubs**, switches, and routers, that connect other devices and computers using connection media are called **networking devices**.
- **Server computers and services devices**—This includes the hardware that provides one or more services to users, such as server computers, printers, and network storage devices.
- **Networking services software**—This includes the software that provides connection and communication services for users and devices.

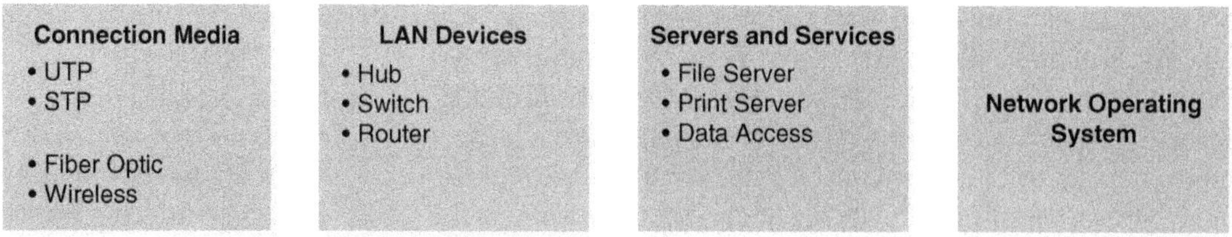

Connection Media	LAN Devices	Servers and Services	
• UTP • STP • Fiber Optic • Wireless	• Hub • Switch • Router	• File Server • Print Server • Data Access	**Network Operating System**

FIGURE 10-2

Common components in the LAN Domain

Many physical devices in the LAN Domain are combinations of several types of components. These components should work together to provide easy access to desired resources and still maintain the security of your organization's information. **Figure 10-2** shows common components you will find in the LAN Domain.

Connection Media

The purpose of any network is to allow multiple computers or devices to communicate with each other. Networked computers and devices are connected and have the appropriate software to communicate. In the past, networked computers and devices were connected using some type of cable. Many of today's networks contain a mix of cables and wireless connections. The cables or devices you use to connect computers and devices to form a network are collectively called **connection media**. Although the technical details of network connections are beyond the scope of this discussion, it is important to have a general understanding of a network's components.

Wired LAN Connections

There are four basic cabling options for physical network connections. Each option has its own advantages and disadvantages. From an information security perspective, a wired LAN connection is more secure than a wireless LAN connection. To access a network device through a wired connection, you must physically enter the facility and plug into the network. For practical purposes, a large organization's network has both wired and wireless LAN connections.

Choosing to use physical cables for part of your network, you will have to run cables to each device. Running cables between devices takes careful planning to do it right. Make sure when you explore cabling options that you evaluate the cost of installing all the cables and connection hardware to support both your current and future needs. **Table 10-1** lists the four basic cable options, along with the advantages and disadvantages of each one.

Wireless LAN Connections

Organizations have discovered that granting mobile access to business applications can increase productivity and revenue. A LAN is all about connectivity across the enterprise. The easier you can be connected to a LAN, the faster you can start accessing and exchanging

TABLE 10-1	Basic network cabling options.	
CABLE TYPE	**DESCRIPTION**	**ADVANTAGES AND DISADVANTAGES**
Unshielded twisted pair (UTP)	This is the most common type of network cable. UTP generally consists of two or four pairs of wires. Pairs of wires are twisted around each other to reduce interference with other pairs. The most common type of UTP is Category 5 UTP, which supports 100 megabits per second (Mbps) for two pairs of wires and 1,000 Mbps for four pairs.	• Lowest cost • Easy to install • Susceptible to interference • Limited transmission speeds and distances
Shielded twisted pair (STP)	This is the same as UTP, but with foil shielding around each pair and optionally around the entire wire group to protect the cable from external radio and electrical interference.	• Low cost • Easy to install • More resistant to interference than UTP • Same speed limitations but supports longer run lengths
Coaxial	This is a single copper conductor surrounded by a plastic sheath, then a braided copper shield, and then the external insulation.	• Higher cost • Difficult to install • Very resistant to interference • Higher speeds and longer run lengths
Fiber optic	This is a glass core surrounded by several layers of protective materials.	• Highest cost • Easy to run cable, although installing end connectors requires special tools • Immune to radio and electrical interference • Extremely high speeds and long run lengths

information. Wireless and mobile computing have changed the way we see LANs. This view affects our perception of LAN and Remote Access Domain issues.

Wireless connectivity allows you to view the LAN more broadly than the computer on your desktop. Handled devices allow you to extend your LAN network out of the office and

Communication Protocol

A communication protocol isn't as complex as the name implies. The technical details of each protocol can be quite complex, but the concept is simple. A **protocol** is just a set of rules that parties use to communicate. You use protocol rules every day. For example, suppose you want to invite a person to attend a meeting. If that person is a close friend, you would use an informal greeting and style of conversation. If, on the other hand, the person is an elected official, you would use a far more formal greeting and conversation style. You decide how to communicate based on your own protocol rules. We browse the web every day. Note the address bar often starts with "http" or "https," which are communication protocols for the Internet.

into the business. In other words, you can connect to the network and access or exchange information where the product or service is being made or delivered. Here are a few examples of how using wireless technology can extend the LAN into the business:

- **Health care**—Health care providers can access real-time patient information or medical research from a patient's bedside. These devices enhance collaboration for more accurate diagnoses. These devices can also track medical equipment to ensure availability at critical times.
- **Manufacturing**—Wireless connectivity allows employees to share real-time data on the factory floor.
- **Retail**—Wireless access to a LAN helps retailers place intelligent cash registers where there is no network wiring. This network access allows retailers to manage inventory, check customers out faster, and print the latest promotion coupons from the register.

Extending the LAN has many advantages over just connecting a standard desktop. LANs today can carry voice, video, and traditional computer traffic. Voice over Internet Protocol (VoIP) allows you to place and receive phone calls over a LAN or WAN. This has become popular for both home and business because of the cost savings over traditional telephone systems. Rather than incurring high flat-rate fees and per-minute call charges, most VoIP services charge a low flat-rate fee. We continue to see new companies enter the market offering less expensive voice and video solutions over the Internet.

Wireless connections are common in today's LAN environments, where flexibility is an important design factor. Wireless connections allow devices to connect to your LAN without having to physically connect to a cable. This flexibility makes it easy to connect computers or other devices when running cables is either difficult or not practical for temporary connections.

> **NOTE**
>
> LANs today can also carry video feeds, such as those from security cameras. As LANs are extended, security policies must be extended to cover the new risks.

Common Network Server and Service Devices

LANs provide easy access to shared resources and shared services. Shared centralized services make it possible for multiple users to share information and physical resources at a lower cost than duplicating information or purchasing devices for every workstation. Shared resources can include both server computers and services devices. Both offer value to a group rather than as a dedicated resource.

Depending on your network audit, one or more of the network services may be in scope. For example, DLP then auditing the mail service may be in scope. On the other hand, if your focus is on data, than a database server may be in scope. Understanding the types of services and aligning risk is an important step in the audit planning process. The following is a list of servers and a brief description of their services for devices commonly found on the network, as follows:

Web Server

A web server, as the name implies, is used for accessing the Internet. The web server can also be used to create internal web services, which are typically referred to as an "intranet."

Proxy Server

A proxy server acts as a bridge between a host server and a client-server. This server adds a layer of security since the information that is requested can be filtered by the proxy server.

FTP Server

FTP servers are used to transfer files from one computer to another. Uploaded files move from your computer to the server, while downloaded files are extracted from the server onto your device.

Application Server

An application server connects a client to software applications. This allows clients to run software without the need to install it on their local devices.

File Server

A file server stores data files for multiple users. They allow for faster data sharing and the archiving of common files. These data are typically unstructured, meaning, the files can be any content the user has created, such as spreadsheets, presentations, or text documents.

Database Server

Database servers function as large storage for data that are structured. These data are typically used in many applications, such as customer information, health records, employee information, and financial data.

Mail Server

A mail server stores and delivers mail for clients through email service platforms. Because mail servers are set up to continually connect to a network, individual users can access their email without running any systems through their own devices.

Print Server

A print server connects user devices and allows users to print on a shared printer. These servers give businesses the ability to use a single printer to serve an entire department.

Domain Name System (DNS) Server

DNS servers transform readable computer domain names into computer language Internet Protocol (IP) addresses. The DNS server takes search data from a user and finds the target device through an IP address lookup.

Dynamic Host Configuration Protocol (DHCP) Server

DHCP servers issue, track, and manage IP addresses for all internal network devices.

Collaboration Server

A collaboration server allows teams to share files and information in real time. Microsoft Teams services is an example of a collaboration server.

Monitoring and Management Server

Monitoring and management servers record any activity on network devices. They are also used by network administrators to manage configurations on network devices.

Remote Access Server and Services

These servers provide secure encrypted communications with users outside the network. This is typically referred to as creating a virtual private network (VPN) connection with the network.

Networking Services Software

The last category of components in the LAN Domain is **networking services software**. This category consists of components that really aren't connection or hardware components. All the network computers and components don't do anything without the network software to provide the ability to communicate. The networking services software changes a group of connected devices into a network of devices that communicate to accomplish tasks.

A **network operating system (NOS)** provides the interface between the hardware and the Application Layer software. The NOS provides many of the same functions an operating system provides on a standalone computer. In fact, the roles of

 NOTE

Novell was a leader in early NOS products and many early LANs ran Novell NetWare as their NOS. Today's Novell NOS product is Open Enterprise Server and is based on the SUSE distribution of Linux.

the operating system and NOS are so similar that nearly all of today's operating systems contain NOS functionality. Today's networking components generally run either a version of Windows or UNIX/Linux operating systems.

NOS products provide extensive support for resource access and management as well as credential management at various levels. NOSs support low-level authorization as well as higher-level authentication standards such as **Kerberos** and Active Directory. Choose the NOS that fits in best with your existing IT infrastructure.

LAN Traffic and Performance Monitoring and Analysis

After you start using a LAN to share resources, how do you know if you are upholding your security policy? You'll learn how to use preventive controls later in this chapter, but you should also use detective controls to validate how your users are using your LAN. Traffic and performance monitoring utilities allow you to watch the traffic flowing across your network. You can watch the traffic in real time or collect it in log files for later analysis.

FYI

Monitoring any resource requires system resources. You will affect your network's performance any time you collect traffic to analyze. Also, you must save a copy of network messages you plan to analyze at a later time. Because networks transport potentially high volumes of information, your saved network messages can require large amounts of disk space to store. It is generally a bad idea to save all network traffic. You should save complete copies of network traffic only when you are investigating a problem and need the extended detail for your analysis.

---

technical TIP

If you're interested in getting more technical information on packet sniffers and packet analyzers, you can find a list of popular tools at http://sectools.org/sniffers.html.

There are two common types of monitoring tools available for monitoring LANs: packet sniffers and network software log files. A **packet sniffer** is software that copies specified packets from a network interface to an output device—generally a file. A sniffer may copy all packets or may select certain packets based on a specific filter, such as source, destination, or protocol. Because sniffers copy the actual packets from the network, you get to see all of the addressing and routing information as well as the contents of each message. If the message is encrypted, you won't be able to read the contents, but you will see the encrypted data.

The other common option is to change settings in network software to create audit logging entries for certain packets. You can change configuration settings to log all traffic or just certain conditions. You should only log information you must record to avoid slowing down your network.

After you have a collection of packets, you can use packet analysis software to make sifting through the sniffer output or log files easier. Most analysis software allows you to sort and query data according to your own requirements. You can analyze packets originating from a specific computer or destined for a specific port, or you can analyze queries based on any of the packet's attributes. Using monitoring and analysis tools helps verify appropriate LAN use and identify inappropriate LAN use.

LAN Configuration and Change Management

Suppose you find inappropriate network packets during your LAN traffic analysis. For example, say your traffic analysis revealed a collection of packets originating from an IP address that is not valid for your network. In most cases, LAN controls should only allow traffic originating from and addressed to valid addresses. If you initially set up your LAN controls to properly filter network addresses, something is wrong.

One of the first things you should check is the current settings of your routing rules. You should be able to tell if you have defined your routing rules properly. If you find that the rules have changed, determine when the rules changed, who changed them, and why were they changed.

One attack method is to access network devices and change packet filter rules to permit malicious traffic. Another important control in the LAN Domain is network device configuration control and change management. You should implement a formal process to change network configuration settings. A change control board should approve each change. In addition, you should allow only a small number of privileged users to access network devices with the authority to change settings. You should also define your network devices to create audit log entries any time you change a configuration setting. A formal change procedure and configuration change audit will limit unexpected changes to your network configuration and provide an audit trail when changes allow unwanted network traffic.

Network audits should review the related LAN policies, standards, and guidelines to ensure compliance. Contrasting LAN configuration to these requirements will validate that the change management process is working effectively.

LAN Domain Policies

The LAN Domain refers to the organization's local area network (LAN) infrastructure. A LAN policy should outline the processes and requirements to ensure sensitive data and applications are appropriately segmented and protected.

Control Standards

A key component in the control standards for the LAN will define firewall controls, denial of service protection, Wi-Fi security control, and more.

A Firewall Controls standard describes how LAN firewalls should handle application traffic. This kind of traffic includes web, email, and Telnet traffic. The standard should also describe how the firewall should be managed and updated. The following are examples of statements from a typical Firewall Control standard:

The default policy for the firewall for handling inbound traffic must block all packets and connections unless the traffic type and connections have been specifically permitted.

Typically, good firewall hygiene always blocks the following types of traffic:

- Inbound traffic from a non-authenticated source system with a destination address of the firewall system itself. This type of packet normally represents some type of probe or attack against the firewall. One common exception to this rule would be in the event the firewall system accepts delivery of inbound email (SMTP on port 25). In this event, the firewall must allow inbound connections to itself, but only on port 25.

- Inbound traffic with a source address indicating that the packet originated on a network behind the firewall. This type of packet likely represents some type of spoofing attempt.

- Inbound traffic containing ICMP (Internet Control Message Protocol) traffic. Since ICMP can be used to map the networks behind certain types of firewalls, ICMP must not be passed in from the Internet, or any untrusted external network.

A Denial of Service (DoS) Protection standard describes controls that protect against or limit the effects of DoS attacks. This standard also addresses Smurf attacks and distributed denial of service (DDoS). Here are some examples of controls statements from this type of standard:

Routers and firewalls must be configured to forward IP packets only if those packets have the correct source IP address for <Organization> network.

Only allow packets to leave the network with valid source IP addresses that belong to the organization's network. This will minimize the chance that the network will be the source of a spoofed DoS attack.

> **NOTE**
>
> A Smurf attack, named after the program that exploits the problem, is a DoS attack on a network.

Baseline Standards

LAN Domain control standards may refer to specific technical requirements for network devices, including servers. Where there is a specific technology component, you'll need a baseline standard to document the security settings for those devices. How networks policies, standards, and guidelines are documented will vary from organization to organization. The larger and more regulated the organization is, the more formal the documentation. The following are some examples of baseline documents to be included in the network audit scope:

- **Wi-Fi Access Point (AP) Security Configuration Guide**—Describes each product and version of supported APs

- **Intrusion Detection System (IDS) and Intrusion Prevention System (IPS)**—Describes technical controls for LAN-attached IDSs and IPSs
- **Baseline Configuration(s)**—Describes each LAN-attached device product family, such as Windows Server, UNIX server software, routers, firewalls, IDSs, IPSs, and so on
- **Remote Maintenance**—Describes the actions that should be taken for each type of LAN-attached device in the event of crisis or emergencies, where the organization may need immediate access to remote maintenance, and diagnostic services to restore essential operations or services
- **Audit Storage Capacity**—Describes the requirements for allocating sufficient audit record storage capacity and configuration of auditing tools and devices to reduce the likelihood of capacity being exceeded
- **Content of Audit Records**—Describes the need to produce audit record details for each audit record generating device to ensure that it contains sufficient information to establish what events occurred, the sources of the events, and the outcomes of the events
- **Firewall Baseline Security Standards**—Describes technical controls for each firewall, version, and manufacturer
- **Router Baseline Security Standards**—Describes technical controls for each router, version, and manufacturer
- **Server Configuration Settings**—Describes the technical controls for each server product family
- **Server Baseline Configuration(s)**—Describes the baseline configuration for each server product family

Guidelines

Guidelines for implementing control standards are useful for system administrators, network administrators, and their managers who have responsibilities for maintaining LAN-attached devices. Unlike standards or policies, they provide more flexibility and deviation. The guideline provides insight into the network architecture. The following are a few examples of guideline documents:

- **Security Assessments Guidelines**—Provides recommendations on how security assessments should be conducted, how the information in them should be protected, and what the assessment process should focus on assessing
- **Information System Backup Guidelines**—Provides recommendations for system backups, offsite storage, retrieval, periodic testing of backup media, and so on
- **Firewall Architecture and Management Guidelines**—Provides information on firewall architectures, when they should be used in the organization and recommendations for ongoing management and maintenance
- **Router Architecture and Management Guidelines**—Provides information on router types and architectures, when they should be used in the organization and recommendations for ongoing management and maintenance

- **IDS and IPS Architecture and Management Guidelines**—Provides information on IDS and IPS architectures, types, when they should be used in the organization, and recommendations for ongoing management and maintenance

- **Wi-Fi Security Guidelines**—Provides information on Wi-Fi systems architectures, types, when they should be used in the organization and recommendations for ongoing management and maintenance

- **Demilitarized Zone (DMZ) Guidelines**—Recommends how to design a DMZ architecture, the typical systems that are operated in the DMZ, and how network communications should be designed for security

- **Intrusion Detection Systems Guidelines**—Recommends how to design an IDS system of sensors, collection stations, alert mechanisms, and recommendation on how alerts should be managed and how to tune devices to eliminate or reduce false positives

- **Intrusion Prevention Systems Guidelines**—Describes the types of IPSs, their uses, how they operate, and under what conditions the organization wishes to deploy them

- **User Proxy Server Guidelines**—Offers recommendations on implementing a user proxy for Internet access, tips on establishing access credentials, and tips on suspending or revoking access

- **Content Filtering Guidelines**—Provides recommendations on content filtering options, ways to maintain the list of banned sites, and ways to request access to blocked sites needed for business purposes

LAN Management, Tools, and Systems

Managing a LAN means ensuring it fulfills the goals for which it was designed. It also means continually updating the LAN's configuration to satisfy new and updated goals. LAN management covers several related activities, including the following:

- Monitoring LAN performance
- Changing configuration settings to optimize performance
- Changing configuration settings to support new requirements
- Adding necessary controls to address security issues
- Maintaining components of a current recovery process
- Adding, changing, and removing hardware components as requirements dictate
- Mapping LAN components

Bandwidth is limited, so the way it's shared among your users should always be carefully considered. Bandwidth usage and distribution monitoring can help you determine whether you need to expand your network. It can also help you determine whether any individual applications or devices are experiencing bandwidth problems that need to be addressed.

> **NOTE**
>
> Bandwidth is a measurement that quantifies how much information can be transmitted over the network. When a LAN reaches its maximum bandwidth, it becomes susceptible to many kinds of transmission errors and delays.

When you have a clear understanding of bandwidth usage, you'll have insight into which applications should and should not be prioritized as well as where congestion is occurring. Managing your network traffic flow effectively can even help you boost the performance of your network.

To correctly assess bandwidth demand, compare wired and wireless connections because this will help you spot any bottlenecks. Network security scanning software or network monitoring software can help you gain a full understanding of which network elements you should prioritize.

Bandwidth within the LAN, for example, decreases as new services such as VoIP and video are offered.

Security policies are helpful by defining and enforcing what is acceptable use over the LAN. It is not uncommon to have security policies limit the use of live video feeds. Video can take up significant bandwidth. Similar policies limit listening to live music over the network. You can enforce any of these policies at the firewall, cutting off the source of video and music from the Internet without anyone's discretion.

Maximizing C-I-A

One common goal in all domains is the pursuit of the most secure environment possible. Because maximizing the confidentiality, integrity, and availability of your organization's information leads to a secure environment, all of your activities should be to maximize C-I-A.

Maximizing Confidentiality

Ensuring confidentiality in the LAN Domain is one of the simpler tasks. There are basically four steps to ensuring only authorized users can see confidential data:

1. Identify confidential data.
2. Require positive identification for all access requests and define strict access controls for all confidential data identified in Step 1.
3. Use encryption to store all confidential data identified in Step 1.
4. Use encryption to transfer all confidential data identified in Step 1.

You should already be enforcing identification and access controls in the LAN Domain. The new controls involve using encryption. **Encryption** is the process of scrambling data in such a way that they are unreadable by unauthorized users but can be unscrambled by authorized users to be readable again. Specifically, encryption takes **cleartext** data and turns them into **ciphertext** through the use of an algorithm and a key. Cleartext data are simply human-readable data. Ciphertext is the resulting unreadable output.

Encrypting stored data is easy. Today's operating systems support encryption either directly or through integrated software. You can encrypt individual files, folders, volumes, or entire disk drives. After you decide how much data you want to encrypt, explore the various encryption options available for your operating system.

Transmission encryption means never sending information across the network in cleartext, otherwise known as being in the clear. The term *in the clear* means in a format anyone can read during transmission. You can use encryption at the application level or by only allowing encrypted connections between source and destination **nodes**. Many database management systems and document management systems can also refuse to transmit confidential data over unencrypted connections. Regardless of how you implement encryption, you should validate your controls to enforce encryption and use a packet analyzer to verify that your traffic is actually encrypted.

Maximizing Integrity

LAN nodes are just as susceptible to malicious software as any other computers. As LAN nodes become more powerful and based more on standard operating systems, they become more attractive targets. A compromised LAN node can be just a starting point. Once an attacker gets a foothold in your network, it becomes far easier to compromise other parts of your infrastructure.

You should use the malicious code policies and procedures from the Workstation Domain in the LAN Domain as well. The issues are the same. Ensure you have anti-malware software installed on every computer in the LAN Domain. Establish procedures to ensure all anti-malware software and data are kept up-to-date. Because some components in the LAN Domain are devices and not general-purpose computers, you should explore anti-malware features on each device and enable any available features. Your goal is to prevent malicious software from entering your LAN Domain.

Malware is not the only integrity concern. Users can also violate data integrity. Users can be malicious or unaware of their actions. Either way, it is important to control changes to critical data. Good access controls should stop any data changes by unauthorized users. You can also audit changes to critical data by authorized users. Audit data can provide valuable audit trails for later analysis. Good audit trails can help trace unauthorized changes back to their source. Getting to the root of unauthorized changes should provide the input needed to modify or add controls to keep the damage from happening again.

> **WARNING**
>
> Don't forget that malware can enter your LAN Domain in other ways. Computers and devices in the LAN Domain often have USB ports, CD/DVD drives, and other ports an attacker can use to introduce malware. Just as in the Workstation Domain, ensure you control access to external media. Don't allow external media except when you absolutely need it.

Maximizing Availability

It is important to develop and maintain a comprehensive recovery plan to replace lost or damaged data. As you use LANs to store more information in central repositories, it becomes more important to ensure the data are available when users request it. A crucial part of your security plan is creating secondary copies, or backups, of your data in case the primary copy is damaged or deleted. Because more users are sharing the same set of data, any loss affects a larger portion of your organization.

A solid recovery plan contains a schedule for creating backups as well as the procedures for recovering lost or damaged data. All current NOS products include capable utilities to back up and recover data. Third-party vendors also provide solutions that make enterprise-wide backups easier than managing individual computers. Explore the backup solutions available for your choice of server computers and select the one that meets your security needs with minimal administrative oversight.

Most backup and recovery solutions target networked computers. Don't forget to include any network devices with valuable data in your backup and recovery plan. Some network devices store configuration settings and performance data. Backing up these devices can save valuable log and performance data and make reconfiguring a device after a failure much faster. In nearly all cases, it is faster to load backed-up configuration data than to re-enter it manually. Make sure your backup plan includes any devices with data you'll need if a device fails.

Another important aspect of availability is ensuring your users can access LAN resources in an acceptable time frame. If the network is too slow, users can't get to their requested information, and you are not supporting data availability. In some cases, this problem is just due to excessive network use or a lack of network capacity for normal use. In both cases, you must examine the behavior and reduce the load on your network, increase its capacity, or both.

In other cases, a lack of availability results from an attack. Suppose your organization sells automobile insurance. You attract new customers by offering to analyze their existing coverage and providing a competitive quote showing how your coverage saves them money. You depend on your database of coverage costs to generate the analysis report. You cannot conduct business if you cannot access your database. In this case, an attacker who renders your network unusable effectively stops your ability to conduct business. The type of attack that denies access to a critical resource or service is called a DoS attack.

The best defense against DoS attacks is to aggressively enforce access controls and monitor your network for unusual or excessive traffic. You'll need to provide evidence that you've implemented both preventive and detective controls to combat DoS attacks.

Patch Management

Unpatched system vulnerabilities are attributed to 27% of the data breaches according to a Tripwire 2019 study. Patch management is critical when it comes to securing your systems. The primary purpose of patches is to fix known bugs and security flaws in the software. Additionally, applying patches helps maintain regulatory compliance. Many compliance standards require regular updating of software. Implementing patch management is necessary for companies to stay compliant with various industry norms and regulations. Failure to stay in compliance can result in data breaches and regulatory penalties.

Adherence to Documented IT Security Policies, Standards, Procedures, and Guidelines

Compliance in the LAN Domain depends on implementing the best controls. As with all domains, you can meet some goals using different controls. Don't just accept the common controls. Take the time to explore alternative controls for each security goal. Some controls will have more of an impact on your organization than others. If two controls provide the same assurance but have different levels of impact on your organization, choose the one that has less of an impact.

As you analyze controls in the LAN Domain to meet compliance requirements, ensure each control satisfies your security policy. If a control does not support any part of your security policy, you should question its value to your organization. Although different legislation, regulations, and vendor standards have different requirements, **Table 10-2** lists some types of controls you'll likely need to ensure components in your LAN Domain are compliant.

Implementing multiple types of controls decreases the likelihood an attack will be successful and makes your LAN Domain more secure.

Best Practices for LAN Domain Compliance

When auditing network infrastructure, start with the basics of physical topography and understanding the business support requirements. That will help you put an audit finding in the proper perspective. Once complete then align that understanding with LAN policy to contrast the organization's expectations with actual network deployments.

While planning should be broad, the actual network audit should be narrow and focus on specific risks. Network auditing is a marathon, not a spirit. Multiple network audits over time will provide a holistic view of the LAN. Most good size networks are far too complex with thousands of devices to audit in a single engagement.

Additional best practices for consideration in a network audit include the following:

- Distinguish between on-premises and remote hardware. Also, keep in mind that many devices (such as an employee's personal phone) may be connected only intermittently to the network.
- Network devices should be inventoried, including their location.
- Check the last time the device was updated or replaced.

TABLE 10-2 Preventive, detective, and corrective controls in the LAN Domain.		
CATEGORY OF CONTROL	**TYPE OF CONTROL**	**DESCRIPTION**
Preventive	Node-based access controls for LAN nodes User-based access controls for LAN resources Configuration change control Encryption	Only allow authorized nodes to establish connections. Only allow authorized users to access resources. Limit changes to network device configuration settings and filtering rules. Enforce encryption for stored data and transmitted data for confidential information.
Detective	Connection request auditing Object access auditing Performance monitoring Packet analysis Configuration settings monitoring	Log connection failures for all connections and successes for high-value targets. Log access failures for most objects and successes for critical objects. Frequently sample network traffic flow metrics and alert for any unusual activity. Examine packets for known attack signatures and to ensure necessary data are encrypted. Compare LAN device configuration settings with stored baselines to detect any unauthorized changes.
Corrective	Operating system and application patching Attack intervention	Keep applications and operating systems patched to the latest available level. Automatically modify filtering rules to deny traffic from sources generating known attack signature packets.

- Check how the life cycle of a device is tracked and what end-of-life device management is employed.
- Properly label devices with a physical ID tag.
- Make sure device's environmental conditions are adequate, such as network closet temperature.
- Check if a self-assessment on network risks is performed by the business.
- Ensure that data are secure both while in motion on the network and at rest on network endpoints.
- Verify which authentication protocols are in place to grant network access.
- Don't reinvent the wheel. There are network audit checklists readily available through professional organizations and standard boards

CHAPTER SUMMARY

Network infrastructure tends to be highly complex. Networks consist of a mix of physical and virtual devices. Some may run in an on-premises data center, while others are hosted in the cloud. There may be multiple networks in the mix, some public and some private. Performing audits of networking infrastructure helps you ensure that your networking assets are patched and protected. It also provides visibility into your network architecture and identifies bottlenecks that hinder the business from achieving its goals.

In this chapter, we learned the importance of regular network audits. These audits should be a core part of your network management risk strategy. They help you identify opportunities for performance optimization and address potential security vulnerabilities. They also ensure regulatory compliance.

KEY CONCEPTS AND TERMS

Ciphertext	Kerberos	Packet sniffer
Cleartext	Network operating system (NOS)	Protocol
Connection media		Router
Denial of service (DoS)	Networking devices	Switch
Encryption	Networking services software	
Hub	Node	

CHAPTER 10 ASSESSMENT

1. A LAN is a network that generally spans several city blocks.

   A. True
   B. False

2. A local resource is any resource connected to the local LAN.

   A. True
   B. False

3. Which of the following devices repeats input received to all ports?

   A. Switch
   B. Hub
   C. Gateway
   D. Router

4. _____ cabling provides excellent protection from interference but can be expensive.

5. Even the newest wireless protocols are slower than using high-quality physical cable.

   A. True
   B. False

6. Which LAN device commonly has the ability to filter packets and deny traffic based on the destination address?

   A. Router
   B. Gateway
   C. Hub
   D. Switch

7. Which of the following would be the best use for a packet sniffer?

   A. To approve or deny traffic based on the destination address
   B. To encrypt confidential data
   C. To analyze packet contents for known inappropriate traffic
   D. To track configuration changes to specific LAN devices

8. Why is LAN device configuration control important?

   A. Configuration control helps to detect violations of LAN resource access controls.
   B. Configuration control can detect changes an attacker might have made to allow harmful traffic in a LAN.
   C. It reduces the frequency of changes because they are more difficult to implement with configuration control.
   D. Configuration control ensures LAN devices are set up once and never changed.

9. A(n) _____ is a dedicated computer on a LAN that runs network management software.

10. Which of the following controls would comply with the directive to limit access to payroll data to computers in the human resources department?

   A. User-based authorization
   B. Group-based authorization
   C. Media access control–based authorization
   D. Smartcard-based authorization

11. You should back up LAN device configuration settings as part of a LAN backup.

   A. True
   B. False

12. A successful DoS attack violates the _____ property of C-I-A.

13. Where must sensitive information be encrypted to ensure its confidentiality? (Select two.)

   A. While in use on a workstation
   B. During transmission over the network
   C. As it is stored on disk
   D. In memory

14. Why is mapping a LAN a productive exercise?

    A. Visual maps help to identify unnecessary controls.
    B. Visual maps help in understanding your LAN design.
    C. A LAN map is required before physically installing any hardware or connection media.
    D. A visual map is the only way to define paths between devices.

15. How can some smart routers attempt to stop a DoS attack in progress?

    A. They can alert an attack responder.
    B. They can log all traffic coming from the source of the attack.
    C. They can terminate any connections with the source of the attack.
    D. They can reset all connections.

16. The terms Data Loss Protection (DLP) and Data Leakage Protection (DLP) program both refer to a formal program that reduces the likelihood of accidental or malicious loss of data leaving the network.

    A. True
    B. False

17. A(n) _____ is a network of at least two computers connected through a network in a certain area.

18. Which type of network limits what and how computers can talk to each other as an extra type of security measure?

    A. Segmented network
    B. Flat network
    C. Transitional network
    D. 3-D network

19. Which of the following common network devices can be defined as a software or hardware device that filters the traffic in and out of a LAN?

    A. Router
    B. Firewall
    C. Switch
    D. Hub

20. When creating a baseline document to document the security settings for devices, which type of document included in the network audit scope typically will describe each LAN-attached device product family?

    A. Wi-Fi AP Security Configuration Guide
    B. Baseline Configuration
    C. Remote Maintenance
    D. Audit Storage Capacity

Compliance Within the LAN-to-WAN Domain

DATA SUSTAINS THE ORGANIZATION'S business processes and enables it to deliver products and services. Stop the flow of data, and just as quickly, you disrupt the ability to deliver products and services. If the loss of data lasts long enough, the viability of the organization itself comes into question. That is how vital data is for many organizations today.

The **LAN-to-WAN Domain** refers to the technical infrastructure that connects the organization's local area network (LAN) to a wide area network (WAN). One of the principal concerns is controlling the network traffic between the outside network (i.e., WAN) to the private network (i.e., LAN). The LAN-to-WAN denotes, for many organizations, its connection to the Internet or a dedicated circuit to a branch office. While LAN and WAN are references to technologies, for practical purposes think of a LAN as the organization's internal network and the WAN as the Internet or connection to a branch office. The connection to the Internet represents a significant risk to the organization. The Internet has a direct connection to the organization's private network and resources. Protection relies on the organization's ability to put in place layers of controls that filter out unwanted network traffic.

The policies of an organization define the amount of risk they are willing to take by defining the number of layers of control between the organization's network and the Internet. This chapter will examine these layers of control. We will review the policy concern on how to filter the traffic between the Internet and the private network. Additionally, many organizations have an Internet presence. The chapter will discuss the challenge of serving up content on the Internet to customers and businesses. These publicly facing websites provide often access to internal resources such as databases for product information. As a result, they are a prime target for hackers. The chapter will discuss the LAN-to-WAN key controls that harden Internet-facing servers, filter traffic between these networks, and monitor for breaches in security.

Chapter 11 Topics

This chapter covers the following topics and concepts:

- How compliance law requirements relate to business drivers
- Which devices and components are commonly found in the LAN-to-WAN Domain
- What cloud services are
- What LAN-to-WAN configuration and change management are
- Which LAN-to-WAN management tools and systems are commonly used
- What legal considers migrating applications to the cloud are
- How to maximize C-I-A
- How to perform penetration testing and validate LAN-to-WAN configuration
- How to ensure adherence to documented IT security policies, standards, procedures, and guidelines
- What best practices for LAN-to-WAN Domain compliance are

Chapter 11 Goals

When you complete this chapter, you will be able to:

- Understand compliance law requirements and business drivers
- Understand types of filtering
- Explain what content blocking is and examples of where it is applied
- Compare how devices and components found in the LAN-to-WAN Domain contribute to compliance
- Describe methods of ensuring compliance in the LAN-to-WAN Domain
- Summarize best practices for LAN-to-WAN Domain compliance

Compliance Law Requirements and Protecting Data Privacy

It's not enough to keep your information secure within your network. Keeping your information secure means keeping it secure at *all* times. This is especially true as data move between domains in the information technology (IT) infrastructure. As organizations rely more and more on remote resources and applications, it becomes crucial to ensure your data are secure as they travel from location to location. A solid security policy that includes compliance with all appropriate requirements should support efficient and cost-effective

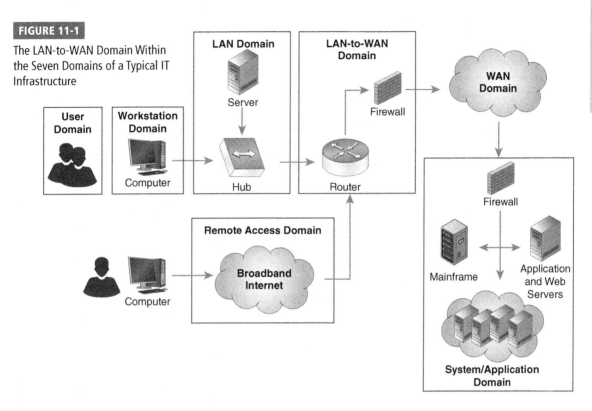

FIGURE 11-1

The LAN-to-WAN Domain Within the Seven Domains of a Typical IT Infrastructure

operations. Implementing the controls necessary to support your security policy in the LAN-to-WAN Domain makes your organization more secure and more effective.

Figure 11-1 shows the LAN-to-WAN Domain in the context of the seven domains in the IT infrastructure.

We value a degree of privacy when it comes to highly personal information about ourselves. For many, what first comes to mind as highly personal information is our financial and medical records. Yet this information is stored in many forms as digital files. Securing and protecting these files is both a trust and legal obligation for an organization. This book focuses on U.S. legal privacy obligations; however, countries throughout the world have similar laws. These laws recognize that data will leave the confines of the local network and define how such data should be transmitted and handled.

In general, it is understood that data privacy must be protected. What is not so clear, however, is what constitutes private data. Depending upon the environment that an organization operates, privacy can take on different meanings. The **American Institute of Certified Public Accountants (AICPA)** describes **privacy obligation** as "ensuring privacy, which concerns the rights and obligations of individuals and organizations concerning the collection, use, retention, disclosure, and disposal of personal information comes with risks." Thus, privacy is about personal information, which might be used to identify an individual. Most privacy examples include the following:

- Name
- Social Security number (SSN)

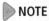
NOTE

The law often plays catch-up as technology and the use of private data expand exponentially. As a result, online service provider agreements may be more of a protection than the regulatory requirements. For example, individuals who take DNA tests to identify their heritage can have their data sold or the data can be used to deny insurance coverage if the DNA shows an increased risk for cancer.

- Home address or geo location
- Email address
- Physical characteristics such as biometrics

Personal information can also be considered sensitive. Consider for example sensitive financial or health information. When combined with personal information, this information becomes personal *and* sensitive. The protection of this data is increasingly important when you consider the risks posed by improper use or unauthorized disclosure to name a few.

For both individuals and organizations, the collection of personal data has many benefits. Individuals can benefit from personalized services and targeted offerings. On the other hand, individuals may be subject to spam and **identity theft** if data are not protected properly. The organizations can be subject to litigation, negative publicity, and even financial loss.

Numerous methods are used to protect privacy data:

- Develop appropriate privacy policies.
- Establish the position of a **privacy officer.**
- Conduct training and awareness around data handling.
- Consider adequate controls around data retention and data destruction.
- Conduct regular risk assessments of access controls.
- Limit data access and sharing to only what is required.
- Consider security technologies such as encryption.

Privacy laws and regulations vary by industry and region. In North America, many states have their own privacy laws. The following are a few examples of privacy laws at the federal and state level:

- **Health Insurance Portability and Accountability Act (HIPAA)**—The Privacy Rule within Title II of the Act is concerned with the security and privacy of health data.
- **Gramm-Leach-Bliley Act (GLBA)**—The Financial Privacy Rule within GLBA is concerned with the collection and disclosure of personal financial information.
- **Children's Online Privacy Protection Act (COPPA)**—The COPPA contains provisions for websites collecting personal information from children under 13 years of age
- **SB1386**—This California law regulates the privacy of personal information.
- **Electronic Communications Privacy Act of 2000**—This Act regulates that protects the privacy of email and other electronic communications.
- **Privacy Act of 1974**—Limits are imposed on personal information collected by U.S. federal agencies.
- **Fair Credit Reporting Act (FCRA)**—The use of consumer credit information is regulated.

- **Personal Information Protection and Electronic Documents Act (PIPEDA)**—This Canadian law addresses how organizations collect, use, and disclose personal information.

It is important that IT audits consider privacy data and the application of appropriate privacy controls within organizations. First, consider the laws and regulations across multiple boundaries in which business is conducted. Further, the coordination among general counsel, compliance team, and IT is necessary to understand both the legal and security repercussions.

Finally, organizations should consider a privacy audit. A privacy audit would focus on the following:

- What are the privacy laws that apply to the organization?
- Are the organizational responsibilities defined and assigned (for example, that of the privacy officer and responsibilities of legal)?
- Are policies and procedures for creating, storing, and managing privacy data applied and followed?
- Are specific controls implemented to securely transmit sensitive data over the Internet?

One of the main concerns when sending data across public networks is confidentiality. Although not all data are confidential, any data you exchange with a remote resource using a WAN is potentially available for anyone else to see over the INTERNET as illustrated in **Figure 11-2**. Consider all WANs to be hostile and insecure. Your organization

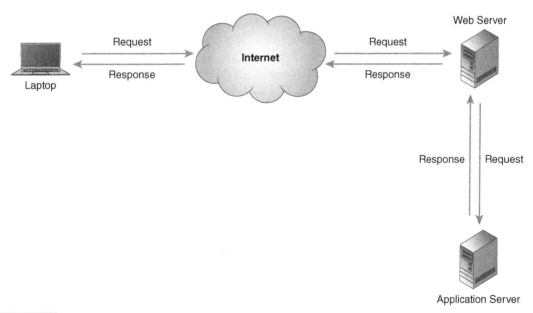

FIGURE 11-2

Exchanging Data with a Remote Service

controls access to your LANs and has some measure of assurance of how private the LANs are. WANs are different. You don't have control over who accesses a WAN or who can access data traveling across it. You must deploy sufficient controls to protect the privacy of any data in the LAN-to-WAN Domain.

Implementing Proper Security Controls for the LAN-to-WAN Domain

The primary control type you will use in the LAN-to-WAN Domain for any data passing through is traffic filtering. There are different devices and types of filtering but make sure you aggressively use filtering to stop any inappropriate traffic from flowing in, out, or through your LAN-to-WAN Domain. A collection of well-placed and well-configured firewall devices can dramatically increase your network's ability to withstand attacks.

Another important control anytime data flows in or out of the LAN-to-WAN Domain is encryption. There are many encryption choices, and the right control depends on how you'll use the data and which component applies the encryption method. Your application may encrypt your data in another domain. You will learn about different approaches later in this chapter. Some solutions require multiple layers of controls. You select the best controls that support a few general principles:

- No data in the LAN-to-WAN Domain should ever be transmitted in cleartext. Anyone can read cleartext data or data that are in the clear.
- When using encryption, select the algorithm based on needs. Don't just select the largest key.
- Assume an attacker can intercept and examine any network messages.

A LAN is effective to connect computers within an office or groups of buildings. However, to connect to a customer, vendor, or office across the country or globally, you need to connect to a WAN. Generally, that means connecting through the Internet.

So how do you move data from a secure LAN through an unsecure WAN to a secure LAN? Typically, you would segment a piece of your LAN called a **demilitarized zone (DMZ).** The term DMZ was taken from the military to describe creating a buffer between two opposing forces. The DMZ sits on the outside of your private network facing the public Internet. These servers provide public-facing access to the business such as public websites. They are especially hardened against security breaches as they are an attack vector. Sitting between the DMZ and internal network are firewalls that filter traffic from the DMZ servers to the private LAN servers. More often than not, the DMZ sits between two layers of firewalls. The first firewall allows limited Internet traffic into the DMZ, and the second highly restricts traffic from the DMZ servers and routes the traffic to the appropriate part of the private network.

A DMZ can control both inbound traffic and outbound traffic. An example of outbound traffic control is content filtering. For example, it may describe the control requirements for employees to limit access to certain websites or to prohibit high bandwidth traffic, such as YouTube videos. Here are several additional examples of policies that deal with LAN-to-WAN connectivity and filtering:

- **Content blocking tools configuration**—Requirements that describe what types of web content should be blocked and how updates are approved

- **Intrusion detection and prevention tools**—Configuration requirements for each product with particular emphasis on that placed in the DMZ
- **Proxy server**—Limit network traffic through specific servers
- **Firewall configurations**—Limit specific network traffic

The auditor should examine procedure and guideline documents. These documents are useful for individuals who must determine how much Internet access should be permitted. The documents establish controls while balancing the risk and the business needs to be connected. The following guideline documents are examples:

- **DMZ Guidelines**—Recommends additional services to be placed in the DMZ and, depending on those services, the additional security requirements
- **Intrusion Detection and Prevention Systems Guidelines**—Recommends how to design an intrusion detection system (IDS) of sensors, collection stations, and alert mechanisms to eliminate or reduce false positives
- **Content Filtering Guidelines**—Recommendations on content filtering options, ways to maintain the list of banned sites, and ways to request access to blocked sites when needed

Devices and Components Commonly Found in the LAN-to-WAN Domain

The LAN-to-WAN Domain represents a point of transition between more secure LANs and far less secure WANs. In this section, you'll learn about the devices and components you'll commonly find in the LAN-to-WAN Domain. Once you've learned about the devices and components, you'll learn about controls to ensure compliance in the LAN-to-WAN Domain.

Routers

A router is a network device that connects two or more separate networks. In the context of the LAN-to-WAN Domain, a router makes the actual connection between the LAN and the WAN. A router can be a standalone network device or it can be software that runs on a computer. In either case, the hardware must contain at least two network interfaces— one for each network. A router works by inspecting the address portion of the packet and forwarding the packet to the correct network.

The process of examining each packet is time consuming and can slow your network down. Newer network devices and software often contain support for **Multiprotocol Label Switching (MPLS)**. MPLS networks add a simple label to each network packet. The routing devices in the network forward packets based on the address in the label as opposed to data in the header portion of the packet. MPLS can dramatically increase the speed and usefulness of your network in two important ways:

- MPLS takes less time to process each packet because the router only has to look at the packet's label.
- MPLS devices create virtual links between nodes that can transport higher-level encrypted packets.

Firewalls

A **firewall** is a network security measure designed to filter out undesirable network traffic. Like a router, a firewall can be a network device or software running on a computer. Firewalls provide an important security capability. You can define rules for each firewall that tell the firewall how to filter network traffic. You can restrict which packets you allow to flow through the LAN-to-WAN Domain. Firewalls give you the ability to aggressively control what types of information can travel between your LANs and WANs.

The simplest type of firewall is a packet-filtering firewall. The firewall examines each packet and decides on an action to take after comparing the packet's attributes with the firewall rules. Rules commonly instruct firewalls to deny or forward packets based on the target application, Internet Protocol (IP) address, and port. You can create rules based on other criteria as well. However, protocol, IP address, and port filtering give you the ability to restrict most unwanted traffic from passing through the firewall.

Proxy Servers

A **proxy server** is a type of firewall that makes requests for remote services on behalf of local clients. The proxy server receives a request from a client and evaluates the request based on its defined rules. If it determines that the request is authorized, the proxy server forwards the packets to the remote server, using its own IP address as the source address. In this way, a proxy server hides the true source's identity. The remote server only sees the IP address of the proxy server. **Figure 11-3** shows how a proxy server forwards requests to remote resources.

The proxy server keeps a record of sent messages in an internal table. Unless an error occurs, the remote server should send a response to the initial request. When the proxy server receives the response, it looks up the true address of the client that sent the original request and forwards the response to the client.

Proxy servers have several uses. Because they process all network traffic between clients and remote servers, they work well as content filters. Proxy servers can filter

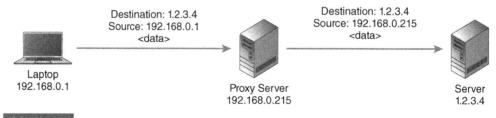

FIGURE 11-3

Network Request Using a Proxy Server

unwanted or inappropriate content using many different types of rules. Web content filters examine web-based traffic and can block web content that does not adhere to your organization's Internet or web acceptable use policy (AUP).

DMZ

A major concern of business is how well protected the servers in the DMZ are. In other words, how well are you protecting my website? Businesses are particularly concerned about website availability and integrity. The websites for many companies represent their public image and major sales channel.

Security policies set strict rules on how DMZ traffic should be limited and monitored. Security policies outline how the DMZ server should be configured and how often security patches should be applied. Security policies also outline how often external penetration testing is conducted. Penetration testing probes and tests the network for weaknesses and vulnerability from the outside looking in. Penetration testing is required by many standards and is considered best practice.

> **NOTE**
>
> A company cannot afford to have "web graffiti" on its site. Web graffiti is a term used when a website has been breached and its content altered usually in a way that embarrasses the business. The last thing a business executive wants to wake up is the company website covered with abusive language or pornographic images.

The LAN-to-WAN Domain marks an important transition for data. Data flowing from a WAN to your LAN moves from an unsecure domain to a secure domain. It is generally a poor idea to allow any users to access resources inside your secure LANs. It is important to positively identify users to properly control access to your organization's resources. On the other hand, many organizations do want to provide internal information to anonymous users. For example, most online retailers want anonymous users from the Internet to visit their sites and browse through their products. How do you allow anonymous users to access your data without compromising it?

The answer lies in creating an area of your IT infrastructure that allows access for anonymous users but aggressively controls information exchanges with internal resources. This special zone is connected to both the Internet and your internal secure network. A DMZ is a separate network or portion of a network that is connected to a WAN and at least one LAN, with at least one firewall between the DMZ and the LAN. **Figure 11-4** shows a simple DMZ with one firewall.

A very common use of DMZs is for web servers. Users from the Internet can access your web server and see pages generated from the web server. The web server can make limited connections to your application and database servers in your LAN. The firewall blocks connections from Internet users to your LAN but allows the web server to connect. One danger is that an attacker could compromise your web server and use it to either connect to your LAN resources or perhaps use the web server to launch attacks on other computers. To help protect your DMZ servers from launching attacks, you can add a second firewall between the DMZ and the WAN. This firewall would filter outbound traffic and would stop attacks originating from within your DMZ. **Figure 11-5** shows a DMZ with two firewalls.

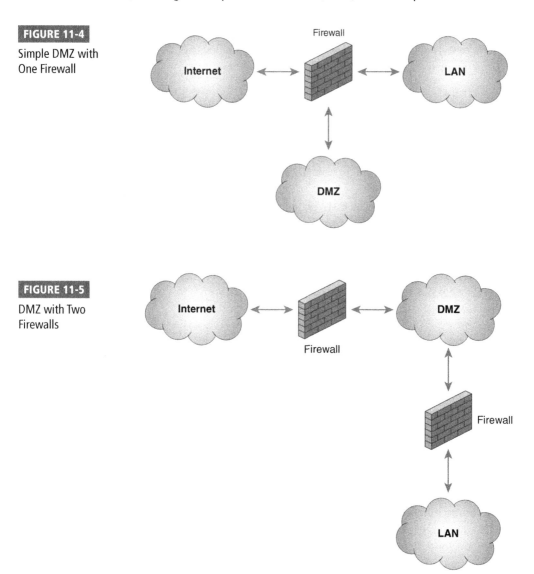

FIGURE 11-4

Simple DMZ with One Firewall

FIGURE 11-5

DMZ with Two Firewalls

Virtual Private Network Concentrator

The Remote Access Domain refers to the technology that controls how end users connect to an organization's LAN remotely. An example would be employees who need to connect to the office network from their homes. This capability has been critical during the COVID-19 pandemic that started in 2020. Remote access has allowed organizations to keep running while protecting their workforce.

A virtual private network (VPN) concentrator is a network device that establishes secure communications between two end points, such as an employee's home network and the company network. Routers can also be used to create a VPN connection. The difference is that VPN concentrators can serve up to thousands of users at the same time beyond the capacity of many routers. It can create VPN tunnels for each employee, securing their connections to the companies' network no matter where they are in the world.

The key benefit of a VPN connection is that all data within the connection (referred to as a VPN tunnel) are encrypted. This protects both the data within the tunnel and the connection. The organization must establish well-defined policies to ensure controls are consistently deployed. Following are typical policy examples related to VPN connections:

- It is the responsibility of employees with VPN privileges to ensure that unauthorized users are not allowed access to the corporate network.
- Multifactor authentication must be used to initiate a VPN session.
- When actively connected to the corporate network, VPNs will force all traffic to and from the workstation over the VPN tunnel; all other traffic will be dropped.
- Dual (split) tunneling is NOT permitted; only one network connection is allowed.
- All computers connected to corporate internal networks via VPN or any other technology must use the most up-to-date corporate-approved anti-virus software.
- VPN users will be automatically disconnected from the corporate network after 30 minutes of inactivity.
- The VPN concentrator is limited to an absolute connection time of 12 hours.
- Only corporate-approved VPN workstation client software may be used.

For discussion purposes, focus less on each of these individual examples and more on types of policies the auditor should expect. Policies should be clear and concise and at a sufficient level of detail that the corresponding control can be tested for operational effectiveness. Additionally, with the expansion of VPNs due to the COVID-19 pandemic, many homes are now extensions of the corporate office. Policies need to cover both physical and technical requirements. For example, the physical requirements for working from home may require users to lock up company documents at home and ban family members from accessing company assets.

Network Address Translation (NAT)

Network address translation (NAT) enables a local area network (LAN) to map internal IP addresses to external IP addresses. Typically, these translation tables are maintained and performed within network routers.

NAT services have three main benefits:

1. To hide internal IP addresses from the outside
2. To allow for more internal IP addresses
3. To merge multiple internal networks to form a single Internet connection.

Internet Service Provider Connections and Backup Connections

The purpose of the LAN-to-WAN Domain in most organizations is to provide a method to connect your LANs to the Internet. Connecting to the Internet is easier than ever before.

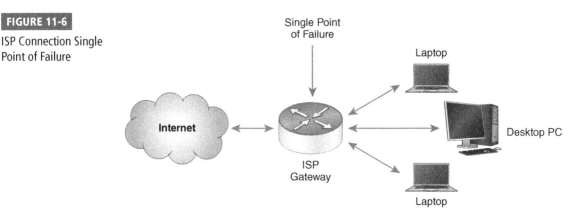

All you have to do is establish an account with an **Internet service provider (ISP)**. The
ISP provides at least one method to connect your device to its network. After you have
connected to its network, the ISP routes traffic from your environment to the Internet.

Your network relies on the connection to your ISP to establish Internet connections.
If the connection to your ISP goes down for any reason, you'll lose your connection to the
Internet. A single ISP connection means a **single point of failure**. With a single point of
failure, many components depend on a single component. If the single component fails,
all other dependent components essentially fail as well. **Figure 11-6** shows a single ISP
connection that represents a single point of failure.

Make sure you develop an alternative Internet connection plan to avoid a single point
of failure. You'll learn how to accomplish this in the "Dual-Homed ISP Connections"
section later in the chapter.

Cloud Services

The use of **cloud services** is mainstream in the United States with 90% of the companies
surveyed by O'Reilly in 2021. The migration to the cloud includes core applications. The
survey indicates that 48% of the companies plan on moving more than 50% of their
applications to the cloud, while 20% have already moved all their applications to the cloud.

What does it mean to move to the cloud? In the survey, it was clear the migration
referred to corporate applications. Hosting applications in the cloud is only one potential
service available to a company migration to the cloud. Additionally, the three main cloud
services models include:

- **Infrastructure as a Service (IaaS)**
- **Platform as a Service (PaaS)**
- **Software as a Service (SaaS)**

IaaS cloud services provider manages all the networking, data storage, and servers
typically found in a traditional data center. The data center facilities are owned by the
cloud service provider. The company manages the running of the servers and system and
application software.

CLOUD SERVICE	IaaS	PaaS	SaaS
Application software			x
Operating system software		x	x
Server hardware and maintenance	x	x	x
Data storage hardware and maintenance	x	x	x
Network hardware and maintenance	x	x	x

TABLE 11-1 High-level comparison among IaaS, PaaS, and SaaS.

x = Cloud service provider responsibilities.

PaaS cloud service providers manage everything under IaaS plus run servers and system software. The company manages the application software.

SaaS cloud service providers manage everything under IaaS and PaaS plus run the application software. The company becomes a user of the application software with varying application privileges.

These definitions can vary depending on the cloud service provider. For example, some cloud providers offer Network as a Service (NaaS). NaaS is a subset of IaaS in which only network services are provided. **Table 11-1** illustrates a high-level comparison between the three cloud services models.

Intrusion Detection Systems/Intrusion Prevention Systems

Firewalls are extremely effective at filtering out known unwanted traffic. However, attackers are getting more and more sophisticated all the time. A firewall is only as good as its rules. Because most firewall rules are based on static attributes, they aren't effective at protecting a network from all types of attacks.

For example, suppose an attacker compromises one of your trusted servers and installs a distributed denial of service (DDoS) agent. On command, the agent starts sending large volumes of messages to different hosts. Your firewall sees all the messages but forwards them because they originated from a trusted server. The result is a successful DDoS attack.

A type of network measure that can help in this situation is an **intrusion detection system (IDS)**. An IDS is either a network hardware device or software that monitors real-time network activity. It compares the observed behavior with performance thresholds and trends to identify any unusual activity. If it does identify unusual activity, it sends a notification to someone who can explore the situation and react appropriately. Some systems provide the ability to automatically take action. An **intrusion prevention system (IPS)** extends the IDS capability by doing something to stop the attack. In the preceding example, the IPS could modify firewall rules to deny any traffic originating from the compromised server. This simple action would stop the attack.

Data Loss/Leak Security Appliances

As the volume of information flowing around networks increases, so does the concern that sensitive data will leak out of the protected environment into the public domain. Compliance requirements often place restrictions on data and how you must handle it. For example, the Payment Card Industry Data Security Standard (PCI DSS) requires your organization to protect credit card numbers both at rest and in transit. You can ensure your applications and databases protect credit card numbers, but what about other forms of data transfer? How do you protect credit card numbers in email messages?

Data leak security appliances (also called *data loss security appliances*) are network devices or software running on computers that scan network traffic for data-matching rules. The rules differ for each organization but would likely include patterns for matching credit card numbers, Social Security numbers, and other sensitive information for organizations enforcing PCI DSS compliance. Other requirements for protecting sensitive data would result in additional rules. The data leak security appliance helps detect and prohibit data that would otherwise leak to the public due to oversight or error. It is one more layer in a multilayered approach to security.

Web Content Filtering Devices

As you learned earlier, a web content filter is a specific type of proxy server. In addition to forwarding web requests to a remote web server, the filter scans all traffic and applies content rules. These content rules conform to the organization's Internet AUP. Web content filters are common in many organizations that provide Internet access. The goal is to provide Internet access that is necessary or desired for appropriate users while denying inappropriate Internet use.

A web content filter evaluates content based on several different criteria, including the following:

- **Blacklist**—This provides a list of uniform resource locators (URLs) or Domain Name System (DNS) entries from which all transfers are blocked.
- **URL filter**—This involves scanning and evaluating URLs for inappropriate content using a dictionary of inappropriate search items.
- **Content keyword filtering**—This involves evaluating text in content for inappropriate content using a dictionary of inappropriate search terms.
- **Content analysis**—This involves evaluating text and nontext content for inappropriate content.

Data classification is a useful way to rank the sensitivity of data to the organization. When data are properly labeled with classification, they can be filtered as they leave the organization. Data classification be an important tool to stop sensitive information from leaving the organization. For example, there is often a requirement in companies to block emails that are sent to external users if the email contains an attachment with confidential data or customer account information. But how do you know what type of data is contained in an email? Classifying data is one approach with allows the software to examine the contents of an email and block certain data types from leaving the internal network.

While data classification can be a powerful tool, it can be challenging to enforce. Classifying data can be time-consuming if not fully integrated into the day-to-day activities of the company. Executive support is key to policy enforcement. At some point in the enforcement process, you need to change behaviors. This takes some form of disciplinary action. Even pulling someone to the side and coaching workers run the risk of negatively impacting morale. It is important that you lay the foundation for such discussions in advance. You accomplish this through the executive of the department explaining the importance of data classification and how it helps the company to protect its customers and comply with the law. This executive can send a clear message that there is zero-tolerance for ignoring such policies. The executive can also be clear that when violations of policies are brought to their attention they will be taken seriously. This type of message establishes a tone at the top.

> **TIP**
>
> Learn more about tools that can filter and block email based on data content by visiting partner websites of major email vendors, such as the Microsoft partner website Infotechtion at the following link: https://www .infotechtion.com/post /data-loss-prevention-block -email-attachments-with-a -sensitivity-label.

Traffic-Monitoring Devices

Traffic-monitoring devices monitor network traffic and compare performance against a baseline. Traffic monitors can help detect network issues by identifying performance problems and alerting administrators to the problem. Network problems can be caused by the following:

- Denial of service (DoS) or DDoS attacks
- Device or communications failure
- Bandwidth saturation

In any case, it is important to know when a problem develops. Traffic-monitoring devices can often alert administrators to emerging problems that can be addressed before they become critical.

LAN-to-WAN Traffic and Performance Monitoring and Analysis

Monitoring the traffic that flows through the LAN-to-WAN Domain can be a demanding task, but it is one that is a vital part of ensuring your environment's security. A secure network is one that provides smooth operation and allows only authorized traffic. If any part of your network were to be down even for a small period of time, productivity within your organization would decline. In the case of critical business functions, network problems could cause service interruptions and could result in noncompliance. To be proactive, it is important to monitor how traffic moves throughout the network and to verify that your network is meeting your organization's security goals.

Traffic monitoring and analysis is the process of capturing network traffic and examining it to determine how users and applications are using your network. The two main monitoring techniques are network device based and nondevice based. Network devices, especially routers and gateways, often include monitoring functionality you can use to keep track of your network's health. Nondevice techniques require that you add hardware or software to capture traffic and analyze it. Any computer in the LAN-to-WAN Domain can act as a traffic-capture device.

After you capture traffic, your analysis software can examine it in real time or save it to a file for later analysis. Monitoring and analyzing network traffic in the LAN-to-WAN Domain is very similar to monitoring and analyzing traffic in the LAN Domain. The goal is to detect problems before they become critical. Your efforts should focus on identifying degrading performance that might affect data availability or traffic that might indicate attack activities.

LAN-to-WAN Configuration and Change Management

The LAN-to-WAN Domain exists to provide a structured transition between your LAN and a WAN, such as the Internet. Much of the functionality in the LAN-to-WAN Domain depends on the configuration of the devices in the domain. Each device or software component operates based on configuration settings and rules. Any change to settings or rules changes the way the domain components operate.

After you configure the components in the LAN-to-WAN Domain to operate securely, it is important to prohibit unauthorized changes to the domain configuration. Any configuration changes you make will change the way components operate. Changes can be beneficial or detrimental. You must enforce a change-management process to ensure you only make authorized changes to any configuration and that you document all changes for later auditing.

The change-management process is fairly simple and contains only a few steps. Each step is important and contributes to the overall security of your environment. Here are the basic configuration-management steps required to make any changes to device configuration settings or rules:

1. The requestor submits a configuration setting or rule change request. It is important to document each change and the reason for the change. Auditing configuration changes and comparing the impact of similar changes requires as much historical information as possible.

2. The **configuration control board (CCB)** reviews each request and either approves or denies it. The CCB can be a group of people or a single person with the responsibility to evaluate changes.

3. The implementers—generally security administrators—receive approved change requests for implementation and make the approved changes.

4. Before making any changes, security administrators should validate the current configuration against the latest authorized baseline. This step identifies any unauthorized changes.

5. Security administrators should validate any configuration changes in a test environment whenever possible.

6. After applying authorized changes, security administrators should create a new authorized baseline.

7. The implementers should validate the changes made to ensure they satisfy the original request.

Coordinated Attacks

Many attacks against enterprise data really consist of multiple coordinated attacks. Suppose an attacker wants to launch a DoS attack to disable your organization's web servers and stop you from conducting business on the Internet. The attacker attempts a direct DoS attack that your IPS devices in the LAN-to-WAN Domain immediately identify and stop.

The attacker searches for other vulnerabilities and finds a way to use social engineering to install a Trojan horse on the IPS device. The Trojan horse provides a back door that the attacker can use to log on to the IPS and change configuration settings. The attacker modifies the IPS rules to not block the attacking computers. The next attack succeeds in bringing down your web servers. This attack is successful because of a lack of controls at several levels. The last level of control that is missing is positive configuration management for the IPS.

Although it might seem like an intrusive process, requiring all configuration changes to go through a change-management procedure allows you to audit all authorized changes and deploy only approved changes. The overall configuration-management process should also include periodic audits of each component's configuration against the latest baseline to identify unauthorized changes. In this way, you can ensure your LAN-to-WAN components maintain a secure configuration.

LAN-to-WAN Management, Tools, and Systems

Managing the LAN-to-WAN environment basically involves the same tasks as managing the LAN environment. In addition, managing the LAN-to-WAN environment involves efforts to ensure the additional components in the LAN-to-WAN Domain are protecting the internal domains from the external domains. The LAN Domain, as the name implies, focuses on LAN-specific topics. The LAN-to-WAN Domain includes WAN access components and security needs.

Managing the LAN-to-WAN Domain means ensuring authorized data passes smoothly through the domain's components and on to its destination. This means ensuring you have defined just the right firewall rules. Use the principle of least privilege to write firewall rules. Your rules should allow through the firewall only the traffic that is necessary to perform authorized business functions. In today's distributed environments, that goal is difficult to achieve. Users and applications tend to establish and use multiple connections with remote services and resources. Your firewall rules should allow all of the different connections you'll need and can take some fine-tuning to get right.

FCAPS

Managing a network involves several related tasks and can become confusing without a plan. The **International Telecommunication Union Telecommunication Standardization Sector (ITU-T)** (one of three divisions of the International Telecommunication Union, primarily responsible for communications standards) and the International Organization for Standardization (ISO) developed **FCAPS**. FCAPS is a network-management functional model. FCAPS is an acronym that represents the focal tasks necessary to effectively manage a network. FCAPS stands for the following:

- **Fault management**—This includes activities to detect, log, communicate, and potentially fix network problems to keep the network running effectively. Fault management directly addresses the availability property of security by minimizing downtime.
- **Configuration management**—This includes activities to monitor network component configuration settings to track and manage the state of your network.
- **Accounting management**—This includes activities to measure how your users are using your network to support regulation compliance and billing.
- **Performance management**—This includes activities to measure and report on network performance to support optimization.
- **Security management**—This includes activities to control access to network resources and limit access exclusively to authorized users.

Network-Management Tools

Many tools are available to help manage your network. Look for the tools that best fit into your environment and provide the functionality you need to best manage your environment.

Although these tools represent functionality that is useful in the LAN-to-WAN Domain, many of them are useful to manage networks in other domains as well. Select the tools that work best to help keep your networks secure and operating smoothly.

Access Rights and Access Controls in the LAN-to-WAN Domain

As remote access and the use of VPN has gained prominence during the pandemic of 2020, so too has the need to ensure remote authentication is working effectively. Do you truly know that individual is an employee or a hacker pretending to be an employee? When accessing the network within the office there is less of a concern. In most corporate offices you have guards, locked doors, badges, and visibility as to who is sitting at the workstation. But over the Internet how do you know who is on the other side of the wire?

To address this concern many companies, require **two-factor authentication**, also referred to as **multifactor authentication**, for remote access.

Two-factor authentication requires end users to authenticate their identity using at least two different types of credentials. The most commonly accepted types of credentials are as follows:

- **Something you know**—Refers to something only you are supposed to know such as your ID and password combination. Security awareness education should tell you to never share your password with anyone.

- **Something you have**—Refers to a unique device that you must have in your physical possession to gain access. An example is a security token that might flash a unique number every 60 seconds. Alternatively, confirmation to log on may be sent to your cell phone.

- **Something you are**—Refers to some sort of biometric such as a finger printer.

Two-factor authentication provides a high level of confidence that the remote user is an employee. This combination of enhanced remote authentication and network VPN connectivity can be powerful tools to ensure company networks are protected. In the context of the LAN Domain, your organization can exert substantial control over which computers and users can establish connections. The situation is slightly different in the LAN-to-WAN Domain. Although it is still possible to require strict access controls, the design of the LAN-to-WAN Domain includes active connections to a WAN. That means the components in this domain are exposed to the WAN, which in many cases is the Internet.

Internet-facing components are network components in your organization's IT infrastructure that users can access via the Internet. These components experience a higher number of threats due to this increased visibility. To make matters worse, many enterprise applications that provide Internet connectivity encourage at least some anonymous connections. This exposure to anonymous users makes it more difficult and more important to secure the components in the LAN-to-WAN Domain.

The transitional nature of the LAN-to-WAN Domain calls for collections of controls to meet security needs. You need the ability to evaluate several attributes of a connection request's source before granting access to your network. You should define different access profiles based on your policies to meet the needs of different types of network users. **Network access control (NAC)** is a solution that defines and implements a policy that describes the requirements to access your network. NAC defines the rules a connecting node must meet to establish a secure connection with your network. It also allows you to proactively interrogate nodes that request a connection to your network to ensure they don't pose a risk. You can use NAC to classify connecting nodes based on the level of compliance with your access rules. NAC allows you to evaluate node attributes that include the following:

- Anti-malware protection
- Firewall status and configuration
- Operating system version and patch level
- Node role and identity
- Custom attributes for enterprise configuration

You can choose from many products to implement NAC. NAC software alone won't secure your networks, but it does give you the ability to define and enforce policies that can get you closer to your security goals.

Maximizing C-I-A

As with all other domains in the IT infrastructure, your main goal in the LAN-to-WAN Domain is to deploy and maintain controls that support all of the C-I-A properties of security for your data. The LAN-to-WAN Domain contains several components that play critical roles in providing secure access to your organization's data. Maintaining that security requires diligence and the right controls.

Minimizing Single Points of Failure

One of the main functions of the LAN-to-WAN Domain is to provide access, or connectivity, between the LAN and the WAN domains. One property in the C-I-A triad is availability. Resources and data are available only if users can successfully establish connections between the two domains. If any device in the LAN-to-WAN Domain is required to make a connection, that device must be functional to fully support data availability. To minimize any downtime due to device failure in the LAN-to-WAN Domain, ensure every node has an alternate whenever possible. Any node that does not have an alternate becomes a single point of failure. If the node fails or becomes unavailable, it affects the entire domain. Evaluate each node to see if a redundant node would remove the single point of failure. Allow unique devices only if there are no other available alternatives and implement compensating controls to protect the availability property.

Dual-Homed ISP Connections

Many organizations employ a single connection to their ISP. If the connection device goes down, so does the Internet access for the entire organization. In the preceding section, you learned to avoid single points of failure. That goal applies to your ISP connection as well. The solution is to establish at least two ISP connections, as shown in **Figure 11-7**.

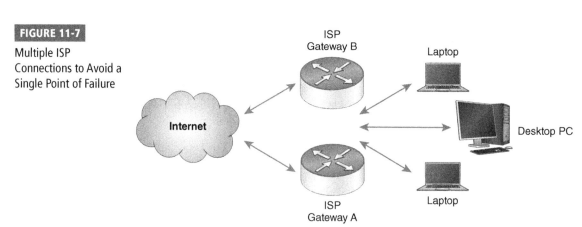

FIGURE 11-7

Multiple ISP Connections to Avoid a Single Point of Failure

A **dual-homed ISP connection** is a design in which a network maintains two connections to its ISP. If one gateway or connection fails, the other can still connect to the Internet.

FYI

Methods of choosing which ISP connection to use can be very simple. The round-robin method simply keeps a list of all available ISP connections. When you use one connection, the system remembers to use the next connection in the list the next time someone wants to connect. When you reach the end of the list, just start over. This method cycles through the list of ISP connections over and over.

The other simple method is to remember the number of times you have used each ISP connection. When a user wants to connect to an ISP, you select the connection with the lowest number of uses. This simple method helps you use all of your connections equally.

In the simplest case, you use the primary connection for normal Internet access. You use the secondary connection only if the primary connection fails. You can implement this solution easily, but it does waste the available bandwidth on the secondary connection because it sits unused most of the time. Another option is to use both connections at all times. Your ISP connection devices can decide which connection to use based on many criteria. More-sophisticated connection-management software can use the best ISP connection based on available bandwidth. This method provides load balancing as well as fault tolerance. Less-sophisticated connection-selection methods may involve simple round-robin or connection-count algorithms. Regardless of the method you use, having a secondary ISP connection can protect you from WAN connection failures.

If you decide to set up dual-homed ISP connections, you can choose from two different options:

- **Use two connections to the same ISP**—Two connections to the same ISP might save money but are still vulnerable to interruption if your ISP fails.
- **Use two connections to different ISPs**—Maintaining two connections to different ISPs will cost more and require more maintenance due to working with different vendors, but will protect your environment if one ISP goes down.

Examine using dual-homed ISP connections to maximize your data availability.

Redundant Routers and Firewalls

A common bottleneck in any network is the router or firewall. In many networks, these devices require that all traffic pass through them. Although that practice does make maintenance and configuration easier, it introduces one or more single points of failure. If all traffic from the Internet passes through one router and that router crashes, how can your Internet users connect to you? The answer is, they can't.

The easiest way to see the most obvious single points of failures for network connections is to map your network. It is easy to see on a network map where node failure would result in a fragmented network. After you identify routers and firewalls that are single points of failure, you should introduce redundant nodes to your network. Every single point of failure should have at least one alternate device. Having redundant devices allows your network to continue in the case of a device failure. If there are two paths from point A to point E and one path fails, all traffic can use the other path. Implementing redundant devices addresses availability by protecting your network from device failure. In addition, you gain the additional benefit of spreading out traffic among the redundant devices and possibly increasing overall performance. In both cases, redundant network devices can protect the availability of your network.

Web Server Data and Hard Drive Backup and Recovery

You should have a recovery plan in place for every device and computer in your organization. **Business continuity plans (BCPs)** and **disaster recovery plans (DRPs)** enable you to recover from disruptions ranging from small to large.

One crucial part of a BCP or a DRP involves recovering data and configuration settings from a secondary copy saved in case you lose your primary copy. This secondary copy of data to be used in case of primary data loss is commonly called a *backup image* of data, or just a *backup*. The value of a backup in the recovery process depends on how current it is. Because you'll lose any work that occurred after your last backup when you recover data, it makes sense to back up frequently.

One of the more common servers in the DMZ is the web server. Web servers provide a generic front end to many enterprise applications and resources. Web servers provide the first visible point of contact for many remote clients and are necessary to bridge the outside Internet user community with the far more structured collection of application components in your organization's secure network. If your organization's web server is down, your organization's web presence is down too. To maximize the availability of your organization's web presence even in the face of disasters, it is important to ensure you have a current recovery plan for all the web servers in the LAN-to-WAN Domain. A current recovery plan is one that you support with frequent backups—and one that you test on a regular basis. A solid schedule for backups and a plan to recover your web servers in the case of an interruption that involves data loss will maximize your organization's uptime.

Use of VPN for Remote Access to Organizational Systems and Data

You have seen several topics that relate to data availability but nothing yet that relates to the other two properties of the C-I-A triad, integrity and confidentiality. Information that travels to and from the Internet or another WAN can potentially be accessed by pretty much anyone. The best protection for information on a WAN is to use encryption. You can allow remote users to access resources on your LAN through the LAN-to-WAN Domain by setting up a **virtual private network (VPN)**.

 NOTE

VPNs provide secure access to remote users and are particularly pertinent to the Remote Access Domain.

A VPN is a persistent connection between two nodes. The nodes can be on the same network or on separate networks. Many VPNs also encrypt all the traffic that flows along the connection. Because the traffic is encrypted, no unauthorized users can see the information. In this manner, encryption supports data confidentiality. Attackers can modify the data along its route, but without knowing what the data actually contains, the changes would not have a real purpose other than to destroy data. When the altered data reaches the end of the VPN and is decrypted, the VPN endpoint detects the change and takes action. The endpoint can either request that the data be re-sent or throw an error. Either way, you detect the unauthorized change and protect the data's integrity.

Penetration Testing and Validating LAN-to-WAN Configuration

Testing security controls and configuration settings is crucial to ensuring you have the right controls in place. One particular type of testing simulates actions an attacker would take to attack your network. This type of test is called a *penetration test* because the purpose of the test is to attempt to penetrate, or compromise, your security controls. In fact, conducting periodic penetration tests is a requirement for compliance with several standards. PCI DSS is one example of a standard that requires annual penetration tests to validate security controls.

> **NOTE**
>
> It is important to keep in mind that a distributed application is one in which the components that make up the application reside on different computers. Consequently, a penetration test of an application can require simulating an attack across multiple servers.

An experienced penetration tester can simulate the actions an attacker would take and verify the strength of your security controls. Such tests validate the controls you have in place as well as indicate areas of weakness you should address. You should seek approval first, then design several types of penetration tests to ensure your security controls are doing the job.

Never conduct a penetration test unless you have written authorization from the network and system owners. Penetration tests will likely raise alarms. If you're not authorized to perform the tests, it could result in liability issues and even criminal prosecution. Verbal approval is not enough—get it in writing. Before you start any penetration testing, get written approval for the specific scope of your tests. Your approval documents should include the following:

- Specific IP addresses or ranges of nodes you will test
- Specific IP addresses of nodes that will conduct the tests
- A list of nodes that should be excluded from the tests
- A list of the techniques used in the tests
- A schedule or time frame approved for the tests to occur
- Points of contact for the testing team and the approving organization(s)
- Procedures for handling collected test data

Performing penetration testing is a highly specialized skill. This is one area where many companies outsource and hire a vendor to perform the service periodically. Additionally, several of these vendors have created on-premise services and solutions that continually monitor the network for potential vulnerabilities and intrusion; for example, the company Rapid 7 is a leader in this field and more information can be found on this topic at https://www.rapid7.com/.

External Attacks

The more common type of penetration test is from the perspective of the external attacker. The penetration tester, also called the *pentester*, launches a series of attacks from outside the target's network. In most cases, the pentester conducts the tests from a computer connected to the Internet. The tester simulates the actions an attacker would take when developing an attack on your organization.

Although each penetration test is different, many tests follow similar paths. Here is a common flow a penetration tester follows to develop attacks:

1. **Reconnaissance**—Here, the tester collects as much information about the target environment as possible. At this stage, the tester is collecting both technical and nontechnical information. Both types of information can help the tester determine how the organization operates, where it operates, and which characteristics the organization and its customers value. The purpose of the attack will drive the process. In an actual attack, if an attacker wants to extract or modify data, all efforts will be directed toward the data of interest. If the attacker wants to harm the organization, the target of the attacks will be what the organization values. An organization that markets safety to its clients would suffer from confidential data disclosure, whereas an organization that prides itself on high availability would suffer most from being shut down. Information gathered by the tester or attacker in the reconnaissance phase drives all subsequent activities.

2. **Footprinting**—After collecting general organizational information, the next step is to learn as much as possible about the target's technical architecture. At this point, testers use tools to query and identify as many identified nodes in the target network as possible. The process of **footprinting** means determining the operating system and version for each node. Operating system information helps identify a node's possible purpose and the next step is to learn more about the node.

3. **Scanning and enumeration**—The next step collects detailed information about each node. Testers can use automated tools to scan each node, identifying open and active ports. Testers can also query open ports to determine which services are running on a selected node. In this manner, testers can develop a detailed map of the target's technical environment and get a good picture of what hardware and software make up the target's infrastructure.

4. **Vulnerability identification**—Once the testers have all the available information on operating systems and running software and services, the next step is to explore known vulnerabilities in the target's environment. For example, if scanning and enumeration reveals the target is running Microsoft Internet Information Services (IIS) web server version 6.0, the testers would search for known vulnerabilities with that specific version.

5. **Attack planning**—A complete attack plan would include all identified vulnerabilities in the target environment, sorted by exploit difficulty and impact. In most cases, testers will start with the easiest attacks that produce the largest impact. The attack plan is a sorted list of attacks that the testers will carry out along with the procedures to execute the attack and collect results information.

6. **Attack execution**—The execution phase follows the attack plan and launches each attack against the target environment. Testers grade the success of each attack and the effectiveness of security controls to mitigate the attack.

7. **Collecting and presenting results**—The final step in a penetration test is to compare the attack plan with the attack results. Testers will collect all result information from each attack and present a report of overall test performance. The report should analyze the effectiveness of existing controls and make recommendations for any changes that would increase security.

Blocking malicious traffic using IP intelligence is highly complicated and an emerging approach for many companies. Keeping up with all the latest attacks and keeping a skilled workforce can be expensive and overwhelming. Consequently, companies are hiring firms to perform these specialized activities. Network traffic would be routed to the vendor's Internet connection and once validated as safe would be forwarded to the company's network. This reduces the company's network traffic to what is considered legitimate and safe. The company F5 is a leader in this field and more information can be found on their website at https://support.f5.com/csp/article/K10978895.

Internal Attacks

Not all attacks occur from external sources. Many attacks originate from within an organization's own networks. These types of attacks can originate from compromised computers running malware or from attackers who have bypassed access controls and gained a foothold inside your network. In either case, attacks from within your organization can be more dangerous than attacks from the outside.

Internal traffic and activities are generally regarded as more trusted than external traffic. The general idea is that if a user has successfully satisfied stringent access controls, that user should be trusted. This general trust makes internal attacks dangerous if an attacker is able to circumvent access controls and operate from within your internal networks.

To measure your organization's ability to handle internal attacks, you should conduct internal penetration tests as well as external tests. There are two main types of attacks that may originate from within your organization:

- **Internal attacks on your organization**—An **internal attack** is one in which an attacker is able to compromise your access controls and either establish a presence inside your networks or place malware on an internal computer. In either case, the attacker has access to your resources at a higher level of trust than a general external user. Internal attacks generally target your organization.

- **Internal-to-external attacks on another organization**—An attacker might choose to use your infrastructure to launch an **internal-to-external attack** on another organization. There are two main reasons for using one organization to attack another. First, an attacker could use your organization to launch an attack in an attempt to hide the attack's true origin. Second, the main goal of the attack could be to place the blame on your organization and cause you to incur embarrassment and possibly other consequences.

Regardless of the reasons, internal penetration testing of your security controls is to ensure both types of attacks will not succeed. Your goal is to ensure internal attacks on your organization will not compromise your security and attacks on other organizations will not be allowed past your networks. Both external and internal penetration testing ensure your environment is secure from attacks in both directions.

Intrusive Versus Nonintrusive Testing

Penetration tests are simulations of attacks. In most cases, attacks on information systems and infrastructures are intended to cause damage of some sort. That means if you fully simulate attacks, there will likely be some impact that results. Any test that simulates an attack and results in damage is an **intrusive test**. A test that only validates the existence of a vulnerability is a **nonintrusive test**.

 TIP

Although creating a test environment takes substantial effort, today's use of virtualization can make the process far easier. You can create a collection of virtual machines that replicate your real environment and provide a good test bed for penetration testing.

For example, suppose your organization runs the Apache web server. Penetration testers discover a vulnerability in the version of Apache running on your primary web server. The vulnerability, if exploited, will cause the web server to crash. Scanning and enumerating your web server computers to collect data is generally a nonintrusive test, whereas exploiting the vulnerability and actually crashing the web server is an intrusive test.

As you develop a penetration plan, assess the impact of each test and carefully consider whether you want to allow intrusive tests against your environment. If all your security controls are sufficient, even intrusive tests will fail to affect your environment. But any deficiency in your controls could allow an intrusive test to have a negative impact on your systems or networks. The best way to handle such intrusive tests in a safe manner is to perform them against a test environment that is an exact copy of your production environment.

Configuration Management Verification

You learned about the importance of managing network information earlier in this chapter. Recall the FCAPS approach to network management. The C in FCAPS stands for configuration. RANCID and Canner are tools that help manage network configuration settings. It is important to aggressively control your network devices' configuration settings. RANCID and Canner, along with other available tools, can help you create baselines of configuration settings and compare changes over time. You should develop a schedule and process to frequently compare configuration baselines and verify all changes to your network's configuration.

A solid network configuration-management process makes it easy to classify any configuration changes as authorized or unauthorized. You just compare baseline differences to your authorized changes list to see which changes occurred that were not authorized. Because every configuration change has some effect on what traffic flows through your LAN-to-WAN Domain, it is important to manage authorized changes and detect any unauthorized changes. Implementing the FCAPS approach will help formalize the process and make your networks more secure.

Adherence to Documented IT Security Policies, Standards, Procedures, and Guidelines

Compliance in the LAN-to-WAN Domain depends on implementing the best controls. As with other domains, explore alternative controls for each security goal. Many of the LAN-to-WAN security controls affect performance and the ability of your users to access your organization's resources. You must ensure the correct controls are in place to balance all three security properties.

As you analyze controls in the LAN-to-WAN Domain to meet compliance requirements, ensure each control satisfies your security policy. If a control does not support any part of your security policy, you should question its value to your organization.

Implementing multiple types of controls decreases the likelihood an attack will be successful and makes your LAN-to-WAN Domain more secure.

Best Practices for LAN-to-WAN Domain Compliance

The LAN-to-WAN Domain provides the outside world with access to your data. In many ways, the domain filters authorized users from unauthorized ones. Because this domain connects your secure LAN with an untrusted WAN, you must ensure the controls protect your LAN resources. Protecting information in the LAN-to-WAN Domain focuses on maintaining the balance between easy access and solid security. Solid planning, along with aggressive management, can provide both.

The following best practices represent what many organizations have learned. Plan well and you can enjoy a functional LAN-to-WAN Domain that makes LAN information available for use to WAN users. Here are general best practices for securing your LAN-to-WAN Domain:

- Map your proposed LAN-to-WAN architecture before installing any hardware. Use one of the several available network-mapping software products to make the process easier. Identify all of the components' data paths through the domain. Use the map to identify any single points of failure. Update the network map any time you make physical changes to your network.

- Establish a DMZ with at least two firewalls. You should locate one firewall between your WAN connection and the DMZ perimeter and configure it to filter incoming and outgoing traffic between the WAN and the DMZ. Locate the other firewall between your LAN and the DMZ. This internal firewall should filter all incoming and outgoing traffic between the LAN and the DMZ.
- Implement at least two redundant WAN connections. Use load-balancing techniques to use the bandwidth of both connections.
- Configure all DMZ servers and devices to resist attacks from WAN users.
- Develop a backup and recovery plan for each component in the LAN-to-WAN Domain. Include recovery plans for damaged or destroyed connection media. Don't forget to include configuration settings for network devices in your backup and recovery plans.
- Implement frequent update procedures for all operating systems, applications, and network device software and firmware.
- Define routing and filtering rules to restrict traffic passing through the LAN-to-WAN Domain. Most traffic should either terminate or originate in the LAN-to-WAN Domain.
- Monitor LAN-to-WAN traffic for performance and packets for suspicious content.
- Carefully control any configuration setting changes or physical changes to domain nodes. Update your network map after any changes.
- Use automated tools whenever possible to map, configure, monitor, and manage the LAN-to-WAN Domain.
- Deploy at least one IPS for each WAN connection to detect and respond to suspected intrusions.
- Conduct complete penetration tests at least annually to evaluate security control effectiveness.
- Use two-factor authentication for all remote VPN connections.
- Use content blocking tools to reduce data loss.
- Deploy intrusion detection in the DMZ and inside the network.
- Implement data classification to enhance content filtering capability.
- Hire specialized vendors to perform penetration testing.
- Monitor cloud migration strategy and progress toward moving the company's applications to a cloud service provider.

As with all best practices, these are only a starting point. Implement the points that are appropriate for your environment. Doing so will get you started toward establishing and maintaining a secure LAN-to-WAN Domain.

CHAPTER SUMMARY

In this chapter, we learned that the connection to the Internet represents a significant risk to the organization. The Internet has a direct connection to the organization's private network and resources. Protection relies on the organization's ability to put in place layers of controls that filter out unwanted network traffic. In this chapter, we examined the layers of LAN-to-WAN controls. We reviewed the policy concerns on how to filter the traffic between the Internet and the private network. Additionally, we discussed the challenge of serving up content on the Internet to customers and businesses. We examined core capabilities such as creating VPN tunnels for remote workers. We discussed how the different layers of the network work together, such as the use of two-factor authentication to start a VPN connection.

We examined in this chapter both the form and substance of many network controls. The volume of policies and standard topics is enormous. From this, you walked away with a deep appreciation as to the skills needed to maintain such capabilities, such as penetration testing and blocking malicious code. You also learned how to classify data and how such classification can enhance content filtering. Finally, we examined best practices that included several examples that should be found in the policy.

KEY CONCEPTS AND TERMS

American Institute of Certified
   Public Accountants (AICPA)

Children's Online Privacy
   Protection Act (COPPA)

Cloud services

Configuration control board
   (CCB)

Blocking

Business continuity plans (BCPs)

Data leak security appliances

Demilitarized zone (DMZ)

Disaster recovery plans (DRPs)

Dual-homed ISP connection

Electronic Communications
   Privacy Act of 2000

Fair Credit Reporting Act (FCRA)

FCAPS

Firewall

Footprinting

Health Insurance Portability and
   Accountability Act (HIPAA)

Gramm-Leach-Bliley Act (GLBA)

Identity theft

Infrastructure as a Service
   (IaaS)

Internal attack

Internal-to-external attack

International
   Telecommunication Union
   Telecommunication
   Standardization Sector
   (ITU-T)

Internet service provider (ISP)

Intrusion detection

Intrusion detection system (IDS)

Intrusion prevention system
   (IPS)

Intrusive test

LAN-to-WAN Domain

Multiprotocol Label Switching (MPLS)

Network access control (NAC)

Nonintrusive test

Personal Information Protection and Electronic Documents Act (PIPEDA)

Platform as a Service (PaaS)

Privacy Act of 1974

Privacy obligation

Privacy officer

Proxy server

SB1386

Single point of failure

Software as a Service (SaaS)

Traffic monitoring devices

Two-factor authentication (multifactor authentication)

Virtual private network (VPN)

CHAPTER 11 ASSESSMENT

1. A distributed application is one in which the components that make up the application reside on different computers.

   A. True
   B. False

2. Which of the following is commonly the primary security control for data entering the LAN-to-WAN Domain?

   A. Filtering
   B. NAT
   C. Encryption
   D. Address validation

3. Multifactor authentication is the de facto standard to authenticate a remote connection.

   A. True
   B. False

4. A(n) _____ is an isolated part of a network that is connected both to the Internet and your internal secure network and is a common home for Internet-facing web servers.

5. Which type of network device is most commonly used to filter network traffic?

   A. Router
   B. Firewall
   C. Switch
   D. IDS

6. If you only have one connection to the Internet and that connection fails, your organization loses its Internet connection. This is an example of a(n) _____.

7. Which of the following devices detect potential intrusions? (Select two.)

   A. Firewall
   B. IPS
   C. IDS
   D. Load balancer

8. What does it mean when there are differences between the last security configuration baseline and the current security configuration settings?

   A. Unauthorized changes have occurred.
   B. Authorized changes have occurred.
   C. Changes have occurred (either authorized or unauthorized).
   D. Unapproved changes are awaiting deployment.

9. If a company wanted to have control over the server and applications on the server, which cloud service would be the best fit?

   A. Infrastructure as a Service (IaaS)
   B. Platform as a Service (PaaS)
   C. Software as a Service (SaaS)
   D. A and C

10. Which of the following best describes a dual-homed ISP connection?

   A. An ISP connection using two firewalls
   B. Connecting two LANs to the Internet using a single ISP connection
   C. A network that maintains two ISP connections
   D. Using two routers to split a single ISP connection into two subnets

11. Many organizations use a(n) _____ to allow remote users to connect to internal network resources.

12. You only need written authorization prior to conducting a penetration test that accesses resources outside your organization.

   A. True
   B. False

13. NAT is helpful to hide internal IP addresses from the outside world.

   A. True
   B. False

14. The _____ feature speeds up routing network packets by adding a label to each packet with routing information.

15. Requiring a user to enter their user ID/password plus a secret PIN number be considered two-factor authentication.

   A. True
   B. False

Compliance Within the WAN Domain

THE PURPOSE OF A **WIDE AREA NETWORK (WAN)** is simply to allow any user in the world to connect to any application in the world. In practical terms, a WAN connects local area networks (LANs) across large geographical areas. The classic example is the home office with a data center needing to be connected to branch locations. This was traditionally achieved by each branch having a dedicated connection back to the home office to connect to the data center. This hub (i.e., the home office) and spoke (i.e., branch offices) is very reliable and has been the main network model deployed for the last 20 years. This hub-and-spoke network model approach is still widely in use today

With the increasing migration of applications to the **cloud**, a new WAN network model has emerged called **software-defined WAN (SD-WAN)**. The problem is that the old hub-and-spoke network model, while reliable, is not very efficient to serve up Internet applications back to branches. This new network model does not replace the traditional WAN. The SD-WAN model extends the traditional WAN model by taking advantage of the distributed nature of the cloud and using the most efficient route to serve up cloud applications.

This chapter will review the key components of the WAN and SD-WAN network models. This chapter will discuss the trade-off between the models and best practices. Additionally, the chapter will examine how to monitor the WAN environment and what WAN components should be considered as part of an audit such as incident response.

Chapter 12 Topics

This chapter covers the following topics and concepts:

- How compliance law requirements drive business decisions
- Which devices and components are commonly found in the WAN Domain
- What emerging technologies are in the WAN space, such as SD-WAN
- What WAN traffic and performance monitoring and analysis are
- What WAN considerations should be applied to WAN incident response
- What access rights and access controls in the WAN Domain are
- How to maximize C-I-A
- What WAN service provider Service Organization Controls (SOC) compliance is
- How to ensure adherence to documented information technology (IT) security policies, standards, procedures, and guidelines
- What best practices for WAN Domain compliance are

Chapter 12 Goals

When you complete this chapter, you will be able to:

- Understand the difference between WAN and SD-WAN
- Compare how devices and components found in the WAN Domain contribute to compliance
- Describe methods of ensuring compliance in the WAN Domain
- Summarize best practices for WAN Domain compliance

Compliance Law Requirements and Business Drivers

Organizations rely on distributed architecture. Many organizations deploy their enterprise applications as distributed applications. Today many core applications are being migrated to the cloud. Although the actual applications and resources belong in other domains, clients need the ability to access resources and run distributed programs. Providing the ability to connect to geographically diverse resources is the main purpose of the WAN Domain. Although making your resources and data available to more users is a good thing, you must pay close attention to security. Keeping your data secure as they leave your network takes advance planning. Always consider how secure your data are in each of the domains of your IT infrastructure. **Figure 12-1** shows the WAN Domain in the context of the seven domains in the IT infrastructure.

Your responsibility to keep your data secure does not stop when data leave the controlled area of your networks. The WAN Domain represents an area that might be out

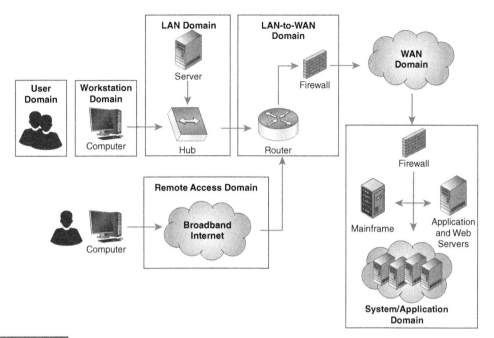

FIGURE 12-1

The WAN Domain within the seven domains of a typical IT infrastructure.

of your control. Your responsibility to secure data means to protect it in such a way that it is secure even when traveling across an untrusted network. Ensuring data are safe even in the WAN Domain makes it possible for your organization to deploy distributed applications that can provide unprecedented functionality to remote users. Implementing the controls necessary to support your security policy in the WAN Domain makes your organization more secure and allows you to provide a higher level of visibility to your data.

Protecting Data Privacy

WANs allows you to connect to your headquarters to several branch offices using a WAN. You connect each of your LANs to the WAN and all your nodes can communicate. The only problem is that you now depend on another organization to communicate. Each time you send a message from your headquarters to a branch office, that message travels across someone else's network. You no longer have control over who sees your network traffic or who can alter it. **Figure 12-2** shows how data traveling from one of your nodes to another across a WAN are out of your control.

Creating secure communications over a WAN is not completely out of your control. Deciding on the best WAN solution for your business depends on your requirements and budget. Security policies outline how each connection type should be configured and protected. The security policies also outline roles and responsibilities. Keep in mind that private WANs security is typically configured by the service provider. Your security policies need to include how to deal with the vendor and how to validate the security configuration.

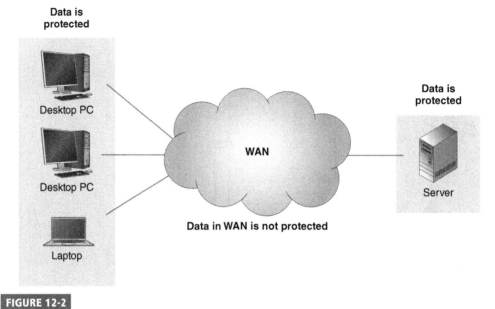

Data is protected

Desktop PC

Desktop PC

Laptop

WAN

Data is protected

Server

Data in WAN is not protected

FIGURE 12-2

Lack of control for data traveling across a WAN.

The biggest question for companies using the Internet to connect their offices is how to keep communication secure and private. A common solution is called a **virtual private network (VPN)**. VPN solutions can be managed in-house. By setting up network devices at both offices, you can create an encrypted tunnel. All communications between the offices are then protected from eavesdropping, and the data passed through the tunnel remain secure. There are dedicated network devices whose only function is to create and manage VPN traffic. These devices are called VPN concentrators. Many firewalls also have the capability to create and maintain a VPN tunnel.

Cloud Computing

The word *cloud* can take many different meanings and depends upon the cloud model. The National Institute of Standards defines cloud computing as "a model for enabling ubiquitous, convenient, on-demand network access to a shared pool of configurable computing resources (e.g., networks, servers, storage, applications, and services) that can be rapidly provisioned and released with minimal management effort or service provider interaction. This cloud model is composed of five essential characteristics, three service models, and four deployment models." The three common cloud service models include the following:

- Infrastructure as a Service (IaaS)
- Platform as a Service (PaaS)
- Software as a Service (SaaS)

SD-WAN

When it comes to WAN, the business is generally concerned with reliability, speed, and cost. An emerging network, SD-WAN in many ways better balances these interests. Several companies are competing for this emerging market, with each providing unique offerings.

To best illustrate and drive a deep understanding of what SD-WAN is and how it differs from the traditional WAN, we will examine Cisco's SD-WAN offering. When we use the term SD-WAN in this chapter, we are referring to Cisco's offering. Nonetheless, for discussion purposes, the Cisco approach to the SD-WAN network model is broad and provides a good illustrative model of the broader SD-WAN architecture.

The traditional WAN would connect the home office to the branches through a circuit. As a company grows into hundreds of branches, the number of dedicated circuit connections can get enormously expensive. Each of these connections must be encrypted. Essentially, we securely connect through the WAN to each branch site. We can look for a cheaper solution using an Internet connection to the home office, but it cannot guarantee reliability like a dedicated circuit.

What is SD-WAN, and how does it differ from the traditional WAN? The game-changer was the migration of core transition data center applications into the cloud. The Internet has been with us for a long time, but the migration of applications to the cloud has changed the way we think about accessing these applications. Today you may be using Office 365, Google Drive, or Dropbox. Many applications can now sit in Google Cloud or Azure.

Traditionally a branch would connect to the home office to access the application, then on the same circuit consume the information. As applications moved to the cloud, the old model no longer made sense in all cases. It does not make sense for a branch to access the home office, the home office to access the cloud, and then return the cloud information back to the branch, especially if the home office is thousands of miles away and the cloud application is hosted close to the branch.

We have to make sure all these connections work seamlessly, reliably, and fast. SD-WAN extends traditional WAN by adding local Internet connections to the branch. The traditional WAN circuit can still exist in the branch. Thus SD-WAN augments WAN capability; the SD-WAN model does not replace the traditional WAN model. You still have routers (referred to as the data plane) that send data from branch to home office. Under SD-WAN, the control plane has become a lot smarter and is no longer part of the router but a standalone management system. From an auditor's lens, these management systems contain the rules that need to be assessed.

This decoupling of routing decisions (i.e., control plane) from the router itself means the router has less CPU-intensive work, which leads to higher performance capability. But simply decoupling the control plane and data plane does not make it smarter. What does make it smarter is that these management systems (including the control plane) can monitor the WAN connections and make smarter decisions.

Sometimes circuits would go down, and we would have failover to the secondary circuit. That works, but then you have other times where performance for some apps might just be poor over one circuit. It wasn't down; it was just degraded. Consequently, it would not failover. The user would see agonizingly slow or no responses. From the user's standpoint, the circuit is unusable. Yet a perfectly good secondary circuit was not accessible because there was no failover. Under SD-WAN, the performance of both circuits is monitored, and traffic routed appropriately. If the primary circuit biomes are degraded, traffic is routed to the secondary circuit.

These routing rules under SD-WAN can also apply to specific applications such as Voice over Internet Protocol (VoIP). We've all experienced VoIP phone calls that sound like an echo or with lots of static. Under SD-WAN, you could set a threshold value, for example, 100 milliseconds of latency or below. When that threshold is exceeded, the VoIP call is routed to an alternative circuit.

From a branch location view, you can have an SD-WAN with the traditional circuit to the home office and an alternate connection to the Internet. The smarter SD-WAN model will automatically route the user to the best connection! What does this mean for the user? If they are accessing an Internet application, they no longer have to travel back and forth to the home office. The user automatically is routed to the Internet if that is the fastest path to the application. Poor local Internet connection. No problem. The user is routed to the home office Internet connection through the traditional WAN circuit. Cisco has reported seeing in some highly distributed environments, as much as 40% improvement in performance using SD-WAN over the traditional WAN.

The SD-WAN model brings more information capability than is possible with a traditional WAN. Under an SD-WAN model, you can apply filtering rules to network traffic. This highly simplifies filters such as URL filters. Rather than applying those filters at every endpoint, such filters can be defined once and applied across the entire WAN traffic.

In sum, many experts look at software-based WAN network models, such as SD-WAN, as the trend in the near future.

Implementing Proper Security Controls for the WAN Domain

The primary control type you will use in the WAN Domain for any data is encryption. You have many encryption choices, and the right control depends on how you'll use the data and which component applies the encryption methods. Your application may encrypt your data, or another component may encrypt the connection in another domain. You will learn about different approaches to encryption later in this chapter. Some solutions require multiple layers of controls. You select the best controls that support a few general principles. These are the same principles that apply in the LAN-to-WAN Domain:

- No data in the WAN Domain should ever be transmitted in cleartext.
- When using encryption, select the algorithm based on needs. Don't just select the largest key.
- Assume an attacker can intercept and examine any network messages.

Figure 12-3 shows a simple diagram of how a VPN tunnel protects encrypted data as it moves across the Internet.

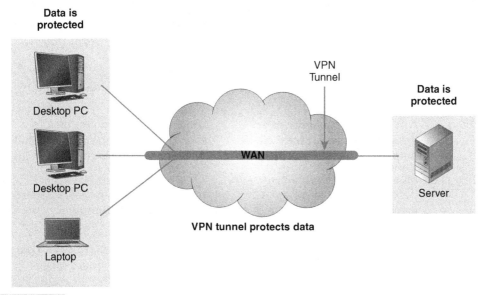

Data is
protected

Desktop PC

Desktop PC

Laptop

VPN
Tunnel

Data is
protected

WAN

Server

VPN tunnel protects data

FIGURE 12-3

Protecting WAN traffic using encryption.

Devices and Components Commonly Found in the WAN Domain

The WAN Domain exists to transport network messages from one node to another. In most cases, the WAN is a network that is owned and managed by some other entity. Your ability to affect the WAN's security is limited or nonexistent. You must ensure that you transmit data across the WAN in a secure fashion using secure protocols and techniques. In this section, you will learn about the devices and components you'll commonly find in the WAN Domain that support communication, both secure and unsecure. Once you've learned about the devices and components, you will learn about controls to ensure compliance in the WAN Domain.

WAN Service Providers

Few organizations have the resources to create and manage their own global WANs. The most common approach to deploying applications and functionality across a WAN is to lease network access from a **WAN service provider**. A WAN service provider provides WAN bandwidth to subscribing organizations. The WAN transports traffic among subscriber nodes and subscribers pay for the service. The WAN service provider handles all routing, connection media, and hardware issues within the WAN. All the subscribers do is connect to the WAN and use it to send and receive traffic.

The three main concerns when selecting a WAN provider are cost, speed, and stability. Other factors should also be considered when selecting a WAN, but these three are often the most important. Each type of WAN has its own characteristics and works best in different types of environments.

TABLE 12-1 WAN options.		
WAN TYPE	**DESCRIPTION**	**COMMENTS**
Dedicated line/ leased line	A point-to-point connection between two physical devices	Most secure, but also one of the most expensive; exclusive access to all bandwidth
Circuit switching	A dedicated circuit established between two points for the duration of a conversation	Lower cost, but requires time to establish circuit and circuit switching is slower than the next two options
Packet switching	Messages travel in variable-length packets along point-to-point or point-to-multipoint links through WAN switches	Can be substantially faster than circuit switching but media is shared and can suffer congestion
Cell relay	Similar to packet switching but with fixed-length cells	Best for transporting voice and data but overhead can reduce speed
VPN over Internet	A VPN established between two nodes	Very inexpensive but performance and stability depend on your Internet connection

> **NOTE**
>
> Although cost is only one factor when considering a WAN provider, it can be a determining factor.

> **NOTE**
>
> With a dedicated line, or a dedicated circuit, you don't share the bandwidth with anyone else. The entire bandwidth is always available for your use.

WAN service providers offer several types of WANs for different budgets and performance requirements. Each type of WAN has its strengths and weaknesses. You need to evaluate each option based on your specific needs to find the best fit for your organization. **Table 12-1** lists the main types of WANs available from WAN service providers.

Pay attention to the cost of WAN service. Some WAN providers offer services for a fixed monthly fee, whereas other products carry a usage charge. Estimate your monthly usage and calculate your costs for each type of service. That is one of the reasons an SD-WAN is so attractive and more scalable. With SD-WAN, the Internet connection already exists at no additional connection cost to the WAN. Dedicated lines or circuit switching are less scalable as the new connection must be ordered, installed, tested, and is an additional cost.

Dedicated Lines/Circuits

Your particular WAN needs will direct you toward the best WAN choice. If your primary need for a WAN is to connect a small number of LANs to one another, dedicated lines might be the best choice. A **dedicated line**, also called a dedicated circuit, is a permanent circuit between two endpoints. A single dedicated line works very well when connecting two LANs, campus area networks (CANs), or even metropolitan area networks (MANs). You can connect more than two networks using multiple dedicated lines.

Dedicated lines are fast, secure, and always available. Because no one else shares your dedicated line with you, your organization has exclusive access to the traffic flowing along the line. Of course, the WAN service provider has access to your traffic as well, but no one else should be able to see your traffic. If your budget and connectivity needs support dedicated lines, they can return some of the best performance of all WAN options.

MPLS/VPN WAN or Metro Ethernet

Multiprotocol Label Switching (MPLS) is a very common network model for many midsize and large companies. If your requirements include connecting more than three or four locations—for example, connecting multiple branch offices to the headquarters— dedicated lines will likely be too expensive. Another option in such a case would be MPLS networks supporting a VPN. MPLS works with many WAN technologies and provides very good overall performance using packet-switching and circuit-switching networks. Although MPLS networks are not optimal for high-bandwidth, large-volume network transfers, they work very well in most environments where you need to maintain connections between several other networks.

WAN Layer 2/Layer 3 Switches

Most discussions of network protocols include a discussion of the **Open Systems Interconnection (OSI) reference model**. The OSI reference model is a generic description for how computers use multiple layers of protocol rules to communicate across a network. The OSI reference model defines seven different layers of communication rules. You will also likely encounter another popular reference model, the **Transmission Control Protocol/Internet Protocol (TCP/IP) reference model**, when discussing network protocols. The TCP/IP reference model defines four different layers of communication rules. Both models are useful to describe how protocols work and how to implement them in network communications. **Figure 12-4** shows the TCP/IP reference model and the OSI reference model.

You might hear hardware devices or software protocols referred to as Layer 2 devices or Layer 5 protocols. These references generally refer to the OSI reference model layer to describe where the referenced hardware or software operates. In the context of WANs, most WAN protocols operate at OSI Layer 2. MPLS actually operates between Layers 2 and 3 and is sometimes called a Layer 2.5 protocol. Most traditional network switches operate at OSI Layer 2, but newer devices use advanced techniques to provide more sophisticated switching capabilities at OSI Layer 3.

Recall that traditional Layer 2 switches use the Media Access Control (MAC) addresses in each packet to forward the packet to its proper destination. One type of Layer 3 switch extends the concept of a traditional Layer 2 switch by implementing fast Internet Protocol (IP) routing using hardware. Most routing using IP addresses requires software to examine each packet. Software is always slower than hardware, and thus, routing has historically been slower than switching. A Layer 3 switch can greatly speed up routing by using advanced hardware to make the routing decision.

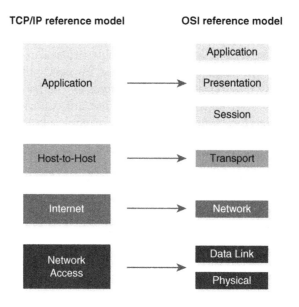

TCP/IP reference model   **OSI reference model**

FIGURE 12-4

TCP/IP and OSI Reference models.

Layered Protocols in Real Life

The idea of layered protocols sounds complex, but it really reflects what happens in normal human-to-human communication. You use layers and translations in subtle ways every time you talk with a different person.

Here is an example that demonstrates the obvious need for multiple layers. Consider how ambassadors communicate in the United Nations. Suppose a U.S. ambassador wants to send a written note to the ambassadors of China, Russia, and Italy. In this example, protocol requires all written messages be presented in French. Here is how the message travels through the United Nations:

1. The U.S. ambassador writes a message in English, then hands the message to a translator. *The ambassador layer passes the message to the translator layer.*

2. The translator translates the message into French, then hands it to an aide to take to the mailroom. *The translator layer passes the message to the aide layer.*

3. The aide makes three copies of the message, addresses each copy, and places the messages in the U.S. outbox in the mailroom. *The aide layer duplicates and passes the messages to the mailroom clerk layer.*

4. The mailroom clerk picks up the messages from the U.S. outbox and places them in the appro-priate inboxes for China, Russia, and Italy. *The mailroom clerk handles the physical transfer.*

5. An aide for each country—China, Russia, and Italy—picks up the message and delivers it to the translator. *The aide layer collects a message from the mailroom and passes it to the translator layer.*

6. The translator translates the message from French into the country's natural language and gives it to the appropriate ambassador. *The translator layer translates the message and passes it to the ambassador layer.*

7. The ambassador for each country reads the message and takes appropriate action. *The ambassador layer reads the message.*

Figure 12-5 illustrates the process.

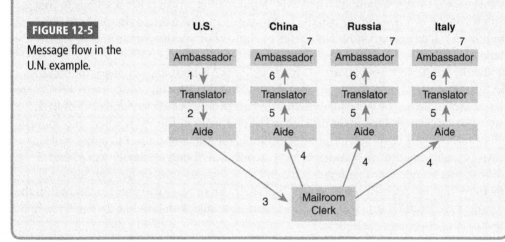

FIGURE 12-5

Message flow in the U.N. example.

WAN Backup and Redundant Links

All components in all domains can fail. If this happens, it's important that each component have a backup or alternate component to replace it. Your WAN connection is no exception. If your organization relies on a single WAN connection and that connection fails, access to your WAN fails.

Keep in mind the importance of redundant and alternate WAN connections in the LAN-to-WAN Domain. The issue bears repeating here. Remember that your organization's ability to use a WAN to communicate with central resources and functions depends on the availability of your WAN to support the connection. A failure anywhere in the WAN violates your organization's data availability. Make sure you take these steps to protect the availability and security of your data across the WAN Domain:

- Ensure the SLA for each WAN service provider meets or exceeds the required uptime goals for each WAN.

- Establish backup or redundant WAN connections—either multiple connections to the same WAN or multiple connections using different WANs.

- Install backup or redundant connection devices in the WAN Domain to ensure connection hardware failure does not result in a failure to connect to your WAN.

WAN Traffic and Performance Monitoring and Analysis

Monitoring the traffic and performance of your WAN Domain can directly translate into concrete results. WAN usage might cost money, but it always costs time. Anytime you can reduce WAN usage, you are saving time and perhaps money as well. Recall that a secure network is one that provides smooth operation and allows only authorized traffic. Access to your WAN is one of the necessary pieces in a distributed environment. If the WAN is down or unreachable, your distributed applications cannot function. Network problems could cause service interruptions and could result in noncompliance. You need to be aware how all parts of your network are working to ensure you are compliant.

Traffic monitoring and analysis for a WAN are nearly identical to the process used with the LAN-to-WAN Domain. The WAN Domain differs from other domains in that you probably don't own or control the hardware or the software in the WAN. Your organization likely pays a subscription fee to connect to another organization's WAN. You pay the WAN service provider either by bandwidth usage or a flat fee for a specified bandwidth limit. Because you are likely to pay for WAN access, proactively managing WAN traffic can reduce your need for additional bandwidth and reduce your WAN costs.

You can implement WAN traffic-monitoring and analysis software and devices in two ways. You can install software or devices on the perimeter of the WAN where you connect to it or rely on your WAN service provider to supply traffic-flow data. You gain far more control monitoring the WAN yourself, but you only have limited capability to affect the WAN's performance. One technique is to send a message to another node on the WAN and have that node echo a response. The first node can analyze the route and duration the message took for the round trip. Comparing sample traffic with baseline data will reveal if the current performance is normal.

Several vendors provide tools to help monitor WAN traffic and optimize your WAN's throughput. Real-time WAN optimization software can analyze current WAN performance and then modify how new traffic is sent across the WAN. These **WAN optimizers** can exclude unnecessary traffic, use compression to maximize bandwidth, cache data, and prioritize traffic to make the best use of your WAN. The result can be a noticeable increase in network speed. In this case, you haven't made the network any faster, but you have used the available bandwidth more efficiently and increased your data throughput.

You can choose from many products to help optimize your WAN usage. Most of these products use similar methods to assess WAN performance such as sending and tracing the path of an echo. Not only can these tools detect performance problems, but by tracing the path, they can identify the fault to a specific hop.

WAN Configuration and Change Management

As with the LAN and LAN-to-WAN Domains, managing network-configuration settings in the WAN Domain is important. You need to proactively manage the components you do control. You can manage the settings of at least these WAN Domain components:

- **WAN access device**—This is the device or computer you use to physically connect to your WAN.

- **WAN account**—Your WAN service provider will provide access for you to configure specific settings to your WAN account. It is important that you create a backup of these settings. Even if your WAN service provider only allows you to manage your account using a webpage, saving screen shots of each configuration page is better than having no record of your settings.
- **WAN optimization device**—Any hardware or software that optimizes WAN traffic belongs to the WAN Domain and is a prime candidate for configuration management.

The strategies and techniques for managing configuration settings and controlling configuration changes should match your activities in the LAN and LAN-to-WAN Domains. As with other domains, managing the configuration settings of your WAN Domain components is an important part of keeping your overall environment compliant and secure.

WAN Management Tools and Systems

Because the WAN service provider bears the responsibility of maintaining the actual WAN, there isn't much left to do to manage components in your WAN Domain. It is important to ensure all the components in the WAN Domain are doing their jobs, but there isn't much you can do to manage the actual WAN. You learned about WAN optimization tools earlier in this chapter. Managing components in the WAN Domain primarily means managing how well your organization uses the WAN resources. There are three main categories of WAN management tasks:

- Providing the best WAN option for specific traffic
- Caring for WAN Domain components
- Optimizing WAN usage

In this respect, the WAN optimization tools are also WAN management tools. Your organization likely has different needs for WANs. As a result, you will likely use different WAN solutions. You may make the decision of which WAN to use in other domains, but the actual access point exists in the WAN Domain. It is important to ensure each WAN access point is configured and optimized to provide the best level of service for your needs.

> ### Mixed WANs
>
> Your organization doesn't have to choose only a single WAN solution. Organizations commonly use multiple WAN solutions to best meet their needs. For example, you might select dedicated lines to connect your headquarters building to your R&D facility, a packet-switching network to connect branch offices that need only data services, and a circuit-switching network for branches that need voice and data services. You could also use a metro Ethernet network for the branch office that is located in the same city as your headquarters building. Such a solution with multiple WANs can give you the best performance for your distributed enterprise needs.

Incident Response Management Tools

No matter how well your data are protected or how well your WAN is designed, eventually, there will be an outage or a breach of security. It could be a human error, a vulnerability within the network device supporting the WAN, or a host of problems outside your control. No organization's WAN connection or information security is considered perfect.

When that incident occurs, your organization will need to respond quickly in a well-thought-out process. The speed and effectiveness of the response will limit the damage. This includes how well you can control the costs and consequences resulting from the incident. To ensure an organization is well prepared, it's typical to create an incident response plan so a well-skilled IT team and their supporting policies ensure that an incident can be quickly identified and contained. It's this team's responsibility to perform a careful analysis of the cause. Understanding the nature of the tack helps make changes to prevent it from reoccurring in the future.

This response team is typically a cross-functional team that is pulled together by people from multiple disciplines. The team is pulled together to respond to major incidents. Minor incidents are typically managed as part of normal operations.

Incident response policies are generally broad, covering a wide variety of security incidents. The WAN incident response plan is typically integrated into the broader response plans. This includes the classification of the incident. You classify incidents to prioritize an immediate response and to prevent a repeat of the incident in the future. To help prioritize the immediate response, you classify the potential impact on the organizations. To help prevent the incident from happening again, you classify the root cause of the incident.

An incident analysis should start immediately upon activating the response team. You must determine quickly the type of threat, the scope of the incident, and the extent of the damage. This will allow you to determine the best response. During this analysis, you are collecting information both for the immediate need to contain the incident and for future forensic analysis.

The collection of forensic evidence is an important part of the response team's responsibility. This means collecting and preserving information that can be used to reconstruct events. The analysis depends on as much information as possible, particularly indicating the following:

- What led up to the event, such as any WAN monitoring that was taking place
- What happened during the event, such as how many circuits were impacted
- How effective the response was, such as communication with the service providers

Access Rights and Access Controls in the WAN Domain

Because there are limited components in the WAN versus SD-WAN, there are also limited opportunities to enforce access control for the domain. There are essentially two places to control access to the WAN. First, you can deploy controls to limit access to the WAN access device. Device and user authentication and authorization controls should limit which users can access the WAN access point. The second way to control WAN access is in the access device itself. The WAN access point has the ability to enforce access controls. In this way, the WAN access device controls which users can get through the device and onto the WAN.

WAN access devices and WAN optimization devices both contain the ability to selectively grant access to the WAN. Although the WAN access device generally operates like a firewall or gateway, WAN optimization devices can make more sophisticated decisions about WAN access. Granting access may include decisions regarding time- or bandwidth-sensitive rights. Some users might be granted WAN access only during slow periods, while other users might get access on demand. You have the ability to grant or deny WAN access based on your security and functional needs.

Implementing more complex controls means you should spend more time testing the controls under different circumstances. If you implement load-based controls using WAN optimization, ensure you test the controls under different network loads, either real or simulated. Use auditing to create logging entries for repeated access denials to ensure your controls aren't hampering your users' ability to do their jobs. As always, avoid auditing too many events. Only audit the ones you'll need to analyze your WAN's ongoing performance.

Maximizing C-I-A

The main goal in all domains is to deploy and maintain controls that support all of the C-I-A properties of security for your data. The WAN Domain contains several components that play critical roles in providing secure access to your organization's data. Maintaining that security requires diligence and the right controls.

WAN Service Availability SLAs

Each WAN service contract includes specific promises of stated levels of service called **service level agreements (SLAs)**. SLAs state what your WAN service provider promises to deliver in terms of various types of services. Most WAN service provider SLAs address the availability property of data security. You should subscribe to a WAN service that guarantees the level of availability your organization requires to conduct business.

Availability SLA terms depend on the type of service you purchase. Most WAN service providers offer customers a choice of service guarantees for different costs to meet different customers' needs. **Table 12-2** shows a sample list of availability service choices. Note that the levels of service differ based on the reliability or recovery options selected.

TABLE 12-2 Availability service choices.

SERVICE	AVAILABILITY	COMMENT
Dual routers/ dual circuits	100%	Redundant hardware and connections provide uninterrupted service.
Single router with backup	99.95%	Backup hardware can replace the primary router with very little downtime. The estimated annual downtime is 4.4 hours.
Single router	99.5%	A single router is a single point of failure— and you must replace failed hardware. The estimated annual downtime is 43.8 hours.

The level of availability you choose will dictate the cost and hardware requirements for your WAN service. Examine the impact of expected or scheduled annual downtime and select the level of service that fits your organization.

WAN Traffic Encryption/VPNs

SLAs define levels of service that protect the availability property of data. Additional concerns when sending data across any WAN include integrity and confidentiality. The main type of control you can use to ensure the integrity and confidentiality of your data is encryption. One of the more common types of encryption in use in the WAN Domain is encrypted traffic over a VPN.

A VPN is a persistent connection between two endpoints, commonly created over a WAN. Although not limited to WANs, VPNs make it easy to establish what appears to be a dedicated connection over a shared-access WAN. VPNs work well in creating persistent connections, also called tunnels, over the Internet or other types of WANs. Many VPNs also encrypt the traffic in the tunnel, making it an attractive option for WAN traffic that may contain sensitive data. Encrypted VPNs are also called **secure VPNs**. Even though others might be able to see the traffic as it travels through the WAN, no one can read it or change it without being detected because the data are encrypted.

> **NOTE**
>
> VPNs provide secure access to remote users and are particularly pertinent to the Remote Access Domain.

Today's networks often support multiple VPN protocols. Consult your WAN service provider for information on which VPN protocols your WAN supports. Use VPNs anytime you need to ensure integrity and confidentiality when sending data over a WAN. **Table 12-3** lists some of the more common VPN protocols in use today.

TABLE 12-3 Common VPN protocols.	
PROTOCOL	**DESCRIPTION**
Layer 2 Tunneling Protocol (L2TP)	This common tunneling protocol defines a connection between two endpoints. You need another protocol, such as Internet Protocol Security (IPSec), to provide encryption services.
Point-to-Point Tunneling Protocol (PPTP)	This Layer 2 protocol defines a tunnel between two endpoints. PPTP is older and generally less secure than L2TP.
Secure Sockets Layer/ Transport Layer Security (SSL/TLS)	This common protocol is used to transport encrypted Hypertext Transfer Protocol (HTTP) traffic. It can also be used to create an encrypted tunnel.
Datagram Transport Layer Security (DTLS)	This protocol is used by Cisco hardware to create a generic VPN that works well in most network architectures.
Secure Socket Tunneling Protocol (SSTP)	SSTP works at the Transport Layer to provide a VPN that works with most firewalls.

WAN Service Provider SOC Compliance

For service providers, it's important to instill trust and confidence in their customers. Service organizations have a vested interest in helping their customers understand that adequate controls and processes are in place. The Service Organization Controls (SOC) report provides such assurance. The Auditing Standards Board of the **American Institute of Certified Public Accountants (AICPA)** issues and maintains these auditing standards.

An SOC report signifies that a service organization has had its control objectives and activities examined by an independent auditing firm. Because so much emphasis is placed on security and compliance with multiple sources of requirements, service providers must demonstrate that they have adequate controls in place to securely handle their customers' data. In addition, the requirements of Section 404 of the Sarbanes-Oxley Act make SOC audit reports even more important to the process of reporting on the effectiveness of internal control over financial reporting.

SOC reports take the form of three different engagements, which produce three different reports. The following are the three types of engagements and associated SOC reports:

- SOC 1 report is the assessment of controls related to financial reporting.
- SOC 2 report builds on SOC 1 and includes controls related to organizational oversight, risk management, vendor management, and regulatory oversight.
- SOC 3 report is a simplified summary of the SOC 2 report and is typically produced for public consumption.

An SOC compliance audit demonstrates that a WAN service provider stands behind its security controls and has confidence in its ability to protect customer data. You should insist on doing business only with WAN service providers who can show evidence of the appropriate SOC reports.

Adherence to Documented IT Security Policies, Standards, Procedures, and Guidelines

Compliance in the WAN Domain depends on implementing the best controls you can and on ensuring your WAN service provider's controls are compliant as well. As with other domains, you should explore alternative controls for each security goal. You must ensure the correct controls are in place to balance each of the three C-I-A security properties.

As you analyze controls in the WAN Domain to meet compliance requirements, ensure each control satisfies your security policy. If a control does not support any part of your security policy, you should question its value to your organization. Different legislation, regulations, and vendor standards have different requirements. Implementing multiple types of controls decreases the likelihood that an attack will be successful and makes your WAN Domain more secure.

Best Practices for WAN Domain Compliance

The WAN Domain allows multiple locations to establish network connections without having to manage the physical networks yourself. Because this domain connects your environment to an untrusted WAN, you must ensure the controls protect your internal resources. Solid planning, along with aggressive management, can provide both easy access across an untrusted WAN and the ability to maintain your data's security.

The following best practices represent what many organizations have learned. Plan well and you can enjoy a functional WAN Domain that makes internal information and resources available for use to WAN users. Here are general best practices for securing your WAN Domain:

- Map your proposed WAN and SD-WAN architecture, including redundant and backup hardware and connections, before establishing service.
- Establish multiple WAN connections to avoid any single points of failure. Use fault-tolerant hardware that can maintain WAN connectivity if connection fails.
- Use load-balancing techniques on the multiple WAN connections to use the bandwidth of both connections.
- Develop a backup and recovery plan for each component in the WAN Domain. Include recovery plans for damaged or destroyed connection media.
- Integrate WAN services into your incident response planning.
- Implement frequent update procedures for all operating systems, applications, and network device software and firmware in the WAN Domain.
- Monitor WAN traffic for performance and packets for suspicious content.
- Carefully control any configuration setting changes or physical changes to domain nodes. Update your network map after any changes.
- Use automated tools whenever possible to map, configure, monitor, and manage the WAN Domain.
- Use WAN optimization devices or software to maximize WAN utilization.
- Deny any unencrypted traffic the ability to travel to the WAN.
- Insist that all WAN service providers provide evidence of the appropriate SOC report.
- Frequently sample WAN traffic flow metrics and be alert for any unusual activity.
- Conduct periodic penetration tests to identify security control weaknesses.
- Keep WAN-connected devices and applications patched to the latest available level.
- Automatically modify filtering rules to deny traffic from sources generating known attack signature packets.

These best practices give you a brief overview of the issues you'll need to consider when implementing WAN access. Consider each of the best practices and add your own that will make your organization safer when transporting data across a WAN.

CHAPTER SUMMARY

One of the most important concerns when sending data across public networks is confidentiality. Although not all data are confidential, any data you exchange with a remote resource uses a WAN; consider all WANs to be hostile and unsecure. Your organization likely controls access to your LANs and has some measure of assurance of how private the LANs are. WANs are different. You don't have the same level of control over who accesses them or who can access data traveling across a WAN. You must deploy sufficient controls to protect the privacy of any data in the WAN Domain.

In this chapter, we examined emerging and breakthrough WAN technologies such as SD-WAN. We reviewed the key components of the WAN and SD-WAN network models. This chapter discussed the trade-offs among the models and best practices. Additionally, the chapter examined how to monitor the WAN environment and what WAN components should be considered as part of an audit, such as incident response.

12

Compliance Within the WAN Domain

KEY CONCEPTS AND TERMS

American Institute of Certified
  Public Accountants (AICPA)
Cloud
Dedicated line
Multiprotocol Label Switching
  (MPLS)
Open Systems Interconnection
  (OSI) reference model

Secure VPNs
Service level agreement (SLA)
Software-defined WAN
  (SD-WAN)
Transmission Control
  Protocol/Internet
  Protocol (TCP/IP) reference
  model

WAN optimizers
WAN service provider
Wide area network (WAN)
Virtual private network (VPN)

CHAPTER 12 ASSESSMENT

1. The WAN Domain commonly contains a DMZ.

  A. True

  B. False

2. One of the most important concerns when sending data across a WAN is confidentiality.

  A. True

  B. False

3. Which of the following is the primary type of control employed in the WAN Domain?

A. Firewalls
B. Encryption
C. Hashing
D. Compression

4. A SD-WAN completely replaces all the components of the older WAN model.

A. True
B. False

5. Which type of WAN generally has the highest speed and is most secure?

A. Dedicated line
B. Circuit switching
C. Packet switching
D. MPLS network

6. The _____ contains the guaranteed availability for your WAN connection.

7. An SD-WAN is more scalable than a WN network model.

A. True
B. False

8. Most WAN protocols operate at which level in the OSI reference model?

A. 7
B. 3
C. 2
D. 1

9. Many experts think _____ network models are the trend in the near future.

10. WAN subscription cost tends to decrease as availability increases.

A. True
B. False

11. By definition, VPN traffic is encrypted.

A. True
B. False

12. Which of the following is an internal control report for the services provided by a service provider?

A. SLA
B. WAN
C. SOC
D. MPLS

13. A(n) _____ plan should be integrated into broader response plans.

14. A SOC ___ report assesses the controls related to vendor management.

Compliance Within the Remote Access Domain

© SidorArt/Shutterstock

I N THE AFTERMATH OF THE COVID-19 pandemic, there has been a dramatic shift toward employees working remotely. According to the Owl Labs survey taken in 2020, 80% of full-time workers expect to work from home at least three times per week. This is almost double the 44% rate from the same survey taken in 2018. While there have been benefits to both the employee and organization, it has come at a price. Many of these remote workers use their personal equipment. More data than ever are leaving the confines of the traditional office setting.

The proliferation of new equipment and pressure on deploying remote access capability has presented challenges for IT teams. They need to make sure that information that leaves the confines of the network is protected and personal devices are clear from malware and viruses. Whether it is personal devices or corporate devices, the organization needs to ensure security tools are installed, managed, and supported remotely.

An important first step to evaluating remote access security is to conduct an audit. This chapter will discuss the key elements you should include in a remote access security audit. This chapter will review those key elements for inclusion in such an audit.

Chapter 13 Topics

This chapter covers the following topics and concepts:

- How remote access relate to business drivers
- Which devices and components are commonly found in the Remote Access Domain
- What remote access and virtual private network (VPN) tunnel monitoring are
- What remote access traffic and performance monitoring and analysis are
- What remote access configuration and change management are
- Which remote access management tools and systems are commonly used

- What access rights and access controls in the Remote Access Domain are
- What Remote Access Domain configuration validation is
- How to ensure adherence to documented information technology (IT) security policies, standards, procedures, and guidelines
- What best practices for Remote Access Domain compliance are

Chapter 13 Goals

When you complete this chapter, you will be able to:

- Identify compliance law requirements and business drivers
- Compare how devices and components found in the Remote Access Domain contribute to compliance
- Describe methods of ensuring compliance in the Remote Access Domain
- Summarize best practices for Remote Access Domain compliance

Remote Access Business Drivers

This dramatic shift that increased the remote workforce has multiple benefits for both the employer and employee. In understanding these benefits we also understand the potential risk. As the old saying goes, "there is no free lunch." For each benefit, we need to consider the risk. For example, an employee may find the peace and quiet in a home office beneficial. At the same time, employees are less supervised and there is less informal collaboration. While everyone's situation may be different, let's consider the potential benefits outlined in **Table 13-1**.

The Remote Access Domain of a typical IT infrastructure contains the components that can bring your distributed environment together and make its resources available to remote users. When your organization provides this level of service, you are enabling remote users to operate more effectively and efficiently without requiring them to physically be at your main location. This capability is a benefit to users who are geographically separated from your physical resources, either permanently or temporarily. Your users can do their jobs from more locations if they can access your resources remotely. The Remote Access Domain provides the access path for your remote users. **Figure 13-1** shows the Remote Access Domain in the context of the seven domains in the information technology (IT) infrastructure.

Take necessary steps to secure your data in all seven domains of the IT infrastructure. Distributing your data far from its secure storage locations exposes it to more threats of attack. You'll likely need to show compliance with one or more requirements that directly address sensitive data sent to remote users. For example, the Health Insurance Portability and Accountability Act (HIPAA) requires controls to protect the privacy of medical data.

TABLE 13-1 Employer and Employee Remote Access Potential Benefit

EMPLOYER	EMPLOYEE
Talent retention	Freedom and flexibility
Cost saving	Cost saving
Reduction in absenteeism	Time saved from not commuting
Loyalty	Location freedom
Productivity	Peace and quiet
Expanded talent pool	Less stress
	Work-life balance
	Personalized environment

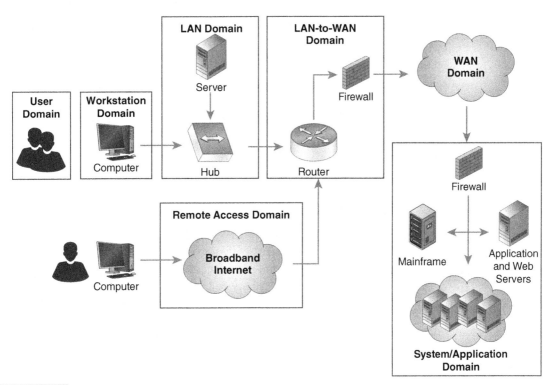

FIGURE 13-1

The Remote Access Domain within the seven domains of a typical IT infrastructure.

The Payment Card Industry (PCI) requires credit card privacy controls. Many states require privacy controls on any personally identifiable data. These are only a few of the requirements you'll need to satisfy when supporting remote users. Your security policy should include all the necessary elements to meet compliance requirements and support efficient and cost-effective operation. Making sure you have the proper controls in place to secure the Remote Access Domain is one important part of an overall plan for data security.

Protecting Data Privacy

A 2021 study from the Tessian Group reports that 48% of employees report being less likely to follow safe data practices while working from home. Additionally, 84% of technology leaders report concerns over the adequacy of data loss prevention controls for the remote workforce.

Assessing remote access monitoring and capability should be a priority given these new remote force realities and risks. Protecting data privacy and an organization starts with strong security controls and security assessment of potential vulnerabilities. The following are steps an organization should take to assess and improve remote access security:

- **Penetration testing**—Test all connectivity points between the end user and the corporate network for vulnerabilities
- **Policy creation**—Clear and concise policies and awareness training on what is permitted for remote work environments such as are allowed to print, secure material, and share with family a workspace
- **Remote device testing**—Test samples of remote user devices for compliance with policies
- **Check protocols and authentication**—Identify how users connect to the corporate network and access sensitive data; dual-factor authentication should be at a minimum the de facto standard
- **Governance**—How are remote workers' access with sensitive information monitored and policies enforced; what are the consequences for a noncompliance to following safe data practices
- **Logging and reporting**—Ensure activities by remote devices are properly monitored and the ability to generate reports and audits required by its compliance obligations

Implementing Proper Security Controls for the Remote Access Domain

Implementing proper remote access controls makes good business sense. Equally important in many industries, it is required by law, and evidence will be required by regulators. Consider the Federal Financial Institutions Examination Council (FFIEC) examination handbook for the financial services industry. Section II.C.15(c) is dedicated to remote access. Specifically the regulatory guidance states:

> Management should develop policies to ensure that remote access by employees, whether using institution or personally owned devices, is provided safely and soundly. Such policies and procedures should define how the institution provides remote access and the controls necessary to offer remote access securely.

The FFIEC guidance, as with many best practices frameworks, lays out a series of requirements. These regulatory requirements include the following control measures:

- Disable remote unused communications.
- Tightly control remote access through management approvals and subsequent audits.
- Implement robust controls over configurations at both ends of the communication.
- Implement remote connections to prevent potential malicious use.
- Log and monitor all remote access communications.
- Secure remote access devices.
- Restrict remote access during specific times.
- Limit the applications available for remote access.
- Use robust authentication methods for access.
- Use encryption to secure communications.

Notice the guidance in the second bullet requires audits of the remote access environment. A formal audit puts management on notice when any major defects are found in the form of audit issues. Additionally, notice the level of control the organization is expected to have of the end-user devices. This may include ensuring virus protection is installed and current, preventing users from installing software on the devices, as well as the use of firewalls, host-based intrusion detection system (IDS), and packet content filtering to identify, monitor, and limit remote access activities.

A secure connection between the remote user and the organization's network will typically mean creating an encrypted point-to-point tunnel through the Internet. The most common form of remote access is through a virtual private network (VPN). The VPN provides an encrypted isolated "tunnel" or connection between a remote user's computer and the internal network.

Although the most common security control in the Remote Access Domain is encryption, don't forget the controls on remote users and the computers they use to access your network from a remote location. Remote users must adhere to your remote access acceptable use policy (AUP). Encryption can help protect your sensitive data, but a user who isn't careful or a poorly secured laptop can leave the data vulnerable.

Devices and Components Commonly Found in the Remote Access Domain

The Remote Access Domain provides access to remote users and remote resources. It exists, in part, to provide a secure way to exchange data with remote components without sacrificing data privacy. This domain consists of several components that work together with your wide area network (WAN) to ensure that your data are private and your environment is compliant. **Figure 13-2** shows the devices and components commonly found in the Remote Access Domain.

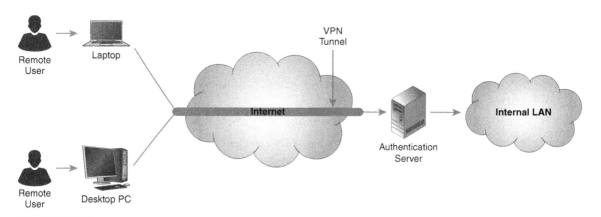

Devices and components are commonly found in the Remote Access Domain.

Control system architectures are different in the sense that in flat networks users would have access across the entire infrastructure. Access was limited by application layers. In a controlled network, when a system does not have adequate access control capability, added protection is provided by limiting network traffic. For example, network firewalls protect systems from inbound communications by preventing all communication methods except those required for the desired functionality.

The following list describes the commonly found security controls required from any system to protect access to critical resources, services, data, or communications. Every system in the chain of communication between a remote user and the end target host should pass through these controls.

- **Identity establishment**—Controls to provide and exchange unique identities
- **Identity validation**—A control designed to ensure the identity of each party
- **Roles (optional)**—Groups of users or systems organized according to their responsibilities
- **Entitlements**—Lists of access rules that govern which groups and individuals are allowed access to certain resources at what times

Remote Users

Remote users refer to enable individuals to access systems where they are not physically capable to connect directly through a tried connection to the network. Employees who traveled often needed to access data from the organization's central database when they were away from the office. This example is a classic case for remote access. The classic solution to this need was to provide a modem or bank of modems attached to the internal network.

An audit should look broadly across the user population to determine who is remotely accessing the corporate network. Understanding the user population will also you to understand how data are handled. Let's consider the following sampling user populations:

1. **IT or security company employees**—These users include people like domain admins, network admins, and others who typically access critical internal systems from inside the office.

2. **Third-party hardware and software vendors**—Third-party vendors for hardware and software typically require elevated privileges within targeted host systems to perform tasks.

3. **Supply chain vendors**—These remote users may need access to the network to monitor inventory and have access to financial and forecast data.

4. **Services vendors**—Vendors that provide specific services such as human resources, legal, and payroll may require access to specific business applications.

5. **Consultants**—Businesses will sometimes need privileged access to support special projects or deliver custom code to be tested.

It's important to assess remote users' access needs based on their roles. In each role an audit should ensure policies are adequate, appropriate management oversight exists, monitoring is in place, and compliance to policies is enforced.

Remote user access should require a higher standard of care than local user access. Local users enjoy the additional protection of the local environment and its security controls to protect data. Remote users do not have these additional layers of protection. You must ensure that your users agree to comply with your remote access AUP and that you have sufficient controls in place to protect the security of your data even in remote locations.

FYI

Be careful when allowing devices to act as remote access devices. Smartphones and tablets can cause problems. Many of these devices are not as secure as they might seem. Although most of today's smart devices that can support VPNs do so well, local data protection support is often lacking. Smaller and more compact devices are ultraportable and easy to misplace. Many of these devices have poor default controls for protecting the data at rest. Initially, many organizations were quick to restrict the use of such devices. That has become less feasible, however. Fortunately, various controls and mobile-device management companies provide solutions to help mitigate the risks.

Remote Workstations or Laptops

The user's computer, laptop, or other device becomes the remote device. Remote devices aren't special devices— they just have the ability to connect to a WAN and establish a connection to some other resource. In fact, more and more tablets and smartphones are used as remote devices to access corporate email and collaboration applications such as MS Teams.

Remote devices need two main capabilities to handle remote connections in a secure manner:

- **Remote devices must be able to handle encryption**—The most common type of encryption used in remote access is the secure VPN. As long as your device supports the VPN you've chosen for remote access and can establish a secure connection, the device passes the first test.

- **Remote devices must be able to protect stored data**—Even when using a VPN, the data get decrypted at the remote device. If your remote device can't ensure data privacy through its own controls, it should not be allowed to retrieve or process your confidential data.

As computers and other devices mature, it is common to see VPN support and local data privacy protection as standard features. You can use operating system encryption or third-party utilities to encrypt data. Either way, most of today's computers with recent operating systems already contain the ability to act as secure remote access devices.

Remote Access Controls and Tools

When it comes to remote access, organizations are concerned about flexibility, reliability, and speed. Wireless connections extend the flexibility to remote devices. Mobile devices and **broadband** are reliable. However, the speed and reliability with which they can access and exchange data depend on location and carrier. Much like cell phone coverage, mobile broadband coverage can be spotty.

This is one area in which security policies need to keep pace with technology and business requirements. Policies must be clear whether personal devices such as a smartphone should be permitted access to organization information.

The Remote Access Domain must include control standards that address VPN connections, multifactor authentication, and token use. For example, a VPN control standard may describe the security requirements for VPN and other remote access connections to the organization's network.

It is the responsibility of employees with VPN privileges to ensure that unauthorized users are not allowed access to the organization's internal networks. VPN use is to be controlled using either a one-time password authentication such as a token device or a public/private key system with a strong passphrase as described in the multifactor authentication to VPN standard.

Each of the following three core controls are included within the remote access environment:

1. **Authentication**—Controls that test the assertion that prove the identity of the remote user.

2. **Authorization**—Controls that grant authenticated users the appropriate and limited access.

3. **Nonrepudiation**—Controls that ensure the user cannot challenge their ownership which in this case is the activity performed during a remote access session. This is achieved through a combination of controls such as authentication with multifactor authentication and encrypted VPN tunnels.

Authentication Servers

The process in the previous section describes authentication for remote users. The two most common methods to authenticate remote users are RADIUS and TACACS+. Both rely on centralized authentication databases and servers to handle all remote users. Either of these approaches works well when there is a large number of remote users or you need to manage remote users in a central location.

RADIUS

Remote Authentication Dial In User Service (RADIUS) is a network protocol that supports remote connections by centralizing the management tasks for authentication, authorization, and accounting for computers to connect and access a network. RADIUS is a popular protocol that many network software and devices support and is often used by Internet service providers (ISPs) and large enterprises to manage access to their networks.

RADIUS is a client/server protocol that runs in the Application Layer and uses **User Datagram Protocol (UDP)** to transport authentication and control information. UDP is a core protocol of the Internet Protocol (IP) suite. It is a connectionless protocol, which provides no guarantee of delivery. Servers with RADIUS support that control access for remote users and devices communicate with the RADIUS server to authenticate devices and users before granting access. In addition to just granting access and authorizing actions, RADIUS records usage of network services for accounting purposes.

 NOTE

The Application Layer is Layer 7 in the Open Systems Interconnection (OSI) reference model, and Layer 4 in the Transmission Control Protocol/Internet Protocol (TCP/IP) reference model.

TACACS+

Terminal Access Controller Access-Control System Plus (TACACS+) is another network protocol that was developed by Cisco. TACACS+ has roots back to an earlier protocol, TACACS, but is entirely different. TACACS+ provides access control for remote networked computing devices using one or more centralized servers. TACACS+ is similar to RADIUS in that it provides authentication, authorization, and accounting services, but TACACS+ separates the authentication and authorization information. TACACS+ also uses TCP for more reliability.

One difference between RADIUS and TACACS+ is of interest in a discussion of security. RADIUS only encrypts the password when sending an access request packet to the server. TACACS+ encrypts the entire packet, making it a little harder to sniff data from a TACACS+ packet.

VPNs and Encryption

Remote users create a VPN tunnel connection to the organization network. This **tunneling** process ensures that your information will be encapsulated so that no one will be able to intercept, alter, or even monitor your activity. Tunneling does more than just hide and tunnel your data from the rest of the Internet. Data in transit are more vulnerable to attacks as the data will travel outside the protected network. The VPN and associated tunnel solve this problem by sending all traffic through the encrypted tunnel.

A VPN is cost-effective by replacing more expensive dedicated point-to-point links. Using a VPN over existing Internet connections adds no additional cost. Two types of VPN are commonly used, and both are secured but require different implementation approaches.

1. **Site-to-site VPN**—Typically used to connect two or more offices. The VPN connection is typically established between two firewalls and remains up constantly.
2. **Remote access VPN**—Typically used by remote users. The connection is typically established manually through the users' laptop or desktop. This would be the type of connection used by employees working from home.

In both these connections the system administrator can choose one of two types of tunnels to be used as follows:

- **Full tunnel**—All traffic coming from the employee's device will go directly to the corporate firewall. This is a completely secured implementation as all the security services of the firewall will be applied to all the traffic coming out from the employee's device.
- **Split tunnel**—Part of the traffic will be encrypted, and part will be sent through the public network. The traffic will be split based on its purpose. A split VPN tunnel is inherently less secure.

ISP WAN Connections

One of the more common ways to establish remote connections is using the Internet. Because it is easy to establish Internet connections and the access points are numerous, it makes sense to at least consider it for your remote connections needs. Historically, there have been several issues that must be resolved to use the Internet as a remote access WAN:

- **Both sides of the connection must use the same WAN**—When using the Internet as the WAN, all each side must do is establish an Internet connection. The LAN-to-WAN Domain already ensures your internal networks are connected to your WAN. All that is left is for the remote node to connect.
- **Encryption is an absolute necessity**—This is because the Internet is a public use network. VPNs work well to transport data securely over the Internet.
- **Reliable access must be available for remote nodes**—Internet access is becoming easier to find than ever before. Many Wi-Fi hotspots exist to enable computers and devices to connect to the Internet.

- **Remote connections must be fast enough to be usable**—This requirement is one that will likely cause the most potential issues. Sometimes, especially in more remote areas, it is difficult to find high-speed Internet access. In such cases, it is important to provide access through low-bandwidth methods to ensure data availability.

Although the Internet might not be the fastest WAN, it is quickly becoming the most cost-effective medium and the easiest to use for remote connections.

Remote Access and VPN Tunnel Monitoring

Preventative controls cannot prevent all security threats and mitigate all security vulnerabilities. To ensure that preventative measures are not bypassed, monitoring needs to be put in place. Remote access monitoring should include the following:

- Prioritize monitoring toward critical assets and services.
- Monitor failed authentication attempts.
- Monitor successful authentication attempts from different sources and alert when the same user logs in.
- Monitor failed access attempts; all devices or processes that manage access control to communications, data, or services should log and/or alert when access is requested that is not allowed.
- Monitor successful access attempts; all devices or processes that manage access control to communications, data, or services should log when access is requested and allowed.
- Log VPN connections to track what users are on the network at what time and for what duration.
- Log any remote logon attempt on end user devices.

Anytime you allow remote access to your internal protected local area network (LAN) by remote users, you increase the risk of security violations. It is important that you know who is using the remote access features you've enabled to access your resources. There's a lot you can monitor with respect to remote access, but the best place to start is by identifying and validating just who is using remote access.

The overall idea is to keep track of who is using your VPNs and what they are doing. For example, suppose your primary VPN is optimized for large volumes of small messages. Your expectation when you enabled the VPN was that users would use it to access your online order management system. VPN and remote access monitoring has shown you that most VPN users are running very large custom reports from your database to analyze data. The VPN is actually transporting large volumes of data for a relatively small number of users. You find that you can change some VPN settings that make it run faster for the way your users are using the VPN. Reports run faster, and your data are more available. **Table 13-2** lists a few programs that help monitor remote access and VPN usage.

TABLE 13-2 Remote access and VPN monitoring tools.

PRODUCT	SOURCE
CodePlex Remote Access Monitor (open source)	http://remoteaccessmonitor.codeplex.com/
SoftSea Remote Access Monitor (free)	http://www.softsea.com/review/Remote-Access-Monitor.html
Cisco VPN Monitor	http://www.cisco.com/en/US/products/sw/cscowork/ps2326/ products_user_guide_chapter09186a00800e680d.html#63236
Simple Network Management Protocol (SNMP)	Not a vendor-specific product

The last entry in Table 13-2 is the **Simple Network Management Protocol (SNMP)**. SNMP is a network protocol used to monitor network devices. Most network devices include SNMP support and can run SNMP agents to report conditions that require attention by another computer or device running network management system software. SNMP uses UDP protocol messages to retrieve information from network devices and for the devices to send updates when conditions you define are met. Although there are many ways to use SNMP, you can configure devices to send an alert to the network manager when remote users connect to your network.

Remote Access Traffic and Performance Monitoring and Analysis

It's important to monitor connections and events related to remote access users to learn about who is accessing your network from remote locations. But to ensure your VPNs are configured to best utilize your VPN bandwidth, it is important to also monitor the traffic flowing along your VPNs. Although you can't monitor the contents of traffic in encrypted VPN tunnels, you can monitor traffic statistics to understand how well your remote users are using VPN bandwidth. You can also detect unusual VPN activity that could indicate malicious activity or excessive use.

> **technical TIP**
>
> You should verify that all traffic flowing along your VPNs is encrypted. It is possible to configure VPN tunnels to transport data without encrypting it first. If you misconfigure your VPN or if an attacker is successful at reconfiguring your VPN, you could be sending data into the WAN unencrypted. Validate that the packets flowing along your VPN are actually encrypted.

Because both endpoints are within domains in your IT infrastructure, you can monitor decrypted packets when they emerge from the end of the VPN tunnel. It is still important that you monitor WAN traffic to understand how your organization uses your WAN connections. VPN traffic monitoring provides additional information on how individual tunnels are behaving within your overall WAN

NOTE

Monitoring VPN traffic does not replace any other types of network monitoring.

usage. Excessive WAN usage might indicate a network usage problem. Further investigation using VPN monitoring could reveal that one remote user using a VPN is attempting to launch a denial of service (DoS) attack on your organization. In this case, WAN traffic monitoring will have revealed a high-level problem, and VPN traffic monitoring will have revealed the cause of the problem. You need to monitor at both levels to get the whole picture.

You can implement VPN traffic monitoring and analysis using the same methods as LAN and WAN traffic monitoring and analysis. You can install software or devices on the perimeter of the VPN where you establish the endpoint. You can also use any of a wide variety of network management software packages that support SNMP to monitor traffic directly from the network devices that transport VPN traffic. Regardless of the methods you employ, monitoring and analyzing VPN traffic is important to ensure your private data are secure and compliant.

Remote Access Configuration and Change Management

It's important to manage the network configuration settings in the LAN, LAN-to-WAN, and WAN Domains. Likewise, managing the changes to your VPN and remote access configuration is crucial to maintaining a secure environment for remote users and resources. When auditing a remote access environment consideration should be given to the following:

TIP

The IT network team has access to network-mapping software products to make the process easier. These tools can update the network map any time physical changes are detected.

- Map remote access architecture, including redundant and backup connections.
- Assess firewalls between your VPN endpoint and the internal network.
- Assess global user accounts.
- Assess the strength of authentication used.
- Assess the limited number of administrative accounts with permissions for remote administration.
- Assess the backup and recovery plan for each component in the Remote Access Domain. Include configuration settings for network devices in the backup and recovery plans.
- Assess whether procedures for all operating systems, applications, and network device software and firmware in the Remote Access Domain are up to date.
- Assess the monitoring of VPN traffic for performance and suspicious content.

- Assess control and configuration setting changes or physical changes to domain nodes. This includes if updates were applied to the network map after any changes.
- Assess encryption for all communication in the Remote Access Domain.

Review the suggested best practices and implement the controls that work best for your environment. Each organization has different needs and will end up with different controls to best ensure functionality and security in the Remote Access Domain.

Remote Access Management, Tools, and Systems

Managing a user's remote access devices requires the same tools as managing network devices. The distinction is with the connection to the remote users' laptops or desktops. While the end user is connected through a VPN tunnel into the corporate network, there is no distinction in management tools. Meanwhile, on the corporate network all the same access management tools and systems are in use.

The challenge occurs when the user cannot connect to the corporate network. How do you provide support in a secure manner? The answer is, it depends. The most common method is for the corporate help desk to securely remote into the user's remote laptop or desktop. Two conditions have to exist for this approach to work:

1. The end user's laptop or desktop must be functional to allow the end user to access the device; in other words, the problem is with the VPN connection and not the device.
2. The device must have Internet connectivity.

When both these conditions are met, the IT help desk has software available or preinstalled on the end user's machine to allow for secure remote access by the IT help desk. A number of products and services provide this type of support, such as "RemoteToPC" and "FixMe.IT." The basic idea behind this type of software and service is to use the Internet as an alternative connection to the remote computer. The connection is still encrypted and typically requires the remote user to grant permission to the device. Once the IT help desk has the access, they repair any configuration problems, including resetting passwords or reloading certificates needed to establish the normal VPN connection to the corporate network.

Corporate IT help desk for remote users' personal phones tend to be more complicated. If the phone problem cannot be quickly resolved, a common approach is to simply reinstall the phone applications.

Access Rights and Access Controls in the Remote Access Domain

The degree to which you grant rights and permissions to remote users depends on your general access model and your operating system. In most cases, remote users accessing your environment via a VPN enjoy the same rights as users on your LAN. The idea behind a VPN is that once it is established, it operates just like a LAN. VPN users are essentially the same as other LAN users. Although it is possible to exclude some users from accessing your network using a VPN at the operating system level, it is generally easier to use the remote access authentication server to define which users can use remote access.

WARNING

Do not include administrative users in a global user list. If you do allow remote administration, you should create administrative accounts specifically defined for remote administration. This practice makes it easier to audit and control remote users with elevated privileges.

The main goal for all networking issues is to keep things simple. Complexity leads to an increased exposure to risk and requires more effort to maintain. Try to keep three lists of users: internal network users, remote access users, and global users. If you don't need to separate most local and remote user rights, then just defining a global user list keeps things simple. After you create the users, you'll need to support remote access. Your operating system provides the ability to define what each user can do through permissions or access control lists (ACLs).

In addition to user rights, your remote access servers can define how you handle remote connections. You should set up VPNs to appear as networks that are separate from your physical LANs. Defining all VPNs in a specific range of subnets gives you the ability to define filtering or access rules that affect just your VPN connections. Defining rules for VPNs gives you the ability to identify and filter suspicious traffic or any traffic that is not authorized. For example, suppose you want to prohibit remote users from using **Server Message Block (SMB)**, a protocol used to map network resources as shares. You could set a rule in a firewall that sits between your VPN endpoint and your LAN to drop any TCP traffic for the default SMB port, 445. In this way, you prohibit any SMB access from your VPNs.

You can use user rights, permissions, ACLs, and firewall rules to restrict what remote users can do. Document what you'll allow remote users to do and use the appropriate controls to enforce your rules. The more remote users can do, the greater the risk to your data security. Allowing remote users to access your environment can increase your organization's effectiveness at the risk of reducing your overall security. Ensure you have the necessary controls in place to limit what remote users can do and to ensure your data are safe regardless of where it travels.

Remote Access Domain Configuration Validation

Validating compliance in the Remote Access Domain includes validating the controls that satisfy compliance requirements. With respect to the Remote Access Domain, most compliance concerns focus on data privacy. It is important to evaluate all controls to ensure that all three properties of the confidentiality, integrity, and availability (C-I-A) triad are satisfied. The Remote Access Domain has three main areas of concern: client-side configuration, server-side configuration, and configuration management verification. Each area focuses on a slightly different component of the Remote Access Domain. Taken together, validating these three areas provides assurance that components in your Remote Access Domain are compliant with the necessary requirements.

VPN Client Definition and Access Controls

Each VPN client stores configuration details to connect to the organization's VPN server. Typically, VPN details include information such as the following:

- Host name or address (primary and backup)
- Logon user name
- Password (optional, dependent on the authentication method)
- Authentication method
- Transport protocol
- Local address options
- Local log settings

Each of the client settings should match the server settings. In some cases, servers support multiple types of clients and will negotiate settings, such as authentication method and transport protocol. It is important that you verify each client's settings to ensure that clients are in compliance with organizational VPN settings standards. One of the easiest ways to verify client settings is to restrict your server settings to deny any connection requests that fall below certain standards. If your clients meet the standards, they can connect. If not, their connections fail.

There are two types of access controls for remote access. The first are the access controls for computers or devices. These access controls define which computers or devices can establish remote connections. Your authentication servers or VPN servers store computer and device access controls. The location depends on the type of VPN and operating system you are using. The second type of access control is at the user or group level. This type of access control is the same as access control in the User Domain. Once a remote user authenticates and is authorized to access resources, the normal operating system access controls take effect.

> ⚠ **WARNING**
>
> Consult the setup and configuration guide for your web server. Some web servers enable all encryption modes by default, including a debugging mode that actually doesn't encrypt traffic. If you leave this option enabled, attackers can trick your web server into sending private data without using Transport Layer Security (TLS) with encryption. Unless you're using a VPN, the web server sends the data in the clear.

TLS VPN Remote Access via a Web Browser

Most web development languages and many applications have the ability to require secure connections. For example, you can require that a particular webpage or cookie can only be sent to a client using a secure connection. If the client attempts to render a secure webpage using an unsecure protocol, the page does not render. You would have to use HTTPS to render the page. In other words, you would have to include HTTPS in the address to reach the page.

To verify compliance with data privacy for remote users, you should enforce the following:

- Require all webpages that access sensitive data to have secure HTTPS connections or have local host addresses. Local host addresses for webpages require VPN connections.
- Require all users to be authenticated before accessing any resources or data.
- Allow only VPN nodes to access sensitive data directly.
- Require operating system– and application-specific access controls to define which users can access sensitive data.

Adhering to these rules will ensure your data are safe from unauthorized remote users.

VPN Configuration Management Verification

Managing all your network devices' configuration settings keeps unauthorized changes from reducing your data's security. RANCID, along with other available tools, can help you create baselines of configuration settings and compare changes over time. You should develop a schedule and process to frequently compare configuration baselines and verify all changes to your network's configuration.

A solid network configuration management process includes managing changes to all configuration settings. A formal process makes it easy to classify any configuration changes as authorized or unauthorized. You just compare baseline differences to your authorized changes list to see which changes occurred that were not authorized.

Adherence to Documented IT Security Policies, Standards, Procedures, and Guidelines

Security doesn't just happen. A secure environment is the result of solid plans and faithful adherence to those plans. If your organization takes the time to plan the best ways to achieve compliance and security assurance, it makes sense to follow those plans. Each component of your plans should address one or more of the basic C-I-A properties of data security. As you select and deploy controls, ensure that each one supports your organization's security policy. Many organizations end up deploying controls that seem good but are not indicated in their policy. Such a situation indicates that either the control is not needed or the policy needs amending. In either case, your controls should be the result of enacting your security policy. Above all else, it is important that your security policy be current and complete. **Table 13.3** lists the types of controls you'll likely need to ensure are compliant in your Remote Access Domain. These controls won't meet every compliance goal but will satisfy many current compliance requirements and make your Remote Access Domain more secure.

Best Practices for Remote Access Domain Compliance

Organizations audit their information security stance to protect the confidentiality, integrity, and availability of their critical information business assets. Auditing and

TABLE 13-3	Common compliance controls in the Remote Access Domain.	
TYPE OF CONTROL	**COMPONENT**	**DESCRIPTION**
Preventive	Proxy server	Prevent any unencrypted traffic from traveling between remote users and your internal network.
	Firewalls	Use a firewall between the VPN endpoint and your internal network to identify and deny unnecessary traffic.
	User-based access controls for all resources	Restrict access to the VPN to reduce traffic and resource exposure.
	Configuration change control	Limit changes to all network device configuration settings and filtering rules. Require approval for all changes before deploying them.
Detective	Performance monitoring	Frequently sample VPN traffic flow metrics and alert for any unusual activity.
	Traffic analysis	Examine traffic for known attack signatures and to ensure data are encrypted.
	Configuration settings monitoring	Compare VPN/remote access device configuration settings to stored baselines to detect any unauthorized changes.
	Penetration testing	Conduct periodic penetration tests to identify security control weaknesses.
Corrective	VPN/remote access component patching	Keep VPN/remote access devices and applications patched to the latest available level.
	Attack intervention	Automatically modify filtering rules to deny traffic from sources generating known attack signature packets.
	Business continuity planning and disaster recovery planning	Develop and maintain plans to survive and continue operations in the face of small or large disruptions. Establish alternative WAN access plans in the case of primary WAN failure.

assessment allow an organization to validate their compliance and ensure they are operating within acceptable risk tolerances. Key questions to answer during an audit are as follows:

- Is remote access limited to authorized users?
- Does remote access using strong authentication such as multifactor authentication?
- Is remote access limited to least privileged?
- Is remote access activity monitored and reviewed?
- Is noncompliance appropriate enforced?
- Are both ends of the communication secure and encrypted?
- Are endpoint devices appropriately configured and protected?

A lot of effort goes into building the remote access environment. No configuration or technical checklist would cover adequately all aspects of the Remote Access Domain. The best network audit approach is to ask the right questions that will lead the auditor to assess the related core technologies, configurations, and processes.

CHAPTER SUMMARY

The need for secure remote user access continues to grow as the workforce shifts to embrace work from home as a new norm. In this chapter, we discussed the benefits and risks that need to be controlled. We discussed the importance of using VPN and the various components and technologies needed to support the remote user environment. We explored the need to protect sensitive data leaving the traditional confines of the corporate network. Finally, we discussed best practices to audit the remote access domain.

KEY CONCEPTS AND TERMS

Broadband

Remote Authentication Dial In User Service (RADIUS)

Server Message Block (SMB)

Simple Network Management Protocol (SNMP)

Terminal Access Controller Access-Control System Plus (TACACS+)

Tunneling

User Datagram Protocol (UDP)

CHAPTER 13 ASSESSMENT

1. The primary concern for remote access is availability.

A. True
B. False

2. Which entity is responsible for controlling access to network traffic in the WAN?

A. WAN optimizer
B. Your organization
C. WAN service provider
D. Network management platform

3. _____ is the primary security control used in the Remote Access Domain.

4. All VPN traffic is encrypted.

A. True
B. False

5. Given adequate security controls, PDAs are appropriate for use as remote access devices.

A. True
B. False

6. Which of the following terms means the process to decide what a user can do?

A. Identification
B. Authentication
C. Clearance
D. Authorization

7. Which of the following protocols is used for encrypted traffic?

A. HTTPS
B. SNMP
C. IP
D. L2TP

8. _____ is a technique that creates a virtual encrypted channel that allows applications to use any protocol to communicate with servers and services without having to worry about addressing privacy concerns.

9. Which of the following protocols works well with firewalls?

A. GRE
B. SSTP
C. L2TP
D. L2F

10. Monitoring VPN traffic requires specialized methods that is different from those used to monitor LAN and WAN traffic

A. True
B. False

11. _____ is a network protocol used to monitor network devices.

12. The use of global user accounts can simplify user maintenance.

A. True
B. False

13. Which protocol is commonly used to protect data sent to web browsers when not using VPNs?

A. IPSec
B. PPTP
C. GRE
D. TLS

14. Which of the following controls would best protect sensitive data disclosure to unauthorized users using remote computers?

A. Encryption
B. Strong passwords
C. Firewalls
D. Configuration management tools

15. Which protocol does SNMP use to transport messages?

A. TCP
B. UDP
C. TLS
D. GRE

16. What are some benefits to allowing employees remote access during stay-at-home work?

A. Freedom and flexibility
B. Cost saving
C. Personalized environment
D. All the above

17. What is it called when an organization improves its remote access security by identifying how users connect to the corporate network and access sensitive data?

A. Policies
B. Penetration testing
C. Authentication
D. Governance

18. The most common form of remote access is through a VPN.

A. True
B. False

19. What type of control within the remote access environment grants authenticated users the appropriate and limited access?

A. Authentication
B. Authorization
C. Nonrepudiation

20. What type of control within the remote access ensures that users cannot challenge their ownership, which in this case is the activity performed during a remote access session?

A. Authentication
B. Authorization
C. Nonrepudiation

Compliance Within the System/Application Domain

DO USERS ACCESS DATA?

No. It sounds counterintuitive and perhaps a bit of a trick question, but it is technically true. Access to data is always achieved through an application. This may be an installed application on the workstation, an application in the operating system, or even an application embedded in the BIOS. A user can only read, update, or create data through an application. An application controls the user experience and thus becomes the pivotal point of strength or weakness. This is also true when it comes to cybersecurity. Applications can be a strong or point of weakness when it comes to protecting an organization's customer and company data.

Application audits are conducted to ensure the business' software is properly functioning, complies with the organization's policies, and is legally licensed. These typical audit criteria will increase the value of the software to achieve the organization's goals while reducing the potential for business disruptions and cybersecurity threats.

In this chapter, we will review the key areas to consider in performing application and systems audits. We will discuss how software is maintained and the importance of proper configuration. These common components and others that will be discussed ensure software complies with policies.

Chapter 14 Topics

This chapter covers the following topics and concepts:

- How compliance law requirements relate to business drivers
- Which devices and components are commonly found in the System /Application Domain
- What secure coding benefits are
- What system and application configuration and change management are

- Which system and application management tools and systems are commonly used
- What access rights and access controls in the System/Application Domain are
- How to maximize confidentiality, integrity, and availability (C-I-A)
- What system/application server vulnerability management is
- What data loss protection is
- What the importance of secure coding is
- How to ensure adherence to documented IT security policies, standards, procedures, and guidelines
- What best practices for System/Application Domain compliance are

Chapter 14 Goals

When you complete this chapter, you will be able to:

- Understand the difference between application and system software
- Describe what the software development life cycle is
- Explain how system and service accounts are used
- Identify compliance law requirements and business drivers
- Compare how devices and components found in the System/Application Domain contribute to compliance
- Describe methods of ensuring compliance in the System/Application Domain
- Summarize best practices for System/Application Domain compliance

Compliance Law Requirements and Business Drivers

The System/Application Domain refers to the software needed to collect, process, and store information. It is more than securing communication between the end user and the data used by the software. What collects, processes, and stores data is ultimately software. Performing safe handling of data is not just good business practice but is mandated by laws, rules, and regulations (LRR). Ensuring software complies with LRRs is important to avoid fines and meet regulator expectations.

Let's illustrate this point by examining the common software feature of encryption. Many laws mandate and strongly encourage the use of encryption to protect the confidentiality of data. For example, the **Health Insurance Portability and Accountability Act of 1996 (HIPAA)** has several provisions related to encryptions such as "implement a mechanism to encrypt PHI whenever deemed appropriate." PHI refers to **Protected Health Information**. In simplest terms, PHI is an individual's health records.

Consequently, software used to collect, process, and store PHI data must use encryption whenever possible. When selecting software for this purpose, this feature must be a strong consideration. Often, vendors will highlight that their software is HIPAA compliant. Meaning, they had their software assessed, and for the purpose it intended the software meets all HIPAA regulatory requirements.

So, in this example you acquired the software. You ensured the software is HIPAA compliant. Let's also assume the software is properly configured and used. Is your software compliant with legal requirements? Maybe. Always keep in mind that multiple layers of laws may apply.

Licensing may be a legal layer that may have to be examined. For example, is the use of the software compliant with the legal terms in the license?

Notice the HIPAA requirement quoted stated that encryption should be applied "whenever deemed appropriate." One of the reasons why this encryption requirement is vague and open to interpretation is that it was acknowledged that technology advances. What may be considered appropriate encryption standards today may be different tomorrow. Let us consider software in the cloud, for example, Amazon Cloud or Microsoft Azure.

Locale can also impact compliance with legal requirements and impact business decisions. In the United States, the law imposes controls on the export of certain forms of encryption. Consequently, if your software encrypts and decrypts data across international boundaries, the software may be subject to regulatory requirements. Export restrictions on encryption technologies could be a business driver on where your company can do use certain software.

The System/Application Domain provides the environment for the applications you run as clients on your network and the computer systems that house them. This domain provides the engine for today's distributed applications and enables you to provide individual components of applications as opposed to entire applications in one footprint. **Figure 14-1** shows the System/Application Domain in the context of the seven domains in the IT infrastructure.

Keeping data secure in the System/Application Domain involves ensuring availability and controlling unauthorized access. You've already learned about many of the techniques you'll use in the System/Application Domain. Although other domains focus on keeping data secure as it travels across various networks, the System/Application Domain's main security controls ensure your data's security in storage and in use. As with other domains, you'll likely need to show compliance with one or more requirements that directly address the sensitive data you store and process in the domain. HIPAA requires controls to protect the privacy of medical data, the Payment Card Industry (PCI) requires credit card privacy controls, and many states require privacy controls on any personally identifiable data. These are only a few of the requirements you'll need to satisfy when selecting security controls for storing and using data. A solid security policy that includes compliance with all appropriate requirements should not only be secure, but should

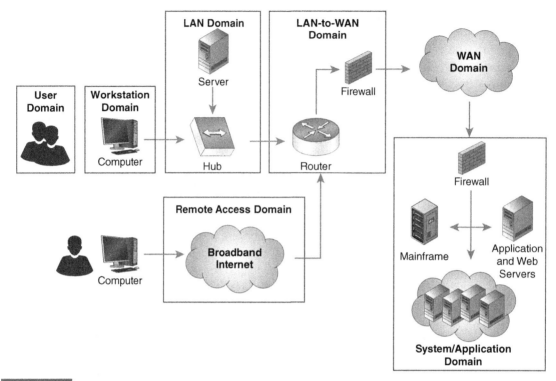

The System/Application Domain within the seven domains of a typical IT Infrastructure.

support efficient and cost-effective operation. Implementing the controls necessary to support your security policy in the System/Application Domain makes your organization more effective by providing useful data that are compliant with relevant requirements.

Application Software Versus System Software

Business software is typically called applications. Software that supports the running of the applications is typically called **system software**, such as software that runs on the operating system of a server. The System/Application Domain refers to all the system and application software-related components.

It's not uncommon to hear system and application terms used interchangeably. They are not the same. For the purposes of this chapter, we use the more precise definition given previously. Generally, any business software that an end user (including customers) uses to access data is considered an application. This includes email, word processing, and spreadsheet software. Conversely, the operating system, the software needed to run the applications, and software that allows computers to communicate over the network, or between devices, is considered system software.

A typical user often leverages both applications and system software seamlessly. Let's consider a user pulling up the Microsoft Word application. The user types a memo then selects print. At an extremely high level, the Word application sends the memo to the operating system, which sends it to the print spooler software that temporarily stores print jobs. The system communicates with the printer that the job is ready to print, and the printer's system prints the memo.

Application software is at the heart of all business applications. Application software can sit on the workstation, server, or be accessed through the cloud. For example, an application can display a screen by which customers and employees can select products and enter data. Once the information is collected, the application transmits the transaction to a server. The server can store the information in a database to be processed later or instantly processed the transaction, store the results, and display information back to the end user. Later an employee can extract data from this ordering application into a spreadsheet to track the total number of orders each month by product type. The application that took the order, the spreadsheet that tracked the orders, and the email that was sent to announce the company had record sales for the month are all examples of application software.

 TIP

An easy way to distinguish between the terms "application" versus "system software" is to focus on two application characteristics. An application has a user interface and typically a single purpose such as email or word processing. All other software is typically considered part of the supporting system.

Protecting Data Privacy

Because the System/Application Domain centralizes much of your data and the processing of that data, you must protect it from disclosure or unauthorized alteration. Recall that ensuring data privacy essentially means allowing only authorized users to view or modify it. You can deploy layers of controls to restrict access to authorized users.

Although controlling access to data and resources can be challenging, in some ways it is a little easier than trying to protect data as you send it to remote locations. You can enforce strict rules that limit which users and programs can access your data. An unauthorized user must access your network, then access a server in the domain, and then run a program or access data in a database. There are several points along the way to place good security controls. You can implement several types of controls that make it difficult for unauthorized users to get to your private data. An important first step is to identify sensitive or private data and then design controls to protect that data.

Implementing Proper Security Controls for the System/Application Domain

The best security controls are simple layered controls. Try to avoid overly complex controls. Complex controls generally require more effort to configure and maintain and often provide more opportunities to fail. Your goal in designing security controls is to ensure they do their jobs and keep your data secure. Although deploying layered controls is generally considered to be sound security practice, be careful that you don't create so many controls that authorized users have difficulty accessing the data they need. Try to search for controls that balance security and usability.

Security controls in the System/Application Domain generally fall into three categories. There are many potential controls, but the most important controls should isolate data, limit access to data, or protect data from loss through redundancy. Each type of control plays a part in keeping your data secure and your organization compliant:

- **Isolate data**—Because much of an organization's sensitive data resides in one or more databases in the System/Application Domain, it is important to place barriers between sensitive data and other entities. You can use firewalls and your network design to isolate data. Your network addressing scheme can separate one or more nodes into their own subnets. A **subnet** is simply a part of a network. Other network devices, such as switches, can physically isolate subnets from other nodes.

- **Limit access to data**—Node and user access controls in the System/Application Domain are similar to access controls for other domains. Operating systems provide mechanisms to restrict object access by users or groups. You can also use network authentication to restrict which computers and devices can connect to servers that contain sensitive data.

 TIP

Regardless of the operating system or controls you use, limit access to your sensitive data. Know which users and which nodes can access your data.

- **Protect data from loss through redundancy**—Because the System/Application Domain exists to provide applications and data for your users, it has to be functional. You'll need plans to ensure users can access your applications and data regardless of what happens. That means you'll need to create redundant copies of data or employ other strategies to protect your organization from loss of data or functionality.

Several other domains support users and their ability to access applications and data. In one view, you can look at the System/Application Domain as the central repository of the data you are trying to protect. The System/Application Domain provides the security controls closest to your data. An attacker who has compromised enough controls to reach this domain doesn't have much further to go. The controls you place in the System/Application Domain could be the controls that make the difference between secure data and data loss. Take the time to plan your security controls well.

Software Development Life Cycle (SDLC)

Software Development Life Cycle (SDLC) is a process to design and develop compliant software. The SDLC consists of phases that depict various stages of the software development process. There are various methodologies published on what is considered an SDLC approach. While many of these methodologies vary, they typically break down software development among the following phases:

- Business requirement analysis
- Software design such as architectural design
- Software development, i.e., coding
- Developer testing
- **User acceptance testing (UAT)**

- Deployment
- Maintenance
- Decommission

As illustrated by the listed phases, the SDLC process takes software from cradle to grave. An SDLC audit can maximize the success of a project by detecting its potential risks and weaknesses in the software before deployment. A software development process audit offers independent validation of the testing process and shows areas where it could be optimized. While not an exhaustive list, the following are several important SDLC components that should be audited:

- Business requirements are clear and comprehensive.
- Architectural design is consistent with the technology infrastructure and supportable.
- Testing criteria are well defined.
- UAT testing is representative of the real world and what would be found in production.
- Deployment contingency planning is in place in the event that the new software has to be backed out due to unforeseen problems.
- Maintenance requirements have been defined prior to deployment.
- Decommission plans have been considered when the software reaches end-of-life, such as how the data will be archived if needed for later recovery.

> **NOTE**
>
> It is far less expensive to catch a problem in the early SDLC phases than after deployment. The auditor should strive to provide notice of potential problem areas so they can be addressed before they grow to become significant costly problems to fix and affect the business negatively.

In the **business requirement analysis** phase, the systems analyst or IT professionals gather business objectives and define the information requirements needed to design the application. A requirements document is produced that summarizes the analysis of the IT project. This document should include success criteria established by the business such as speed of processing times and volume of data to be collected, processed, and stored.

In the **software design** phase, a technical design is created. The design will address every business requirement. Additionally, the design phase will validate the feasibility of the business requirements from cost to the organization's ability to support the software. For example, a technical feasibility study examines whether the current information technology (IT) infrastructure makes it feasible to implement the software or if a new infrastructure is required. A legal feasibility study examines any legal ramifications of each business requirement and how the technical design must address these legal mandates such as the implementation of encryption. An operational feasibility study determines if the current business processes, procedures, and skills of employees are adequate to successfully maintain the software. A schedule feasibility study relates to the firm's ability to meet the proposed deadline set by the business to build and deploy the new software.

WARNING

Too often developers use production customer data while coding and testing the software. Test data should be used whenever possible. In those rare cases when production data are required for testing, cybersecurity controls should be put in place to ensure the data remain secure.

In the **software development** phase, developers will start to build the entire system by writing software code. Additionally, the developer will work with other IT professionals to configure the supporting IT environment such as setting up the database or data feeds. The developer will obtain or create test data to understand how the code must collect, transmit, and store the information. While not technically in the testing phase, typically snippets or portions of code will be tested throughout the development progress.

In the **developer testing** phase, the developer's goal is to ensure the functionality of the software is operating to the requirements and expectations of the business. Sound testing includes unit, integration, and functional testing, defined as follows:

- Unit testing means the testing of individual modules or functions within the application in isolation to confirm that the code each portion of the code is working.

- Integration testing means the testing of how the different modules are working together as a group.

- Functional testing means testing an end-to-end function or process to confirm that the code is working within the software and with external dependencies, such as external data sources.

The UAT phase is the final stage of any software development before deployment. Actual business users test the software to determine if it does what it was designed to do in the real world. This is where the business users determine if the software meets their expectations. The users should stress the software such as exceeding the number of the expected users to determine if the software can handle the unexpected volume.

TIP

Negative testing is commonly overlooked in developer and UAT phases. Negative testing uses invalid input, or undesired user behaviors, to check the code for unexpected errors. A simple example might have a business user attempt a function for which their security permissions should not be allowed. Too often testing focuses on testing how code works versus how the code should prevent certain functions from working.

In the **deployment** phase, there is typically a Go-Live or production sign-off. No system should be deployed without this user acceptance. Once deployed, the software will be closely monitored and, if needed, backed out if there are major problems caused by the software. Once successfully deployed, there should be a postimplementation review. This review should include how well the SDLC phases worked to this point, including whether all business requirements and any cost-saving anticipated were met.

The **maintenance** phase is the care and feeding of the software. This may include applying updates or patches to fix bugs or improve information security. Maintenance schedules are published, and maintenance windows are established so the users know when the application will be down. Good software design can reduce the amount of maintenance required. For example, creating automated feeds that adjust key functions, such as dynamically feeding product prices. Dynamically updating pricing tables could eliminate the need to bring down the software to load an internal pricing table within the software.

In the **decommission** phase, the application is at end of life and will be retired. Decommissioning process will notify the users that the application will no longer be available by a certain date. Leading up to the decommissioning date, the users are often moved to another application that provides the same or improved functionality. During the decommissioning process, data are moved and archived as required by the business and by law.

Devices and Components Commonly Found in the System/Application Domain

The System/Application Domain contains the application components that your organization runs and the computer systems on which the applications reside. This domain also contains computers, devices, and software components that support the domain's application software. The rest of this section lists the devices and components you'll commonly find in the System/Application Domain and some of the controls to ensure compliance. **Figure 14-2** shows the devices and components commonly found in the System/Application Domain.

Computer Room/Data Center

The components in the System/Application Domain commonly reside in the same room. The room in which central server computers and hardware reside is called a **data center**, or just a computer room. This data center can be a facility owned by the organization or service provided. Many companies today are migrating applications to the cloud, which eliminates the need for or reduces the size of the data center. Because the software and data in this domain are central to your organization's operation, the hardware must stay operational. A well-equipped data center generally has at least the following characteristics:

- **Physical access control**—Secure data centers have doors with locks that only a limited number of people can open. Electronic locks or combination locks are common to easily enable a group of people access to the room. Physical access control reduces the likelihood an attacker could physically damage data center hardware or launch an attack using removable media. Inserting a universal serial bus (USB) drive that is infected with malware is one type of attack. Limiting physical access to critical hardware can mitigate that type of attack.

Hardware	Software	Infrastructure
• Mainframe • Minicomputer • File Server • Uninterruptible Power Supply • Storage Device	• Application • Source Code • Database Management System	• Data Center • Backup Data Center

FIGURE 14-2

Devices and components commonly found in the System/Application Domain.

- **Controlled environment**—Heating, ventilating, and air conditioning (HVAC) services control the temperature and humidity of a secure data center. Data centers routinely have dozens or even hundreds of computers and devices, all running at the same time. Keeping the temperature and humidity at proper levels allows the hardware to operate without overheating. Data centers also need dependable electrical power. A data center requires enough reliable power to run all computers and devices currently located in the data center, leaving room for growth.

- **Fire-suppression equipment**—A data center fire has the potential to wipe out large amounts of data and hardware. Extinguishing a fire helps protect the hardware assets and the data they contain. Unfortunately, water could damage computing hardware as much as fire, so sprinklers aren't appropriate in data centers. A common solution is the deployment of a roomwide fire-suppression gas to displace the oxygen in the entire room.

- **Easy access to hardware and wiring**—Data center components tend to change frequently. Data center personnel must upgrade old hardware, add new hardware, reconfigure existing hardware, and fix broken hardware. Each of these tasks generally involves moving hardware components from one place to another and attaching necessary wires and cables. Data center computers generally don't have cases like desktop computers do. Often they look like bare components on rails. This design allows them to be used in rack systems. A **rack system** is an open cabinet with tracks into which multiple computers can be mounted. You can slide computers in and out like drawers. Using rack systems makes it easy to manage hardware. Because there tends to be a lot of wiring in a data center, many use a raised floor design. Using raised floors with removable access panels makes it easy to access wires and increases the overall airflow throughout the data center.

- **High-speed internal LAN**—Many computers in the data center are high-performance server computers. To optimize communication between servers, high-bandwidth networks, such as fiber-optic networks, are common within the data center.

When designing a data center, make sure it can support all the components you need today and in the foreseeable future. Data centers that are flexible and scalable allow your organization to change and grow to reflect business demands.

---

technical TIP

When designing a disaster recovery plan, *always* protect people first. Computers, devices, and data can all be replaced. People cannot. A common gas used for years in data center fire-suppression systems is **halon**. Although halon works well to suppress fire, it is hazardous to humans and the environment. Due to the dangers associated with halon, other gas fire-suppression options have emerged to replace it. In fact, the manufacture of a common type of halon, Halon 1301, is banned, and all new fire-suppression systems must use an alternative substance.

Redundant Computer Room/Data Center

A disaster recovery plan contains the steps to restore your IT infrastructure to a point where your organization can continue operations. If a disaster occurs that causes damage and interrupts your business functions, it is important to return to productive activities as soon as possible. If your organization can't carry out its main business functions, it cannot fulfill its purpose. A solid disaster recovery plan (DRP) carefully identifies each component of your IT infrastructure that is critical to your primary business functions. Then, the plan states the steps you can take to replace damaged or destroyed components.

Several options are available for serious disasters that damage or destroy major IT infrastructure components. These are a few of the most common options, starting with the most expensive option with the shortest cutover time:

- **Hot site**—This is a complete copy of your environment at a remote site. Hot sites are kept as current as possible with replicated data so switching from your original environment to the alternate environment can occur with a minimum of downtime.
- **Warm site**—This is a complete copy of your environment at a remote site. Warm sites are updated with current data only periodically, normally daily or even weekly. When a disaster occurs, there will be a short delay while a switchover team prepares the warm site with the latest data updates.
- **Cold site**—This is a site that may have hardware in place, but it will not likely be set up or configured. Cold sites take more time to bring into operation because of the extensive amount of configuration work required for hardware and software.
- **Service level agreement (SLA)**—This is a contract with a vendor that guarantees replacement hardware or software within a specific amount of time.
- **Cooperative agreement**—A cooperative agreement is between two or more organizations to help each other in case a disaster hits one of the parties. The organization that is not affected by the disaster agrees to allow the other organization to use part of its own IT infrastructure capacity to conduct minimal business operations. There is usually a specified time limit that allows the organization that suffered damage time to rebuild its IT infrastructure.

Figure 14-3 shows disaster recovery options in terms of switchover time and cost.

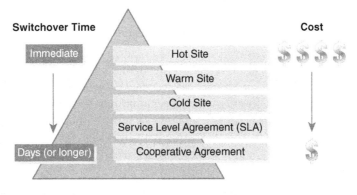

FIGURE 14-3

Disaster recovery options.

Regardless of which option best suits your organization, the purpose of a disaster recovery plan is to repair or replace damaged IT infrastructure components as quickly as possible to allow the business to continue operation.

Uninterruptible Power Supplies and Diesel Generators to Maintain Operations

There is a lot of confusion between a DRP and a business continuity plan (BCP). The two plans work closely with each other and depend on each other for success. You can summarize the difference between the two plans as follows:

- A DRP for IT ensures the IT infrastructure is operational and ready to support primary business functions. A DRP for IT focuses mainly on the IT department.
- A BCP is an organizational plan. It doesn't focus only on IT. The BCP ensures the organization can survive any disruption and continue operating. If the disruption is major, the BCP will rely on the DRP to provide an IT infrastructure the organization can use.
- A DRP is a component of a comprehensive BCP.

To summarize, a comprehensive BCP will take effect any time there is a disruption of business functions. An example is a water main break that interrupts water flow to your main office. A DRP takes effect when an event causes a major disruption. A major disruption is one where you must intervene and take some action to restore a functional IT infrastructure. A fire that damages your data center is an example of a disaster.

One type of interruption addressed by a BCP is a power outage. If a data center loses power, computers cannot operate, and the environment can no longer support the hardware. With no power, there is no HVAC, lights, or anything else that relies on electricity. It is important to plan for power outages and place corrective controls to address a loss of power. Two main methods address a power outage. The first method addresses short-term outages, whereas the second method addresses longer-term outages:

- **Uninterruptible power supply (UPS)**—A UPS provides continuous usable power to one or more devices. UPS units for data centers are typically much larger than workstation UPS units and can support several devices for longer periods of time. A UPS protects data center devices from power fluctuations and outages from several minutes to even several hours for large, expensive units.
- **Power generator**—Generators, which commonly use diesel fuel to create electricity, can deliver power to critical data center components for long periods of time. When a power outage lasts longer than a UPS can power devices, generators can produce electricity as long as they have fuel. Generators are generally not extremely long-term solutions. They will provide power until either regular power is restored or you can move to an alternative data center that has reliable power. If you must locate a data center in a place that does not have reliable power, however, generators can become the primary power source.

Mission-critical data centers require multiple levels of protection to ensure continuous operation. UPS devices and generators are integral parts of a BCP that keep an organization in operation.

Mainframe Computers

Several types of computers make their homes in data centers. The largest type of computer is the mainframe computer. The term *mainframe* dates back to the early days of computers and originally referred to the large cabinets that housed the processing units and memory modules of early computers. The term came to be used to describe large and extremely powerful computers that can run many applications supporting thousands of users simultaneously. Mainframe computers also have the characteristic of being extremely reliable. Most mainframe computers run without interruption and can even be serviced and upgraded while still operating.

Because the hardware, software, environmental requirements, and maintenance for mainframe computers are all expensive, only the largest organizations typically can justify their use. Mainframe environmental and power requirements created the need for early dedicated data centers. Today's mainframe computers are powerful hosts for multiple operating systems that run as **virtual machines**. A virtual machine is a software program that looks and runs like a physical computer. A large mainframe computer can run many virtual machines and provide the services of many physical computers.

Minicomputers

Many organizations realize they need more computing power than basic workstations or PC-based hardware but aren't ready to commit to a mainframe computer. The first minicomputers started appearing in data centers in the 1960s as an alternative to mainframe computers. Minicomputers are more powerful than workstations but less powerful than mainframe computers. They fit somewhere in the middle and address the needs of medium-sized businesses.

Before the 1980s, minicomputers and mainframe computers were the only types of computers that could handle multiple users and multiple applications at the same time. Smaller computers could only handle single users and one application at a time. The 1980s saw the growth of more capable hardware and operating systems for low-cost computers. These small, inexpensive computers are called *microcomputers* and still dominate the personal computer and workstation markets.

Minicomputers still exist to address the needs of medium-sized businesses, but they aren't as common as they were in the past. Some of today's minicomputers are distinct hardware platforms, and some are actually high-end microcomputers running operating system versions that cater to high performance and reliability. Either way, minicomputer performance and cost fill a need between workstations and mainframe computers.

Server Computers

Some computers in a data center aren't multipurpose computers but fill specific roles. Computer roles most commonly focus on satisfying client needs for specific services. Computers that perform specific functions for clients are generally called *server computers*, or just *servers*. Common servers you'll find in today's environments may include the following:

- File servers
- Web servers
- Authentication servers
- Database servers

- Application servers
- Mail servers
- Media servers

These are only a few of the types of servers in many data centers. Server computers help organizations by allowing a computer to focus all of its resources on a single task, providing a specific service to clients. A collection of separate server computers, each providing a different service, can increase the performance of the entire environment by removing interservice conflicts and competition for a single computer's resources. Isolating services on separate server computers can also limit the effects of attacks. An attack that compromises a server computer running a single service will have less impact than a compromise of a single computer running many applications and services.

Data Storage Devices

Data centers are convenient places to locate shared storage devices. The central location, managed environment, and higher general level of security make the data center an ideal environment for protected shared storage. Many networks offer managed storage devices that are shared among network users. Shared devices can be attached to file servers or be separate from server computers. Shared storage devices can be disk drives, tape libraries, optical jukeboxes, solid state storage, or any other mechanism used to store data.

One common method to provide shared storage capability to network users is using a **storage area network (SAN)**. A SAN is a collection of storage devices that is attached to a network in such a way that the devices appear to be local storage devices. In effect, the storage devices form their own network that the operating system accesses just like local drives. The SAN devices protect the data by limiting how clients can access the storage devices. SANs can make it easy to keep shared data available and secure.

Another storage device method is referred to as **network-attached storage (NAS)**. While they are both network-based storage solutions, a SAN typically uses Fiber Channel connectivity, while NAS typically ties into the network through a standard Ethernet connection. A SAN stores data at the block level, while NAS accesses data as files.

Applications

Computer applications have matured along with computer hardware capability. Early computing systems placed all data and software capabilities on a central host computer. Clients used simple terminals to connect directly to the host computer to run applications. Application design has changed through several generations to its current level of maturity, the distributed application model. Each architectural change depended on advances in networking support and changed the way applications use networks and resources. Application architectures differ in the location of critical resources. Critical application resources are as follows:

- **Data storage**—The interface to physical storage devices, such as disk drives
- **Data access**—Software to access stored data, such as database management systems or document management systems

- **Business logic**—Application software that accesses and processes data
- **User interface**—Application software that interacts with end users

Table 14-1 lists major application architectures and their impact on network resources.

TABLE 14-1	Application architectures.				
	SERVICE LOCATION				
ARCHITECTURE	**DATA STORAGE**	**DATA ACCESS**	**BUSINESS LOGIC**	**USER INTERFACE**	**COMMENTS**
Host based	Host	Host	Host	Host	Everything runs on the host. Host-based applications are easy to maintain and secure but are not very scalable.
Client based	Server	Client	Client	Client	This architecture is also called disk-less workstations. This architecture didn't last too long because even a few clients can saturate a network with all disk accesses occurring over a network.
Client/server	Server	Server	Client	Client	This common model attempts to separate application execution from data access and storage. In a classic client/server model, the client runs all of the application code. Although workstations have become powerful, this model is slow when the application needs large amounts of data that must be transferred across the network.
Distributed	Server	Server	Server	Client	Distributed computing attempts to solve the network saturation problem by reducing the amount of information transferred across the network. Large volumes of data can be transferred between a database server and an application server in the data center without having to use the rest of the network. Reduced network usage can result in much better performance. Keeping more data within the data center's network increases the data's security as well.

> **technical TIP**
>
> Not all source code files are compiled into programs computers can run. Some languages actually interpret source code files, while other environments just assemble source code instructions into machine-readable instructions. Regardless of your particular environment, all programs start off as source code files.

Although not all applications are fully distributed, the trend for new development efforts is to deploy distributed applications. More and more applications are specifically written to run on application server computers. This move toward distributed applications has an impact on security and compliance. Although many organizations use application servers in a secure data center to run application components, others may just run applications on a generic network computer. Each application must ensure it protects the security of the data it handles.

Source Code

Application software is a collection of computer programs that fulfills some purpose. Programs that computers can run are the result of a process that starts with programmers creating text files for programs, called **source code**. Source code files are then compiled into programs that computers can run.

 TIP

The best way to secure applications from unintended changes is to keep your development environment separate from your production, or live, environment. You'll learn more about how to do this in the section that covers configuration and change management. Separating the different environments is mandatory for Sarbanes-Oxley Act (SOX) compliance.

The process of changing how an application program runs starts with changing the source code files that correspond to the program you want to change. The programmer would then follow the prescribed procedure to convert the source code into a program the computer can run. This process works for attackers as well. Although it is possible to modify a computer program directly, it is far more difficult than modifying the source code. An important step in securing applications is to remove the source code. Without source code, it is very difficult to modify an application.

Databases and Privacy Data

Very few applications run as standalone programs. Nearly every application accesses data of some sort. Enterprise applications may access databases that are hundreds of gigabytes or even terabytes in size. Databases that store this much data are valuable targets for attackers and should be the focus of your security efforts in the System/Application Domain. Data are crucial assets in many of today's organizations. An organization's ability to keep its data secure is critical to its public image and is mandatory to maintain compliance with many requirements.

Because the database is where many organizations store sensitive data, it is the last barrier an attacker must compromise. In a secure environment, an attacker must compromise several layers of security controls to get to the actual database. Even though the hope is that an attacker never gets that far, you should implement additional controls to ensure you protect the data in your database from local attacks. The database should be the center of your security control efforts. You should take every opportunity to restrict access to the sensitive data in your database, including using controls provided by your database management system.

You'll learn about specific database controls in the "Access Rights and Access Controls in the System/Application Domain" section later in this chapter. Just because your database resides in a secure data center, you shouldn't assume it is safe. Use the security controls available to you at every level possible. Your job is to make an attacker's job as difficult as possible

Secure Coding

For the fifth straight year, the U.S. Department of Commerce's National Institute of Standards and Technology's (NIST's) National Vulnerability Database recorded 18,376 vulnerabilities as of December 8, 2021, which surpassed the 2020 record of 18,351. That averages more than 50 new cybersecurity vulnerabilities every day in 2021. With that in mind, the principle of **secure coding** helps software developers anticipate and code counter measures to make applications less susceptible to attack.

In simple terms, secure coding is the practice of writing a source code that is compliant with the best security principles for a given function and interface. Secure considers how software will be coded, how to detect and defend against cyberattack.

The principle of secure coding assumes every input is suspect and a potential attack vector for a would-be hacker. For example, one strategy is to "validate input" to make sure that it comes from a trusted source. Another strategy is to check for buffer overflow vulnerability. A good developer thinks like a hacker and eliminates any potential unauthorized access.

To illustrate lets consider a simple SQL-injection vulnerability and type of attack. A SQL injection attack consists of inserting SQL queries as part of the input data. For example, assume your application has a search function for a name of a customer that can be up to 30 characters in length. The application takes input fields and forms a SQL call against a database like MS SQL Server or Oracle. Now let's type the input as expected: We type "Dwayne Johnson the Rock!" into the name field and his customer information pops up. All good. But what would happen if we typed a well-formed SQL statement instead of a name such as "DELETE FROM Customers." Potentially the entire customer table was just deleted.

For discussion purposes, we will not show how to create a well-formed SQL injection statement into an input field as this is not a book to teach hacking methods. SQL injection attacks are one of the most prevalent vulnerabilities. A successful SQL injection exploit can read sensitive data from the database, modify database data, and delete database data. The essential point is that secure coding should prevent such vulnerabilities. This includes

TIP

Secure coding techniques must be applied as the code is written and not an afterthought being added. Secure coding consideration must be part of the code design as much as in the code itself. As such, software developers and testers must always be searching for in-code security vulnerabilities that could be exploited.

coding software that ensures inputs entered should be validated against expected input types:

- SQL statements should not appear in text input fields.
- Field types and lengths should match expected inputs.

Secure code will help to prevent many cyberattacks from happening because it removes the vulnerabilities that attack vectors rely on. If the software has a security vulnerability it can be exploited. As the security community becomes more cognizant of common vulnerabilities, best practices and improved secure coding techniques are published. A good developer continually researches vulnerability and the latest secure coding techniques.

Additional secure coding practices include strong coding practices related to the following:

- Input validation
- File integrity checking such as checksum
- Encryption
- Authentication
- Password management
- Session management
- Error handling
- Audit logs
- System configuration
- Database security
- File management
- Memory management

Does that seem like a lot to keep in mind when coding an application? It is. Fortunately, today we have scanners that can automate the source code analysis looking for common vulnerability and poor coding habits. These tools in addition to reducing vulnerabilities also help the developer create cleaner and more optimized code.

TIP

The NIST government website has a list of industry-leading source code analysis tools that can be found at https://www.nist.gov/itl/ssd/software-quality-group/source-code-security-analyzers.

System and Application Configuration and Change Management

Any organization that develops or modifies software applications must follow a configuration management method to ensure the integrity of their software. Far too many organizations lack the formal procedures to control changes to their software. Compliance requires formal change procedures. For example, SOX requires that any changes made to software be documented and tracked in such a way that changes can be undone. Further, SOX requires that all development activities and personnel be completely separate from your production environment. Although compliance requires these actions, they are really just good practices.

Software development and maintenance have evolved as more of an art than a science in many organizations. Small organizations with very few software developers commonly approach the development process informally because it is easy to keep track of a few programs and a few people. As an organization grows, the software development and maintenance activities become more complex. It becomes evident that informal procedures no longer provide the level of control needed to maintain a dynamic application's integrity. One formal method to control the software development life cycle is **software configuration management (SCM)**. SCM provides the activities and requirements to formalize the entire software development process.

SCM requires that all development occur in a separate environment from production. In the most secure environments, the development area is on a server separate from where the completed application runs in production. When developers complete software changes, the changes should move to an isolated testing and quality assurance (QA) environment. Testing and QA personnel test modified software to ensure it complies with the change request requirements and with existing application requirements. Many software changes to fix bugs or add functionality actually cause unintended problems. It is the responsibility of the testing and QA personnel to validate that the newly modified software performs as intended.

Once software changes have been tested and approved, they can be moved into production. SOX requires complete separation between developers and the production environment. Software developers are not allowed to access the production environment at all. Another role, such as a configuration gatekeeper, must move the software to the production environment. This security control limits the ability for software developers to accidentally place untested software in production. Untested code could violate any or all of the three C-I-A properties of data security. The separation between developers and production also stops malicious software developers from placing unauthorized software in production environments.

Regardless of your operating or development environment, it is imperative that your organization implement software configuration management software and controls to manage any changes to software. A solid set of tools will help manage changes, keep untested software from harming your data, and make it far easier to remove and replace offending software if an undiscovered bug does end up in the production environment.

System and Application Management, Tools, and Systems

Managing the components of the System/Application Domain means ensuring that the computers and devices are operating properly and that the application components are running efficiently. These tasks can be grouped into the following goals:

- Ensure your computers and devices are operating properly.
- Ensure your data center network is operating properly, including interfaces to the networks outside your data center.
- Ensure your application components are operating properly.

Proactive monitoring provides assurance that everything is working as planned and raises alerts anytime issues are identified. **Application performance monitoring software** is the highest level monitoring and analysis tool. If your application performance monitoring software reports that all is well, you have the assurance that application components, networks, and computers and devices are all operating properly. If a component has issues, your applications won't operate properly. Although it is possible that an issue can develop that does not immediately manifest an application problem, most application performance monitors can periodically run basic tests on idle applications to ensure that all is well.

If your application performance monitoring software does indicate a problem, the course of action may include any of the following:

- Alert appropriate personnel to initiate troubleshooting procedures on the problematic application.
- Launch network monitoring and analysis software to evaluate network components and connections.
- Launch system monitors or interrogators to evaluate data center computers.

The tools you can use include application performance monitoring software as well as system and network monitoring software. Managing computers, devices, networks, and software in the System/Application Domain doesn't introduce any new tools or topics. The practice of ensuring domain components are operating properly consists of tools and techniques that are appropriate and in use for other domains as well. Using these tools and techniques can help ensure the System/Application Domain is providing your users with application components to fulfill business requirements.

Access Rights and Access Controls in the System/Application Domain

The System/Application Domain is perhaps the most protected domain in relation to users. Both local and remote users must pass through several domains to access any components in the System/Application Domain. That means it is reasonable to expect users and attackers to have already encountered several layers of security controls to make it this far. Recall that a good security plan involves several layers of controls. You should deploy solid controls that protect each domain. However, it isn't good enough to rely on security controls in other domains. Although it is reasonable to expect the System/Application Domain components to be relatively safer than Internet-facing components, you still must protect all components in each domain.

System Account and Service Accounts

The systems and service accounts are different. They are nonhuman accounts that are used to support the system and applications. Because applications can be coded to refer to either of these types of accounts, for discussion purposes we will define both accounts but focus on service accounts within applications.

A **system account** is a user account that is created by an operating system during its installation, such as the root account on Linux or administrator account on

Windows. Developers should not code system accounts into the application logic. System accounts are generally highly privileged accounts.

A **service account** is a nonhuman account. Ideally, these accounts should be configured as noninteractive accounts, meaning a user cannot sign into these accounts. They can only function when coded in an application or system.

The distinction between system accounts and service accounts can be blurred as system accounts are sometimes used to run operating system services. Often an application will need to access data and other services on behalf of the user. In these instances, a service account (sometimes referred to as an "application account") can be used. For example, an application can use a service account to access data from a database on behalf of the user. This may simplify the coding while putting accountability for access management within the application.

Following the path, it is easy to see that an attacker can get right to your web server in the DMZ. To make your distributed application available to the maximum number of people, your firewalls will likely leave your web server ports wide open. All an attacker has to do is compromise your web server to potentially connect right to your application server. One well-placed attack can threaten your System/Application Domain. That's why having layered security controls in every domain is essential.

Your System/Application Domain should implement access controls for nodes and users. You should use Network Access Control (NAC) software, such as PacketFence or Sophos NAC Advanced, with positive authentication to ensure no rogue nodes are allowed to access System/Application Domain components. To address attacks from your web server, your application server should enforce user access controls. In addition, your application should enforce its own user access controls. You should define one set of users for remote access through a web server and another set of users for internal access. That way, you can separate the rights and permissions and also audit remote user access more aggressively. The most secure position is to assume all access requests are potentially hostile and then evaluate each one with aggressive access controls.

Maximizing C-I-A

Identifying security controls to protect data can be confusing. As with other domains, one effective way to ensure you have the right controls in place is to review how well you are maximizing the C-I-A properties of data security. If you can demonstrate that your controls are addressing the needs for data confidentiality, integrity, and availability, you have addressed the basic needs for data security.

WARNING

Local system accounts can be very powerful, and their use should be limited. A service running in the context of the local system account has unrestricted access to local resources. For example, a service running as "LocalSystem" on a domain controller, for example, has full access to Active Directory Domain Services. As a result, a compromised local account could threaten the entire network.

NOTE

In many cases, addressing the C-I-A properties of data security meets compliance requirements as well. Don't neglect to review your compliance requirements when examining security controls, as some requirements might call for additional security controls.

Access Controls

Access controls play an important part in the System/Application Domain. Earlier in this chapter, you learned how an attacker could compromise your web server and attempt to access System/Application Domain components directly. If an attacker is able to compromise a computer in your DMZ and exploit a vulnerability that provides access into another domain, solid access controls can limit the damage that attack can do. Many attackers will attempt to escalate user privileges to establish a connection to another computer or another domain to alter or access data.

---

technical TIP

Your access controls should carefully limit which users can connect to servers in the System/Application Domain from a web server. Do not allow users with escalated privileges to connect from your DMZ. Only allow escalated-privilege users to connect from a protected web server that can be reached only by VPN. These controls reduce the potential for an attacker to connect to sensitive servers from Internet-facing components.

In addition to NAC devices limiting connections to System/Application Domain components and operating system access controls for user logons, all applications should implement access controls. Application access controls can limit access to specific data elements. In a database environment, applications can employ access controls at the record or row level. For even more fine-tuned control, some applications and databases support access control at the field or column level. Application controls can limit which users can read data and which users can write data. Proper use of access controls at all levels can protect the confidentiality and integrity of your data. As long as you employ strong authentication techniques, user identity and access controls help keep your data secure.

Database and Drive Encryption

Access controls protect the confidentiality and integrity of data as long as the operating system enforces the controls. If an attacker is able to acquire a copy of data outside the scope of the operating system, access control cannot protect the data's security. There are two main ways to acquire data outside the scope of the operating system.

The first attack method is to boot the computer that contains the data using removable media. Removable media, such as a CD, DVD, or USB drive, can contain an alternative operating system that allows the attacker to access any file with no access controls. A successful attack such as this allows an attacker to copy any desired data, regardless of how confidential it is. There are two main defenses to this type of attack. The first defense is to limit physical access to critical servers. Most data centers employ physical controls such as locked access doors that only a select few people can open. If an attacker cannot physically access a computer, this type of attack fails. The second defense is to employ operating system–level encryption.

A second type of attack can result in accessing large amounts of confidential data. This second type of attack involves acquiring a copy of a backup image. Many organizations make the mistake of not securing backups once they are created. You should transport backup media to another physical location to protect it from a physical disaster. The purpose of creating backup images is to provide a redundant copy of your data if a disaster destroys the primary copy. Suppose a flood destroys your entire data center. If your backup images were stored in the data center, they could be destroyed as well. Transporting backups to remote locations for storage increases the likelihood they'll be usable even after a disaster at the main data center. If an attacker can steal a copy of your backup media as it is being transported from the data center to the storage location, all of your data could be revealed. Data on backup media is easy to access.

There are at least two controls to stop this type of attack. The first control is to secure all backup media during transport. Treat backups with care. Investing in a method of secure transportation is far less expensive than one security breach. Many companies provide secure transportation and storage for backup media. Consider using such a service to ensure your backups don't fall into the wrong hands. The second control to protect backups is to use data-protection methods such as encryption or tokenization. Several types of encryption and tokenization solutions are available for different needs. Some protect entire backup media or files on a disk, while others protect individual data elements. **Table 14-2** compares the six most common options for data protection.

Protecting data by such means can help ensure only authorized users can access the data. This type of control assists you in protecting the confidentiality and integrity of your data.

System/Application Server Vulnerability Management

No software is perfect. All software, whether an application or an operating system, is susceptible to software vulnerabilities. Because today's applications and operating systems are so complex, it is likely that multiple vulnerabilities exist in any version. Attackers know how difficult it is to develop secure software, and they expend substantial effort trying to find vulnerabilities to exploit.

Software developers are engaged in a continuous cycle to keep their software as secure as possible. Attackers run exhaustive tests against software to uncover any vulnerabilities. When they find a vulnerability, they develop an attack that exploits it. They launch an attack, and some computer systems become victims. The victims report what has happened to the software provider, and the software provider modifies its software to remove the vulnerability. The software provider tests its new software and releases it as a patch. Then the cycle repeats itself. Attackers are continuously looking for vulnerabilities, and software providers are continuously fixing the vulnerabilities they find.

Operating System Patch Management

Operating systems have substantial access to the hardware they control. Compromising an operating system basically means owning that computer. An attacker who successfully compromises an operating system can often use that computer for other attacks as well. You should frequently check your operating system's website for newly released patches and apply those patches. An operating system that has the latest available patches is less vulnerable to the newest attacks.

TABLE 14-2 Common options to protect data.

PROTECTION TYPE	DESCRIPTION	WHAT IT PROTECTS
File encryption	Encrypts individual files. If the file encryption is part of the operating system, such as Windows Encrypting File System (EFS), the encryption key is derived from the user password and files are not readable when the user is not logged on.	Alternate boot attacks or any attack that bypasses operating system access controls
Folder/directory encryption	Encrypts entire folders/directories. An example is Windows EFS in folder encryption mode.	Alternate boot attacks or any attack that bypasses system access controls
Volume/drive encryption	Encrypts entire volume or drive, such as Windows BitLocker or TruCrypt.	Alternate boot attacks or any attack that bypasses system access controls
Application encryption	Encrypts individual pieces of data based on the application's requirements.	Any attack that bypasses the application access controls; also protects backups from attack
Database encryption	Encrypts the entire database. If implemented by the database management system, this is often called **Transparent Data Encryption (TDE)**.	Any attack that bypasses the database management system access controls; also protects backups from attack
Backup encryption	Encrypts backup media as you create the backup image.	Protects backups from attack
Tokenization	A different approach from encryption. Replaces sensitive values with fake data that looks and behaves like the real data element. This helps to maintain business processes and the usability of the data.	Protects individual data elements from a wide range of threats

Set up each computer to download and apply patches automatically or set up a procedure that ensures you apply operating system patches to all computers as soon as they are available. The longer you delay patching any computer, the longer that computer remains vulnerable to newly released attacks.

Application Software Patch Management

Application software can contain vulnerabilities as well. As with operating systems, it is advisable that you acquire the latest application software patches from your application software vendor and apply them as soon as possible. This process is relatively easy for off-the-shelf software. It can be more difficult for software you have modified. Regardless of the role you play in modifying application software, it is important to have a plan in place to keep your software free from known vulnerabilities. Remember, if you know about a vulnerability, chances are some attacker knows about it too.

Data Loss Protection

The business has two main concerns when it comes to information collected, stored, and processed. Is the information *safe* and can you prevent it from *walking out* the door? Seems like a fairly easy question to ask, but a lot more complicated to answer.

This chapter has discussed at length methods of keeping information *safe*. Security policies and secure coding practices ensure risks are evaluated and reduced. Security policies ensure alignment with the business requirements. When there are risks to be taken the security policies ensure a risk assessment is performed so that a balanced decision can be made by the business.

In this section, we focus on the second business concern of how to prevent information from *walking out*. Security policies define what's often called either a **Data Loss Protection (DLP)** program or a Data Leakage Protection (DLP) program. The term refers to a formal program that reduces the likelihood of accidental or malicious loss of data.

The concept of DLP comes from the acknowledgment that data are often copied, changed form, moved, and stored in many places. Often these sensitive data leave the protection of the application database and end up in emails, spreadsheets, and personal workstation files. It is these data that live outside the hardened protection of an application that most concerns business.

A typical DLP program provides several layers of defense to prevent data from walking out:

* Inventory
* Perimeter
* Encryption of mobile devices.

The DLP **inventory** component attempts to identify where sensitive data may be stored. This includes scanning workstations, email folders, and file servers. The process requires inspecting the content of files and determining if they contain sensitive information such as social security numbers.

The DLP **perimeter** component ensures that data are protected on every endpoint on your network, regardless of the operating system or type of device. It checks as data move, including writing data to email, CDs, USB devices, instant messaging, and print. If sensitive data are being written to an unauthorized device, the technology can either stop and archive the file or send an alternate.

Through the logging and analysis server, it monitors real-time events and generates detailed forensics reports. Loggin cannot stop data from leaving but can determine what happened after the data have left.

Adherence to Documented IT Security Policies, Standards, Procedures, and Guidelines

Adherence to documented policies, standards, procedures, and guidelines is important to achieve compliance and a secure environment. That goal is just as important in the System/Application Domain. Although most of the other domains in the IT infrastructure are similar to domains in other organizations, the components in the System/Application Domain tend to be very specific to each organization. The applications any organization runs define the services that organization can provide. In some ways, the System/Application Domain defines the organization to the outside world.

Because the components in this domain are so specific to the organization, in many cases it is imperative to create specific documents to direct actions that apply to the System/Application Domain. Security policies state high-level goals for security. Standards state specific performance metrics to meet goals. Procedures document the steps to meet stated performance metrics. Guidelines provide general direction for situations that don't have specific procedures. Develop documents that address each of the three C-I-A data security properties and each compliance requirement. Plan how you're going to meet compliance requirements before taking action.

After you take the time to create the documents to direct IT activities, you should make every effort to follow the documents. If they have errors or need to be updated, make the necessary changes to keep them as current as possible. Following documented actions will always result in behavior that is more secure and compliant than simply making it up as you go.

Best Practices for System/Application Domain Compliance

The System/Application Domain is broad from the application to all supporting services within the operating system. This domain provides a final layer of control needed to secure the customer's data and the organization's sensitive information. Applying the best practices will reduce failure rates, optimize development time, and provide secure code. As a result, the collective best practices will lead to processes that over time will promote a security-conscious culture.

The following is a list of best practices examples that auditors should consider when assessing the System/Application Domain:

- Compliance with software licenses
- Software complies with regulatory requirements
- Use of encryption where feasible
- Assessment of all SDLC phases
- Security and backup of source code
- Adoption of secure coding practices
- Use of code analyzers to identify software vulnerabilities
- Limiting the use of local system accounts

- Configuration of service accounts such as making service accounts noninteractive
- Deployment of DLP tools
- Monitoring for new secure coding practices
- Not using production data in an application test environment
- Ensuring systems and applications are patched regulatory
- Ensuring applications have appropriate logging and monitoring
- Layered security to support applications such as enhance database security
- Validating all data input

CHAPTER SUMMARY

We learned in this chapter how important it is to break up the systems and applications components into manageable pieces within the domain. We examined each of the domain components and why they exist. We understand that security policies must be aligned to the business requirements. Most importantly we see how security policies can highlight regulatory and leading practices to guide the business in controlling these risks.

The chapter also examines the changing nature of business through cloud technologies. We examine the SDLC process and how it balances the business need with the changing threat landscape. We understand the importance of security policies keeping pace with the increase in vulnerabilities year after year. We better understand the expanding role of secure coding and how these coding practices protect customer data and an organization's information. Finally, we talked about the importance of having a DLP program. The DLP program helps us reduce the likelihood of data walking out the door.

KEY CONCEPTS AND TERMS

Application performance
  monitoring software
Application software
Business requirement analysis
Data center
Data Loss Protection (DLP)
Decommission

Deployment
Developer testing
Halon
Health Insurance Portability and
  Accountability Act of 1996
  (HIPAA)
Inventory

Maintenance
Network-attached storage
  (NAS)
Perimeter
Protected Health Information
  (PHI)
Rack system

Secure coding

Service accounts

Software design

Software configuration management (SCM)

Software development

Software Development Life Cycle (SDLC)

Source code

Storage area network (SAN)

Subnet

System account

System software

Transparent Data Encryption (TDE)

User acceptance testing (UAT)

Virtual machines

CHAPTER 14 ASSESSMENT

1. The main concern of data security in the System/Application Domain is integrity.

   A. True
   B. False

2. Because the System/Application Domain is the innermost domain, security controls are not as important.

   A. True
   B. False

3. A solid multilayered security plan means that an attacker will likely encounter several security controls before reaching the System/Application Domain components.

   A. True
   B. False

4. A(n) _____ is a subdivision or part of a network.

5. Application software and system software mean the same thing.

   A. True
   B. False

6. Every disaster recovery plan should protect _____ first.

7. Secure coding techniques should be applied after developer testing and before UAT testing.

   A. True
   B. False

8. The _____ SDLC phase is the final stage of any software development before deployment.

9. Creating a(n) _____ program will reduce the likelihood of accidental or malicious loss of data.

10. A(n) _____ generally resides in the DMZ and provides the interface between remote users and an application server.

11. Which type of full database encryption doesn't require any user interaction?

   A. TDE
   B. OLE
   C. AES
   D. DES

12. Which benefits do application performance monitoring software provide? (Select two.)

   A. Measure end-user response time
   B. Measure senior management browsing habits
   C. Measure end-user traffic volume
   D. Measure application-installed code base

13. According to SOX requirements, which type of user accounts are prohibited from accessing the production environment?

   A. Database administrators
   B. Software developers
   C. Network administrators
   D. End users

PART THREE

Beyond Audits

Ethics, Education, and Certification for IT Auditors

TECHNOLOGY HAS TRANSFORMED OUR lives and businesses alike. The simple truth is, nowadays, most businesses are so reliant on their technology that without access to their data and online services a company will struggle to operate. For many organizations, the impact of any long-term technology failure could be devastating. Consider a 2019 CNBC article that quoted the insurance carrier Hiscox; the article stated that 60% of small businesses go out of business within six months of a cyberattack.

With such high stakes it is important to find a qualified auditor to assess the health and adequacy of the technology control environment. As in any profession, the skills of a knowledgeable information technology (IT) auditor cannot be undervalued. However, in a career with an ever an evolving technology landscape, auditors must also continuously evolve their skills and knowledge base. Therefore, it is prudent to consistently keep up with new laws and regulations to ensure IT security compliance.

Professional certifications ensure auditors continually acquire new knowledge bases and ensure the disciplines are applied consistency across an industry. This is especially important because as an auditor, you play an integral role in upholding the security of an organization. Keeping up with your certifications, knowledge of current practices and ethics, and continued fieldwork lends credibility to your auditing work. Organizations also rely on IT auditors to perform their work ethically with independence, integrity, and objectivity.

In this chapter, you will learn about certifications and careers in the auditing profession. You will also examine professional ethics and codes of conduct that auditors are required to uphold.

Chapter 15 Topics

This chapter covers the following topics and concepts:

- Criticality of IT in organizations
- Why professional ethics and integrity are important for IT auditors
- What codes of conduct exist for employees and IT auditors
- How to become certified or accredited for IT auditing

Chapter 15 Goals

When you complete this chapter, you will be able to:

- Identify the required skills and knowledge for a career in IT auditing
- Understand the difference between code of conduct and a code of ethics
- Identify codes of ethics from various professional organizations
- Identify the components that make up a mature code of conduct and why organizations establish them
- Understand the differences between auditing associations and other professional bodies
- Differentiate between certifications available to auditors and IT professionals
- Identify educational opportunities and resources available to IT auditors

Professional Associations and Certifications

Professional associations for auditors promote the profession and establish standards that their members must abide by as well. The standards include exemplary ethical and professional behaviors. These organizations serve to educate and inform members of the most current approach to auditing and certify their members as competent to perform audits in their discipline.

Professional associations are common across many professionals where the discipline requires adherence to rigorous standards. These associations promote public confidence in the profession. Consider when it is tax time and you need to complete your income tax. Would having a certified public account (CPA) prepare your tax return provide more confidence that your taxes per completely correctly?! Yes. Equally important, in the event there was a problem with your income tax return, using a CPA demonstrates you took every effort to get it right. This approach could shift some of the risks to the CPA. The same applies to performing audits. Having a certified auditor perform the work provides management with confidence in the completeness and accuracy of the work performed.

It also demonstrates to regulators that management is making every effort to be compliant with policies, industry norms, and the law.

This chapter will discuss three of the most common audit professional associations that IT auditors will encounter: **Institute of Internal Auditors (IIA)**, Information Systems Audit and Control Association (ISACA), and **International Information System Security Certification Consortium [(ISC)²]**. The certification issued by these three professional associations are common and considered the *gold-standard* across many industries.

It is common for an auditor to have multiple certifications. Consider a doctor who is a general practitioner family doctor versus a heart surgeon. In the first case, the professional needs broad foundational knowledge, and the latter case needs highly specialized knowledge about surgery and the heart. The same exists for audit certifications, which can be broad and general or highly specialized. In either case, most public and large companies require auditors to be certified. Consequently, as a job requirement auditors often must have one or more audit certification.

Certifications are not just obtained by auditors across multiple disciplines. Certifications are often used by non-auditors to obtain a better understanding of risks. This also goes for auditors who want to obtain a deeper understanding of specific technologies. Regardless of whether you are configuring technology or auditing that technology, in both cases a deep understanding of the technology and associated risks are required.

Table 15-1 illustrates how multiple certifications can create synergies and build an auditor's skills. The table includes common certifications issued by IIA, ISACA and (ISC)².

When starting their career, auditors may choose to obtain a CIA certification. Once in auditing, individuals often start to specialize and choose to obtain a CISA because their focus may be on performing infrastructure audits. An infrastructure auditor may further specialize in information security and obtain a CISSP. While these certifications build on each other, they are not dependent on each other. In other words, individuals who want to specialize in IT audits may choose to jump to a CISA or CISSP and skip obtaining a CIA certification. While the CISSP is not technically an audit certification, it does focus on

 TIP

A local association chapter offers members of a professional association a local venue in which to network and exchange ideas. Local chapters often offer additional and low-cost educational opportunities for members. Often local chapters will have an open house event to invite nonmembers to participate and recruit new members into the professional association.

TABLE 15-1	Common auditor certifications.	
ISSUED BY	**CERTIFICATION**	**SPECIALIZATION SKILLS**
IIA	Certified Internal Auditor (CIA)	Foundational audit
ISACA	Certified Information Systems Auditor (CISA)	IT audit
(ISC)²	**Certified Information Systems Security Professional (CISSP)**	Information security

foundational information security knowledge, which makes it a popular certification to obtain for auditors and non-auditors alike.

Worldwide, IIA serves more than 200,000 members, ISACA more than 145,000 members, and (ISC)² more than 160,000 members. The certifications from these three professional associations are considered the gold standard for auditors.

Professional Ethics, Code of Conduct, and Integrity of IT Auditors

Ethics and **code of conduct** have the intent to control behavior but are different. Ethics are value statements that help an auditor make decisions. Code of conduct outlines expected behaviors and mandated actions given a specific situation. For example, an ethical value statement may say that auditors must maintain their independence. The code of conduct may say that auditors may not accept gifts. In this way, ethics and code of conduct complement each other. In this example, by not allowing gifts that may influence an auditor's opinion, auditors can maintain their independence,

In addition to having the required knowledge base, being ethical is essential to the auditing profession since organizations must place a high level of dependability and reliance on an IT auditor's work. At its core, ethics is about having an independent, unbiased, fair, and balanced opinion.

Professional organizations for IT auditors, such as ISACA and the IIA, also have codes of ethics to promote an ethical culture in the profession of IT auditing and are adopted by organizations that provide auditing services. The IIA, for example, has four key principles within its code of conduct that auditors are expected to uphold:

- **Integrity**—The integrity of IT auditors establishes trust and thus provides the basis for reliance on their judgment. Auditors with integrity shall
  - Perform their work with honesty, diligence, and responsibility;
  - Observe the law and make disclosures expected by the law and the profession;
  - Not knowingly be a party to any illegal activity or engage in acts that are discreditable to the profession of internal auditing or the organization; and
  - Respect and contribute to the legitimate and ethical objectives of the organization.

- **Objectivity**—IT auditors exhibit the highest level of professional objectivity in gathering, evaluating, and communicating information about the activity or process being examined. Internal auditors make a balanced assessment of all the relevant circumstances and are not unduly influenced by their own interests or by others in forming judgments.
  - Objective auditors shall not participate in any activity or relationship that may impair or be presumed to impair their unbiased assessment. This participation includes those activities or relationships that may conflict with the interests of the organization.
  - Objective auditors shall not accept anything that may impair or be presumed to impair their professional judgment.

- ○ Objective auditors shall disclose all material facts known to them that, if not disclosed, may distort the reporting of activities under review.
- **Confidentiality**—IT auditors respect the value, sensitivity, and ownership of information they receive and do not disclose information without appropriate authority. Auditors upholding confidentiality shall
  - ○ Be prudent in the request, use, and protection of information acquired in the course of their duties and
  - ○ Not use the information for any personal gain or in any manner that would be contrary to the law or detrimental to the legitimate and ethical objectives of the organization.
- **Competency**—IT auditors apply the knowledge, skills, and experience needed in the performance of internal audit services. Competent auditors shall
  - ○ Engage only in those services for which they have the necessary knowledge, skills, and experience;
  - ○ Perform internal audit services per the International Standards for the Professional Practice of Internal Auditing; and continually improve their proficiency and the effectiveness and quality of their services.

IT auditing must provide an independent and objective assurance by following these principles. Auditors are not there to criticize the organization, but to add value through improving operations in order to help them be successful moving forward. Therefore, it is vital that they do not approach the work with an agenda but retain a fair and balanced position. A properly executed audit will ultimately help an organization achieve its goals by establishing a methodical approach to assess the efficacy of an organization's risk management, control, and governance processes.

Ethical Independence

Understanding the importance of independence is still crucial in obtaining accurate results as well as instilling confidence in the results. Independent auditors should not have a vested interest in the outcome of the audit, such as working as the auditor being a direct report to those being audited.

Prior to executing an audit, IT auditors should identify possible impacts to independence, address any potential hindrances to independence compliance, and then convey the potential effect of residual hindrances to the appropriate parties.

When referring to the term "independence" in the audit world, it means there is autonomy from situations that can hinder risk assessment and other auditing tasks unbiasedly. In simple terms, it means being fair-minded. To accurately perform the requirements of the IT audit, the auditor must have a certain level of independence away from higher-ups. A system of checks and balances is a great way to achieve this. For example, a system of dual reporting on both ends can be developed. Risks must be managed at all access levels.

A conflict of interest may occur if a member performs a professional service for a client or employer and the member or his or her firm has a relationship. If the member believes that the professional service can be performed with objectivity, and the relationship is disclosed to and consent is obtained from such client, employer, or other appropriate parties, the rule shall not operate to prohibit the performance of the professional service.

Codes of Conduct for Employees and IT Auditors

A code of conduct should be consistent with the **code of ethics**. The code of conduct is often part of the larger ethics and compliance program within an organization. A well-rounded code of conduct does the following:

- Clearly states the company's mission
- Includes a statement from senior management
- Stresses the company's values and principles
- Provides guidelines on ethical and expected conduct, including rules of conduct
- Provides examples of ethical and unethical behavior

IT auditors belonging to professional organizations or holding certifications are required to adhere to professional codes of ethics. Standards set forth by these organizations further guide the conduct of IT auditors. In addition, most organizations, including all of the major accounting and consulting firms, have employer-driven codes of conducts.

Employer-/Organization-Driven Codes of Conduct

Companies listed on public stock exchanges are, in many cases, required to adopt a code of conduct. Both the NASDAQ and the New York Stock Exchange (NYSE) require this. Specifically, they require that listed companies implement and make available to the public their code of conduct for all directors, officers, and employees.

> **NOTE**
>
> All employees, including auditors, are expected to comply with their organization's code of conduct. Auditors, however, are also responsible for verifying and testing their clients' codes of conduct.

Requirements aside, a code of conduct provides organizations with several benefits. First, it enhances the organization's values and beliefs, and it helps establish a strong culture based on the vision and mission of the organization. Next, a well-implemented code of conduct will build respect as well as enhance the organization's reputation. Finally, it will help guide the organization and its people away from unethical and illegal behavior.

An organizational code of conduct might be included in the employee handbook. Additionally, policy should establish that employees confirm they have read and will comply with the code of conduct. Organizations should reinforce the code occasionally. Many organizations accomplish this through annual verification as well as ongoing training.

For example, KPMG is one of the largest auditing firms in the world. The company's *Global Code of Conduct* states that it "sets forth our core values, shared responsibilities, global commitments and promises. Additionally, the code provides you with general guidance about the firm's expectations, situations that may require particular attention, additional resources and channels of communication, as well as illustrative questions and answers." The guide is a colorful, easy-to-read pamphlet available for download from kpmgs-code-of-conduct.pdf (home.kpmg). The code of conduct dated October 2021 contains 64 pages and an exhausted list of ethical standards that an employee must adhere too. Below are key highlights:

- **Message from Chair and CEO**—This introduces KPMG's goal of being regarded as the one of the best Big Four public accounting firm. It further reiterates the strong corporate commitment to an ethics and compliance program to achieve that goal.
- **Core Values**—This describes the KPMG approach to do the "right thing" which defines the company's culture by identifying values that reflect who it is, what it does, and how it does it. It emphasizes the importance of integrity, excellence, working together, and how the work makes things better.
- **Responsibilities**—This provides key policies and responsibilities for which individuals and management are held accountable. This section describes personal values and integrity as the foundation of business conduct.
- **Getting Help**—This section explains the importance of speaking up, preventing retaliation, and how to open up channels of communication.
- **Our People**—This reiterates the importance and value of people and the need to embrace diversity and treat each other with respect.
- **Our Clients**—This describes commitments and standards around behaving lawfully and ethically and delivering quality service. It also includes other important expectations of conduct, including the importance of maintaining independence and client confidentiality.
- **Our Community and Marketplace**—This describes the expectation that all employees behave as responsible corporate citizens and the importance of building strong communities and achieving the firm's goal through fair competition.
- **Our Firm**—This section outlines expected behaviors to safeguard information and the firm's reputation through honest dealing, accurate reporting, and responding to regulators.

Employee Handbook and Employment Policies

Many organizations also convey expected standards of conduct through corporate policies such as acceptable use policies. The organization may also include these expectations within an employee handbook. In many cases, an organization's code of conduct and acceptable use policies also apply to vendors or other organizations with which they do business. In fact, in describing the "KPMG Way" from the previous section, KPMG describes its core values as representative of "We do our best work when we do it together:

in teams, across teams, and by working with others outside our organization.." This also means that IT auditors, who may spend a considerable amount of time at a client organization, not only must represent themselves consistently with their own code, but also must be aware of their client's expectations.

Certification and Accreditation for Information Security

With the continued growth of cybercrimes and increased focus on regulators' mandates to protect individuals' data privacy, information security auditing remains a top priority for many organizations. It is imperative for a business to be proactive in addressing any such potential threats and attacks and have an effective cybersecurity strategy in place. This is exactly why an IT security audit can be helpful. It not enough just to know how to audit. It is equally important to understand how information security controls should work. This is true whether you are auditing or charged with managing an information security control environment.

Both Computing Technology Industry Association (CompTIA) and (ISC)² offer technology specific certifications that are commonly obtained by auditors.

FYI

Those without the years of experience required for (ISC)² certifications may obtain Associate of (ISC)² status. This program is ideal for those switching careers and for college students. This achievement requires candidates to pass the CISSP certification and adhere to the (ISC)² code of ethics. For many, it provides an ideal opportunity to attract potential employers.

A goal of (ISC)² is to protect the integrity and value of these certifications as well as the professionalism of the information security industry. As a result, the organization requires credential holders and candidates to adhere to the (ISC)² code of ethics. There are four mandatory principles or code of ethics canons:

- Protect society, the commonwealth, and the infrastructure.
- Act honorably, honestly, justly, responsibly, and legally.
- Provide diligent and competent service to principals.
- Advance and protect the profession.

The four principles of ethical behavior come with additional guidelines to help resolve ethical dilemmas. The goal is to encourage correct behavior through research, teaching, advancing the profession, and valuing the certifications. The guidelines also discourage certain behaviors. For example, they discourage associating or appearing to associate with criminals or criminal behavior. They also discourage attaching vulnerable systems to the public network, providing unwarranted reassurance, and promoting unnecessary fear, uncertainty, and doubt.

The guiding principles for each requirement are listed on the (ISC)² website at *http://www.isc2.org/ethics/default.aspx*. The code of ethics states that complying with these guiding principles is not required, nor does compliance ensure ethical conduct. (ISC)² provides the principles to help members resolve ethical dilemmas they may face during the course of their careers. The (ISC)² board of directors, however, may use the principles to judge the behavior of members.

To protect the reputation of the profession, (ISC)² provides a procedure for ethics complaints. (ISC)² will only consider complaints directly related to one of the four principles. The board of directors established an ethics committee to oversee the process and provide recommendations to the board.

> **NOTE**
> Fear, uncertainty, and doubt, or **FUD**, is a common expression within IT circles. FUD is a tactic often seen in politics, sales, and marketing. People use FUD to encourage unfavorable opinions and speculation about a particular topic, often for self-serving interests.

Auditors have an important duty to evaluate organizational controls. These controls affect the confidentiality, integrity, and availability of IT assets and information. As a result, IT auditing professionals must understand both technology and accounting concepts. In many cases, it's not just desirable but necessary for IT auditing professionals to demonstrate certain levels of competence. If you choose to become certified, you will demonstrate your willingness to improve your knowledge and skills. This provides career benefits as well. It proves your expertise in specific areas to your organization, prospective employer, and clients.

Certification programs are available that focus solely on IT. Certification programs are also available that focus on auditing. Additionally, certifications exist that blend the two. Such certifications are more aligned to information system auditing and assurance.

Professional certifications have been around for a long time across many different fields. In the IT field, the number of certifications has skyrocketed over the past decade. This is due in part to the many vendor certification programs that are oriented toward specific technologies. These programs are managed by the corresponding vendors, and the programs benefit the vendors from a marketing aspect.

There are also many nonvendors, also called vendor-neutral, certifications. The **Computing Technology Industry Association (CompTIA)** provides one of the oldest nonvendor IT-related certification programs. CompTIA is a nonprofit organization that provides vendor-neutral certification exams. In addition, the organization provides educational programs and market research and has been involved in activities to advance the IT profession. CompTIA's beginnings go back to 1982. It introduced its first exam, the A+ certification, in 1993. CompTIA was truly a pioneer in the IT security industry. CompTIA certifications include the following:

- **CompTIA A+**—This covers basic operating systems and computer installation, troubleshooting, and communication.
- **CompTIA Network+**—This covers managing and maintaining the basic network infrastructure.
- **CompTIA Security+**—The **CompTIA Security+ certification** covers computer and network security, cryptography, and assessments and audits.
- **CompTIA Server+**—This covers the more advanced computing concepts related to servers.

- **CompTIA Linux+**—This covers the management of Linux operating systems.
- **CompTIA CTT+**—This covers presentation and communication skills for both traditional and virtual class environments.
- **CompTIA CySA**—This covers the behavior analytics to improve information security.
- **CompTIA PenTest**—This covers penetration testing to identify vulnerabilities.
- **CompTIA Project+ certification**—This covers the role of project manager.
- **CompTIA Cloud+**—This covers the topics required to implement and maintain cloud technologies.
- **CompTIA Data**—This covers data analysis and how data drives business decision-making.
- **CompTIA Cloud Essentials**—This covers the secure implementation and maintenance of cloud technologies.
- **CompTIA IT Fundamentals**—This covers broad IT skills.
- **CompTIA Advanced Security Practitioner (CASP)**—This covers advanced security topics and solutions across complex environments.

FYI

Certification is not the same as licensure. Licensure is permission to practice within a specific field. Licensure is required for fields that involve a high level of specialization and that may pose a danger to the individual or the public. Both, however, indicate that an individual has demonstrated a certain level of knowledge or ability. Consider that a license is required to drive a vehicle. Common professions that require licensure include medical practitioners and aviation pilots.

Those interested in IT auditing and assessment may find the Project+ and the Security+ certifications especially beneficial. Unlike some of the more advanced certifications discussed in the next section, these certifications are a great starting point. The other certifications that CompTIA offers can also benefit auditing and assessment professionals required to prove knowledge in more specialized areas.

FYI

Most certifications require periodic renewal. Many professional certifications, as part of the renewal process, also require the certification holder to prove continued education. Evidence of continued learning is submitted to the professional association to demonstrate you are keeping up with the latest developments in your field. Such evidence includes additional classes in a subject and attending specialized conferences. Professional associations often require a certain number of hours of education per year. These hours are referred to as **continuing education units (CEUs)** or continuing professional education (CPE).

Many certification programs are increasingly seeking **American National Standards Institute (ANSI)** accreditation. ANSI oversees thousands of standards and guidelines across nearly every business sector. ANSI accreditation is based on ISO/IEC international standards to ensure that certification programs are of high quality. ANSI accreditation helps maintain the value of certification programs as ANSI accreditation is recognized as a stamp of approval for a quality certification program.

> **NOTE**
>
> In 2007, ANSI accredited the CompTIA A+, Network+, and Security+ certifications.

The following sections discuss three well-known and well-respected organizations that offer programs that require a candidate to sufficiently demonstrate competencies in the auditing of information systems. A complete list of professional certifications is beyond the scope of this chapter.

Certification and Accreditation for Auditors

Both IIA and ISACA provide certification designed specifically for auditors. While these certifications are useful for non-auditors, these professional associations gear their certification and continual education opportunities toward the audit community. This chapter will review the most common IIA and ISACA certifications for auditors. **Table 15-2** provides a broader list of certifications which can be found on the organizations' websites.

IIA

Established in 1941, long before the Internet, when most processes were performed manually, IIA is an international professional association for auditors. The IIA's mission is to "provide dynamic leadership for the global profession of internal auditing." To achieve this mission, the IIA supports many activities that promote the value of the internal audit function. Activities include a wide range of educational and developmental opportunities. The IIA is well known, and considered the gold standard for many audit departments and regulators for its published standards and guidance provided to internal auditors.

The IIA provides guidance through the International Professional Practices Framework. This framework includes mandatory and strongly recommended guidance. Mandatory guidance includes the definition of internal auditing, the code of ethics discussed earlier, and various standards. Standards provide the framework for performing internal auditing functions. They include the basic requirements of internal auditing, including further explanations to clarify terms and concepts.

> **FYI**
>
> For many years, the IIA provided a website and publication named *ITAudit*. The publication is now called *Internal Auditor* magazine. The website is located at *https://iaonline.theiia.org/*. It includes archived issues of ITAudit dating back to 1998.

TABLE 15-2 IIA and ISACA certifications.	
ASSOCIATION	**CERTIFICATION**
IIA	Certified Internal Auditor (CIA)
IIA	Certified Government Auditing Professional (CGAP)
IIA	Certified Financial Services Auditor (CFSA)
IIA	Certification in Control Self-Assessment (CCSA)
IIA	Certification in Risk Management Assurance (CRMA)
IIA	Certified Professional Environmental Auditor (CPEA)
IIA	Certified Process Safety Auditor (CPSA)
ISACA	Certified Information Systems Auditor (CISA)
ISACA	Certified in Risk and Information Systems Control (CRISC)
ISACA	Certified Information Security Manager (CISM)
ISACA	Certified in the Governance of Enterprise IT (CGEIT)
ISACA	Cybersecurity Practitioner Certification (CSX-P)
ISACA	Certified Data Privacy Solutions Engineer (CDPSE)
ISACA	Information Technology Certified Associate (ITCA)
ISACA	Certified in Emerging Technology (CET)

The IIA's recommended guidance includes position papers, practice advisories, and practice guides. The position papers include general topics on governance, risk, and control. They also include explanations of the different roles and responsibilities within the auditing community. The practice advisories assist auditors in applying the standards specific to approaches and methodologies. Finally, the practice guides provide details for internal audit activities. Pertaining to the IT auditor, the IIA provides a series of audit guides specific to IT called **Global Technology Audit Guides (GTAGs)**. These guides provide audit-related guidance pertaining to technology management, control, and security. Another series of guides deal with specific areas related to IT risk and control and is called **Guide to the Assessment of IT Risk (GAIT)**.

Certified Internal Auditor (CIA)

The **Certified Internal Auditor (CIA)** certification, according to the IIA, is "the only globally accepted certification for internal auditors and remains the standard by which individuals demonstrate their competency and professionalism in the internal auditing field." The CIA exam covers internal auditing practices and issues as well as risks and solutions.

The CIA certification is made up of four parts. The first three parts are modeled on the IPPF. Candidates may receive credit for the fourth part if they have obtained another related specialty certification. This includes one of the other three IIA certifications or a number of other non-IIA certifications. The **Certified Public Accountant (CPA)** designation from the American Institute of Certified Public Accountants (AICPA) qualifies, for example. Another example is the CISA certification from ISACA, which is explored further in the next section.

The four parts of the CIA exam process are as follows:

- Part 1—Essentials of Internal Auditing
  125 questions, 2.5 hours (150 minutes)
- Part 2—Practice of Internal Auditing
  100 questions, 2.0 hours (120 minutes)
- Part 3—Business Knowledge for Internal Auditing
  100 questions, 2.0 hours (120 minutes)

To become certified, candidates must meet the following requirements:

- **Exam requirements**—Candidates must complete the exam with a passing score.
- **Educational requirements**—Candidates must have a bachelor's degree, or an associate degree combined with A-level certificate
- **Experience requirements**—Candidates must have 12 to 60 months' work experience depending on the educational degree obtained. All experience needs to be verified using a form on the IIA website.
- **Professional conduct requirements**—Candidates must abide by the IIA code of ethics. They must also provide a completed IIA character reference form.

The IIA makes exceptions for experience and educational requirements for certain equivalents. In both cases, proper documentation is required.

The following three specialty certifications offered by the IIA also require a bachelor's degree or higher, adherence to the IIA code of conduct, and a completed character reference form.

Certification in Control Self-Assessment (CCSA)

The **Certification in Control Self-Assessment (CCSA)** is for practitioners of **control self-assessments (CSAs)**. A CSA provides a method for those internal to an organization to assess risks and controls on their own. Internal auditors are often involved from a more consultative standpoint and can use the CSA program for focusing audit work on more high-risk areas. Candidates for the CCSA exam must obtain one year of control-related business experience, which could be experienced with CSA, auditing, or risk management.

Certified Government Auditing Professional

The **Certified Government Auditing Professional (CGAP)** certification is for public sector internal auditors. This exam tests areas of audit knowledge unique to the public sector. This includes grants and legislative oversight. Candidates must obtain two years of auditing experience in a government environment. This can include federal, state, or local government.

Certified Financial Services Auditor

The **Certified Financial Services Auditor (CFSA)** exam tests a candidate's audit knowledge and abilities concerning financial services. Candidates must obtain two years of auditing experience in a financial services environment. In addition to testing on these four domains, the candidate must choose from one of three financial service areas. These include banking, insurance, or securities. The exam includes additional questions specific to the chosen discipline covering the relevant products, processes, and regulatory environments.

Certification in Risk Management Assurance

The **Certification in Risk Management Assurance (CRMA)** exam tests the candidate's ability to evaluate and provide advice on organizational governance and enterprise risk management. CRMA candidates are required to pass Part 1 of the CIA exam and the separate CRMA exam.

ISACA

ISACA is a professional association that provides many resources for information systems auditors and IT security and governance professionals. ISACA publishes technical journals, standards, guidelines, and procedures. The organization also promotes research and provides educational programs as well as several professional certifications. ISACA is widely recognized as a result of its popular CISA exam.

ISACA publishes several best-practice framework guidelines. These include COBIT, ITAF, Risk IT, Val IT, and most recently COBIT 5, which combines many of the frameworks into one. In addition, ISACA provides several other educational opportunities and professional resources:

- **Standards**—These are for IT auditors as well as information systems control professionals. The standards provide mandatory requirements for IT audits.
- **Research**—This includes research papers to promote the development of timely topics relevant to IT governance, control, assurance, and security professionals.
- **Publications**—These include the *ISACA Journal*, a bimonthly publication for audit, control, security, and IT governance professionals. Additionally, ISACA offers a bookstore containing professional development and reference material. There is also an online library, which provides web access to a wide collection of books.
- **Chapter membership**—This includes membership in chapters around the world that sponsor local education events and seminars and conduct regular meetings.
- **Training and conferences**—These include various conferences that appeal to those new to the field as well as experienced professionals. Additionally, ISACA provides training opportunities such as certification review courses, onsite training, and online courses.
- **Certifications**—These include a handful of certifications for information governance, risk, security, and auditing.

Each ISACA certification requires experience, ethics, education, and an exam. The candidate must pass an exam, adhere to the code of professional ethics, and prove relevant experience. Upon certification, the candidate must also adhere to the continuing professional education program. The continuing education program ensures that certification holders maintain knowledge and skills within the certified area. Each exam is based on a job practice. The job practice provides the foundation for the experience requirements and is the basis of the exam. The job practice is organized by a series of statements that test both knowledge and skills. These are known as task and knowledge statements, which are grouped together and make up parts of the exam, known as domains.

CISA Certification

The **Certified Information Systems Auditor (CISA)** program is well accepted and mature; it's been available since 1978. This certification program is arguably the benchmark for an information systems audit certification for audit, control, and security professionals. In fact, ISACA lists several facts recognizing the significance and importance of the CISA certification. Examples include the following:

> **NOTE**
> ISACA offers its certification exams only twice a year. The exams are available in various cities around the world.

- CISA has won or been a finalist in the Best Professional Certification Program from *SC Magazine* for a number of years.
- The National Stock Exchange of India requires CISA certification to conduct system audits.
- CISA is an approved certification for the U.S. Department of Defense Information Assurance Workforce Improvement Program.
- Payment Card Industry Data Security Standard accepts CISA as a validation requirement for qualified security assessors.
- The U.S. Federal Reserve Bank requires all assistant examiners to pass the CISA exam before they can be eligible for commissioning.

> **NOTE**
> Of the ISACA certifications, only the CISA is specifically focused on the IT auditing profession. This does not mean that an IT auditor would not be eligible or benefit from the other certifications. In fact, all the exams cover areas that are relevant to IT auditors.

To qualify, a candidate needs at least five years of professional information systems auditing or security work experience. ISACA provides a list of available substitutions. Candidates may substitute a maximum of one year of information systems experience. Certification holders are also required to adhere to the ISACA information systems auditing standards. CISA covers the following domains:

- **Information Systems Audit Process**—This provides assurance that IT and associated data are protected and controlled. Specifically, this includes making sure that system audit services are within audit standards, guidelines, and best practices.
- **Governance and Management of IT**—This ensures that a governing program is in place. This includes the structure, policies, processes, and monitoring to achieve effective governance.
- **Information Systems, Acquisition, Development, and Implementation**—This ensures that practices from systems development and acquisition to disposal are adequately in place.
- **Protection of Information Assets**—This ensures that a security policy framework is in place. This also ensures that appropriate controls are in place to protect the confidentiality, integrity, and availability of information systems and data.

- **Information Systems Operations and Business Resilience**—This ensures that the business will continue despite disruptions.

Certified Information Security Manager

The **Certified Information Security Manager (CISM)** certification is designed for information security managers. Candidates also need to prove a minimum of five years of information security experience, which must include three years of experience in three or more of the focus areas or domains. This exam also allows for substitutions. For example, two years may be substituted for a CISA, a CISSP, or a postgraduate degree in information security.

Certified in Risk and Information Systems Control

Certified in Risk and Information Systems and Control (CRISC) is a broad certification program, appealing mostly to IT professionals. CRISC tests for knowledge of enterprise risk as well as the life cycle of information systems controls to mitigate risk. Candidates also need to prove at least five years of IT or business experience and at least three years of experience in one or more of the CRISC focus areas.

Governance of Enterprise IT Certification

The **Certified in the Governance of Enterprise IT (CGEIT)** certification is targeted to IT governance professionals. This includes those involved in the leadership and processes to help make sure that the IT organization is aligned with an organization's strategies. Candidates need to prove at least five years of experience in a governance support role of an organization's IT department.

CHAPTER SUMMARY

It is recognized that an organization's technology needs to operate effectively and protection of its information is critical to its survival. While efficiency is improved by implementing new technology solutions, so does the increased potential for security gaps. Auditors play an integral role in discovering those gaps before they occur so they can be remediated before they cause undue harm. Organizations must have confidence and rely on the work performed by the auditor. As such, auditors must be both skilled and ethical.

As the IT audit profession continues to grow, it is supported by several professional organizations. Auditing knowledge is often demonstrated through obtaining certifications, which provide consistency across the industry. Educational opportunities are numerous for those just entering the profession as well as those looking for growth. Organizations such as the IIA and ISACA provide a tremendous number of resources for the profession. Understanding what certifications exist and how to follow the law makes it easier to maintain an ethical position. Ultimately, maintaining ethics in auditing means performing with independence, integrity, and objectivity.

KEY CONCEPTS AND TERMS

American National Standards Institute (ANSI)

Certification in Control Self-Assessment (CCSA)

Certification in Risk Management Assurance (CRMA)

Certified Financial Services Auditor (CFSA)

Certified Government Auditing Professional (CGAP)

Certified in Risk and Information Systems and Control (CRISC)

Certified in the Governance of Enterprise IT (CGEIT)

Certified Information Security Manager (CISM)

Certified Information Systems Auditor (CISA)

Certified Information Systems Security Professional (CISSP)

Certified Internal Auditor (CIA)

Certified Public Accountant (CPA)

Code of conduct

Code of ethics

CompTIA Project+ certification

CompTIA Security+ certification

Computing Technology Industry Association (CompTIA)

Continuing education units (CEUs)

Control self-assessments (CSAs)

Ethics

FUD

Global Technology Audit Guides (GTAGs)

Guide to the Assessment of IT Risk (GAIT)

Institute of Internal Auditors (IIA)

International Information Systems Security Certification Consortium (ISC)^2

CHAPTER 15 ASSESSMENT

1. Which of the following is *not* considered a soft skill needed by IT auditors?

A. Penetration testing skills

B. Negotiation skills

C. Business writing skills

D. Behavior skills

E. Communication skills

F. Leadership skills

2. A(n) _____ of ethics for IT auditors is important for outlining clear ethical expectations.

3. The Sarbanes-Oxley Act does *not* attempt to define a code of ethics, but rather it references the code of ethics established by the IIA.

A. True

B. False

4. According to IFAC, the rules of behavior that guide the decisions of an organization should do which of the following? (Select the two best answers.)

A. Contribute to the personal fortunes of IT vendors.

B. Contribute to the welfare of key stakeholders.

C. Respect the rights of all constituents affected by the organization's operations.

D. Consider what is best for the organization's stock price.

E. Respect that each individual has a different moral code.

5. A thorough code of conduct would include which of the following?

A. The company's mission

B. The company's values

C. Examples of ethical and unethical behavior

D. All of the above

6. The NYSE requires that companies listed on its exchange publicly make available a code of conduct.

   A. True
   B. False

7. An individual holding which of the following certifications should be familiar with the (ISC)^2 code of ethics?

   A. SSCP
   B. CISA
   C. CISSP
   D. Answers A and C
   E. None of the above

8. Which of the following is *not* a mandatory principle or canon of the (ISC)^2 code of ethics?

   A. Protect society, the commonwealth, and the infrastructure.
   B. Act honorably, honestly, justly, responsibly, and legally.
   C. Provide diligent and competent service to principals.
   D. Advance and protect the profession.
   E. Serve justly, competently, and with pretense.

9. Certification and licensure are essentially the same thing.

   A. True
   B. False

10. Which of the following organizations provides IT-related professional certifications?

    A. CompTIA
    B. ISACA
    C. ANSI
    D. All of the above
    E. Answers A and B only

11. Ethics and code of conduct are considered equivalent.

    A. True
    B. False

12. A candidate for the Certified Internal Auditor certification must first achieve the Certified Information Systems Auditor certification.

    A. True
    B. False

13. To become an ISACA Certified Information Systems Auditor, which of the following is required?

    A. Successfully pass an examination
    B. Adhere to an ethical code
    C. Experience
    D. All of the above

14. Non-auditors such as a systems administrator are allowed to obtain a CISA certification as long as they can show they have the right work experience.

    A. True
    B. False

15. Auditors must obtain a CIA certification prior to obtaining a CISA certification.

    A. True
    B. False

16. What part of the ethical code of conduct refers to how an IT auditor can create trust and reliance on their decisions?

    A. Integrity
    B. Objectivity
    C. Confidentiality
    D. Competency

17. What part of the ethical code of conduct refers to how IT auditors have the abilities and skills to perform internal audit services?

    A. Integrity
    B. Objectivity
    C. Confidentiality
    D. Competency

Answer Key

CHAPTER 1 The Need for Information Systems Compliance

1. B   2. Risk-based approach   3. A   4. IT infrastructure   5. D
6. B   7. B   8. C   9. A   10. D   11. B   12. E   13. D
14. C   15. A

CHAPTER 2 Overview of U.S. Compliance Laws

1. A   2. C   3. FALSE   4. A   5. B   6. B   7. C   8. E   9. D
10. A   11. B   12. C   13. True   14. B   15. E   16. B   17. A
18. B   19. C   20. D   21. CIPA

CHAPTER 3 What Is the Scope of an IT Compliance Audit?

1. Gap   2. C   3. A   4. A   5. B   6. C   7. E   8. B   9. D
10. Framework   11. D   12. A, B, and C   13. A, B, and E   14. Identity
15. B   16. FALSE   17. B   18. D   19. B   20. B

CHAPTER 4 Auditing Standards and Frameworks

1. Framework   2. A   3. B   4. A, B, and C   5. B   6. Goal   7. B
8. B   9. B   10. B   11. Practice   12. D   13. A   14. D
15. A, B, and D   16. B   17. A   18. B

CHAPTER 5 Planning an IT Infrastructure Audit for Compliance

1. E   2. C   3. B   4. B   5. C   6. A   7. D   8. C   9. A   10. A
11. E   12. B   13. A   14. C   15. D   16. C   17. A   18. B

CHAPTER 6 Conducting an IT Infrastructure Audit for Compliance

1. A   2. C   3. B   4. B   5. Penetration test   6. A   7. A   8. A
9. D   10. A   11. Management   12. A   13. A   14. A   15. C
16. A   17. C   18. A   19. B   20. B

CHAPTER 7 Writing the IT Infrastructure Audit Report

1. A   2. B   3. B   4. B   5. A   6. B   7. A   8. C   9. A
10. A   11. A   12. D   13. A   14. B   15. B

CHAPTER 8   Compliance Within the User Domain

1. B   2. Business drivers   3. C   4. A   5. Need to know   6. B   7. D
8. B   9. C   10. A   11. C   12. B   13. C   14. B   15. A
16. A   17. A   18. A   19. A   20. Insider

CHAPTER 9   Compliance Within the Workstation Domain

1. Due diligence   2. B   3. B and C   4. War dialing   5. A   6. B
7. B   8. Integrity   9. A and D   10. Worm   11. Management System
12. B   13. A

CHAPTER 10   Compliance Within the LAN Domain

1. B   2. B   3. B   4. Fiber optic   5. A   6. A   7. A   8. B
9. Software or SD-WAN   10. C   11. A   12. Availability   13. B and C
14. B   15. C   16. A   17. LAN   18. A   19. B   20. B

CHAPTER 11   Compliance Within the LAN-to-WAN Domain

1. A   2. A   3. A   4. Demilitarized zone (DMZ)   5. B
6. Single point of failure   7. B and C   8. C   9. B   10. C
11. Virtual private network (VPN)   12. B   13. A
14. Multi-Protocol Label Switching (MPLS)   15. B

CHAPTER 12   Compliance Within the WAN Domain

1. B   2. A   3. B   4. B   5. A   6. Service level agreement (SLA)
7. A   8. C   9. WAN optimizer   10. B   11. B   12. C
13. Incident response   14. 2

CHAPTER 13   Compliance Within the Remote Access Domain

1. B   2. C   3. Encryption   4. B   5. A   6. D   7. A
8. Tunneling   9. B   10. B   11. SNMP   12. A   13. D   14. B
15. B   16. D   17. C   18. A   19. B   20. C

CHAPTER 14   Compliance Within the System/Application Domain

1. B   2. B   3. A   4. Subnet   5. B   6. People   7. B
8. UAT or User Acceptance Testing   9. DLP   10. Web server   11. A
12. A and C   13. B

CHAPTER 15   Ethics, Education, and Certification for IT Auditors

1. A   2. Code   3. B   4. B and C   5. D   6. A   7. D   8. E
9. B   10. E   11. A   12. A   13. D   14. A   15. B   16. A
17. D X

Standard Acronyms

ACD	automatic call distributor		CBF	critical business function
AES	Advanced Encryption Standard		CBK	common body of knowledge
ALE	annual loss expectancy		CCC	CERT Coordination Center
ANSI	American National Standards Institute		CCNA	Cisco Certified Network Associate
AO	authorizing official		CDR	call-detail recording
AP	access point		CERT	Computer Emergency Response Team
API	application programming interface		CFE	Certified Fraud Examiner
APT	advanced persistent threat		C-I-A	confidentiality, integrity, availability
ARO	annual rate of occurrence		CIPA	Children's Internet Protection Act
ATM	asynchronous transfer mode		CIR	committed information rate
AUP	acceptable use policy		CIRT	computer incident response team
AV	antivirus		CISA	Certified Information Systems Auditor
B2B	business to business		CISM	Certified Information Security Manager
B2C	business to consumer		CISSP	Certified Information System Security Professional
BBB	Better Business Bureau			
BC	business continuity		CMIP	Common Management Information Protocol
BCP	business continuity plan			
BGP4	Border Gateway Protocol 4 for IPv4		CMMI	Capability Maturity Model Integration
BIA	business impact analysis		CNA	computer network attack
BYOD	Bring Your Own Device		CND	computer network defense
C2C	consumer to consumer		CNE	computer network exploitation
CA	certificate authority		COPPA	Children's Online Privacy Protection Act
CAC	Common Access Card			
CAN-SPAM	Controlling the Assault of Non-Solicited Pornography and Marketing Act		COS	class of service
			CRC	cyclic redundancy check
			CSA	Cloud Security Alliance
CAP	Certification and Accreditation Professional		CSF	critical success factor
			CSI	Computer Security Institute
CAUCE	Coalition Against Unsolicited Commercial Email		CSP	cloud service provider
			CTI	Computer Telephony Integration
CBA	cost-benefit analysis			

CVE	Common Vulnerabilities and Exposures	**FISMA**	Federal Information Security Management Act
DAC	discretionary access control	**FRCP**	Federal Rules of Civil Procedure
DBMS	database management system	**FRR**	false rejection rate
DCS	distributed control system	**FTC**	Federal Trade Commission
DDoS	distributed denial of service	**FTP**	File Transfer Protocol
DEP	data execution prevention	**GAAP**	generally accepted accounting principles
DES	Data Encryption Standard	**GIAC**	Global Information Assurance Certification
DHCPv6	Dynamic Host Configuration Protocol v6 for IPv6	**GigE**	Gigibit Ethernet LAN
DHS	Department of Homeland Security	**GLBA**	Gramm-Leach-Bliley Act
DIA	Defense Intelligence Agency	**HIDS**	host-based intrusion detection system
DISA	direct inward system access	**HIPAA**	Health Insurance Portability and Accountability Act
DMZ	demilitarized zone	**HIPS**	host-based intrusion prevention system
DNS	Domain Name Service OR Domain Name System	**HTML**	Hypertext Markup Language
DoD	Department of Defense	**HTTP**	Hypertext Transfer Protocol
DoS	denial of service	**HTTPS**	Hypertext Transfer Protocol Secure
DPI	deep packet inspection	**HUMINT**	human intelligence
DR	disaster recovery	**IaaS**	Infrastructure as a Service
DRP	disaster recovery plan	**IAB**	Internet Activities Board
DSL	digital subscriber line	**ICMP**	Internet Control Message Protocol
DSS	Digital Signature Standard	**IDEA**	International Data Encryption Algorithm
DSU	data service unit	**IDPS**	intrusion detection and prevention
EDI	Electronic Data Interchange	**IDS**	intrusion detection system
EIDE	Enhanced IDE	**IEEE**	Institute of Electrical and Electronics Engineers
ELINT	electronic intelligence	**IETF**	Internet Engineering Task Force
EPHI	electronic protected health information	**IGP**	Interior Gateway Protocol
EULA	End-User License Agreement	**IMINT**	imagery intelligence
FACTA	Fair and Accurate Credit Transactions Act	**InfoSec**	information security
FAR	false acceptance rate	**IP**	intellectual property OR Internet Protocol
FCC	Federal Communications Commission	**IPS**	intrusion prevention system
FDIC	Federal Deposit Insurance Corporation	**IPSec**	Internet Protocol Security
FEP	front-end processor	**IPv4**	Internet Protocol version 4
FERPA	Family Educational Rights and Privacy Act	**IPv6**	Internet Protocol version 6
FIPS	Federal Information Processing Standard		

IS-IS	intermediate system-to-intermediate system
(ISC)²	International Information System Security Certification Consortium
ISO	International Organization for Standardization
ISP	Internet service provider
ISS	Internet security systems
ITIL	Information Technology Infrastructure Library
ITRC	Identity Theft Resource Center
IVR	interactive voice response
L2TP	Layer 2 Tunneling Protocol
LAN	local area network
MAC	mandatory access control
MAN	metropolitan area network
MAO	maximum acceptable outage
MASINT	measurement and signals intelligence
MD5	Message Digest 5
modem	modulator demodulator
MP-BGP	Multiprotocol Border Gateway Protocol
MPLS	multiprotocol label switching
MSTI	Multiple spanning tree instance
MSTP	Multiple Spanning Tree Protocol
NAC	network access control
NAT	network address translation
NFIC	National Fraud Information Center
NIC	network interface card
NIDS	network intrusion detection system
NIPS	network intrusion prevention system
NIST	National Institute of Standards and Technology
NMS	network management system
NOC	network operations center
NSA	National Security Agency
NVD	national vulnerability database
OPSEC	operations security
OS	operating system
OSI	Open Systems Interconnection

OSINT	open source intelligence
OSPFv2	Open Shortest Path First v2 for IPv4
OSPFv3	Open Shortest Path First v3 for IPv6
PaaS	Platform as a Service
PBX	private branch exchange
PCI	Payment Card Industry
PCI DSS	Payment Card Industry Data Security Standard
PGP	Pretty Good Privacy
PII	personally identifiable information
PIN	personal identification number
PKI	public key infrastructure
PLC	programmable logic controller
POAM	plan of action and milestones access tool
PoE	power over Ethernet
POS	point-of-sale
PPTP	Point-to-Point Tunneling Protocol
PSYOPs	psychological operations
RA	registration authority OR risk assessment
RAID	redundant array of independent disks
RAT	remote access Trojan OR remote for IPv6
RFC	Request for Comments
RIPng	Routing Information Protocol next generation for IPv6
ROI	return on investment
RPO	recovery point objective
RSA	Rivest, Shamir, and Adleman (algorithm)
RSTP	Rapid Spanning Tree Protocol
RTO	recovery time objective
SA	security association
SaaS	Software as a Service
SAN	storage area network
SANCP	Security Analyst Network Connection Profiler
SANS	SysAdmin, Audit, Network, Security
SAP	service access point

SCADA	supervisory control and data acquisition	**TCSEC**	Trusted Computer System Evaluation Criteria
SCSI	small computer system interface	**TFA**	two-factor authentication
SDSL	symmetric digital subscriber line	**TFTP**	Trivial File Transfer Protocol
SET	secure electronic transaction	**TGAR**	trunk group access restriction
SGC	server-gated cryptography	**TNI**	Trusted Network Interpretation
SHA	secure hash algorithm	**TPM**	technology protection measure OR trusted platform module
S-HTTP	secure HTTP		
SIEM	Security Information and Event Management system	**UC**	unified communications
		UDP	User Datagram Protocol
SIGINT	signals intelligence	**UPS**	uninterruptible power supply
SIP	Session Initiation Protocol	**USB**	universal serial bus
SLA	service level agreement	**UTP**	unshielded twisted pair
SLE	single loss expectancy	**VA**	vulnerability assessment
SMFA	specific management functional area	**VBAC**	view-based access control
SNMP	Simple Network Management Protocol	**VLAN**	virtual local area network
SOX	Sarbanes-Oxley Act of 2002 (also Sarbox)	**VoIP**	Voice over Internet Protocol
		VPN	virtual private network
SPOF	single point of failure	**W3C**	World Wide Web Consortium
SQL	Structured Query Language	**WAN**	wide area network
SSA	Social Security Administration	**WAP**	wireless access point
SSCP	Systems Security Certified Practitioner	**WEP**	Wired Equivalent Privacy
SSID	service set identifier (name assigned to a Wi-Fi network)	**Wi-Fi**	Wireless Fidelity
		WLAN	wireless local area network
SSL	Secure Sockets Layer	**WNIC**	wireless network interface card
SSL-VPN	Secure Sockets Layer virtual private network	**WPA**	Wi-Fi Protected Access
		WPA2	Wi-Fi Protected Access 2
SSO	single system sign-on	**XML**	Extensible Markup Language
STP	shielded twisted pair OR Spanning Tree Protocol	**XSS**	cross-site scripting
TCP/IP	Transmission Control Protocol/Internet Protocol		

Glossary of Key Terms

A

Acceptable use policy (AUP) | A policy that defines which actions are acceptable and which ones aren't.

Access control lists (ACLs) | Lists of permissions that define which users or groups can access an object.

Acts of Congress | Statutes or public laws enacted by Congress.

Administrator account | Refers to an account with elevated privileges used to manage a system, application, or other users' configurations; for example, an account that can install software, configure an application, or reset another user's password.

American Institute of Certified Public Accountants (AICPA) | A professional association of accountants that set financial audit standards.

American National Standards Institute (ANSI) | A non-profit private organization that promotes and publishes a common set of standards.

Application performance monitoring software | Software that can measure end-user response time for application software server requests as well as end-user traffic volume.

Application software | A computer program that is designed to perform a specific set of tasks.

Assurance | A level of confidence that appropriate and effective IT controls are in place.

Attack vector | A path or approach used by a hacker (i.e., attacker) to gain unauthorized access or disrupt normal computer operations.

Audit | An independent assessment that takes a well-defined approach to examining an organization's internal policies, controls, and activities.

Audit frequency | The rate of occurrence for an audit.

Audit objective | The goal of an audit.

Audit scope | The range of the organization to be included in an audit within a defined time frame.

Authentication | The process of providing additional credentials that match the user ID or user name.

Authorization | The process of granting rights and permissions to access objects to a subject.

Availability | The assurance that information is available to authorized users in an acceptable time frame when the information is requested.

B

Background check | An investigation to divulge evidence of past behavior that may indicate that a prospect is a security risk.

Baseline | A system in a known good state, with the minimum controls relative to the accepted risk applied.

Baseline controls | Countermeasures that apply broadly to the entire IT infrastructure.

Blocking | A general term typically related to preventing data or access.

Broadband | A transmission technique that uses only a portion of the full bandwidth of a channel.

Business continuity plans (BCPs) | Plans that document the steps to restore business operation after an interruption. BCPs, along with DRPs, enable you to recover from disruptions ranging from small to large.

Business drivers | The components, including people, information, and conditions, that support business objectives.

Business requirement analysis | The process of determining the information technology requirements and controls of a business process.

383

C

Card verification value (CVV) | A number printed on a credit card that provides additional authentication when rendering payment for online transactions.

Certification and accreditation (C&A) | An audit of a federal system before being placed into a production environment.

Certification in Control Self-Assessment (CCSA) | An IIA certification that tests professional knowledge of control self-assessments.

Certified Financial Services Auditor (CFSA) | An IIA certification that tests one's knowledge and abilities of audits pertaining to financial services.

Certified Government Auditing Professional (CGAP) | An IIA certification that tests audit knowledge unique to the public sector.

Certified in Risk and Information Systems and Control (CRISC) | An ISACA certification that tests knowledge of enterprise risk and control.

Certified in the Governance of Enterprise IT (CGEIT) | An ISACA certification that tests knowledge of IT governance concepts.

Certified Information Security Manager (CISM) | An ISACA certification that tests required knowledge of information security managers.

Certified Information Systems Auditor (CISA) | An ISACA certification exam considered by many to be the gold standard for IT auditing.

Certified Information Systems Security Professional (CISSP) | An (ISC)² certification considered by many to be the gold standard for information security management.

Certified Internal Auditor (CIA) | An IIA certification exam that covers internal auditing practices and issues.

Certified public accountants (CPAs) | A designation earned by qualified accountants in the United States after passing an accounting certification exam and meeting other professional requirements.

Chief privacy officer (CPO) | A senior-level position responsible for the overall management of an organization's privacy program.

Children's Internet Protection Act (CIPA) | An act of Congress to address concerns about minors' access to explicit online content.

Children's Online Privacy Protection Act (COPPA) | A United States federal law designed with the intent to protect children. COPPA is maintained and enforced by the FTC. COPPA requires websites and other online services aimed at children less than 13 years of age to comply with specific requirements of the law.

CIA | The confidentiality, integrity, and availability (C-I-A) properties that describe a secure object. Also referred to as availability, integrity, and confidentiality (A-I-C).

Ciphertext | The unreadable output that results from encryption. Encryption turns cleartext data into ciphertext through the use of an algorithm and a key.

Cleartext | Human-readable data.

Clinger-Cohen Act of 1996 | A U.S. law that improves upon the acquisition, use, and disposal of federal IT resources.

Cloud | General term typically referring to either the public Internet or private network that acts a unified ecosystem.

Cloud services | Common services that are typically found in the cloud.

Code of conduct | A statement of procedures and guiding principles to influence the culture and behavior of an organization's employees.

Code of ethics | A statement of general principles that pertain to an organization and its constituents.

Committee of Sponsoring Organizations (COSO) | An organization that provides guidance to executive management on organizational governance, internal controls, and risk management.

Compensating controls | Alternative countermeasures to minimize risk.

Compliance | The act of adhering to internal policies, applicable laws, regulations, and industry requirements.

CompTIA Project+ certification | A CompTIA certification that tests knowledge of project management.

CompTIA Security+ certification | A CompTIA certification that tests basic IT security concepts.

Computer assisted audit tools and techniques (CAATT) | Automated computerized tools and techniques that auditors use to aid them in their auditing function.

Computing Technology Industry Association (CompTIA) | A nonprofit professional association known for its many certifications covering a wide range of topics.

Confidentiality | Assurance that information is not disclosed to unauthorized sources.

Confidentiality agreement | A legally binding document in which the parties agree that certain types of information will pass among the parties and must remain confidential and not divulged. Also commonly called a non-disclosure agreement (NDA).

Configuration and change management | Governance process that establishes an orderly method of reviewing, approving, logging, and applying technology changes.

Configuration control board (CCB) | A person or group of people who reviews each change request and approves or denies the request.

Configuration management database (CMDB) | A central repository of system configuration items.

Connection media | The adapters and wires or wireless media that connect components together in the LAN Domain.

Continuing education units (CEUs) | Measurements used in continuing education programs such as certifications.

Control objectives | Objectives that state the high-level organizational goals of information system measures.

Control Objectives for Information and Related Technology (COBIT) | A framework that provides best practices for IT governance and control.

Control self-assessments (CSAs) | Methods for organizations to assess risk and controls on their own.

Controls | Actions or changes put in place to reduce a weakness or potential loss. A control is also referred to as a countermeasure.

Critical Security Controls | A list of 20 security controls primarily addressing the technical control area.

Cybersecurity | The practice of protecting computers and electronic communication systems as well as the associated information.

Cybersecurity Framework | Developed by NIST, a framework that provides a voluntary structure for reducing the risks to critical infrastructure.

D

Data center | One or more rooms with protected access and a controlled environment for computers and other IT devices. Also called a computer room.

Data leak security appliances | Network devices or software running on computers that scan network traffic for data-matching rules.

Data Loss Protection (DLP) | A set of tools and processes to ensure unauthorized sensitive data does not leave the confines of the organization secure network.

Decommission | Relates to the proper retirement and disposal of software and hardware once it is no longer needed.

Dedicated line | A permanent circuit between two endpoints.

Demilitarized zone (DMZ) | A separate network or portion of a network that is connected to a WAN and at least one LAN, with at least one firewall between the DMZ and the LAN.

Denial of service (DoS) | An attack that generally floods a network with traffic. A successful DoS attack renders the network unusable and effectively stops the victim organization's ability to conduct business.

Deployment | Refers to the process of implementing new software or hardware.

Descriptive control | A measure to be applied to a system that is high level and provides a lot of flexibility.

Developer testing | Refers to the testing performed by a developer to ensure operating as designed.

Dial-up modems | Older technology used to connect to a network through a telephone line.

Disaster recovery plans (DRPs) | Plans that document the steps you can take to replace damaged or destroyed components due to a disaster to restore the integrity of your IT infrastructure. DRPs, along with BCPs, enable you to recover from disruptions ranging from small to large.

Dual-homed ISP connection | A design in which a network maintains two connections to its ISP.

Due diligence | Reasonable steps taken to ensure adherence to requirements.

E

E-Government Act of 2002 | A U.S. law that improves the management of electronic government services by establishing a framework that requires the use of the Internet and related technologies to improve citizen access to government information services.

Electronic Communications Privacy Act of 2000 | A U.S. Law, also referred to as HR 5018, that further defines the privacy of an individual's data including government access to such data.

Encryption | The process of scrambling data in such a way that they are unreadable by unauthorized users but can be unscrambled by authorized users to be readable again.

Enterprise risk management (ERM) | The governing process for managing risks and opportunities.

Ethics | Moral beliefs and rules with regard to what is right and wrong.

Ethics Working Group | A consortium to define information security as a recognized profession within IT and to establish a generally accepted framework of ethical behavior.

Executive summary | A concise yet informative review intended for senior level management or those with decision-making power.

External compliance | Refers to the process of ensuring an organization complies with requirement set by an external organization such as compliance with U.S. laws.

F

Fair Credit Reporting Act (FCRA) | U.S. legislation that defines national standards for all consumer reports.

Family Educational Rights and Privacy Act (FERPA) | An act of Congress to protect the privacy of education records.

FCAPS | The acronym for a network management functional model that stands for fault, configuration, accounting, performance, and security.

Federal Information Processing Standards (FIPS) | Technical standards published by NIST and approved by the Secretary of Commerce.

Federal Information Security Management Act of 2002 (FISMA) | An act of Congress to recognize the importance of information security to the interests of the United States.

Finding | A documented conclusion that highlights deficiencies, abuse, fraud, or other questionable acts.

Finding and issue | Refers to audit observations that detail a specific set of non-compliance to standards.

Fingerprinting | The process of identifying the operating system and general configuration of a computer.

Firewall | A network security measure designed to filter out undesirable network traffic.

Footprinting | The process of determining the operating system and version of a network node.

Framework | A conceptual set of rules and ideas that provide structure to a complex and challenging situation.

FUD | An acronym used to describe fear, uncertainty, and doubt.

G

Gap analysis | A comparison between the actual outcome and the desired outcome.

Global Technology Audit Guides (GTAGs) | IIA-published documents that provide audit guidance for IT auditors.

Governance | The process through which an organization's processes and assets are directed and controlled.

Gramm-Leach-Bliley Act (GLBA) | An act of Congress to protect the financial aspects of consumer information held by financial agencies.

Guide to the Assessment of IT Risk (GAIT) | A standardized approach to walking through IT risks including assessing risk severity and prioritization.

Guideline | A document that support standards and policies but is not mandatory.

H

Halon | A gas commonly used in data center fire suppression systems. Due to halon's toxic properties, one type of halon has been banned and is no longer produced. Alternative gases are becoming more common.

Health Insurance Portability and Accountability Act (HIPAA) | An act of Congress that helps citizens maintain their health coverage as well as improve the efficiency and effectiveness of the American healthcare system.

Hub | A box with several connectors, or ports, that allows multiple network cables to attach to it. A hub is basically a hardware repeater. It takes input from any port and repeats the transmission, sending it as output on every port, including the original port.

I

Identification | The process of providing user credentials or claiming to be a specific user.

Identity theft | The taking of one's personal information for unauthorized use.

Information resource management | A process of managing information to improve performance.

Information Systems Security Assessment Framework (ISSAF) | A method for evaluating networks, systems, and applications.

Information Technology Laboratory (ITL) | An organization within NIST that performs research to help set U.S. standards.

Information Technology Laboratory (ITL) Bulletins | NIST publications that provide in-depth coverage of important topics.

Infrastructure as a Service (IaaS) | Cloud services related to providing network and management services to support an organization's infrastructure.

Institute of Internal Auditors (IIA) | A professional body for internal audit professionals that offers guidance on relevant topics.

Integrity | Assurance against unauthorized modification or destruction.

Intellectual property rights (IPRs) | The exclusive privilege to intangible assets.

Internal attack | An attack in which an attacker is able to compromise a system's access controls and either establish a presence inside the network or place malware on an internal computer.

Internal compliance | Refers to complying with an organization's internal standards.

Internal-to-external attack | An attack in which the attacker uses an organization's infrastructure to launch an attack on another organization.

International Electrotechnical Commission (IEC) | An international, nonprofit organization that publishes global standards on electrotechnology, or all things electronic and electric.

International Information Systems Security Certification Consortium (ISC) | A nonprofit professional and certification body that provides related programs for information security professionals.

International Organization for Standardization (ISO) | The world's largest publisher of worldwide standards.

International Telecommunication Union Telecommunication Standardization Sector (ITU-T) | One of three divisions of the International Telecommunication Union, primarily responsible for communications standards.

Internet service provider (ISP) | An organization that provides a connection to the Internet.

Intrusion detection | A set of tools and processes to detect unauthorized access.

Intrusion detection system (IDS) | A network hardware device or software that monitors real-time network activity and compares the observed behavior with performance thresholds and trends to detect unusual activity that might represent an intrusion.

Intrusion prevention system (IPS) | A network hardware device or software that monitors real-time network activity, compares the observed behavior with performance thresholds and trends to detect unusual activity that might represent an intrusion and takes action to stop the attack.

Intrusive test | Any test that simulates an attack and results in damage.

Inventory | The process of identifying all assets of an organization including all software and hardware assets.

ISACA | A global professional organization that provides resources and guidance relating to IT governance.

ISO/IEC 27001 | Good practices that provide an accepted baseline against which IT auditors can audit.

ISO/IEC 27002 | Good practices for information security management.

IT infrastructure | Refers to all the hardware and software to support an organization's IT operations.

IT universe | All the resources or auditable components within an organization.

Kerberos | A popular computer network authentication protocol that allows nodes to prove their identities to one another.

LAN Domain | An IT domain composed of the equipment making up the local area network.

LAN-to-WAN Domain | An IT domain that bridges between the LAN and the WAN.

Least privilege | A principle that dictates that users have access only to what they need to perform their duties.

Local area network (LAN) | A computer network for communications between systems covering a small physical area.

M

Maintenance | Refers to the support to keep current software and hardware such as applying vendor patches.

Malware | A term that refers to a collection of different types of software that share the goal of infiltrating a computer and making it do something.

Management system | Refers to the software tools and process to manage technology assets.

Multifactor authentication | A type of authentication that uses more than two methods to authenticate a user.

Multiprotocol Label Switching (MPLS) | A network mechanism that adds a simple label to each network packet, making routing of the packet faster than routing based on data in the header portion of the packet.

N

National Institute of Standards and Technology (NIST) | An organization that promotes innovation and competitiveness through the advancement of science, standards, and technology to improve economic security and quality of life.

Network Access Control (NAC) | A combination of security controls that define and implement a policy that describes the requirements to access your network.

Network-attached storage (NAS) | Refers to network attached data storage that is shared across the network.

Network operating system (NOS) | Software that provides the interface between the hardware and the Application Layer software.

Network scan | An automated method for discovering host systems on a network.

Networking devices | Hardware devices that connect other devices and computers using connection media.

Networking services software | Software that provides connection and communication services for users and devices.

NIST 800-30 | A guide developed by NIST for the management of risk for IT systems.

NIST 800-53 | Recommended security controls, developed by NIST.

NIST 800-53A | A guide for assessing security controls, developed by NIST.

NIST 800-115 | A technical guide published by NIST on conducting information security tests and assessments.

Node | Any computer or device that is connected to the network.

Non-disclosure agreement (NDA) | Another name for a confidentiality agreement.

Nonintrusive test | A test that only validates the existence of a vulnerability.

Object | The target of an access request, such as a file, folder, or other resource.

Objectives | A set of goals. Used as part of an assessment to determine what needs to be accomplished to validate a control.

Open Source Security Testing Methodology Manual (OSSTMM) | A peer-reviewed method that takes a scientific approach to security testing.

Open Systems Interconnection (OSI) reference model | A generic description for how computers use multiple layers of protocol rules to communicate across a network. The OSI reference model defines seven distinct layers.

Owner | A user who has complete control of an object, including the right to grant access to other users or groups.

P

Packet sniffer | Software that copies specified packets from a network interface to an output device, generally a file.

Payment Card Industry Data Security Council (PCI DSC) | The organization responsible for the development and maintenance of security standards for the payment card industry.

Payment Card Industry Data Security Standard (PCI DSS) | Industry-created standards to prevent payment card theft and fraud.

Penetration test | A method for assessing information systems in an attempt to bypass controls and gain access.

Perimeter | Refers to the hardware and software that acts as a buffer between the public external network and private internal network.

Personal Information Protection and Electronic Documents Act (PIPEDA) | A Canadian law that set the standard on how to collect, use, and disclose personal information.

Permissions | The definitions of what object access actions are permitted for a specific user or group.

Plan-do-check-act (PDCA) | An iterative process for continuous improvement.

Platform as a Service (PaaS) | Cloud services related to providing server platforms to an organization.

Policy | A document that regulates conduct through a general statement of beliefs, goals, and objectives.

Prescriptive control | Detailed and specific measures to be applied to a system.

Pretexting | The act of using false pretenses to obtain confidential information.

Privacy Act of 1974 | A U.S. Law that defines an the collection, usage, and dissemination of an individual's information that is stored in federal agencies systems.

Privacy management | The process of protecting the rights and obligations of individuals and organizations with regard to how they manage personal information.

Privacy obligation | Is a term that refers to professional standards to maintain the confidentiality of personal information.

Privacy officer | A senior-level management position within an organization responsible for handling privacy laws and their impact on the organization.

Procedure | A document that provides step-by-step instructions for how standards and guidelines are put into practice.

Protected health information (PHI) | Individually identifiable health information.

Protocol | A set of rules that govern communication.

Proxy server | A type of firewall that makes requests for remote services on behalf of local clients.

Public Company Accounting Oversight Board (PCAOB) | An organization that provides oversight for public accounting firms and defines the process for compliance audits.

Q

Qualified Security Assessor (QSA) | Entities qualified and authorized to perform PCI compliance assessment.

R

RACI matrix | A table used to document tasks and the personnel responsible for the assignments. RACI stands for responsible, accountable, consulted, and informed.

Rack system | An open cabinet with tracks into which multiple computers can be mounted instead of mounting them in individual cases.

Regulatory agencies | Oversight agencies that deal with administrative law, codifying, and enforcing rules.

Remote Access Domain | An IT domain that covers the access infrastructure for users accessing remote systems.

Remote Authentication Dial In User Service (RADIUS) | A network protocol that supports remote connections by centralizing the management tasks for authentication, authorization, and accounting for computers to connect and access a network.

Risk | An uncertainty that might lead to a loss. Losses occur when a threat exploits vulnerability.

Risk appetite | The degree of risk that an organization is willing to accept to achieve its goals.

Risk assessment | An analysis of threats and vulnerabilities against assets. A risk assessment allows the risks to be prioritized.

Risk management | The practice of identifying, assessing, controlling, and mitigating risks. Techniques to manage risk include avoiding, transferring, mitigating, and accepting the risk.

Risk tolerance | The range of acceptance of risks to keep an organization within its appetite for risk.

Rotation of duties | The process of rotating employees into different functions or job roles.

Router | A network device that connects two or more separate networks.

S

SB1386 | Refers to a California law that sets standards on the handling of an individual's private information.

Scope creep | When the original plans or goals of a project expand. Common with projects, particularly poorly planned projects.

Secure coding | Methods of enhancing security as part of the software development process.

Secure VPNs | VPNs in which all traffic is encrypted.

Security configuration management (SCM) | The processes and techniques for managing security-related configuration items that directly relate to controls or settings.

Separation of duties | The process of dividing roles and responsibilities so a single individual can't undermine a critical process.

Server Message Block (SMB) | An Application Layer protocol commonly used to provide access to file shares and printers.

Service accounts | Refers to non-human accounts that support an application's automated functions, also known as a system account.

Service level agreement (SLA) | A portion of a service contract that promises specific levels of service.

Service Organization Control (SOC) reports | Auditing standards maintained by the AICPA.

Simple Network Management Protocol (SNMP) | A network protocol used to monitor network devices.

Single point of failure | Any component on which service relies. If the single component fails, all other dependent components essentially fail as well.

Social engineering | The act of manipulating people into divulging information.

Software as a Service (SaaS) | Cloud services that provide software services to an organization.

Software configuration management (SCM) | A formal method for managing changes to a software application.

Software design | Refers to the process of defining business requirements and software components to meet requirements.

Software development | Refers to the process of coding of the software to meet the design requirements.

Software Development Life Cycle (SDLC) | Standardizes processes that define the life of software from its creation, deployment, maintenance, and retirement.

Software-defined WAN (SD-WAN) | Software that defines and controls a wide-area network.

Source code | Text files of programs that developers compile into application programs that computers can run.

Special Publications | A series of standards developed by NIST.

Standard user account | A human account without administrative privileges.

Standard | A document that supports a policy. It consists of mandated rules, which support the higher-level policy goals.

Statement on Standards for Attestation Engagements No. 16 (SSAE 16) | A report that is intended to provide assurance to organizations (user entities). This report replaces the SAS 70 report.

Storage area network (SAN) | A collection of storage devices that is attached to a network in such a way that the devices appear to be local storage devices.

Subject | A user or object that requests to access a file, folder, or other resource.

Subnet | A subsection, or part, of a network.

Switch | A networking device that forwards input it receives only to the appropriate output port.

System account | Refers to non-human accounts that support an application's automated functions, also known as a service account.

System software | Software used to run other software which most often refers to the operating system of a platform.

System/Application Domain | An IT domain that covers network systems, applications, and software for users.

T

Terminal Access Controller Access-Control System Plus (TACACS+) | A network protocol developed by Cisco. TACACS+ provides access control for remote networked computing devices using one or more centralized servers.

Threat | Any activity that represents a possible danger.

Threat actions | The methods of carrying out a particular threat.

Threat identification | The process of identifying all threats to the organization.

Traffic-monitoring devices | Devices that monitor network traffic and compare performance with a baseline.

Transmission Control Protocol/Internet Protocol (TCP/IP) | The basic protocol, or language, of modern networks and the Internet.

Transparent Data Encryption (TDE) | A method of encrypting an entire database that is transparent to the user and requires no input or action.

Trojan horse | Software that either hides or masquerades as a useful or benign program.

Tunneling | A technique that creates a virtual encrypted connection and allows applications to use any protocol to communicate with servers and services without having to worry about addressing or privacy concerns.

Two-factor authentication | A type of authentication that uses two types of authentication to authenticate a user.

Type I authentication (what you know) | The information that only a valid user knows. The most common examples of Type I authentication are a password or PIN.

Type II authentication (what you have) | A physical object that contains identity information, such as a token, card, or other device.

Type III authentication (what you are) | A physical characteristic (biometric), such as a fingerprint, handprint, or retina characteristic.

 U

Uninterruptible power supply (UPS) | A device that provides continuous usable power to one or more devices.

User acceptance testing (UAT) | Testing performed by the end-user to validate the functionality meets business requirements.

User Datagram Protocol (UDP) | A core protocol of the Internet Protocol suite. UDP is a connectionless protocol, which provides no guarantee of delivery.

User Domain | An IT domain that covers the end users of information systems.

User proxy | Allows a user to connect through another account.

V

Virtual machines | Software programs that look and run like a physical computer.

Virtual private network (VPN) | A persistent connection between two nodes that allows bidirectional communication as if the connection were a direct connection with both nodes in the same network.

Virus | A software program that attaches itself to or copies itself into another program for the purpose of causing the computer to follow instructions that were not intended by the original program developer.

Vulnerability | A technology weakness.

Vulnerability analysis | The examination of weaknesses or flaws.

Vulnerability scan | An automated method for testing a system's services and applications for known security holes.

W

WAN Domain | An IT domain that covers the equipment and activities outside the LAN and beyond the LAN-to-WAN Domain.

WAN service provider | An organization that provides access to its wide area network for a fee.

Wide area network (WAN) | A network covering a large area often connecting multiple LANs.

Workstation Domain | The operating environment of an end user. in 2002.

Worm | A self-contained program that replicates and sends copies of itself to other computers, generally across a network.

Zero-day vulnerability | Refers to a system vulnerability for which no patch or fix has been released.

References

15 U.S. Code Chapter 94, Subchapter I—Disclosure of Nonpublic Personal Information, n.d. Legal Information Institute. https://www.law.cornell.edu/uscode/text/15/chapter-94 /subchapter-I (accessed May 4, 2015).

American Institute of Certified Public Accountants. Generally Accepted Privacy Principles. n.d. American Institute of Certified Public Accountants. Accessed April 19, 2015. http://www.aicpa.org/interestareas/informationtechnology/resources/privacy /generallyacceptedprivacyprinciples/Pages/default.aspx.

————. New SOC Reports for Service Organizations Replace SAS 70 Reports, 2011. American Institute of Certified Public Accountants. Accessed April 19, 2015. http://www.cpa2biz .com/Content/media/PRODUCER_CONTENT/Newsletters/Articles_2011/CPA/Feb /SOCReplaceSAS70Reports.jsp.

————. SOC Reports Information for CPAs, n.d. American Institute of Certified Public Accountants. Accessed April 19, 2015a. http://www.aicpa.org/InterestAreas/FRC /AssuranceAdvisoryServices/Pages/CPAs.aspx.

Beresford, Dennis R., Nicholas deB. Katzenbach, and C. B. Rogers, Jr. Report of Investigation by the Special Investigative Committee of the Board of Directors of WorldCom, Inc., March 13, 2003. U.S. Securities and Exchange Commission. Accessed April 19, 2015. http://www.sec .gov/Archives/edgar/data/723527/000093176303001862/dex991.htm.

Cannings, Rich, Himanshu Dwivedi, and Zane Lackey. *Hacking Exposed Web 2.0: Web 2.0 Security Secrets and Solutions*. New York: McGraw-Hill Professional, 2008.

Cannon, David L., Timothy S. Bergmann, and Brady Pamplin. *CISA: Certified Information Systems Auditor Study Guide*. Indianapolis: Sybex, Wiley Publishing, 2006.

Celender, Jennifer. Information Privacy Topics, A Discussion, 2002. SANS Institute. Accessed April 19, 2015. http://www.sans.org/reading_room/whitepapers/privacy/information _privacy_topics_a_discussion_687.

Children's Internet Protection Act, 2001. Internet Free Expression Alliance. Accessed April 19, 2015. ifea.net/cipa.pdf.

Clarke, Steve. *End-user Computing: Concepts, Methodologies, Tools, and Applications*. Hershey, PA: IGI Publishing, 2008.

Committee of Sponsoring Organizations of the Treadway Commission. About Us, 2010. Committee of Sponsoring Organizations of the Treadway Commission. Accessed April 19, 2015. http://www.coso.org/aboutus.htm.

————. Guidance, 2010. Committee of Sponsoring Organizations of the Treadway Commission. Accessed April 19, 2015b. http://www.coso.org/guidance.htm.

Contesti, Diana-Lynn, Douglas Andre, Eric Waxvik, Paul A. Henry, and Bonnie A. Goins. *Official (ISC)2 Guide to the SSCP CBK*. Boca Raton, FL: Auerbach Publications, Taylor & Francis Group, 2007.

Davis, Chris, Mike Schiller, and Kevin Wheeler. *IT Auditing: Using Controls to Protect Information Assets*. New York: The McGraw-Hill Companies, 2007.

Ethics Working Group. Ethics Working Group, n.d. Ethics Working Group. Accessed April 19, 2015. http://ethics-wg.org/.

Fair and Accurate Credit Transactions Act of 2003. 2003. U.S. Government Publishing Office. Accessed April 19, 2015. http://www.gpo.gov/fdsys/pkg/PLAW-108publ159/pdf/PLAW -108publ159.pdf.

Family Educational Rights and Privacy Act. n.d. U.S. Department of Education. Accessed April 19, 2015. http://www2.ed.gov/policy/gen/guid/fpco/ferpa/index.html.

Federal Deposit Insurance Corporation. Gramm-Leach-Bliley Act (Privacy of Consumer Financial Information). n.d. Federal Deposit Insurance Corporation. Accessed April 19, 2015. https://www.fdic.gov/regulations/compliance/manual/pdf/VIII-1.1.pdf.

Federal Financial Institutions Examination Council. "Information Security: II.C.15(c) Remote Access." Accessed April 25, 2022. https://ithandbook.ffiec.gov/it-booklets/information -security/ii-information-security-program-management/iic-risk-mitigation/iic15-logical -security/iic15(c)-remote-access.aspx.

Gallegos, Frederick, and Sandra Senft. *Information Technology Control and Audit*, 3rd ed. Boca Raton, FL: Auerbach Publications, Taylor & Francis Group, 2008.

Gavin, J. "60 Percent of Small Businesses Fold Within 6 Months of a Cyber Attack. Here's, How to Protect Yourself." *Inc.* 2018. https://www.inc.com/joe-galvin/60-percent-of-small-businesses -fold-within-6-months-of-a-cyber-attack-heres-how-to-protect-yourself.html.

Global Information Assurance Certification. "Certifications." Accessed May 4, 2015. http://www.giac.org/certifications.

Hamid, Rafidah Abdul. Wireless LAN: Security Issues and Solutions, 2003. SANS Institute. Accessed April 19, 2015. http://www.sans.org/reading_room/whitepapers/wireless/wireless -lan-security-issuessolutions_1009.

Herzog, Pete. Open Source Security Testing Methodology Manual (OSSTMM). n.d. Institute for Security and Open Methodologies. Accessed April 19, 2015. http://www.isecom.org /osstmm/.

Heschl, Jimmy. COBIT in Relation to Other International Standards, 2004. ISACA. Accessed April 19, 2015. http://www.isaca.org/Journal/archives/2004/Volume-4/Documents/jpdf044 -COBITinRelationtoOther.pdf.

H. R. 2458, n.d. National Institute of Standards and Technology. Accessed April 19, 2015. http://csrc.nist.gov/drivers/documents/HR2458-final.pdf.

H. R. 2458–48. National Institute of Standards and Technology. Accessed April 19, 2015. http://csrc.nist.gov/drivers/documents/FISMA-final.pdf.

IEEE Standards Association. "IEEE Get Program." Accessed April 19, 2015. http://standards.ieee .org/about/get/802/802.11.html.

Information Assurance Support Environment. "Policy and Guidance Home." Accessed May 4, 2015. http://iase.disa.mil/Pages/index.aspx.

Institute of Internal Auditors. "Code of Ethics–English." 2010. Accessed April 19, 2015. http://
www.theiia.org/guidance/standards-and-guidance/ippf/code-of-ethics/.

_____. "The Institute of Internal Auditors". Accessed May 4, 2015. https://na.theiia.org
/standards-guidance/topics/Pages/Information-Technology.aspx.

_____. "Reference Library: Audit Software." Accessed April 19, 2015. http://www.theiia.org
/itauditarchive/index.cfm?act=ITAudit.reflibcategory&catid=7.

_____. "Welcome to the IIA." 2010. Accessed April 19, 2015. http://www.theiia.org/.

International Federation of Accountants. "Defining and Developing an Effective Code of
Conduct for Organizations." 2007. Accessed May 4, 2015. http://www.ifac.org/publications
-resources/defining-and-developing-effective-code-conduct-organizations.

International Organization for Standardization. "ISO/IEC 27002:2013(en)." Accessed April 19,
2015. https://www.iso.org/obp/ui/#!iso:std:54533:en.

_____. "ISO/IEC 27001:2013–Information Technology–Security Techniques–Information
Security Management Systems–Requirements." 2013. Accessed April 19, 2015. http://
www.iso.org/iso/home/store/catalogue_ics/catalogue_detail_ics.htm?csnumber=54534.

International Telecommunication Union. "X.701 Information Technology–Open Systems
Interconnection–Systems Management Overview." 1997. Accessed April 19, 2015.
http://www.itu.int/rec/T-REC-X.701-199708-I.

ISACA. "COBIT 5: A Business Framework for the Governance and Management of Enterprise IT."
2012. Accessed April 19, 2015. http://www.isaca.org/COBIT/Documents/COBIT5-Ver2
-FrameWork.pdf.

_____. "COBIT 5 Introduction." 2012. Accessed April 19, 2015. http://www.isaca.org/COBIT
/Documents/COBIT5 -Introduction.ppt.

_____. "COBIT 5 Resource Center." Accessed April 19, 2015. https://cobitonline.isaca.org.

_____. "Code of Professional Ethics." Accessed May 4, 2015. http://www.isaca.org
/Certification/Code-of -Professional-Ethics/Pages/default.aspx.

_____. "Identify, Govern, and Manage IT Risk Part 1: Risk IT Based on COBIT Objectives and
Principles." 2009. Accessed May 4, 2015. http://www.isaca.org/Journal/archives/2009
/Volume-4/Documents/jpdf094-identify-govern.pdf.

_____. "IS Auditing Procedure Security Assessment—Penetration Testing and Vulnerability
Analysis." 2004. University of North Carolina Wilmington. Accessed May 4, 2015. http://
www.csb.uncw.edu/people/IvancevichD/classes/MSA%20516/Extra%20Readings%20
on%20Topics/Networks/IS %20Audit%20Guideline%20Penetration%20Testing%20&%20
Vulnerability%20Analysis.pdf.

_____. "IT Standards, Guidelines, and Tools and Techniques for Audit and Assurance and
Control Professionals." 2010. Accessed May 4, 2015. http://www.isaca.org/knowledge
-center/standards/documents/it-audit-assurance-guidance-1march2010.pdf.

_____. "Standards for IT Audit and Assurance." Accessed April 19, 2015. http://www.isaca.org
/Knowledge -Center/ITAF-IS-Assurance-Audit-/IS-Audit-and-Assurance/Pages/Standards-for
-IT-Audit -and-Assurance-English.aspx.

_____. The COBIT 5 Process Capability Model. In *COBIT 5: A Business Framework for the
Governance and Management of Enterprise IT*. Rolling Meadows, IL: ISACA, 2012.

(ISC)². "(ISC)² Code of Ethics." 2010. Accessed April 19, 2015. http://www.isc2.org/ethics/default.aspx.

International Organization for Standardization. ISO/IEC JTC 001 "Information Technology." 2010. Accessed April 19, 2015. http://isotc.iso.org/livelink/livelink/open/jtc1.

IT Governance Institute. "About the IT Governance Institute." Accessed April 19, 2015. http://www.itgi.org/

———. "Unlocking Value: An Executive Primer on the Critical Role of IT Governance." Accessed May 4, 2015. http://www.isaca.org/knowledge-center/research/documents/unlocking-value-an-executive-primer-on-the-critical-role-of-it-governance_res_eng_1108.pdf.

Kidder, Rushworth. *How Good People Make Tough Choices Resolving the Dilemmas of Ethical Living.* Clovis, CA: Quill, 2003.

King, Tom. "Packet Sniffing in a Switched Environment." SANS Institute. 2006. Accessed April 19, 2015. http://www.sans.org/reading_room/whitepapers/networkdevs/packet-sniffing-switched-environment_244.

KPMG. "KPMG's Code of Conduct—Our Promise of Professionalism." Accessed May 4, 2015. http://www.kpmg.com/us/en/about/pages/codeofconduct.aspx.

Kurihara, Yutaka, et al. *Information Technology and Economic Development.* Hershey, PA: IGI Publishing, 2008.

"LAN Switch Security: What the Hackers Know That You Don't." *Network World* 24, no. 45 (2007):8.

Leo, Ross. *The HIPAA Program Reference Handbook.* Boca Raton, FL: CRC Press, 2005.

Leventhal, Rajiv. "Moving Hospital Care into the Home: A Pandemic-fueled Surge." healthcareinnovation.com. Published March 18, 2021. https://www.hcinnovationgroup.com/population-health-management/remote-patient-monitoring-rpm/article/21211211/moving-hospital-care-into-the-home-a-pandemicfueled-surge.

Littman, Marlyn Kemper. *Building Broadband Networks.* Boca Raton, FL: CRC Press, 2002.

National Institute of Standards and Technology. "Computer Security Resource Center." Accessed April 19, 2015. http://csrc.nist.gov/.

National Institute of Standards. "Draft Cybersecurity Framework v1.1 core." Accessed April 5, 2020. https://view.officeapps.live.com/op/view.aspx?src=https%3A%2F%2Fwww.nist.gov%2Fsystem%2Ffiles%2Fdocuments%2F2017%2F01%2F10%2Fdraft-cybersecurity-framework-v1.1-core.xlsx&wdOrigin=BROWSELINK.

———. "Federal Information Security Management Act Implementation Project." Accessed April 19, 2015. http://csrc.nist.gov/groups/SMA/fisma/index.html.

———. "Guide for Assessing the Security Controls in Federal Information Systems and Organizations." 2010. http://csrc.nist.gov/publications/nistpubs/800-53A-rev1/sp800-53A-rev1-final.pdf.

———. "Guide for Conducting Risk Assessments." 2012. http://csrc.nist.gov/publications/nistpubs/800-30-rev1/sp800_30_r1.pdf.

———. "Improving Critical Infrastructure Cybersecurity Executive Order 13636: Preliminary Cybersecurity Framework." Accessed April 19, 2015. http://nist.gov/itl/upload/preliminary-cybersecurity-framework.pdf.

_____. "Information Security Handbook: A Guide for Managers." 2006. http://csrc.nist.gov/publications/nistpubs/800-100/SP800-100 -Mar07-2007.pdf.

_____. "The NIST Definition of Cloud Computing." 2011. http://csrc.nist.gov/publications/nistpubs/800-145/SP800-145.pdf.

_____. "Security and Privacy Controls for Federal Information Systems and Organizations." 2013. http://nvlpubs.nist.gov/nistpubs/SpecialPublications/NIST.SP.800-53r4.pdf.

_____. "Special Publications (800 Series)." Accessed April 19, 2015. http://csrc.nist.gov/publications/PubsSPs.html.

_____. "Technical Guide to Information Security Testing and Assessment." 2008. http://csrc.nist.gov/publications/nistpubs/800-115/SP800-115.pdf.

Oud, Ernst. "The Value to IT of Using International Standards." 2005. http://www.isaca.org/Journal/archives/2005/Volume-3/Documents/jpdf053-The-Value-to-IT-Using.pdf.

Paperwork Reduction Act of 1995. U.S. Small Business Administration. Accessed April 19, 2015. https://www.sba.gov/sites/default/files/files/pap.pdf.

PCI Security Standards Council. "PCI SSC Data Security Standards Overview." Accessed April 19, 2015. https://www.pcisecuritystandards.org/security_standards/pci_dss.shtml.

_____. "Welcome to the PCI Security Standards Council." Accessed April 19, 2015. https://www.pcisecuritystandards.org.

Powers, Jr., William C., Raymond S. Troubh, and Herbert S. Winokur, Jr. "Report of Investigation by the Special Investigative Committee of the Board of Directors of Enron Corp." FindLaw. Accessed April 19, 2015. news.findlaw.com/wp/docs/enron/specinv020102rpt1.pdf.

Public Company Accounting Oversight Board. "Auditing." Accessed April 19, 2015. http://pcaobus.org/Standards/Auditing/Pages/default.aspx.

_____. "Auditing Standard No. 2." Accessed April 19, 2015. http://pcaobus.org/Standards/Auditing/Pages/Auditing_Standard_2_Appendix_E.aspx.

_____. "Auditing Standard No. 3." Accessed April 19, 2015. http://pcaobus.org/Standards/Auditing/Pages/Auditing_Standard_3.aspx.

_____. "Auditing Standard No. 5." 2010. http://pcaobus.org/Standards/Auditing/Pages/Auditing_Standard_5.aspx.

_____. "PCAOB Oversees the Auditors of Companies to Protect Investors." Accessed April 19, 2015. http://pcaobus.org/Pages/default.aspx.

"RFC 1087–Ethics and the Internet." Internet Engineering Task Force Tools. 1989. http://tools.ietf.org/html/rfc1087.

SANS Institute. "Critical Security Control: 2.0." Accessed May 4, 2015. https://www.sans.org/critical-security-controls/control/20.

_____. "The Most Trusted Source for Computer Security Training, Certification, and Research." Accessed April 19, 2015. http://www.sans.org/.

SANS Technology Institute. "SANS Technology Institute." Accessed April 19, 2015. http://www.sans.edu/.

Sarbanes-Oxley Act of 2002. SEC. Accessed April 19, 2015. https://www.sec.gov/about/laws/soa2002.pdf.

Sayana, S. Anantha. " *Using CAATs to Support IS Audit.* ISACA. 2003. http://www.isaca.org/Journal/archives/2003/Volume-1/Documents/jpdf031-UsingCAATstoSupportISAu.pdf.

Schneier, Bruce. "The Psychology of Security (Part 1)." Schneier on Security. 2008. http://www.schneier.com/essay-155.html.

Steinberg, Scott. "Cyberattacks Now Cost Companies $200,000 on Average, Putting Many out of Business." CNBC. Published October 13, 2019. https://www.cnbc.com/2019/10/13/cyberattacks-cost-small-companies-200k-putting-many-out-of-business.html.

Strickland, Dale. "Should Employees Work from Home after COVID-19?" CurrentWare. Accessed April 22, 2022. https://www.currentware.com/blog/infographic-benefits-of-a-remote-workforce/.

Subramanian, Ramesh. *Computer Security, Privacy, and Politics: Current Issues, Challenges and Solutions.* Hershey, PA: IGI Publishing, 2008.

Swinhoe, Dan. The Biggest Data Breach Fines, Penalties, and Settlements So Far. CSO. Published January 28, 2022. https://www.csoonline.com/article/3410278/the-biggest-data-breach-fines-penalties-and-settlements-so-far.html.

Talukder, Asoke K., and Manish Chaitanya. *Architecting Secure Software Systems.* Boca Raton, FL: CRC Press, 2008.

Tessian Research. "Why DLP Has Failed and What the Future Looks Like." 2021. https://cdn2.hubspot.net/hubfs/1670277/%5BTessian%20Research%5D%20The%20State%20of%20Data%20Loss%20Prevention%20(DLP)%202020.pdf?__hstc=&__hssc=&hsCtaTracking=aad6453b-4ab2-4f6c-bf1d-e2358d846478%7C36b78c19-de71-4009-bc75-6b3a47950315.

Tipton, Harold, and Micki Krause. *Information Security Management Handbook.* 6th ed. Boca Raton, FL: Auerbach Publications, Taylor & Francis Group, 2007.

———. *Information Security Management Handbook*, 6th ed., vol. 3. Chicago: Auerbach Publications, 2009.

Tyson, Jeff. "How LAN Switches Work," HowStuffWorks. 2010. http://www.howstuffworks.com/lan-switch.htm.

U.S. Department of Health & Human Services. "HIPAA Administrative Simplification Statute and Rules." Accessed April 19, 2015. http://www.hhs.gov/ocr/privacy/hipaa/administrative/index.html.

———. "HIPAA Administrative Simplification." 2013. http://www.hhs.gov/ocr/privacy/hipaa/administrative/combined/hipaa-simplification-201303.pdf.

———. "Standards for Privacy of Individually Identifiable Health Information." 2002. http://www.hhs.gov/ocr/privacy/hipaa/administrative/privacyrule/privruletxt.txt.

———. "Understanding Health Information Privacy." Accessed April 19, 2015. http://www.hhs.gov/ocr/privacy/hipaa/understanding/index.html.

U.S. Federal Communications Commission. "Children's Internet Protection Act (CIPA)." 2015. http://transition.fcc.gov/cgb/consumerfacts/cipa.pdf.

———. "Children's Internet Protection Act." http://www.fcc.gov/guides/childrens-internet-protection-act.

U.S. Federal Trade Commission. "Fighting Fraud with the Red Flags Rule: A How-To Guide for Business." Accessed April 19, 2015. http://ftc.gov/redflagsrule.

U.S. Government Accountability Office. "Financial Audit Manual." 2008. http://www.gao.gov
  /special.pubs/gaopcie/.

U.S. Government Publishing Office. "Electronic Code of Federal Regulations." 2015. http://www
  .ecfr.gov/cgi-bin/text-idx?c=ecfr&sid=11975031b82001bed902b3e73f33e604&rgn=
  div5&view=text&node=34:1.1.1.1 .33&idno=34.

U.S. Securities and Exchange Commission. "The Laws That Govern the Securities Industry."
  Accessed April 19, 2015. http://www.sec.gov/about/laws.shtml.

Wakefield, Robin L. "Employee Monitoring and Surveillance—The Growing Trend." ISACA.
  2004. http://www.isaca.org/Journal/archives/2004/Volume-1/Documents/jpdf041
  -EmployeeMonitoringand.pdf.

Wright, Craig S. *The IT Regulatory and Standards Compliance Handbook: How to Survive Information
  Systems Audit and Assessments.* Burlington, MA: Syngress, 2008.

Index

Note: Page numbers followed by *f* or *t* indicate material in figures or tables respectively